Zambia
a country study

Foreign Area Studies
The American University
Edited by
Irving Kaplan
Research Completed
February 1979

The cover shows the Zambian
coat of arms.

Third Edition, First Printing 1979

Copyright (C) The American University, Washington, D.C. 1979

Library of Congress Cataloging in Publication Data

Main entry under title:
Zambia: a country study.

"DA pam 550–75."
"This volume is one of a continuing series of books
written by Foreign Area Studies, the American Univer-
sity, under the Area Handbook Program."
Second ed., 1974, by I. Kaplan and others published
under title: Area handbook for Zambia.
Includes bibliographies and index.
1. Zambia. I. Kaplan, Irving, 1923–
II. Kaplan, Irving, 1923–   Area handbook for
Zambia. III. American University, Washington, D. C.
Foreign Area Studies
DT963.K26 1979   968.9′4   79–21324

Headquarters, Department of Army
DA Pam 550-75
Supersedes 1974 edition

For sale by the Superintendent of Documents, U.S. Government Printing Office
Washington, D.C. 20402

Stock Number 008–020–00814–1

Foreword

This volume is one of a continuing series of books written by Foreign Area Studies, The American University, under the Area Handbook Program. Its title, format, and substance reflect modifications introduced into the series in 1978. The last page of this book provides a listing of other country studies published. Each book in the series deals with a particular foreign country, describing and analyzing its economic, military, political, and social systems and institutions and examining the interrelationships of those systems and institutions and the ways that they are shaped by cultural factors. Each study is written by a multidisciplinary team of social scientists. The authors seek to provide a basic insight and understanding of the society under observation, striving for a dynamic rather than a static portrayal of it. The study focuses on historical antecedents and on the cultural, political, and socioeconomic characteristics that contribute to cohesion and cleavage within the society. Particular attention is given to the origins and traditions of the people who make up the society, their dominant beliefs and values, their community of interests and the issues on which they are divided, the nature and extent of their involvement with the national institutions, and their attitudes toward each other and toward the social system and political order within which they live.

The contents of the book represent the work of Foreign Area Studies and are not set forth as the official view of the United States government. The authors have sought to adhere to accepted standards of scholarly objectivity. Such corrections, additions, and suggestions for factual or other changes that readers may have will be welcomed for use in future revisions.

William Evans-Smith
Director, Foreign Area Studies
The American University
Washington, D.C. 20016

Acknowledgments

The authors are grateful to individuals in various government agencies and private institutions who gave of their time, research materials, and special knowledge to provide data and perspective. The authors also wish to express their gratitude to members of the Foreign Area Studies staff who contributed directly to the preparation of the manuscript. These persons include Frederica M. Bunge who, in her capacity as assistant director for research, reviewed all the textual material; Sheila L. Ross and Diane Ullius Jarrett, who edited the manuscript; and Harriett R. Blood, who prepared the graphics. The team appreciates as well the assistance provided by Gilda V. Nimer, librarian, and Ernest Will, publications manager.

Special thanks are owed to Ramona Hutko who, under the direction of Michael T. Graham of The American University Department of Art, designed the cover for this volume, as well as the illustrations on the title page of each chapter. The inclusion of photographs in this study was made possible by the generosity of various individuals and public and private agencies. We acknowledge our indebtedness especially to those persons who contributed original work not previously published.

Contents

PRECOLONIAL ZAMBIA TO CA. 1890—The Stone Age—The Iron Age to ca. 1500—Peoples and Polities, ca. 1500–1800—THE COMMERCIAL REVOLUTION: THE LATE EIGHTEENTH AND NINETEENTH CENTURIES—THE COLONIAL INTERLUDE, CA. 1890–1964—Missionary Penetration—Cecil Rhodes and the Scramble for Southern Africa—Company Rule, 1895–1924—Colonial Office Protectorate, 1924–53—The Decade of Federation, 1953–63—INDEPENDENCE: THE FIRST DECADE, 1964–74—The Politics of Independence—State and Economy—Zambia in Regional and World Politics

THE PHYSICAL SETTING AND POPULATION—Terrain and Drainage—Climate—Ecological Zones and Settlement—POPULATION—Density and Distribution—Migration and Urbanization—LANGUAGE—Maternal or First Languages—The Role of English in Zambia—Vernacular Lingua Francas—SOCIAL STRUCTURE—Family and Marriage—Lineage, Clan, and Descent System—Residual Precolonial Administrative/Political Structures—"Tribes" and "Tribalism"—THE DUAL SOCIETY: FROM RACE TO CLASS AND URBANIZATION—MAJOR ETHNIC GROUPS—Bemba—Nyanja—Tonga—Lozi—Peoples of North-Western Province—Urban Africans—Whites—Asians—OTHER FORMS OF SOCIAL DIFFERENTIATION—Sex Roles—The Generation Gap—RELIGION—Traditional Religious Beliefs—Christianity—Developments in the Late 1970s—Size of Religious Constituencies—OTHER VOLUNTARY ASSOCIATIONS—EDUCATION—HEALTH

List of Figures

Preface

When research for the *Area Handbook for Zambia* was completed in November 1968, Zambia had been independent for four years, and its economic situation was good enough to assume that it had the wherewithal and time to carry out the developmental and nationbuilding program contemplated by its leaders. Five years later, when the "Summary of Events: November 1968–November 1973" was written, a variety of difficulties—social, political, and economic—had appeared, but the sharp drop in world copper prices, the rise in the costs of imported goods, and the full burden of Zambia's support for the forces opposing the white minority regime in Southern Rhodesia had not yet made themselves felt.

This study supersedes the *Area Handbook for Zambia,* updated in the "Summary of Events: November 1968–November 1973." The earlier work was prepared by a team composed of Milena Choumenkovitch, Gordon C. McDonald, James L. McLaughlin, Barbara Marvin, Harold D. Nelson, and Diane D. Novotny under the chairmanship of Irving Kaplan. The summary of events was prepared by Gilda Nimer, Richard Tierney, and Benjamin Nimer under the direction of the latter.

Zambia: A Country Study is based on a variety of published and unpublished sources. Some data were provided and ambiguities clarified through consultation with individuals having firsthand knowledge of Zambia. Some gaps in information and resulting problems remain, however, and these have been noted in the text. Given the limits of time and space, some aspects of Zambian society and culture have been treated briefly or not at all. Where available books and articles provide amplification of detail or interpretation presented in a chapter, the author has noted them in a paragraph at the end.

The authors have tried to limit the use of foreign and technical terms. These are briefly defined where they first appear in a chapter, or reference is made to the Glossary, included for the reader's convenience.

All ethnic and language names in Zambia originate in Bantu languages characterized by the use of class prefixes that vary with the language (thus several Bemba—abaBemba, an individual—umuBemba, the language—iciBemba; similarly baLozi, muLozi, siLozi; for the Ndembu, also called Lunda—aLunda, kaLunda, ciLunda). These prefixes are omitted in this study; the root—e.g., Bemba—is used for plural, singular, and language, its reference obvious from the context.

Many of Zambia's languages have been transcribed in an orthography using all or part of the international African alphabet. The Zambian government has officially accepted this standard, but not all usage yet conforms to it. The letter that may give the reader of this study pause is *c,* used in the international alphabet as the equivalent of *ch* in English. In older sources, therefore, *iciBemba* may be seen as *ichiBemba.* In particular the term *citemene,* widely used in Zambia to refer to an indigenous mode of agriculture, is Bemba in origin and is spelled that way in its language of origin and in many English-language sources, but sources prepared by Europeans frequently use *chitemene.*

All measures are given in the metric system (see table 1, Appendix). Place-names conform to the usage in the publications of the United States Board of Geographic Names.

Irving Kaplan

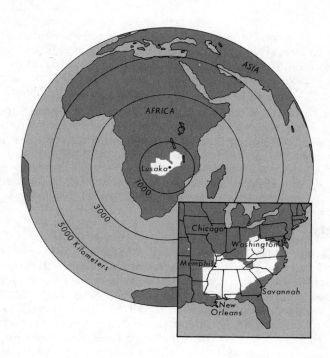

Country

Formal Name: Republic of Zambia.

Short Form: Zambia.

Term for Nationals: Zambians.

Preindependence Political Status: In the late nineteenth century various parts of what was to become Northern Rhodesia were directly or indirectly under the control of Cecil Rhodes' British South Africa Company. In 1924 Northern Rhodesia became a British Protectorate, a status formally retained through the period of the Central African Federation of Rhodesia and Nyasaland; federation began (despite black African opposition) in October 1953 and was dissolved on December 31, 1963. Zambia became independent on October 24, 1964.

Capital: Lusaka.

Geography

Size: 752,614 square kilometers.

Topography: Largely plateau, some flat, some undulating, most ranging between 900 and 1,500 meters. Mountainous areas chiefly along borders with Tanzania (Mbala Highlands in northeast) and Malawi (Mafingi Mountains in east). Lowlands are rift valleys— Luangwa River Valley in east, middle Zambezi valley in south— both bounded by escarpments to the north. Most rivers drain via Zambezi River to Indian Ocean. The network of streams and lakes in the northeast drains via Zaïre River to Atlantic Ocean.

Climate: Cycle of wet and dry seasons and associated variations in temperature give Zambia three seasons: cool and dry from April to August; hot and dry from mid-August through October or November; warm and rainy from October through March or April. Longest rainy season and heaviest annual rainfall in northwest and north of Lake Bangweulu in east. Lowest rainfall in southern and low-lying eastern areas, where drought sometimes occurs.

Society

Population: Mid-1978 estimate of 5,381,000, based on 1969 full and 1974 sample censuses; 3.1 percent annual growth rate in mid- and late 1970s. Urbanization high owing to intensive development of copper mining; 1969 urban population nearly 30 percent; 1974 estimate more than 35 percent; by 1978, 40 percent (62 percent of urban population in copperbelt). Rural densities vary from fewer than two per square kilometer to fifty or more in a few locations; denser populations in commercial agricultural areas of the line of rail (see Glossary) and far southeast and where fishing supplements agriculture (as in upper Zambezi plain and lakes and marshes of northeast).

Languages: Each ethnic group has own dialect or language; as many as eighty-four African dialects identified. English is official language and has become increasingly important. Seven official vernaculars are recognized; most important are Bemba (northeast and copperbelt), Nyanja (Cewa) (east and central cities, e.g., Lusaka), Lozi (west and Livingstone), and Tonga (south).

Ethnic groups: Seventy-three officially recognized ethnic groups, defined by varying criteria. None politically or economically predominant; Bemba speakers (the largest linguistic community although not all ethnic Bemba) make up less than 19 percent of the population.

Religion: Approximately half claim to be Christians, roughly one-half to two-thirds Roman Catholic, the rest in various Protestant and independent churches; many Christians, however, participate in some indigenous religious activity and share local beliefs. The remainder may be considered adherents of one of the indigenous religious systems.

Education and Literacy: Great expansion of educational system after independence in 1964 (Zambia formerly dependent on Southern Rhodesian institutions for higher levels of education). Government has attempted universal free primary education (seven years) and preparation of Zambians to replace expatriate personnel, but a number fail to continue beyond lower primary (five years), and relatively few go beyond lower secondary levels. One university and a number of specialized postsecondary institutions.

Health: Government attempts to provide medical service at little or no cost in rural as well as urban areas. Urban hospitals, large rural hospitals, and Flying Doctor Service under government auspices; many smaller units operated by missions and major employers. Paramedical personnel largely indigenous despite great expansion in services. Major medical problems include chronic illnesses, such as malaria, schistosomiasis, and dietary insufficiency as well as acute diseases, such as measles, typhoid, and dysentery.

Government and Politics

Form: One-party participatory democracy formally established on December 13, 1972. Centralized government under President Kenneth Kaunda. Separate party and government structures, both headed by president. In principle Central Committee of United National Independence Party (UNIP) makes policies that Cabinet implements. In practice Cabinet has had policymaking powers that government reorganization of January 1979 tried to curtail. Unicameral National Assembly includes both elected (the great majority) and presidentially appointed members. President also appoints secretary general of UNIP, prime minister, and secretary of state for defense and security.

Administrative Divisions: Nine provinces (includes capital of Lusaka and surrounding area) subdivided into urban and rural districts (see fig. 1).

Politics: Some elements of a democratic society despite banning of legal opposition. Dissent centers mostly on high economic price paid for involvement in liberation struggle of neighboring countries and measures enacted for implementation of Kaunda's egalitarian ideology of Humanism.

Legal System: Supreme Court, High Court, four classes of magistrates' courts, and local (customary) courts. Substantive law consists of legislation enacted before independence, acts passed by Zambian legislature, and aspects of English common law. Local modified (customary) law provides basis for decisions in local courts.

Major Features of International Relations: Opposition to white domination in southern Africa major concern of foreign policy despite Zambia's economic dependence on links to white-dominated states. Hence providing asylum and support for guerrilla forces have paralleled attempts to achieve peaceful transition. Relations with Western countries close, particularly Great Britain. Attempts to diversify have led to good relations with People's Republic of China (China) and formal, somewhat cool relations with Soviet Union.

International Memberships: United Nations and affiliated organizations, Organization of African Unity, European Economic Community (associate member), and African Development Bank. Zambia one of front-line states along with Tanzania, Mozambique, Angola, and Botswana.

Economy

Salient Features: Mixed economy dominated by parastatal companies in all sectors except construction and agricultural production. Sharp division between modern, urban-oriented industrial and commercial agricultural activities, located chiefly along the line of rail, and rural subsistence sector of agriculturalists and pastoralists. Development efforts seriously impaired from mid-1970s by transportation problems and cumulative effects of adverse price fluctuations of single major export, copper. Private sector long downgraded as basically incompatible with philosophy of Humanism, but overriding economic problems led in late 1970s to reassessment of sector's value and assignment of important role during Third National Development Plan (1979–83).

Agriculture: Some 60 percent of population dependent on agriculture but its contribution of less than one-eighth of gross domestic product (GDP) smallest reported among low-income countries. Annual growth rate stagnated during first decade after independence at average of about 2.7 percent, below population growth; some improvement from mid-1970s after government increased agricultural producer prices. About one-half of marketed domestic production grown by commercial sector of small number of expatriates, Zambians, and state farms. Principal staples maize, millet, sorghum, cassava, beans, and peanuts; commercial crops maize, tobacco, cotton, and peanuts.

Livestock and Dairy Farming: Large national herd of 1.6 to 1.9 million head of cattle, mostly owned by traditional farmers. Annual offtake in traditional sector low, furnishing under one-half of beef supply available to commercial market; remainder provided by expatriate commercial stockraisers and state farms having combined herd of under 300,000 head. Milk widely used, but marketed domestic supply far short of demand, and milk reconstituted from imported materials accounted for almost three-quarters of sales. Commercial dairy farms run largely by expatriates; some state-run operations.

Fisheries and Forestry: Some 50,000 persons engage in fishing—half of them in full-time commercial operations—in major lakes, rivers, and swamps. About one-fifth of roughly 60,000-ton annual catch used in fresh or frozen form, remainder sun or smoke dried; most of catch distributed in urban areas. Forests cover over half of country but consist mostly of second-growth savanna woodland used chiefly for firewood and poles. Expanding plantations of exotic species expected to support paper manufacturing industry sometime in 1980s.

Mining and Manufacturing: Mining industry—copper—dominant economic activity; accounted for over one-third of GDP between 1965 and 1974 but dropped to roughly one-eighth in 1975–78 period because of low copper price. Manufacturing industries included sugar and oil refineries; cement, fertilizer, glass, and mining explosive plants; breweries; food processing factories; textile mill; and automotive assembly plants. Most large-scale establishments dependent on imported materials.

Energy Sources: Self-sufficient in electric power production; varying amounts exported to neighboring states. Installed hydroelectric generating capacity over 1.6 million kilowatts in 1978; other capacity roughly 100,000 kilowatts. Total output in 1977 almost 8.7 billion kilowatt-hours. Industry (mainly copper) used about 90 percent of domestic consumption, commercial establishments and homes roughly 10 percent. Rural electrification limited by low per capita income of subsistence farmers and only slight demand by traditional population using shifting cultivation. Coal output met domestic demand; all petroleum imported.

Foreign Trade: Copper sole important source of foreign exchange earnings: from 1965 to 1978 it accounted for more than 90 percent of annual export receipts. Principal destinations of exports in late 1970s were Japan, United Kingdom, remainder of European Economic Community (EEC—also known as Common Market); trade with China of some importance. Main imports by value: machinery and transport equipment, manufactured goods, mineral fuels, chemicals, and foodstuffs. Major suppliers: United Kingdom, EEC, United States, Japan, and South Africa.

Transport and Communications

Railroads: Two main lines totaling about 1,960 route kilometers: trunkline from Rhodesian border (where it ties in to southern African rail network) to copperbelt, thence via Zaïre to Benguela railroad across Angola; Tanzania-Zambia Railway Authority (TAZARA) line extending from trunkline northeastward to Tanzanian border (and to Dar es Salaam port).

Roads: Over 35,000 kilometers, of which about one-seventh asphalted, another one-fifth improved. Main network included paved north-south road from copperbelt to Rhodesian border, with major paved branches northeastward to Tanzanian border, eastward to Chipata (and Malawi border), westward to Mongu. Lusaka and provincial capitals connected by paved roads.

Air Services: Government-owned Zambia Airways provides services to roughly twenty towns; private charter operations also furnish flights to some 120 to 130 airfields. International services by Zambia Airways and several international airlines through sole international airport at Lusaka.

Telecommunications: Estimated 77,400 telephones in early 1978; direct dialing in larger towns and between Lusaka and copperbelt centers. International telephone and cable service to most of world; telex in most commercial centers. Radio stations at Lusaka, Kabwe, Kitwe, and Livingstone; estimated 140,000 receivers in 1977. Television stations at Lusaka, Kabwe, and Kitwe; television sets estimated under 30,000. Earth satellite station at Mwembeshe, in operation from 1974.

National Security

Armed Forces: Zambia National Defense Force (ZNDF) includes the Zambia Army—12,800—and the Zambia Air Force—1,500. Service in the armed forces voluntary. Two civilian components —the Home Guard and the Zambia National Service (ZNS)—also included under ZNDF.

Units: Army has eight battalions that are self-contained combat groups including integral support units. Air force has two combat squadrons, two transport squadrons, one fixed-wing liaison squadron, and one helicopter squadron.

Equipment: Mostly British. Acquired ten Soviet tanks in late 1970s. Rapier missile system acquired in early 1970s, inoperative in 1978 because of lack of spare parts and maintenance. Tiger Cat missile system delivered after Rhodesian raids in late 1978 inoperative until crews can be trained in Great Britain.

Military Alliances: Not formally aligned. Has informal association with Angola, Botswana, Mozambique, and Tanzania in opposing white minority regimes in southern Africa.

Police: Zambia Police Force is a national organization, under the Ministry of Home Affairs. Strength about 10,000.

Armed Militia: Home Guard, strength unknown.

Introduction

AS THE DECADE of the 1970s was coming to an end, Zambia confronted a very difficult economic situation and was still embroiled in the costly turmoil arising out of its support for the efforts of African nationalists to free neighboring Southern Rhodesia from domination by a white minority. Less salient but still of some importance was the country's involvement in the politics of the struggle for independence in Namibia (South-West Africa). Zambia's economic problems were in part a consequence of its longtime participation in the sanctions against Southern Rhodesia and the failure of other transport links—of enormous importance to a landlocked state—to make up for the loss of the rail connection through that territory.

More important in the long run has been Zambia's excessive reliance on a single product—copper—as its chief source of foreign exchange and of indigenous capital for development. With the exception of a few years, Zambia's first decade (1964 to 1974) as an independent state was marked by good copper prices. The effects of world inflation, increasing the cost of fuel and of imported capital goods, began to be felt only in 1973. Despite frequent references to the need to diversify exports and to develop other sectors of the economy, particularly agriculture, the Zambian elite in these favorable circumstances tended to stress copper production. Moreover, where investment in other productive activity did occur, the emphasis was on capital-intensive industry. When world copper prices declined sharply in the mid-1970s, the basic weakness of the Zambian economy was clearly revealed.

A good deal of Zambia's operating and capital budgets went to education, health, and other infrastructure. In an effort to make up as rapidly as possible for the fact that Zambia's educational system was, in 1964, weaker than that of any other British colony recently come to independence, the development of that system was heavily stressed. President Kenneth Kaunda and others considered formal education, appropriately modified to meet Zambia's needs, crucial to both nationbuilding and economic development. Despite the expenditure, a decade and a half has not been enough to bring the growing Zambian population to the desired educational level. Moreover the reorientation of the curriculum has still to be accomplished.

The expansion of the educational system on the one hand and its limitations on the other have contributed, with other factors, to the rapid and distorted process of urbanization. Educated at best through junior secondary school (a total of ten years of schooling) or, more often, through the seven primary grades or less, large numbers of young people in search of jobs have been making their way to the urban areas—chiefly those in the copperbelt (see Glossary) but also to the capital, Lusaka, and to other towns. Industrial, technical administrative, and other skills were indeed in demand (and often provided by expatriates), but these school leavers lacked them; given the capital-intensive character of manufacturing developed since independence, there has been comparatively little need for unskilled workers.

By 1974 more than 35 percent of the Zambian population was urban, most of it located in the towns along the line of rail (see Glossary), and it was likely that the proportion approached 40 percent by the end of the 1970s. There was little to hold young men and (increasingly) young women in the rural areas. The lip service given the importance of agriculture notwithstanding, relatively little had been done to develop Zambian agriculture and to make the farmer's life attractive. In a few areas, particularly along the line of rail, Africans have become involved in commercial cultivation, responding to adequate conditions of cultivation and to the urban demand for their products. Even so, much of Zambia's commercial production was accomplished by European farmers. Elsewhere (with some exceptions) the nature of soils and climate set limits to successful commercial or even thriving subsistence cultivation. A sustained attack on the problem was lacking, in part because the elite was only peripherally interested. In addition the focus on urban activity and the welfare of urban dwellers led to pricing policies for agricultural commodities that discouraged many Zambian farmers.

These policies, which favored the urban consumer, constituted only one element contributing to—or, perhaps more accurately, reflecting—the cleavage between urban and rural Zambians. The greatest differences—economic and other—lay between subsistence cultivators and the educated elite who occupy the highest positions in government and party, parastatal corporations, and private enterprise (where, however, many high-level professionals and technicians were expatriates). The subelite (those occupying mid-level positions in all sectors) and the so-called labor aristocracy (the unionized copper miners and some others) were also distinguished from subsistence cultivators, from the elite, and from each other economically, culturally, and socially. There were perhaps smaller gaps in income between many urban dwellers (the elite excepted) and the relatively few successful African farmers, but there were differences in economic interest and in other respects.

The rural-urban and class distinctions were not the only ones in Zambian society. Like many other former colonial territories, Zambia was made up of a great variety of peoples speaking different languages (most of them mutually unintelligible despite their common membership in the Bantu language family). These indigenous communities were not permanently fixed bounded entities (tribes, as they have been called, or ethnic groups) but constituted groups of historically varying scope, composition, and identity. The names and boundaries that have characterized them in the twentieth century were in many cases imposed by colonial officials who found it convenient to categorize and label the peoples they ruled.

The shifting character of these entities notwithstanding, their varied experience and modes of adaptation before, during, and after colonial rule often led them to assess political, economic, and social situations and opportunities in ethnic terms. This kind of sectionalism continued to mark politics and, sometimes, social relations after independence. A very strong effort has been made to minimize its significance, and ethnicity or regionalism did not dominate Zambian politics in the late 1970s; nevertheless ethnic or regional cleavage as a significant basis for political alignment, now latent, could once again become manifest. Perhaps one of President Kaunda's relative successes has been that he is able to defuse sectionalism, largely because he claims and is seen to be Zambian ("above tribe"). That cannot always be said of most other members of the elite who, despite their membership in an educated status group and their common use of English, are often perceived as representing specific sections in government or party and who might be willing, were it not for Kaunda, to make sectional appeals in a struggle for political power.

The philosophy of Kaunda's Humanism in principle underlies the goals for—if not the organization of—Zambian polity, society, and economy. It insists and expects not only that sectionalism give way to a sense of common humanity but also that economic and social divisions and tendencies to self-aggrandizement give way to cooperation and egalitarianism. In practice the rhetoric of Humanism is ubiquitous in attempts to motivate (or castigate) Zambians, but its goals have not been approached—let alone reached—in part because they may not be widely shared or deeply felt.

If the effects of sectionalism have been damped, that has been accomplished only by substituting what the Zambian governing elite calls one-party participatory democracy for the multiparty system that prevailed until late 1972. The parties other than the United National Independence Party (UNIP) had the flavor and some of the substance of sectionalism, and even UNIP was seen in sectional terms by some Zambians. Kaunda may have been personally disposed to democratic processes, but multiparty politics seemed to express not so much reasonable competition as sheer divisiveness and therefore to stretch the limits of Zambia's fragile unity.

One-party participatory democracy left room for expression of disapproval; overtly in the right of voters to vote "no" in a presidential election and, more subtly, by refusal to participate in the elections. Both techniques have been used, but the expression of disapproval was not so strong as to oust Kaunda from office. By the late 1970s the stresses and strains of Zambian society attendant on the economic difficulties that came after the decline in copper prices and the attacks (without defense or reprisal) on Zambian soil by Rhodesian forces led to the possibility that the presidential election of late 1978 might result in either heavy abstention or a strong negative vote. The turnout was not as high as the ruling party might have wished but exceeded that for elections in the early 1970s, and the negative vote, although fairly high in some districts, was not as great as some observers expected.

Kaunda survived, but the issues that had seemed to make his survival problematic persisted. He dealt with some of those connected with Zambia's support of Zimbabwean guerrillas against the Rhodesian regime but could not or would not deal with others. Reaffirming that support, he nevertheless was constrained to permit a crack in Zambia's closure of the border with Southern Rhodesia so that fertilizers and other items crucial to Zambian agriculture could reach his landlocked country from South African ports. Having given refuge to Africans from Zimbabwe and sanctuary to Joshua Nkomo's Zimbabwe African People's Union (ZAPU), he had laid Zambia open to air attacks by Rhodesian forces that began in late 1978 and persisted into 1979; neither ZAPU's nor Zambia's forces could deal with these attacks. Apparently Kaunda's government would have to tolerate Rhodesian encroachment, although observers have suggested that some Zambians resented either the failure to fight back or the need to suffer such attacks. In the latter case what is at issue is the weariness of Zambians who may have supported Kaunda's solidarity with the guerrillas in the beginning but had not bargained for the long-term burden such solidarity entailed.

Sooner or later the Rhodesia-Zimbabwe issue will be settled. Of longer term interest is the precarious state of the Zambian economy. In early 1979 copper prices, which had been low for roughly four years, showed signs of rising again; but such a rise, though helpful in the short run, might well tempt the Zambian elite to the same excessive dependence on a single commodity that had contributed to the economy's difficulties in the mid- and late 1970s. The Third National Development Plan (1979–83) much talked about but not yet published at the end of February 1979, would presumably take into account the fallacy of relying exclusively on copper. Diversification was one theme of the plan, and renewed emphasis on agricultural development was another. Major reforms in the educational system and other improvements in infrastructure requiring large capital outlays were to be put in abeyance for the time being. Even with increases in copper prices and aid from international organizations, however, economic development that would bring satisfying rewards to enough of the Zambian people might not come soon enough to avert the widening of existing cleavages and consequent potential instability.

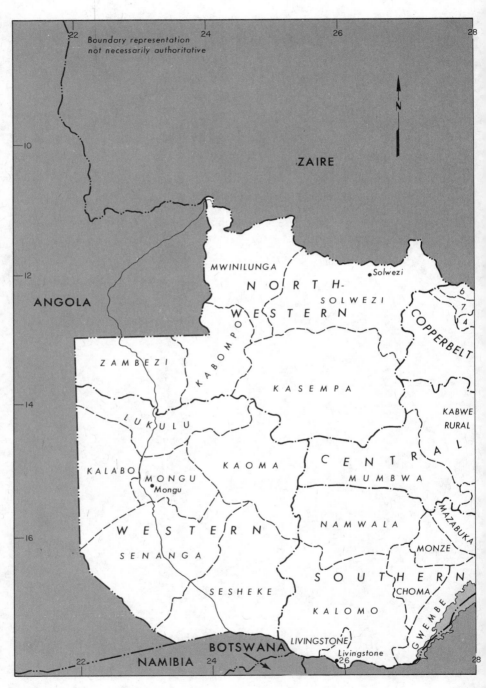

Figure 1. Major Administrative Divisions

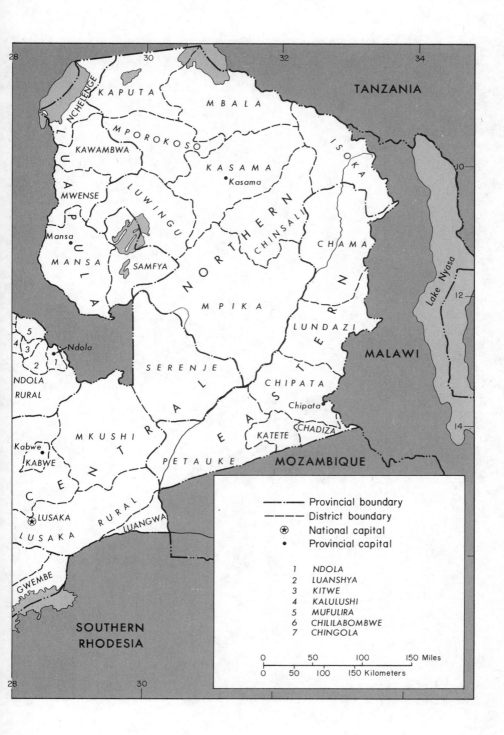

TANZANIA

NCHELENGE

KAPUTA

MBALA

MPOROKOSO

KAWAMBWA

ISOKA

KASAMA
• Kasama

MWENSE

LUWINGU

N O R T H E R N

CHINSALI

CHAMA

Lake Nyasa

Mansa
•

MANSA

SAMFYA

M P I K A

LUNDAZI

E A S T E R N

MALAWI

5

4 3
• Ndola

2 1

NDOLA
RURAL

S E R E N J E

CHIPATA

Chipata
•

CHADIZA

Kabwe
•

MKUSHI

KATETE

KABWE

PETAUKE

MOZAMBIQUE

C E N T R A L

⊛ LUSAKA

RURAL

LUSAKA

LUANGWA

GWEMBE

SOUTHERN
RHODESIA

—·—·— Provincial boundary
— — — District boundary
⊛ National capital
• Provincial capital

1 NDOLA
2 LUANSHYA
3 KITWE
4 KALULUSHI
5 MUFULIRA
6 CHILILABOMBWE
7 CHINGOLA

0   50   100   150 Miles

0   50   100   150 Kilometers

Chapter 1. Historical Setting

Luvale mask used in ceremonial dances

THE HISTORY OF Zambia until relatively recent times is better conceived of in terms of broad social and cultural phases and processes than as a succession of individual polities or personalities. These are seen most clearly in the patterns of change and persistence in technology, production, trade, material culture, and sociopolitical organization that mark both the content and the chronological structure of Zambian history. That change and persistence are manifest today in such crucial issues as the effect of foreign trade and investment on local production and culture, the fragility of an economy based on a single export, the constraints imposed by dependence on exterior lines of communication and trade, the political and economic role of foreigners, the development and deployment of human and natural resources, and the role of the state in governing, mediating, and resolving the conflicts attendant thereon.

Geography—political and social as well as physical—is the bedrock of Zambian history. Occupying a landlocked position on the central African plateau, Zambia lies at the heart of the mining complex that stretches across the subcontinent from Zaïre to South Africa. Zambia's history is an integral part of, and indeed has been largely shaped by, the history of central Africa. In colonial times Zambia's interior lines of communication were less developed than its exterior ties, while its insular position with respect to regional and intercontinental trade made it subject to external forces and market conditions. In recent years Zambia has become an integral part of the political economy and international system of southern Africa.

Production and external trade have long provided the material basis of Zambia's culture and history. The diffusion of new technology, such as metallurgy and the practice of agriculture, and the introduction of new crops—maize, cassava, peanuts, sweet potatoes, sugarcane, rice, cotton, and tobacco—gradually transformed the essential basis of human society. External demand for ivory, slaves and, more recently, copper tied Zambia to a far-flung network of regional and transoceanic trade routes and markets extending from East Asia to the Americas.

Changing technology and material culture were also accompanied by changes in social organization and value systems. Indeed, in historical perspective, human society in Zambia has been characterized by increasing social differentiation and specialization of economic, social, and political structures, the elaboration of more formal institutions and complex patterns of social stratification, and the use of more advanced technology.

The history of Zambia can be divided into three broad chronological phases: precolonial, colonial, and the period of independence. The precolonial period, which spanned several millennia before about 1890, can be subdivided conveniently into the Stone Age and subsequent Iron Age. Zambia's Stone Age inhabitants were hunters and gatherers whose material culture showed progressive refinement and advances until yielding in the first millennium A.D. to Bantu-speaking, iron-using intruders who made the most significant contributions to the language, culture, and biology of the country's present-day population. These people introduced not only new metallurgical techniques but also new pottery styles, agriculture, stockraising, and more complex organizational forms and institutions including chieftainship, state, and kingdom.

Iron Age technology was introduced to Zambia in two distinct stages. The first wave of Bantu-speaking migrants brought rather simple smelting techniques early in the first millennium. Later, between about 700 and 1200, more complex ironworking techniques arrived and spread. Thus by the thirteenth century the ancestral populations of Zambia exhibited a relatively advanced material culture and social structure based on agricultural production, setting the scene for the emergence of discrete societies and polities.

State systems may have been established in the Shaba region of the Zaïre watershed during the eighth or ninth century A.D. Perhaps influenced by developments in Shaba, or responding to essentially similar conditions, kingships likewise emerged by the thirteenth century in the surrounding Zaïre basin and central lake districts and perhaps on the central Angolan plateau. During the next few centuries offshoots of these kingdoms moved south and southwest into Zambia. There they established new states and chiefdoms, by force or invitation, among the Later Iron Age farmers. These dynastic migrations mark the historical origin of most of the identifiable ethnic communities of present-day Zambia. Long-distance trade expanded during this period also, first with the Arabs and Africans who dominated Indian Ocean and coastal commerce, and after the sixteenth century with the Portuguese based in Angola to the west and Mozambique to the east. The new trade routes and markets brought new foreign imports in exchange for ivory, slaves, copper, and other products.

During the eighteenth and nineteenth centuries a commercial revolution occurred in the central African interior in the wake of mercantile penetration by Afro-Arabs (largely Swahili speaking) from the east coast and renewed Portuguese demand. Moreover new pressures in the nineteenth century irrevocably broke Zambia's comparative isolation from the direct impingement of external influences and culminated in the imposition of European rule. Zambia attracted a new class of foreign intruders: African raiders from the south, African and Arab warlord-merchants from the northeast, and finally European explorers, missionaries, and conquerors. The trade in slaves and ivory intensified, drawing Zambia into the world economy. Ngoni raiders crossed the Zambezi River from the south. From the northeast came traders and slavers from Zanzibar and the Tanganyika coast, breaking traditional trading patterns in the interior. Yeke traders in Katanga (present-day Shaba in Zaïre) encroached upon the domains of the *mwata kazembe* (usually called *kazembe*) kingdom in the Luapula Valley, severed its historical ties with the Lunda sovereign (the *mwant yav*), and intervened in the internal politics of the kingdom. Other Zambian peoples like the Bemba and Bisa capitalized on the new commercial opportunities to expand their economic and political position in the northeast. In the southeast new groups of warrior-traders called Cikunda lived by predatory slaving and hunting ivory. Sotho remnants known as the Kololo crossed the Zambezi in the west and occupied the Lozi kingdom for three decades. Ndebele incursions also plagued western and southern Zambia. The net result of these traumatic upheavals was that Zambia was plunged into a period of turmoil and subjected to unprecedented foreign intrusion just as the European scramble for Central Africa reached its peak. By conquest and diplomacy Zambia was subdued by the British in the 1890s, bringing this historical era to a close and inaugurating Zambia's colonial period, which lasted until 1964.

At first Zambia was administered by the British South Africa Company and was called Northern Rhodesia. Company rule was superficial but exploitative, and in 1924 the British Colonial Office assumed responsibility for administering the territory. The discovery of major copper deposits in the 1920s led to the emergence of the copperbelt as the economic and political center of the territory in the 1930s. As African political consciousness matured into nationalism, the insecure European minority sought closer association with the entrenched white settler regime in Southern Rhodesia. Thus in 1953 the two Rhodesias joined Nyasaland (Malawi) to form the Central African Federation of Rhodesia and Nyasaland, despite the misgivings and opposition of Northern Rhodesia's Africans.

The federation lasted only ten years. Elections in late 1962 resulted in an African majority in the Legislative Council and a shaky coalition between the two African nationalist parties. The council demanded secession from the federation, internal self-government under a new constitution, and a new parliament based on democratic franchise. In December 1963 the federation was dissolved, and Northern Rhodesia finally became independent in October 1964 as the Republic of Zambia under President Kenneth Kaunda.

Independence inaugurated another era in Zambia's history. By 1973 Zambia had become a "one-party participatory democracy" under Kaunda's United National Independence Party (UNIP), organized opposition having been eliminated by a combination of electoral, constitutional, and executive actions. Copper continued to dominate Zambia's economy, which Kaunda sought to bring under state control by nationalization. Zambia also assumed a central role in the regional politics of southern Africa, supporting the armed struggle for majority rule and skillfully maintaining its nonaligned course between East and West.

Precolonial Zambia to ca. 1890

The Stone Age

Archaeologists conventionally divide the African Stone Age into Early, Middle, and Late Stone Age periods. In Zambia the earliest human artifacts consist of a variety of stone tools called hand axes, which have been found in the Kalomo and Zambezi river valleys. This tool kit, dating back perhaps 200,000 years, is characteristic of the Acheulian phase of Early Stone Age technology that occurred widely throughout the continent. It represents the work of *Homo erectus,* the same species that produced the more spectacular hand axes at Tanzania's Olduvai Gorge more than 500,000 years ago.

Kalambo Falls, which has yielded tools and other remains dating perhaps to 100,000 years ago, is one of Africa's most significant Early Stone Age sites (see fig. 2). There well-established hunting and gathering communities flourished, perhaps supplementing their diet by fishing and scavenging. Wooden clubs and spears along with throwing stones constituted the essential hunting technology, and a diversified stone tool kit including flake knives, choppers, cleavers, and scrapers was employed. More important, however, is the fact that Kalambo Falls has yielded the first evidence of the use of fire in sub-Saharan Africa. The discovery of fire —with its manifold uses for cooking, warmth and protection, burning brush, and chasing and hunting game—was one of early man's most dramatic advances.

About 125,000 years ago a transition to more specialized stone industries having greater regional variation occurred in southern Africa as people spread out from lake and riverine environments to occupy "dambos" where large shallow depressions collected and retained rainfall, ensuring a long-term if not perennial water supply. The uppermost Acheulian levels of the Kalambo Falls sequence reveal an intermediate tool complex known as Sangoan. This new tool kit, also widespread in sub-Saharan Africa, was characterized by large chopping tools probably used to make wooden implements that have not survived.

Local variation is a hallmark of the Middle Stone Age in Zambia. In some areas at least, Sangoan techniques gave way to proto-Stillbay tool kits made from stone flakes rather than cores. The oldest human skeletal remains in southern Africa also date from this period. At Kabwe (formerly Broken Hill) an almost complete skull and other bones dating to perhaps 125,000 years ago were discovered in 1921. Broken Hill Man represents the species formerly called *Homo rhodesiensis,* also found in east and south

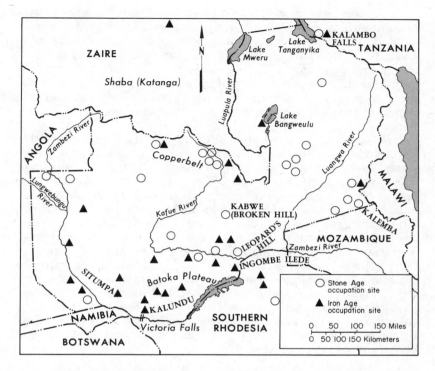

Figure 2. Important Stone Age and Iron Age Sites

Africa, and resembles Neanderthal Man *(Homo sapiens neander-thalensis)*, which became extinct in Europe, North Africa, and western Asia about 35,000 years ago.

The final and most widespread Middle Stone Age industry in Zambia is the Stillbay, dating to about 35,000 years ago. The Still-bay tool kit was characterized by greater variety in scrapers and flake tools. Other regional variations also occurred. At Kalambo Falls, for instance, the distinctive large leaf-shaped points or blades of the Lupemban industry had Sangoan roots, but the industry reflects adaptation to a more heavily wooded or forest environment.

The Late Stone Age was heralded by the transitional Magosian industries dated to about 20,000 B.C. at Kalemba rock shelter, Leopard's Hill Cave, and Kalambo. By 15,000 B.C. the Late Stone Age had begun in Africa and elsewhere in the Old World. The prepared-core method was retained, but smaller cores and flakes predominated. This new tool complex included small, thin sharp blades (microliths) for knives and spears. Such microlithic techniques also made possible the invention of composite tools of wood and stone or bone; previously these materials had been only used separately in toolmaking.

7

In Zambia several distinctive Late Stone Age industries have been identified, of which two are widespread and have been well studied. The Nachikufan variant, typified by woodworking tools and ground stone axes, was concentrated in the wooded areas of north, east, and central Zambia and indicates an emphasis on food gathering. In the open country of the southwest there evolved the more appropriate hunting technology of the Wilton culture, which was widely distributed throughout eastern and southern Africa.

The tempo of human history increased remarkably during the Late Stone Age. By that time *Homo sapiens,* modern man, had established his mastery over varied environments by devising and adapting specialized tools and techniques for survival and sustenance. Human culture and society diversified and became more complex, and the rate of technological change accelerated. Simple hand axes gave way to composite tools, which in turn were followed by the invention of the still more complex bow and arrow. To be sure, food gathering and fishing remained important. But these Late Stone Age advances enabled modern man to improve his hunting techniques, exploit new habitats and food sources, enjoy a more varied and healthful diet, and increase in numbers. Skeletal remains indicate that these Late Stone Age hunters resembled the people called the San or Khoisan (and referred to by whites as Bushmen), still found in remote and scattered enclaves throughout southern Africa.

The Iron Age to ca. 1500

Zambia occupies a central place in the Iron Age of southcentral Africa. It lies astride Africa's historic north-south migration routes and lines of communication running from the Nile Valley and the Horn of Africa through the lake region of eastern Africa to southern Africa. The Zambezi-Zaïre watershed also forms a natural zone of human migration and cultural diffusion. Geographically and historically Zambia was well positioned to receive and mediate the revolutionary changes of the Iron Age.

In this context, the Iron Age is to be understood as a shorthand expression for the composite changes in southern African culture and society beginning in the early first millennium A.D. These changes include the introduction of ironworking, pottery, and new forms of economic life centered on agriculture, the domestication of animals, and stockkeeping; major human migrations with their attendant demographic, linguistic, social, and cultural diffusions and transformations; and the emergence and spread of more complex forms of political organization, such as chieftainship, states, and even empires. The rate of historical change quickened, as major human and technological advances were measureable in centuries instead of millennia.

Although scholarly opinion is not unanimous, it is widely agreed that Iron Age technology spread to the subcontinent along with the migrations from what is now Zaïre of negroid peoples who spoke related Bantu languages. (Their ultimate point of origin probably lay still farther north.) Apparently these people had made the transition from hunting and gathering to food production during the first millennium B.C., while still in the Late Stone Age. However, the acquisition of ironworking technology from the north enabled these cultivators to expand rapidly and to spread their way of life throughout central and southern Africa.

Pottery remains serve the same function in the study of the Iron Age as stone tools for the Stone Age. These fragments have enabled scholars to identify, classify, and date several distinctive Iron Age traditions in the subcontinent. Radiocarbon dates and the distribution of early Iron Age sites in southcentral Africa suggest a rather sudden introduction and rapid spread of ironworking technology throughout the region during the first centuries of the Christian era.

Thanks to the archaeological investigations of J. Desmond Clark, Brian Fagan, David Phillipson, Joseph Vogel, and others, the Zambian Iron Age is especially well known. The evidence indicates that the spread of Iron Age culture in Zambia took place in two broad phases. The initial occupation by early Bantu migrants occurred in successive movements into the country from the north, west, and south between the fourth and sixth centuries A.D. A second major wave of migration of Bantu-speaking farmers, indicated by distinctive Later Iron Age pottery styles, took place in the second millennium. These later settlers may be identified as the more or less direct ancestors of Zambia's modern-day inhabitants. Here again, though, two different Later Iron Age migrations are indicated by the contrast between the pottery styles of the far south and the rest of the country.

There are four major regional variants in the Zambian Iron Age. Southern Zambia, distinguished by the best known Iron Age sequence in sub-Saharan Africa, was settled (on the Batoka Plateau) in the fifth century by Iron Age farmers. Sixth-century immigrants from the south then settled the region northwest of Victoria Falls, whence their distinctive pottery tradition spread to the Batoka Plateau during the late first millennium. In the early second millennium this pottery tradition was replaced by yet another, which is ancestral to the historically known pottery styles of the region. The present-day peoples and cultures of southern Zambia seem therefore to be descended from these Later Iron Age immigrants who displaced or absorbed the remaining Late Stone Age and Early Iron Age populations.

The fifth-century Iron Age settlements on the Batoka Plateau are those of the so-called Kalundu group, whose pottery style resembles that of contemporaneous pottery in central and northeastern Zambia, suggesting a common origin in Shaba. Between the ninth and twelfth centuries the Kalundu was supplanted by the Kalomo pottery tradition, which spread north across the plateau and may represent a late phase of the Shongwe style from the Victoria Falls region. The diffusion of this new pottery style may have been associated with drought-related population movements and perhaps the displacement or absorption of the Kalundu culture-bearers, but it did not otherwise signal a shift in the material basis of culture.

The sixth-century Rhodesian immigrants who settled around Victoria Falls and later spread north introduced the Shongwe pottery tradition, which may have been a later phase of the Situmpa style practiced to the northwest. The people of the Shongwe tradition, apparently of mixed negroid-bushmanoid stock, enjoyed a semipermanent village life based on an agricultural economy, which also depended heavily on hunting and fishing. The smelting and working of iron were widespread, and sporadic if not sustained trade and bartering may have existed.

Early in the second millennium the pottery traditions of southern Zambia were rapidly supplanted by a new style that seems ancestral to that of the present-day Tonga-speaking peoples of that region. The evidence suggests large-scale population movements into Zambia from the north or northwest, hence the appellation "Tonga Diaspora" tradition. The astonishing continuity in the pottery tradition of the Batoka highlands and Victoria Falls area since the twelfth century indicates broader cultural and demographic continuities as well.

Like their Later Iron Age contemporaries, the Tonga Diaspora peoples practiced mixed farming but little trade. Their culture was distinguished by intensive agriculture and stockkeeping, the latter perhaps encouraged by the introduction of cattle-milking from the northeast in the early second millennium. These peoples may also have introduced cotton cultivation and spinning, pipe smoking, and new rituals associated with the many clay cattle figurines found at their sites. Wealth and status distinctions assumed some importance at this time also, suggesting incipient social stratification.

Somewhat later at Ingombe Ilede the political economy of long-distance trade seems to have precipitated the process of state formation in southern Zambia. Burial mounds dated to the fourteenth or fifteenth century reveal advanced technology and social structure, as well as clear evidence of long-distance trade with Shaba to the north and with the east coast. Ingombe Ilede flourished at the same time as the more renowned Mwene Mutapa empire in Rhodesia and may have been the northern outpost of the regional gold trade for the Arab merchants who penetrated the Zambezi early in the second millennium. Among the most suggestive finds are copper crosses, which hint at the existence of standardized currency, and iron bells, which were symbols of chieftainship in Zaïre whence they were probably imported. Of technological interest are skills shown in drawing copper wire and making alloys and in the flange-welding technique of the iron bells. Indeed, it has been hypothesized that Ingombe Ilede was linked with the southward movement of chiefly clans or segments from Shaba, which seem to have introduced chieftaincy to Zambia in later centuries.

Unlike in the south, in northeastern Zambia the coming of the Iron Age did not result in the rapid replacement of Late Stone Age technology or populations. As evidenced by the Kalambo Falls Early Iron Age tradition, which spread over the plateau between the Luangwa and Luapula rivers, Stone Age and Iron Age peoples and traditions coexisted, the former gradually giving way to the latter over several centuries. This transition is evident not only in stratified archaeological sites but also in stylistic changes in the rather remarkable rock paintings found almost exclusively in northeastern Zambia.

The third major regional variant of the Zambian Iron Age is found between the copperbelt and the lower Kafue river, in the central part of the country. Here the impact of Early Iron Age immigrants was more immediate and profound than in the north. The relative absence of remains from Stone Age cultures and the abundance of Iron Age sites dating from the fifth and sixth centuries suggest a rapid displacement or absorption of the former. It also seems that the technologies for smelting copper and iron were introduced simultaneously in central Zambia during the latter part of the first millennium.

After the eleventh century, however, a new pottery tradition spread over most of northeastern and central Zambia. The distribution of this distinctive Later Iron Age pottery, classified as the Luangwa tradition, suggests that it diffused east and south from Shaba with a new wave of migration. The Luangwa tradition was associated not only with the spread of more advanced metalworking techniques, but also with new slash-and-burn cultivation methods. Moreover its resemblance to the modern pottery styles of these regions further suggests that its makers were ancestral to many present-day inhabitants. In short much of eastern and northern Zambia seems to have been settled in the early second millennium by a new population whose sociopolitical organization and technology enabled them to exploit the wooded environment more effectively than their Early Iron Age predecessors, who were probably absorbed by the newcomers.

Finally in western Zambia Early Iron Age pottery of the Lungwebungu tradition, found also in the adjacent regions of Zaïre and Angola, was probably associated with migrations from the south or west in the mid-first millennium. Here, in contrast to northeastern and central Zambia, there is a marked continuity between Early Iron Age and modern pottery styles. This implies a long process of cultural evolution uninterrupted by outside migrations or drastic internal changes. The fact that modern practitioners of this Lungwebungu tradition are men suggests further that this was the pattern also among the Early Iron Age peoples elsewhere in Zambia.

In summary, by the early second millennium Zambia was settled by peoples who may be considered the cultural and physical ancestors of its modern inhabitants. Although there was no sharp break between the Late Stone Age and the Early Iron Age, the transition to ironworking, agriculture, and stockkeeping certainly occurred at a more rapid rate than the succession of the various Stone Age industries. Material culture and socioeconomic organization also advanced to new levels of complexity, as evidenced by the commercial, technological, and social sophistication of the peoples of Ingombe Ilede and the Tonga Diaspora in the south.

Peoples and Polities, ca. 1500–1800

During the next few hundred years the peoples of Zambia emerged into the full light of history. After the fifteenth century the archaeological record can be supplemented by both oral traditions and written records of European observers. In this connection, it is important to consider the meaning of "tribal" identity and traditions. The term *tribe* has been used to refer variously to peoples who speak a common language or acknowledge the authority of a single chief, or even to the name given to a group of people by outsiders. Such identities change, indicating that so-called tribal history is really the history of changing identities rather than of discrete social groups. As Andrew Roberts, the foremost historian of Zambia, has written, "tribes" are "byproducts of social and cultural change" or "states of mind" rather than "actual social organizations."

The traditions of origin of modern-day Zambians provided a sense of identity as well as cultural and moral explanations of institutions, practices, and social relationships. Stories of so-called tribal migrations in particular probably refer to the movements of dynastic or chiefly offshoots who established their authority over societies lacking chiefs or with chiefs having limited jurisdiction and authority. The history of these dynastic groups became accepted as the tribal history.

Before the advent of chieftainship political relations within and between Zambian societies were governed by the lineage organization (see Social Structure, ch. 2). Beginning perhaps as early as the fifteenth century and accelerating after the seventeenth, chieftainship spread throughout Zambia. By the nineteenth century chiefly institutions had supplanted the lineage as the characteristic political institution among most of Zambia's peoples. Chiefs varied greatly in the nature and scope of their authority but usually embodied religious and ceremonial functions as well as legal and administrative ones.

Traditions indicate that most Zambian chieftainships can be traced to migrations of chiefly lineages or clans and related political ideologies from the upper Zaïre basin between 1500 and 1800.

Chieftainship, indeed kingship, may have emerged in Shaba under indigenous inspiration and forces as early as the eighth or ninth century. The impetus for such large-scale political organization seems to have come from the requirements of regulating relations among strangers and traders who congregated at the extraction sites of scarce natural resources, such as salt, copper, and iron, or at commercial crossroads and markets. Political organization based on kinship alone could not manage such relations; kingship could.

By the thirteenth century states had crystallized among several other societies in the Zaïre basin and central lake region and perhaps on the adjacent Angolan plateau as well. Statehood seems to have emerged and spread less by conquest than by the peaceful imposition of certain awe-inspiring ideas, political ideologies, modes of social organization, and methods of governing. For Zambia, it was the diffusion of Luba and Lunda dynastic segments and political culture from southern Zaïre that precipitated the historical process of state formation and chiefly rule.

The chieftainships of central and northeastern Zambia trace their origin to the Luba empire in southeastern Zaïre, where the imperial kingship tracing itself to Ilunga Mbidi had developed. The ideology of Luba kingship, perhaps derived from the early Shaba states, was based on *bulopwe,* a hereditary ruling quality transmitted in a single descent line. This concept had two dynamic ramifications. On the one hand it strengthened royal lineages and justified the exercise of authority over unrelated peoples and lineages. On the other hand—and this is crucial to the proliferation and territorial dispersion of chieftainship—it encouraged succession disputes and the migration of unsuccessful dynastic contenders to establish their own chiefdoms elsewhere. It was this institutionalized process of dynastic fission and migration that resulted int he spread of chieftainship to many parts of Zambia (see fig. 3).

The earliest known kingdom in Zambia was the mysterious Maravi (Malawi) kingdom of Kalonga that developed south of Lake Malawi and probably dates to a fourteenth-century Luban migration. Its western subjects eventually became the Cewa, whose sixteenth-century chieftainship under the *undi* (a title derived from the name of the first chief) survives as the oldest offshoot of the early Kalonga state. Among other Zambian peoples with more or less remote Luban ancestry are the Bemba and Bisa, both of whom occupy center stage in the history of the northeast, as well as the Ambo, Kaonde, Lala, Lamba, Lenje, Lima, Nsenga, Sala, Soli, Swaka, and Ushi.

The Bemba emerged as the dominant people in northeastern Zambia after the eighteenth century. Chieftainship developed in the late seventeenth century under the Luba clan chief Citimukulu; that name became the title of the Bemba paramount chief. At first the Bemba state was loosely structured, ritual and kinship were more important than secular authority and central-

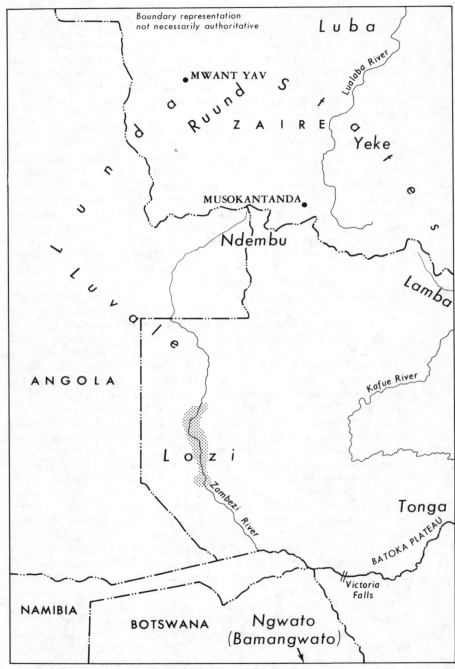

Figure 3. African Polities, Eighteenth and Nineteenth Centuries

SOUTHERN
RHODESIA

International boundary
Luba Ethnic or ethnolinguistic group
• Capital of specific state or chiefdom
Floodplain
Swamp

0   50   100   150   200 Miles
0   50 100 150 200 Kilometers

ized institutions, and many subordinate chiefs split off to establish independent chiefdoms. Unlike the Lozi and Ngoni conquest states, Bemba chiefs assimilated to the culture and language of the local population. The kingship itself circulated among the royal lineages, often resulting in dynastic succession wars until the early nineteenth century when one of these lineages monopolized royal succession. At the same time territorial and commercial expansion enabled the *citimukulu* to enlarge the imperial administration with appointed kinsmen and thus strengthen the kingship and his royal lineage.

To the south of the Bemba several Bisa chieftainships emerged out of the same process of Luban expansion. During the eighteenth century the Bisa played a major role in the devleopment of long-distance trade between northeastern Zambia and the east coast. The spread of chiefly institutions among the Bemba and Bisa also spurred the development of chieftainships among other peoples in the northeast and northwest, such as the Iwa, Mambwe, Namwanga, Senga, and Shila.

In northwestern Zambia the inspiration for chieftainship emanated from the Lunda of southwestern Zaïre. Like the Luba, the Lunda developed centralized political institutions and transmitted them south and west. The Lunda nourished and expanded the authority of their king, the *mwant yav,* through the notion of "perpetual kinship" in which titled positions were linked in kinship terms, thus integrating unrelated individuals and groups into the extended royal family. The Lunda also capitalized on the idea, widespread in Central Africa, of "owners of the land" by retaining subordinated local chiefs under supreme royal authority and incorporating them into the perpetual kinship network. Thus indigenous customs, beliefs, and institutions were adapted to the purposes of statecraft and imperial administration. Lunda migrations spawned fewer chieftainships than did those of the Luba, but Lunda chieftainships retained more concrete historical, cultural, and economic ties to their ancestral home.

According to oral tradition, in the late sixteenth century a royal marriage alliance between the senior Lunda chief and a Luba alienated several Lunda groups that then migrated toward the southwest. In fact Lunda political models were propagated through a large portion of the western savanna by emigrant chiefs, court conquests, and cultural borrowing. During the seventeenth century this Lunda diaspora gave rise to the Cokwe and Mbangala chieftainships in Angola, to the Luvale, Ndembu, and Lunda of northwestern Zambia, and to the *musokantanda,* a "perpetual son" of the *mwant yav,* who became paramount over the northern Kaonde chiefs in Zambia. Trade and firepower further encouraged the statebuilding process among the Cokwe and Mbangala, who obtained guns and new food crops, such as maize and cassava, through their commercial ties with the Portuguese in Angola.

The most important Zambian kingdom of Lunda origin was that

of the *kazembe,* which was established in the Luapula valley during the last major wave of Lunda migration and conquest in the mid-eighteenth century. *Kazembe* was a royal title awarded by the *mwant yav* to a man who helped the Lunda gain control over the salt deposits on the upper Lualaba in the early part of the century. The *kazembe* continued to expand his domain eastward, subduing other peoples like the Shila and gaining control of local copper mines. The transfer of this title to a successor ensured the continuity of the incipient kingdom, which then prospered by its access to European trade goods (including guns from the west) and by the adoption of cassava as the staple crop. Unlike the Bemba, the kingdom of the *kazembe* was a classic conquest state with a monodynastic kingship modeled on that of the *mwant yav,* titled territorial governors who also served as kingmakers, and an imperial officialdom bound together by enduring kinship ties.

The other major locus of political power in western Zambia was the Lozi kingdom. Although there may have been remote ties with the Lunda political tradition, the Lozi state emerged on the fertile upper Zambezi flood plain as a result of local evolution and an extended period of migration from the north beginning in the late seventeenth century. By the late eighteenth century a royal bureaucracy based on merit supplanted the original titled aristocracy. The Lozi kingdom was a remarkably centralized imperial state, with graded officialdom and councils, an extensive tributary system, and corvée labor for military service and public works.

The Commercial Revolution: The Late Eighteenth and Nineteenth Centuries

Earlier phases of Zambia's past were characterized by important changes in Stone Age technology, the introduction of metallurgy along with agricultural and pastoral economies, and the emergence of historic peoples and polities. These long-term transformations had at least one thing in common: they were essentially African, that is, deeply rooted in the historical and cultural traditions of the continent by the time they began to influence the course of Zambian history. In the eighteenth century, however, external forces began to shape the contours of Zambian history, and by the end of the nineteenth century Zambia had been drawn into the world economy and subjected to colonial rule in the wake of the industrial revolution and European imperialism.

The commercial revolution of the eighteenth and nineteenth centuries in Central Africa did not occur in a historical vacuum. Since the Early Iron Age, trade had been an increasingly important factor in Zambian history. Local and regional trade in salt, fish, meat, and other foods, iron ore and metalwork, copper ornaments, cloth, pottery, baskets, and other domestic consumption goods had flourished for centuries in many areas since the first millennium without benefit of uniform currencies and regular markets. The extent of this local production and exchange was of no small moment in this process, for the capacity of Zambian societies to adapt successfully to the complexities of long-distance trade was largely a function of the scale of their domestic economies.

Early in the second millennium external commercial contacts between the interior and the Indian Ocean were expanded and intensified, as reflected in the rise of the trading site at Ingombe Ilede. This new international commerce was based on the unique and exotic products of the respective trading areas: thus gold and ivory of Central Africa were exchanged for glass beads, seashells, porcelain, and luxury cloth from Asia. After the sixteenth century Portuguese commercial penetration from both west and east added still another dimension to the internationalization of Zambia's economies. By the early eighteenth century the Portuguese had wrested the gold trade of Central Africa from the Muslim merchants on the Mozambican coast, extended their chain of forts and trading posts up the Zambezi beyond the confluence of the Luangwa, and opened southern and central Zambia directly to export copper, ivory, and gold.

The implications of foreign penetration soon became evident. In eastern Zambia the Cewa kingdom of the *undi* had taken advantage of the Portuguese demand for ivory in the seventeenth century to expand its trade and hegemony. But gold was discovered in the early eighteenth century, and the *undi* unwisely allowed the Portuguese to exploit the mines in cooperation with his subordinate chiefs. This arrangement effectively undermined not only the *undi's* commercial monopoly but also the integrity of the state. This was a striking prelude to things to come.

The expansion of long-distance trade in northeastern Zambia in the eighteenth century was also a response to overseas demand for ivory and copper. Here Yao and Bisa merchants joined to form a transcontinental trade route linking the east coast with the west through the *kazembe's* ties with the *mwant yav*. The *kazembe*, however, sought to bypass these middlemen and gain direct access to the Portuguese on the lower Zambezi, an ambition that coincided with Portuguese strategic and commercial aims to open the interior.

But the grand designs never materialized. Despite successive expeditions by the Eurafrican *pombeiros* (interior traders) Mello and Teixeira, the father-and-son team of Goncalo Pereira and Manuel Pereira, and Francisco de Lacerda in the late 1790s, and the first transcontinental journey from Luanda in Angola to Tete in Mozambique by Pedro Baptista and Anastacio Francisco from 1804 to 1811, Portuguese trade with the *kazembe's* kingdom dwindled to almost nothing. Again, changing external demand was fateful. By the early nineteenth century slaves had surpassed ivory and gold as the chief Portuguese exports from the lower Zambezi. When at least two other Portuguese missions to the *kazembe* failed to establish regular commercial relations, and powerful neighbors like the Bemba encroached on his dominions, the *kazembe's* kingdom declined.

Trade with the west coast also increased as a result of growing external demand and enterprising middlemen. Serving the same function as the Bisa in the east, the Ovimbundu of Angola expanded their ivory and slave trade in the eighteenth century, linking the Portuguese on the Atlantic coast with markets in the interior. Among the peoples of western Zambia who participated in this widening commercial network were the Lozi, Lamba, Luvale, and several Lunda states.

During the nineteenth century Zambia was beset by new and even more threatening external forces. Foreign commercial and military penetration overturned many of the established states in the area, radically altering the balance of power within and among Zambia's polities and reorienting its historical east-west links on a north-south axis. The quickening pace of the industrial revolution in Europe and North America increased demand for African labor and raw materials, thus intensifying the pillage of the interior of the subcontinent. During most of the century it was rapacious African and Muslim traders and warriors from eastern and southern Africa who threatened to overrun and dominate Zambia. But in the end it was British mercantile imperialists who did.

Northeastern Zambia was drawn into the Arab, Swahili, and Nyamwezi commercial empires expanding west and southwest from Zanzibar and the Tanganyika coast. The Kazembe-Bisa-Yao trade alliance broke up under the new pressures and incentives. The Yao adopted the ruthless raiding practices of the coastal slavers and devastated the area west of Lake Malawi. The Bisa also exploited trading opportunities with the newcomers and extended their range of operations eastward to the coast.

By contrast the *kazembe's* kingdom, the dominant power in the Luapula valley in the early nineteenth century, was eclipsed by a combination of outside forces. By mid-century Zanzibari Arabs frequented his capital, engaging in political as well as economic enterprises. At the same time Nyamwezi merchants from Tanganyika penetrated Shaba, where these trading colonists became known as the Yeke. Under chief Msiri, Yeke trade relations with the *kazembe* degenerated into exploitation as Msiri used his superior commercial and military position, buttressed by firearms, to sever the *kazembe's* western links with the *mwant yav* and Angola and to absorb some of the *kazembe's* tributaries into his own empire.

It was not long before these foreign powers intervened in the internal politics of the weakened kingdom. In 1872, with the aid of Swahili and Arab mercenaries under the Afro-Arab merchant warlord Tippu Tib, the exiled Lunda prince Lukwesa killed the reigning *kazembe* and seized the throne. This coup was unprecedented on two accounts: it was the first time that foreign arms had decided succession to the *kazembe's* throne and the first time that a rebel successfully gained the kingship. Thus began a new era of instability, as the loyalist prince Kanyembo Ntemena obtained military aid from the Bemba and deposed Lukwesa, who in turn sought Yeke assistance. Insecurity in the capital was mirrored in the countryside, where building with mud instead of wood and grass was introduced to afford greater protection to villages.

The Bemba, however, followed the pattern of the Bisa and Yao in capitalizing on the new Arab trade by exchanging slaves and ivory for guns. In the latter part of the century, while the *kazembe's* kingdom suffered internal strife and foreign encroachment, the Bemba entered a period of renewed territorial aggrandizement, even defeating Ngoni invaders after a series of wars between 1850 and 1870. This period also witnessed a remarkable expansion and consolidation of the *citimukulu's* royal power, as the bureaucracy and provincial governorships were filled by non-royal appointees who displaced hereditary and local figures.

Zambia also suffered some consequences of the vast upheaval (called the *mfecane*) in southeastern Africa precipitated by the rise of the Zulu under their renowned chieftain Shaka. In the early 1820s Zwengendaba's Nguni fled north from Natal. They crossed the middle Zambezi in late 1835 and continued their migration northward between Lake Malawi and the Luangwa River until settling in southwestern Tanzania, where they became known as the Ngoni. Zwengendaba's death in about 1845 touched off a succession dispute during which several disaffected groups hived off and migrated north, east, and southeast. The largest segment, under Mwambera, settled in northern Malawi whence they raided the Senga, Tumbuka, Cewa, and Bemba. Mperembe led his followers on an extended migration, raiding the Bemba, Bisa, Lungu, and Mabwe before he was finally defeated by a Bemba coalition under king Citapankwa and settled permanently in Malawi. Meanwhile Zwengendaba's eldest son Mpezeni pushed southwest through Bemba country, crossed the Luangwa, and by 1880 had subdued Mkanda, the northern Cewa chiefdom that had asserted its independence of the *undi's* paramountcy in the early nineteenth century. This remarkable Ngoni expansion was achieved by the use of radically new forms of military organization and tactics: a permanent organization for war based on age-regiments, the incorporation of war captives into the regimental structure, and hand-to-hand combat with short stabbing spears.

Southeastern Zambia also experienced depredations in the second half of the century. In 1862 the Portuguese reoccupied Zumbo, the Zambezi post abandoned in the mid-1830s, in order to exploit the interior for ivory and slaves. Ruthless slaving produced large-scale social dislocation and predatory reactions. Hence the emergence of the Cikunda, a new "tribe" of slave soldiers whose mixed ethnic backgrounds were submerged in a common quest for plunder. Under such notorious leaders as Matakenya and Kanyemba, the Cikunda visited devastation among the peoples of the middle Zambezi valley and into central Zambia.

Nor was western Zambia spared the ravages of invasion. Here the Lozi kingdom had expanded into an empire by the late eighteenth century and had become the dominant regional power. The material basis of Lozi hegemony was further strengthened in the early nineteenth century by the introduction of new crops from the West and the adoption of new weapons and tactics. However, the kingdom was plunged into civil war after the death of the tenth king, Mulambwa (ca. 1830), just as invaders from the south arrived.

These invaders were Sebitwane's Kololo, originally a Sotho people caught up in the *mfecane*. Like the Ngoni, the Kololo fled north in the early 1820s and crossed the Zambezi in the 1830s. Finding the Lozi state divided in a three-way succession war, Sebitwane occupied the kingdom and established his own conquest state. The new rulers had to contend not only with Lozi resistance but also with other raiders from the south, the Ndebele under Mzilikazi. Sebitwane successfully defended his new kingdom against these threats and sought to establish commercial relations with African and European gun traders. His son Sekeletu succeeded in 1851 and continued Sebitwane's policy of seeking direct trade links with the west coast, exercising a monopoly on the ivory trade, and cooperating with such Europeans as David Livingstone, the celebrated missionary and explorer.

But Kololo rule was destined to last only three decades. Unable to pacify and integrate their subjects and distracted by Ndebele marauders, the conquerors soon lost their kingdom. In 1864, the year after Sekeletu's death, a Lozi army under Njekwa inflicted a decisive defeat on the Kololo and enthroned the Lozi prince Sipopa.

Restoration of Lozi kingship did not restore order, however. Sipopa represented only one of the three main factions contending for the throne. Neither his transfer of the capital nor his alliance with the English trader George Westbeech could prevent the revolt in 1876 during which he was killed. It was not until 1885 that the period of civil war ended with the succession of Lubosi to the throne. The new king took the name Lewanika, purged his rivals, revived the monarchy and royal ceremony, reformed the army, promoted European trade (including arms imports), expanded cultivation, settlement and transport, and restored a measure of unity and stability to the kingdom. But even this resurgence of Lozi power could not forestall the impending British takeover. Following the precedent of his trusted fellow monarch and ally, Khama of the Bamangwato (a Tswana chiefdom in what would become Botswana), Lewanika signed a mineral concession and protectorate treaty with the British South Africa Company in 1890.

Finally the Batoka Plateau peoples of the south, who formerly enjoyed relative security, also suffered widespread devastation and depopulation from raids by Sebitwane's Kololo in the 1830s and later by the Ndebele. Unlike the case of the Lozi, these raids did not result in conquest, and a measure of peace returned after mid-century before the Lozi civil war, renewed Ndebele incursions, and Cikunda depredations afflicted the area in the last decades of the century.

In short, during the nineteenth century Zambia absorbed the Ngoni and Kololo invasions from the south, endured the penetration of the merchant warlords from the east and north, experienced the ravages of intensified slave raiding in the interior, and was drawn into a world economy dominated by the Western industrial states. But violence and dislocation were not evenly distributed; indeed, some peoples like the Bisa and Bemba profiteered during this time of unprecedented turmoil. The negative impact of these changes was also partially offset by the increase in production and commerce, the opening of new trade routes, and the adoption of new food crops that permitted the diversification and intensification of agriculture. Thus internally as well as externally Zambia experienced an increase in the scale of political and economic organization. This remarkable and widespread expansion of relations and institutions was a prelude to changes of even greater magnitude under colonial rule.

The Colonial Interlude, ca. 1890–1964

The constellation of external forces pressing on Zambia in the mid-nineteenth century was formidable. It was the British, however, at the very end of the century, who occupied the area between the Zambezi, the Zaïre watershed, and the central lake region to give Zambia its peculiar configuration.

Missionary Penetration

The British takeover was as sudden and irreversible as it was late, but it was preceded by almost a half-century of probings by missionaries and explorers. Foremost among these was Livingstone, whose three major journeys into the interior of Central Africa between 1853 and his death in 1873 aroused missionary zeal in addition to commercial greed and official interest. Missionary penetration soon increased. In the 1875–76 period two Scottish mission stations were established in the Shire valley in Malawi, and the London Missionary Society, for which Livingstone had pioneered, founded two missions on Lake Tanganyika in the 1880s.

Missionary advances from the south, however, affected Zambia more directly. François Coillard of the Paris Missionary Society, who had worked among the Basotho (of modern Lesotho) since 1858, visited the Lozi kingdom in 1878 and again in 1885. With the support of Westbeech and the blessing of Lewanika, he established a missionary outpost in 1886 at Sefula near the Lozi capital. F. S. Arnot, a Scot of the fundamentalist Plymouth Brethren, also worked among the Lozi with the aid of Westbeech, successfully excluding the French and Belgian Jesuits.

Cecil Rhodes and the Scramble for Southern Africa

These missionary advances notwithstanding, it was British strategic and commercial interests that brought southcentral Africa into the British empire. In 1895, in response to the German annexation of South-West Africa (Namibia) the previous year and the threat of a German alliance with the Boer Transvaal republic, Britain declared a protectorate over Bechuanaland (Botswana). This act of defensive imperialism precluded the possibility of a German-Boer transcontinental link that would leave Great Britain isolated at the Cape route to India. The discovery of gold in the Transvaal in 1886, and the treaty between the Transvaal and the Ndebele king Lobengula, led the British to press their claims even farther north.

At this point the entrance of Cecil Rhodes on the scene accelerated the pace of the British advance. An industrialist and unabashed imperialist, Rhodes had come to Africa in 1870. By 1888 he had gained control of the Kimberley diamond industry, obtained a mineral concession from Lobengula, and openly sought to extend British influence across the entire continent from the Cape to Cairo. In 1889 Rhodes received a royal charter for his British South Africa Company, giving him treaty powers with which to act on behalf of the British government. At Rhodes' instigation, the British consul in Mozambique, Harry Johnston, signed treaties with the chiefs between Lakes Malawi and Tanganyika, thus driving a British wedge between German East Africa (Tanganyika) and Belgian King Leopold's Congo Free State. Additional treaties in 1890 secured northwestern Zambia for the British, bringing the British sphere across the Zambezi to Katanga. Because Rhodes' representative was involved in an armed brawl with an important chief in which the latter was killed, the chief's successor signed a treaty with the Belgian king's agent, leading to the exclusion of that portion of the copperbelt on the Congo side of the Congo-Zambezi watershed from Rhodes' domains and to the peculiar intrusion of what came to be known as the Congo Pedicle (later the Zaïre Pedicle—see Glossary) between the eastern and western lobes of Zambia. Among the treaties that Rhodes' agents did sign was Frank Lochner's with Lewanika, establishing the Barotseland Protectorate over the Lozi. In 1890 also Rhodes' Pioneer Column established Fort Salisbury, marking the beginning of Southern Rhodesia. Within the next few years British treaties with Germany, Portugal, and Belgium settled most of Zambia's boundaries.

Company Rule, 1895–1924

The British South Africa Company was a convenient, effective, and inexpensive instrument for carrying out British imperial designs without direct government involvement. In the scramble for Central Africa, Britain claimed Zambia not for its intrinsic value but to deny it to European rivals. Having achieved this negative aim, administration of Transzambezia was left to Johnston, commissioner in Nyasaland (Malawi), while the company was preoccupied in the south with a major Ndebele revolt. It was not until 1895 that the company resumed responsibility for the northern territory, which in 1897 was designated Northern Rhodesia.

Company administration was more nominal than real, reflecting entitlement rather than effective control. Gradually, however, Northern Rhodesia was effectively occupied. The Bemba and the *kazembe's* Lunda kingdom submitted to the company's authority by 1899. Only Mpezeni's Ngoni offered resolute resistance, which was crushed by military force in 1898.

Among the Lozi the mineral concession and protectorate status were double-edged swords, depriving the kingdom of its independence and resources while simultaneously conferring special privileges. Although further concessions by Lewanika in 1898 and 1900 reduced his power and resources still more, the new agreements obliged the company to develop education and trade and, more importantly, to set aside a "reserved area" where mineral prospecting was prohibited. Thus the Lozi retained a measure of autonomy; by giving up an empire Lewanika retained his kingdom.

Administrative problems were formidable at the territorial level. For all practical purposes the company regarded its northern domain as an adjunct or outlying province of its more promising Southern Rhodesia. And the awkward shape of Northern Rhodesia, reflecting different historical traditions and the by-products of the scramble, simply compounded matters. In 1899, therefore, Northern Rhodesia was administratively divided into North-Eastern Rhodesia, with headquarters at Fort Jameson, and North-Western Rhodesia, administered initially from Kalamo and after 1907 from Livingstone. In 1911, however, the two territories were rejoined as Northern Rhodesia with headquarters at Livingstone, another reflection of the southern orientation.

Nor did the company attend to economic matters with zeal. In the first place, company rule was an instrument for exploitation rather than for development. Moreover Northern Rhodesia offered little prospect for profitable investment. In comparison with Katanga, South Africa, or Southern Rhodesia, the meager resources of this landlocked territory could be developed only at considerable cost. Taxation of the African population was therefore introduced in 1900, at first in the northeast and later throughout the territory.

Northern Rhodesia soon made its economic mark as a source of labor for the mines elsewhere and as a link between the mining centers of the subcontinent. By 1910 South Africa, Bechuanaland, Mozambique, and Southern Rhodesia were linked by rail through Northern Rhodesia to the Katangan capital of Elisabethville. The mines and railroad created a new demand for food supplies, but this was met by a small number of white settler farmers rather than African producers. Not permitted to compete with the settlers, Africans were forced from the land and became migratory laborers to earn the cash necessary to survive in a commercial economy and to pay the taxes levied by alien authorities. Only in a few areas, chiefly among the Tonga of Southern Province, were African agriculturalists able to overcome political and other obstacles to commercial farming, and a small but important peasantry emerged by mid-century in these districts.

Under company rule Barotseland continued its special but increasingly untenable status within Northern Rhodesia. When the company attempted to introduce taxation in 1904, Lewanika successfully argued that he should be the designated agent for collecting the new "hut tax," although he received only a small share. Gradually, however, Lewanika surrendered his land and his powers of civil and criminal jurisdiction over Africans except in the reserved area. When he died in 1916, Lewanika retained but a shadow of his former regal majesty and had been reduced to the status of a tolerated "tribal" chieftain.

Politically and economically the tiny European minority numbering only a few thousand exercised overwhelming power over about 1 million Africans. It was not these subjected Africans, however, but the company overlord toward whom the settlers directed their political energy. Inspired by the political gains of the larger and more vigorous European population in Southern Rhodesia, where in 1910 the settlers attained an elected majority in the Legislative Council, the northerners agitated for a greater voice in the governing of the territory. An advisory council was therefore established in 1918, but it lacked real power and was but a temporary palliative. Meanwhile proposals for amalgamating the two Rhodesias became the chief point of contention between the company and the settlers.

The company sought amalgamation as a means to lower administrative expenses and to put the territories in a better position to negotiate unification with South Africa, which had become an independent union in 1910. But at this time the settlers in both Rhodesias opposed such plans, each for their own reasons. The southerners feared that amalgamation would retard their movement toward self-government, which they did achieve in 1923; the settlers in the north feared domination by the south and sought instead to exchange company for Crown overlordship. The company too was anxious for relief of its burdens. Thus in 1924 Northern Rhodesia became a protectorate under the Colonial Office. A legislative council was formed, largely of officials, but the settlers elected five members. Needless to say, Africans were excluded. Through this device the settlers enhanced their political position vis-à-vis both the new colonial government and the disenfranchised African majority.

Colonial Office Protectorate, 1924–53

The switch from company to Crown exacerbated the plight of the African population. The first governor, Sir Herbert Stanley, sought to transform Northern Rhodesia into a "white man's country" bridging South Africa and Southern Rhodesia with British East Africa. He therefore encouraged European immigration and established reserves to ensure European control of the most productive and strategic areas near towns and the line of rail (see Glossary). By 1930 some 60,000 Africans had been forced to move from lands that had been reserved for white settlers. The consequences were adverse from an economic and ecological as well as a human standpoint. African farmers were placed at an even greater competitive disadvantage with Europeans, and the increased population pressure on the less fertile African reserves soon led to the depletion of these lands. To make matters more painfully and visibly wasteful, the anticipated large-scale white immigration did not occur, so that prime lands from which Africans had been expelled were underutilized or reverted to nature. The economy of the protectorate did not operate profitably until the late 1920s; by then, however, it was copper rather than agriculture that was responsible for the profit.

The rapid emergence of the copperbelt was the dominant economic and political factor in Northern Rhodesia after the 1920s. The discovery of major copper deposits, new prospecting and extracting techniques, and rising world demand for copper made large-scale operations feasible and profitable. The railroad, originally built to service the mining complexes to the north and south of Northern Rhodesia, could now be used to overcome the transport problem of the landlocked territory.

The opening and development of the copperbelt were the work of heavily capitalized corporations. Under the company, prospecting and mining in Northern Rhodesia were carried out on a limited scale by a few small companies until 1923, when the company decided to grant large concessions to major concerns backed by substantial capital. In 1925 Alfred Beatty, founder of Selection Trust, restructured the firm with American support. Two years later Ernest Oppenheimer, the South African gold industrial magnate, incorporated a Rhodesian branch of his Anglo American Corporation. By the end of the 1920s the copperbelt was dominated by these two interconnected corporate giants.

After a period of fits and starts, copper production and world demand increased in tandem. By the early 1930s copper exports had regained their previous peak and accounted for 90 percent of the territory's export trade. Output doubled between 1933 and

1938 to meet the market demands of the United Kingdom and Europe. Rearmament and World War II stimulated production even more, bringing Northern Rhodesia into the ranks of the world's major copper producers.

Wage labor and labor migration soared with the growth of the copper economy. By 1930 the roughly 22,000 Africans working in the copper mines constituted one-third of the African wage earners in the protectorate. After the depression of the 1930s the copper boom pushed the number of African wage laborers to nearly 33,000 by the early 1940s. Thousands of others were employed along the line of rail, servicing the mines and towns that sprang up along the route.

Despite this tremendous expansion of wage labor within Northern Rhodesia, the territory continued to export labor on a large scale. By the mid-1930s the Tanganyikan goldfields employed 10,-000 Northern Rhodesian workers, and thousands more worked on sisal plantations there. Several thousand others labored in Katanga, more than 50,000 in Southern Rhodesia, and thousands more in South Africa. In all, as many Northern Rhodesians worked outside the territory as inside, and more than half of the able-bodied males worked away from their home areas.

The railroad and the copperbelt combined to form an enclave economy within Northern Rhodesia. The railroad itself had begun the process, becoming a fundamental divide of social geography as towns and settlements cropped up. By 1921 nearly 90 percent of the European population lived along the line, and nearly half of these were concentrated in the three towns of Livingstone, Broken Hill, and Lusaka. The growth of the copper industry in the 1920s hastened the process, and by 1931 half of the white settlers, who by now numbered more than 14,000, were concentrated in the copperbelt alone.

Prosperity bred vast disparities between the copperbelt-rail enclave and the rest of the territory and between European and African living conditions. Indeed the African population received little in return for its contribution to the economy. The Africans who flocked to the new towns and mines encountered discrimination in all its forms. Housing construction always lagged behind residential needs, and the housing that was available to Africans was segregated and inferior even to rural African standards. Neither the mining companies, the railroad, nor the colonial government provided adequate facilities and social services. Education was left to the relatively few mission schools, which offered only primary education. Lacking the wherewithal and the opportunity to gain the requisite training, Africans remained unable to compete on equal terms with the white settlers. Their elementary skills qualified them only for menial, manual, and marginal jobs that paid little. In short, the African labor force was virtually condemned to servile occupations and perpetual wage discrimination.

Social segregation and economic deprivation also were mirrored on the political plane, where Europeans monopolized the instruments of power. The protectorate was under the ultimate legal authority of the British Parliament and administered by the Colonial Office. The colonial governor, the senior official in the territory, presided over an executive council, composed of civil servants, and a legislative council, dominated by officials but including in its membership from the beginning at least five elected settlers. Political participation was restricted to wealthy white farmers and businessmen. The poor farmers, mineworkers, and tradesmen had neither the means nor, at first, the inclination to engage in politics. Africans were not represented at all until the mid-1930s when a series of strikes and riots won a grudging concession: the addition of one unofficial member to the Legislative Council to represent African interests; and he too was a European.

The Colonial Office had inherited from the company a system of direct administration of the African population. In the late 1920s, however, in keeping with the new philosophy of indirect rule being applied throughout Great Britain's African empire, Northern Rhodesia too implemented this allegedly more efficient, effective, and enlightened system of native administration. The doctrine of indirect rule was based on the assumption that the African population could be ruled, reformed, and perhaps redeemed by the benevolent colonial government working with and through the traditional authority structures. Hence chieftainship was the key to indirect rule: established chiefs were incorporated into the colonial administration and, where chiefly institutions were not present, they were created by official appointment.

Indirect rule was introduced to Northern Rhodesia by J.M. Maxwell, who succeeded Stanley as governor in 1927 after serving as colonial secretary of the Gold Coast (Ghana). Based on this experience in West Africa, Maxwell proceeded to implement indirect rule before his departure in 1932, although the system was not put into practice throughout the protectorate until 1936. Under this new regime, the governor was empowered to establish native courts as well as superior and subordinate Native Authorities. Indirect rule may have been conceived as humane and efficient (and thus inexpensive, always a consideration), but it could never achieve its ultimate goal of guiding Africans toward self-rule under their traditional authorities. Indeed the system was self-defeating: chiefs who were co-opted into the colonial hierarchy lost legitimacy in the eyes of their people, especially when invested with powers far exceeding the indigenous norms of chiefly authority; and appointed chiefs had even less chance of acceptance. It is no wonder that the records of the colonial period are littered with references to ineffective chiefs. From the point of view of the colonial officials, they could hardly have been otherwise. Moreover the facile assumption that traditional institutions could withstand and successfully manage the drastic changes of development proved equally wrong.

Relations between the colonial government and the settlers were often strained too. Basically the authorities and the settlers differed over the nature and the purpose of the colonial relationship. British officials, however paternalistic and insensitive they may have been, felt at least some obligation to look after the welfare of the African majority. The settlers, however, were concerned primarily with advancing their own interests under what they considered more responsible forms of government. The situation became especially tense in 1930 when the Colonial Office, addressing a similar problem in Kenya, formally proclaimed the "paramountcy" of African interests under British trusteeship. Although the Joint Select Committee of Parliament softened the language of the Colonial Office in a report issued the next year, the implications were not lost on the white settler population. The question of union with Southern Rhodesia was therefore revived in the 1930s, leading in 1936 to an agreement between the unofficial members of the Northern Rhodesia Legislative Council and representatives of Southern Rhodesia to seek amalgamation under the latter's constitution. Two years later the Colonial Office dispatched the Bledisloe Commission to the Rhodesias to study the issue. Although no recommendations were made, the commission did note the widespread African opposition to union. The outbreak of World War II in 1939 ended further discussions of the matter, at least for a while.

African protest against white colonial rule was expressed in religious and social movements before overt political action was taken. The revival of traditional religion and the appearance of syncretistic sects were among the earliest manifestations of the Africans' predicament. Witchcraft and antiwitchcraft movements flourished. Perhaps the most widespread of these was the *mucapi* cult, which swept across eastern and northeastern Northern Rhodesia from Nyasaland in the early 1930s. This movement, and others like it, indicated the extent to which new forms of social solidarity were required to replace traditional chiefs and institutions.

Among the most popular and powerful religious organizations, and the one with the most direct political implications, was the Watch Tower Bible and Tract Society. Better known as Jehovah's Witnesses, African Watch Tower adherents prophesied the approaching end of time, when Africans would be saved and Europeans damned. Although it forbade political activity and civil disobedience, the Watch Tower was regarded as subversive by the colonial authorities, who banned its publications and curtailed the activities of its leaders. However, the indigenous leaders and organizations of the Watch Tower sect and its evangelical appeal attracted many followers. In 1935 the Watch Tower convened its first territorywide meeting in Lusaka, to which the headquarters of the protectorate had just been transferred from Livingstone.

More orthodox Christian groups also provided a new vehicle for the expression of African religious needs. In the 1920s Ernest Muwamba established the Union Church of the copperbelt, filling a gap where European missions had yet to enter. Cooperation between the Union Church and Protestant missions eventually led to the formation of the present-day United Church of Zambia. In the meantime, however, Muwamba and some of his followers left the Union Church and joined the African Methodist Episcopal (AME) church. The latter had prospered earlier in South Africa and in 1928 was firmly established in Northern Rhodesia by John Membe. Appealing especially to newly organized Africans and welfare associations, the AME church expanded into one of the largest organized religious groups in Zambia.

Although sporadic and uncoordinated at first, more explicit forms of social activism were adopted by the various secular welfare associations that flourished mainly in the townships along the line of rail after the 1920s. Not surprisingly the Northern Rhodesians who first obtained sufficient education to secure professional positions were the moving spirits behind these new organizations. By 1904 some of the graduates of the Livingstonia mission's training institute on the northwest shore of Lake Malawi had begun teaching. In 1906 a new school was opened in Chinsali under David Kaunda, the father of Zambia's first president. Sensitized to racism and the plight of Africans under colonial rule, Kaunda joined with Donald Siwale and Hezekiya Karosa to found the Mwenzo Welfare Association in 1912. The association experienced an erratic existence until it finally came to an end in the late 1920s. Like other welfare associations of the time, it lacked a clear purpose and widespread popular support and was more concerned with social than political issues.

By the 1930s several other African welfare societies were established along the urban corridor of the copperbelt and railroad. Composed largely of clerks and teachers, among whom Livingstonia graduates were prominent, these organizations had more specific programs, actively protested discriminatory practices, and occasionally succeeded in obtaining some amelioration of adverse working conditions. Despite some notable local achievements of these native welfare associations in Ndola (where Muwamba's leadership was again crucial), Luanshya, Livingstone, and Lusaka, their influence was still limited. This fact was painfully evident in the 1933 failure to form the territorywide United Welfare Association of Northern Rhodesia because the government simply refused to recognize it. The Northern Rhodesian African Congress, an organization of Tonga farmers, chiefs, and teachers established by Ellison Milambo and George Kaluwa in 1937, foundered for the same reason.

By the late 1930s, however, genuine political movements had

emerged in the copperbelt, the real locus of political power in Northern Rhodesia. African discontent crystallized in the mining towns, where workers staged their first strike in 1935. The government responded by expanding and consolidating the so-called tribal elements of urban administration and in 1938 introduced urban courts under tribal councillors and urban advisory councils of tribal elders. A labor department was also formed in 1940.

The unprecedented outbreak of African labor power spurred the European mineworkers to form the Northern Rhodesia Mineworkers' Union in 1936; this was aimed as much against African workers as against the management of the mining companies. In 1940 the European union struck at Mufulira and Nkana. African workers soon followed suit in a weeklong and violent strike during which soldiers killed seventeen strikers at Nkana. After the report of the Commission of Enquiry sent from Great Britain, some reforms and improvements were effected, but they were regarded as inadequate by the Africans and threatening by the whites.

Meanwhile the African welfare societies formed in the copperbelt mining towns were becoming more effective spokesmen for workers than the urban advisory councils and other tribal representatives. In rural areas welfare societies developed among the educated elites: teachers, pastors, small merchants and, especially in Southern Province, would-be commercial farmers. By 1946 the territorywide network of rural and urban welfare associations was mobilized by Dauti Yambo, a teacher and founder of the Luanshya society. Meeting in Broken Hill, their representatives formed the Federation of African Societies, an early precursor of the nationalist political parties soon to emerge.

For its part the government continued to seek additional means to manage African political stirrings. In 1944 African regional-provincial councils were established with mixed membership representing the urban advisory councils, Native Authorities, and welfare societies. And in 1946 delegates from these provincial councils began to attend the territorywide African Representative Council, which convened more or less annually until 1958. The council became an effective organ for the expression of African protest against the racial, social, and political discrimination of the colonial regime; it was purely advisory, however, and powerless to change the system.

The African labor movement also expanded and became better organized. In 1943 the African Shop Assistants' Association was formed on the copperbelt, a forerunner of the first genuine trade union of shop assistants founded in 1948 with the sanction of Britain's Labour Government. By the end of that year African unions had been established in all four mines, and in 1949 they merged to form the Northern Rhodesia African Mineworkers' Union under Lawrence Katilungu. Recognized along with several other unions as the negotiating units for their respective trades, it became the most powerful trade union in the subcontinent and a major force in the nationalist struggle that led to independence. The abolition of tribal representatives on the copperbelt in 1953 was a somewhat belated confirmation of their anachronistic position and of the real power of the unions.

The white settlers made equally impressive political gains during the 1930s and 1940s. On the one hand they sought to prevent the African majority from securing real political power, and on the other hand they pressed forward their own political claims against colonial tutelage. Specifically their objectives were to gain control of the Legislative Council, to merge with Southern Rhodesia in an enlarged white settler state independent of the Colonial Office, and to obtain the mining royalties still paid to the British South Africa Company. The most prominent European political figures in this struggle were Roy Welensky, the trade union leader, and Stewart Gore-Browne, a former army officer, both of whom were elected to the Legislative Council in the mid-1930s.

The settlers' efforts to get control of the Legislative Council failed. Although the council expanded in the 1930s and 1940s, by 1945 there were still only eight elected members as against nine officials. Moreover, in 1948 the African Representative Council elected two members to the Legislative Council, bringing to five the number of members representing African interests. The settlers achieved partial success in gaining a share of the company's royalties after 1949. But the biggest political issue was that of amalgamation with Southern Rhodesia; there the settlers won a temporary victory.

The question of union was an enduring political issue beginning in the days of company rule. Although dormant during the war, the amalgamation movement picked up momentum in the late 1940s. Whereas Northern Rhodesia's settlers had earlier feared economic domination by their southern kinsmen, the copperbelt boom strengthened their position and made union more attractive and certainly a preferable alternative to African majority rule. Southern Rhodesians, for their part, became more favorably disposed toward union with Northern Rhodesia after 1948, when the electoral victory of the Afrikaner Nationalist Party in South Africa portended a withdrawal from the English-speaking world. Conferences in Lusaka in 1948 and Victoria Falls in 1949 endorsed plans for a Rhodesian federation, although African political leaders uniformly denounced such devices to perpetuate European domination.

The British government had resisted Rhodesian amalgamation proposals because the Europeans constituted such a tiny minority, especially in Northern Rhodesia, but there was support for a federal arrangement instead between the two Rhodesias and Nyasaland, with the proviso that Africans share power with the whites. However, the Conservatives who replaced the Labour Government in 1951 were less inclined to insist on the protection of African interests. During 1952 and 1953 discussions and conferences worked out the modalities of such a federation, which held out the mere promise of "partnership" with the African majority of the three territories. Accordingly, the Central African Federation of Rhodesia and Nyasaland was inaugurated in late 1953 with Godfrey Huggins, former governor of Southern Rhodesia, as federal prime minister. Welensky became minister of transport and development; three years later he succeeded Huggins as federal prime minister. The special status of Barotseland was confirmed in its official designation as the Barotseland Protectorate by a separate Order-in-Council.

The movement toward federation under European auspices did not go unchallenged. The Northern Rhodesian African National Congress, the African Representative Council, various welfare associations, and individual African spokesmen raised a common voice of protest against the amalgamation proposals and boycotted official planning conferences. The national congress was a direct descendant of the Federation of African Societies, which had reconstituted itself in 1948 as the Northern Rhodesia Congress with explicitly political aims. Although drawing its strength mainly from towns, the new congress was linked to the rural areas via the welfare society network. This expansion of its popular base was facilitated by the accelerated rate of social change and heightened political awareness after World War II resulting from the spread of education, radio, and urbanization. In 1951 the Northern Rhodesia Congress renamed itself the African National Congress (ANC) and elected Nkumbula as president. Although African efforts to thwart federation failed, within a few years the nationalist movement was to mount a determined and ultimately successful campaign to achieve independence under majority rule.

The Decade of Federation, 1953–63

At first federation paid off handsomely for the settlers. African resistance had been ineffective, and the nationalists were disorganized and demoralized. Investment increased, and the copper industry expanded. European migration also boosted the settler population, from 49,000 in 1953 to 72,000 in 1958. And perhaps more immediately important, the white settlers enjoyed the benefits of an expanding job market and improved standard of living.

But after a few years the Rhodesian marriage of convenience began to show signs of strain. Ironically not only did it fail to meet the long-term expectations of the white settlers in Northern Rhodesia, but it provoked a surging tide of African nationalism that eventually undermined the federation itself. In the first place, although federation was seen by the settlers as a means of casting off the British yoke, the Colonial Office retained control of Northern Rhodesia. The Europeans did increase their Legislative Council membership to twelve, but African representatives got six seats. Even more galling was Southern Rhodesia's domination.

Constitutionally and politically Southern Rhodesia held sway over the federal parliament and government. In 1954 Salisbury was designated as the federal capital; it soon became the major industrial and commercial center, aided in part by the relocation of business from the north. Worse still, the early copper boom in the north was used to subsidize and finance development south of the Zambezi. The end of the copper boom in the late fifties made enforced sharing of declining revenues even more unpopular. Partnership had proven illusory even among the whites.

Africans were embittered to a greater degree. The expansion of wage employment during the late 1940s and early 1950s virtually ceased. Although rising labor costs benefited some Africans, the gap between whites and blacks actually widened. Educational progress was also slow and, compared to that for the settlers, woefully inadequate. For Africans, "partnership" was a cynical farce.

Initially African reaction to federation was muted. Protests and sit-ins were organized by Nkumbula and Kenneth Kaunda, but these were limited to the northeast and did not attract much attention. Demonstrations, boycotts, and strikes became more frequent in the mid-1950s, however, prompting the government to investigate ANC and jail Kaunda and Nkumbula for two months.

By the late 1950s the ANC had regained its strength and had branches throughout most of the country. This revival stemmed from discontent in the wake of the economic decline and from the influx of highly educated young leaders like Sikota Wina and Simon Kapwepwe, who were committed to achieving independence for the African majority.

The year 1958 marked a turning point in the nationalist movement. Nkumbula's agreement to participate in elections based on the new Northern Rhodesian constitution, which provided for limited African franchise, split ANC. A radical faction led by Kaunda, Kapwepwe, and Wina called for a boycott of the election, defected from congress, and formed the Zambia African National Congress (ZANC). The new party, with Kaunda as president and Kapwepwe as treasurer general, soon became the rallying point for the more ardent nationalists. It also brought sectional divisions into the open. ANC continued to draw its support from Nkumbula's home area in Southern Province and from North-Western Province. ZANC enjoyed more support in the copperbelt and in Northern Province.

In the meantime, in 1957 Ghana had become the first black African state to emerge from colonial rule. Its charismatic leader, Kwame Nkrumah, convened the All-African Peoples' Conference in Accra in December 1958 to promote African independence and continental unity; among the participants were Kaunda, Nkumbula, and Hastings Banda of Nyasaland. Encouraged by this experience, Kaunda returned to Northern Rhodesia to intensify

ZANC's opposition to federal-colonial rule and to boycott the March 1959 elections. When a state of emergency was declared in Nyasaland and Southern Rhodesia amidst fears of anti-European violence, the governor of Northern Rhodesia banned ZANC and had its officers (including Kaunda) and forty-five other party members arrested. Despite these repressive measures and the energetic electoral registration campaign organized by the government and Nkumbula's congress, most eligible African voters did not enroll.

The ban on ZANC forced the nationalists to continue the struggle under different organizational forms. In May 1959 Barry Banda, a former ANC member, created the African National Freedom Movement. The United African Congress was formed by Dixon Konkola, president of the Rhodesian African Railway Workers' Union. These parties merged to form the United National Freedom Party in June 1959, at about the same time that Paul Kalichini organized the African National Independence Party. Within a few months these two parties had also merged to form the United National Independence Party (UNIP). Another breakaway group from congress under Mainza Chona soon joined UNIP. By January 1960 Kaunda and Kapwepwe were released from jail and elected to the same leadership posts in UNIP that they had held in ZANC.

By this time the British government began to express its doubts about the future of the federation. In 1960, therefore, it dispatched the Monckton Commission, which noted the strong African opposition to the federation and the need for constitutional reforms including provision for secession. Discussions held in London in December 1960 showed that the differences between the federalists and the African nationalists in Northern Rhodesia were irreconcilable. Great Britain was prepared to move forward with a new constitution giving Africans a legislative majority but backed down under pressure from Welensky, then the federal prime minister, whose tactics included a show of military force in the copperbelt. The British concession led to mass demonstrations and disturbances throughout the country, and Kaunda flew to London to argue for constitutional revisions. This time the African reaction was telling, and the proposed constitution was altered again to their advantage, while Welensky denounced this "blackmail through violence."

The Northern Rhodesian general election of October 1962 marked the first electoral confrontation between Africans and Europeans. While UNIP actively sought the support of white voters in the copperbelt, Welensky's United Federal Party (UFP) promoted Nkumbula's old congress. UNIP won more than half the popular votes but failed to get a majority of the legislative seats, which were allocated on the basis of race. However, by forming a united front with Nkumbula's ANC, Kaunda prevented a UFP-ANC alliance and thereby achieved an African majority. The fate of the federation was now a foregone conclusion, and it was dissolved by the British government on December 31, 1963.

The new coalition government was an uneasy one, however, as Nkumbula periodically threatened resignation and a merger with UFP. In January 1964 another election was held on the basis of universal adult suffrage. This time UNIP won 55 of the 75 seats, and Kaunda became prime minister of the first predominantly African cabinet. The path was now open for the achievement of complete independence, which was set for October 24, 1964.

Meanwhile three major issues confronted the emerging new nation. Barotseland presented an immediate problem because of its special status dating back to 1890 and most recently confirmed under the federation. Although the *litunga* (Lozi paramount chief) had supported federation in the hope of ultimate independence, many of his younger subjects realized that an independent Barotseland would not be economically viable. In the elections of 1962 and 1964 UNIP won overwhelming Lozi support, and in April 1964 the *litunga* reluctantly agreed to renounce the special treaty relationship with the British Crown and to accept integration into the new state of Zambia.

A more difficult and volatile problem was posed by the Lumpa church, an independent sect founded in 1953 by Alice Lenshina to rid the country of witchcraft. Swelled by mass conversions in the northeast and the copperbelt, especially from among the Bemba, membership in the Lumpa church reached an estimated 50,000 to 100,000 by 1959. Initially perceived by UNIP in a friendly way, the movement ran awry of the independence government not only because of its overzealous witch-hunting but, more importantly, because its political indifference was interpreted by ardent nationalists as treasonous. By mid-1964 tensions between the church and UNIP broke out in widespread violence during which more than 700 people were killed. The church was banned, and its leaders, including Lenshina, were imprisoned. Many Lumpa adherents fled across the border and sought refuge in Zaïre.

Finally there was the question of the British South Africa Company's mineral rights and royalties. The UNIP government was determined to gain full entitlement for Zambia. Negotiations with the company were accompanied by a large-scale propaganda attack on its dubious claims. Finally, at a Government House garden party on the very eve of independence, a dramatic agreement was reached between finance minister Arthur Wina and the company chairman: in return for token compensation of 4 million equally shared by the British and Zambian governments, the company surrendered its rights to the new state. Taken together with rising copper prices and the lifting of output restrictions by the two copper mining companies, full royalty entitlement considerably enhanced the economic prospects for Zambia.

Independence: The First Decade, 1964–74

Independence for Zambia was not simply an event marked by the lowering of the Union Jack and the raising of the Zambian flag. Rather, that ceremony heralded the beginning of a long struggle for true independence. Essentially the struggle was carried out on three levels: politically, it meant the consolidation of the internal authority of the new state and government; economically, it meant the establiishment of state control over national resources and assets and the reduction of dependence on copper and on economic ties with the white south; and internationally, it meant a strong commitment to African liberation elsewhere on the subcontinent and a nonaligned course in world politics. These three aspects of Zambian independence were by no means discrete; indeed their interrelationships were so complex as to make distinctions among them merely analytic.

The Politics of Independence

The struggle for national unity and stability is reflected in the UNIP rallying slogan, "One Zambia—One Nation." It is also manifest in the authoritarian tendencies of the new government. Zambia's independence constitution provided for a unitary state with a strong chief executive, and a cabinet selected from but not responsible to the National Assembly. Remarkably the constitution specifically named Kaunda as first president.

Slogans and centralized institutions aside, regionalism remained a powerful political force in Zambia, where such sectional divisions have deep historical roots. Since early precolonial times different historical migrations, cultural traditions, and political entities divided the west, northwest, northeast, east, and south. These differences were compounded and magnified during the colonial period, when increased mobility and labor migration expanded social horizons and facilitated the spread of the major regional languages. Hence Lozi, Nyanja (Cewa), Bemba, and Tonga became the main languages spoken in their respective regions (see Languages, ch. 2).

The emergence of the copperbelt as the economic center of the country also had a profound effect on the political geography of modern Zambia. The predominance of Bemba speakers among the mineworkers and urban migrants made for ready mobilization by UNIP nationalists. Conversely the relative absence of urban and industrial development in the south, from which ANC drew its support, made political organization more difficult. Thus ANC came to regard UNIP as a "Bemba party," while UNIP considered its rival as a "Tonga party." To be sure, ANC never presented an electoral threat to UNIP, but its hold on the south belied UNIP's claim to be a truly national party.

Divisive interparty and intraparty tendencies also became apparent a short time after independence. Party fission and fusion were not new processes in Zambian politics, as evidenced by earlier periods of party turmoil, especially during the late 1950s. The initial two-party coalition was challenged in July 1966 when two Lozi members of parliament (MPs), one ANC and one UNIP, formed the opposition United Party (UP), which quickly gained popular support in the west. UNIP responded by persuading ANC to support a constitutional amendment requiring compulsory resignation for MPs who changed party affiliation. Both defectors were defeated by UNIP candidates in February 1967 by-elections, which were accompanied by violence and intimidation, revealing UNIP's questionable commitment to a multiparty system. Subsequently six MPs belonging to the ANC crossed the floor to join UNIP, which then won only two of their seats in the by-elections.

Meanwhile UNIP experienced an internal crisis at the party's triennial general conference in August 1967 when elections for the central committee revealed bitter sectional rivalry. Leading Bemba-speaking members, feeling relatively unrewarded for the contribution of "their people" to the independence struggle, teamed up with the minority Tonga-speaking faction to unseat Nyanja- and Lozi-speaking officers. The blatant sectional appeals made during the fracas not only generated intraparty hostility but damaged UNIP's prestige as well. Another enduring consequence was even more profound and debilitating for the Zambian political system: it opened an era of frequent reshuffling of the Cabinet, as Kaunda sought to stem rivalries and balance "tribal" representation. Kapwepwe's accession to the vice presidency seemed to confirm the critics' allegations that UNIP had become a "Bemba party."

In 1968 party politics became even more intense. Sectional fissures in UNIP widened when a "Unity in the East" movement erupted in Eastern Province to challenge "Bemba domination." Kaunda averted a major crisis by a dramatic resignation, returning on conditions that minimized opportunities for party leaders to conduct sectional campaigns. Some months later fighting broke out in the copperbelt between UNIP and UP supporters during the general election campaigns. The government responded in August by banning the UP, whose members transferred their allegiance to the ANC.

The December 1968 general election, the first since independence, was an important measure of the nature and direction of Zambian politics. Although UNIP won by a large margin, eighty-one seats to ANC's twenty-three, the latter gained control of Barotse Province (renamed Western Province in 1969) while retaining (though by a smaller margin) its traditional stronghold in the south. Thus an ANC electoral alliance of the west and south seemed to join the east against UNIP's base in the northeast. Moreover the electoral campaign revealed that both parties regarded the multiparty system with suspicion if not contempt, UNIP because it sought the establishment of a one-party state and ANC because it doubted that a UNIP government could ensure fairness.

Violence and intimidation also marred the election campaign, and voter turnout declined in comparison with the independence elections even though the number of registered voters was 15 percent higher than in 1964. The elections also marked the demise of the ten seats reserved for the European National Progress Party. Kaunda reacted by reshuffling the Cabinet with even greater frequency.

Tensions within the ruling party came to a head in 1969 when vice president Kapwepwe resigned over alleged persecution of his fellow Bemba. Although persuaded by Kaunda to withdraw his resignation, Kapwepwe lost his major portfolios. In 1970 Kapwepwe resigned again, this time permanently, and in August 1971 he emerged as the leader of the new United Progressive Party (UPP) that had been formed in the copperbelt by UNIP dissidents. The UNIP government reacted swiftly by raising a clarion call for a one-party state and detaining without trial about 100 UPP leaders and activists. Kapwepwe himself was not arrested, nor was UPP immediately banned, but Kapwepwe was the only one of five UPP candidates to win a seat in the December by-elections.

As the First Republic entered its last year in 1972, UPP was banned and Kapwepwe was detained along with 122 followers. In March vice president Mainza Chona, who had replaced Kapwepwe in late 1970, was appointed to chair the National Commission on the Establishment of One-Party Participatory Democracy. After extensive open hearings throughout the country, the commission produced its report, which became the basis for legislation in December officially establishing the one-party participatory democracy as the governmental structure of the Second Republic.

The new constitution, modeled on the Chona Commission report, was promulgated in May 1973; in June ANC leader Nkumbula, seeing no alternative, followed several other party members in crossing over to UNIP. Kapwepwe, who had been released from detention earlier in the year, continued to denounce the one-party constitution but announced his retirement from politics. Elections under the new constitution took place in December. Running unopposed, President Kaunda was elected to a third term in office, although one-fifth of the voters opposed him. Voter apathy again was strikingly apparent in 1973 when only 39 percent of the registered voters went to the polls, as opposed to 82 percent in 1968 and 94 percent in 1964.

Thus the inauguration of the one-party participatory democracy under the Second Republic was a watershed in the political history of independent Zambia. This major transformation of the national political structure can be seen as a reconciliation, however imperfect or transient, of the conflict between tendencies toward national unity under a dominant leadership and sectional rivalry under multiparty politics.

Notwithstanding the new constitutional arrangements, sectionalism seems destined to remain the social basis of Zambian politics, perhaps even more salient than the rural-urban cleavage. Powerful historical, geographic, economic, linguistic, cultural, and institutional factors made sectional politics an enduring if not always salient feature of Zambia's political landscape in the 1960s and 1970s. Perhaps even more immediately important, the perception of sectionalism remains strong, whatever the actual conditions. Thus whether Zambia remains a single-party state or reverts to a multiparty system is a matter of institutional artifact of greater interest to political archaeology than to political history or sociology. Such arrangements are but the variable and inherently unstable structural framework erected on the endemic sectional foundation of Zambian politics.

It is in this context that the political leadership and philosophy of President Kaunda must be viewed. Kaunda has been the central figure in this fragmented polity. His stature, authority, political adroitness, and lack of "tribal" connections make him a truly national personality. As sectional politics have become more divisive, Kaunda has concentrated more power in the offices of the presidency and party leader and taken on the role of arbiter among the contending forces. The president has also developed a philosophy called Humanism, which has been promulgated as the national philosophy. Zambian Humanism emphasizes community, unity, and harmony. It stresses cooperation rather than conflict, egalitarianism instead of social rank, and common humanity rather than "tribal" identity. Although one can debate the extent to which Kaunda's Humanism is shared by other Zambians or has guided their behavior, structurally it fits Kaunda's position as a figure transcending region, class, and clan.

State and Economy

The structure of the Zambian economy remained relatively stable during the first decade of independence. Copper continued to be the mainstay of the economy, but fluctuating demand and prices made for feast or famine and complicated development planning. During the first five years after independence copper production, exports, and prices rose; they dropped sharply in the early 1970s but rose again in 1973 and 1974. Nevertheless the central place of copper in the Zambian economy is indicated by the fact that in the first decade it had regularly accounted for 40 to 50 percent of Zambia's gross domestic product (GDP) and more than 90 percent of the value of exports. Copper's contribution to government revenues was also quite high in this period (see National Budget, ch. 4).

Traditionally the mining industry was foreign-owned. Between 1969 and 1973, however, Kaunda carried out a phased program of nationalization. Effective January 1970 the government acquired a 51-percent interest in the two copper companies and appropriated all mining rights in the country. At the time favorable tax and foreign exchange arrangements were offered to foreign shareholders, but these were curtailed in 1973. By these reforms the government extended its control over the crucial mining sector of the economy.

The government's overall objectives were to use the country's mineral wealth to expand economic development programs, especially in the industrial and agricultural sectors, and to reduce its dependence on copper. These goals proved elusive. Although there has been substantial growth in many industrial areas, it has taken place from a very small base and still has a long way to go before it will make a sizable contribution to the economy.

Although roughly 70 percent of the population made a living by subsistence farming, large commercial farms continued to dominate the cash and export markets. Agricultural output grew at a slow rate until the mid-1970s. But population increase nullified these gains, forcing Zambia to become a net importer of food.

Foreign trade during Zambia's first decade of independence showed a relatively stable commodity structure, but the direction of trade shifted markedly from the West to the Far East. By 1970 Japan had replaced the United Kingdom as Zambia's leading export market, owing largely to Japan's need for copper, and in the early 1970s the People's Republic of China (China) too became a major consumer of Zambian products, in good part because of arrangements made in connection with China's construction of a railroad for the Tanzania-Zambia Railway Authority (TAZARA). On the import side Western suppliers continued to dominate, but here, too, Far Eastern products gained ground.

These new trade patterns need to be seen in the context of Zambia's effort to disengage from white-dominated southern Africa. This was no easy task for a landlocked country heavily dependent on transport links through Rhodesia. But after November 1965, when Rhodesian Prime Minister Ian Smith made the Unilateral Declaration of Independence (UDI) from Great Britain, decisive and dramatic action became a matter of necessity. United Nations economic sanctions against the rebel white regime in Salisbury also had the effect of denying Zambia significant trade and transport routes. The sudden cessation by Zambia of fuel imports through Southern Rhodesia almost crippled Zambia's economy, but arrangements were made to haul fuel by road from Tanzania's port capital of Dar es Salaam. By September 1968 an oil pipeline was opened between Dar es Salaam and the copperbelt.

Zambia complied with the international sanctions within the limits of its capacity to endure the consequences. Half of its copper exports were rerouted to go north by road to Dar es Salaam and west by rail through Zaïre to the Angolan port of Lobito. Imports from Southern Rhodesia were also cut back drastically (see Foreign Trade, ch. 4). Not until the mid-1970s, however, did the opening of new coal mines and hydroelectric power stations relieve much of Zambia's dependence on Rhodesian energy supplies. Zambia also acted to minimize its trade with South Africa, from which imports were nearly halved between 1964 and 1973.

In early 1973 economic links with Southern Rhodesia were drastically reduced when the latter closed its border with Zambia in retaliation for Zambia's support of nationalist guerrillas operating in the border regions. Although Salisbury exempted copper from the embargo because it was an important source of foreign exchange for the embattled regime, and a month later lifted the entire embargo, Kaunda boldly took the occasion to close Zambia's border to all Rhodesian traffic. All of Zambia's copper exports were now redirected through Tanzania and Angola. The anticipated opening of the TAZARA line between Dar es Salaam and the copperbelt would ensure the new trade orientation.

Thus Zambia's Second Republic was being inaugurated during a period of political and economic turbulence on the subcontinent. But again these historical changes did not markedly alter the structural problems of Zambia's economy. With a 2.9-percent annual growth rate, Zambia's population reached about 4.5 million in the early 1970s, and the percent change in per capita gross national product (GNP) continued to fall. The imbalances between the rural and urban areas, the income gap between the commercial farmers and the mass of the subsistence cultivators, the stark contrasts between prosperity and poverty within the towns, the wide gulf between the copperbelt and line-of-rail enclave and the rest of the country, and the disparity between the standard of living of the mass of the population on the one hand and the increasingly African wealthy elite on the other all remained to be solved.

Zambia in Regional and World Politics

Landlocked and surrounded by eight other states in the heart of the subcontinent, on the frontier between black and white Africa, Zambia was positioned to play a central role in the southern African regional subsystem. Militant opposition to white minority rule in Rhodesia, South Africa, Namibia, Angola, and Mozambique was the cardinal tenet of Zambian foreign policy. Zambia broke many of its economic links to the white south. Politically and diplomatically Zambia actively supported the African nationalist movements in these territories and provided sanctuary for guerrilla raiders. Increasingly this political confrontation gave way to a military confrontation.

Zambia's position with regard to the minority regimes in southern Africa was clearly spelled out in the 1969 Lusaka Manifesto:

If peaceful progress to emancipation were possible, or if changed circumstances were to make it possible in the future, we would urge our brothers in the resistance movements to use peaceful methods of struggle even at the cost of some compromise on the timing of change. But while peaceful progress is blocked by actions of those at present in power in the States of Southern Africa, we have no choice but to give to the peoples of those territories all the support of which we are capable in their struggle against their oppressors.

With that principle in mind, Zambia took an increasingly tough line against the intransigent Smith regime in Rhodesia and Portuguese colonialism in Mozambique and Angola. Relations with Portugal remained strained until the coup d'etat in Lisbon in April 1974, after which Angola and Mozambique became independent. But relations with Southern Rhodesia and South Africa, in the latter case principally on account of Namibia, deteriorated into frequent border hostilities.

These security threats led inevitably to increased defense outlays and expansion of the armed forces. Zambia's annual military budget increased fourfold between the late 1960s and early 1970s, and the armed forces grew from 5,000 at independence to 16,000 by 1973. Military expenditures as a percent of GNP and government spending also doubled by the early 1970s, and total arms imports reached more than US$50 million by 1973.

In the global arena Zambia has pursued a steadfast policy of nonalignment. Relations with the United Kingdom were affected adversely by the latter's reluctance to take decisive action against its breakaway Rhodesian colony. While its relations with the Soviet Union remained correct if not cordial, Zambia improved its ties with China, mainly in the economic plane in connection with TAZARA. By 1974 China had extended the equivalent of nearly US$280 million in economic aid to Zambia, as compared to US$6 million from the Soviet Union and US$50 million from Eastern Europe. Zambia also received a small amount of military matériel from Peking and Moscow, about US$1 million from each; about twenty-five Zambian military personnel received training in China, and a similar number in the Soviet Union. By the early 1970s about 1,300 Zambian students were attending schools in communist countries.

Zambian attitudes toward the United States have revolved principally around southern African issues. Among the irritants to Zambian-American relations have been the United States reluctance publicly to chastise Portugal, a North Atlantic Treaty Organization ally, for its African policy; an insufficiently aggressive American position against minority rule; and the congressionally sanctioned breach of the Rhodesian embargo in 1972. By 1974, however, the United States had provided more than US$21 million in bilateral economic aid and US$44 million in Export-Import Bank loans.

*   *   *

The prehistory of Zambia is placed in its regional context by David W. Phillipson in *The Later Prehistory of Eastern and Southern Africa*. Phillipson also presents a more detailed survey in *The Prehistory of Eastern Zambia*.

The Zambian Iron Age is especially well documented in detailed site archaeological reports such as Brian Fagan et al., *Iron Age Cultures in Zambia.* Fagan offers a general synthesis of the Iron Age in the Zambezi area in "Zambia and Rhodesia."

The most recent and by far the best general history of Zambia is Andrew D. Roberts' *A History of Zambia.* This comprehensive work offers an excellent and balanced synthesis of Zambian history from the Stone Age through the first decade of independence, ending in 1974. Various aspects of the precolonial history of Zambia are treated in collections of essays edited by Brian M. Fagan, *A Short History of Zambia from the Earliest Times until A.D. 1900,* and by Eric Stokes and Richard B. Brown, *The Zambesian Past: Studies in Central African History.*

Such general works can be supplemented by studies of specific regions and groups. Among the better studies are Andrew D. Roberts' *A History of the Bemba,* Gerald L. Caplan's *The Elites of Barotseland, 1878–1969,* and Mutumba Mainga's *Bulozi under the Luyana Kings: Political Evolution and State Formation in Pre-Colonial Zambia.*

The colonial period of Zambian history, from the late nineteenth to the mid-twentieth centuries, has been studied by many scholars. Lewis H. Gann's *A History of Northern Rhodesia: Early Days to 1953* is a detailed account of British rule. Gann's *The Brith of a Plural Society* is appropriately subtitled *The Development of Northern Rhodesia under the British South Africa Company, 1894–1914.* The role of early missionaries is treated by Robert I. Rotberg in *Christian Missionaries and the Creation of Northern Rhodesia, 1880–1924.* The African side is better covered in Rotberg's *The Rise of Nationalism in Central Africa: The Making of Malawi and Zambia, 1873–1964* and Henry S. Meebelo's *Reaction to Colonialism: A Prelude to the Politics of Independence in Northern Zambia, 1893–1939.* The economic history of colonial rule is the subject of Robert E. Baldwin's *Economic Development and Export Growth: A Study of Northern Rhodesia, 1920–1960* and Elena L. Berger's *Labour, Race and Colonial Rule: The Copperbelt from 1924 to Independence.* Finally George Kay's *A Social Geography of Zambia* is indispensable for an understanding of the relationship between geography and history during the colonial era.

The federation (1953–63) has few apologists among participants and more detached observers. An example of the typical critical work is Patrick Keatley's *The Politics of Partnership.*

The drive toward independence is ably discussed by David C. Mulford in *Zambia: The Politics of Independence, 1957–1964.* A useful sequel that surveys and assesses the first decade of Zambia's independence is the collection of essays edited by William Tordoff, *Politics in Zambia.* Labor and party politics especially are the subjects of Robert H. Bates' *Unions, Parties and Political Development: A Study of Mineworkers in Zambia,* while George C. Bond's *The Politics of Change in a Zambian Community* attempts to place local politics in the Uyombe chiefdom in Northern Province in the wider context of Zambian political trends. The political economy of the mining industry is explored in Richard L. Sklar's *Corporate Power in an African State: The Political Impact of Multinational Mining Companies in Zambia.*

Zambia's external relations, especially in the southern African arena, are ably handled in Jan Pettman's *Zambia: Security and Conflict* and in Richard S. Hall's *The High Price of Principles: Kenneth Kaunda and the White South.*

Lastly the leadership and political philosophy of Kaunda are central to the country's modern history. Kaunda's *Zambia Shall be Free, An Autobiography,* and Fergus MacPherson's biography, *Kenneth Kaunda of Zambia: The Times and the Man,* are essential sources. Kaunda's own writings on Humanism are available in *A Humanist in Africa: Letters to Colin Morris, Humanism in Zambia,* and *Zambia: Independence and Beyond.* Together with Meebelo's edited volume, *Main Currents of Zambian Humanist Thought,* these works provide important material for the study of political ideology in contemporary Zambia. (For further information see Bibliography.)

Chapter 2. Society and Its Environment

Ndembu wood carving

THE NATION'S MOTTO proclaims "One Zambia—One Nation." Yet, from one perspective, there are many Zambias and a variety of physical environments within the nation's borders. Only the patterns most commonly encountered can be characterized here as a guide to the "little Zambias."

Society and environment are closely related. The nature of most Zambian land and its low to moderate fertility have in the past promoted diffuse populations and low densities; the technology of traditional agriculture has depended on extensive land and yielded limited produce. There are some atypical areas differing in both society and environment from the usual. The fertile soils and varied microeconomies of the Zambezi floodplain allowed the development of a dense population and the centralized Lozi kingdom. Similarly the rich fisheries of the Luapula swamps were the economic core for the Eastern Lunda state. The areas of dense population in Zambia in the second half of the twentieth century are those with mineral ores and those corridors on the high plateaus where railroads and roads could most economically be built. In the rural areas, social systems remain in close ecological relationship with the physical environment; in the urban areas, political and economic considerations (such as the siting of bureaucracies or the migration of the rural poor) are often more powerful.

The analysis of the forms and regularities that underlie the social life of Zambian individuals may proceed in two directions: from the whole to the constituent parts (assuming a "Zambian people" and then pointing to differences of language, social structure, or class that divide persons) or from the parts to the whole (starting with individuals and discussing structures and values that lead to common interests and actions). For example, one language unites those who speak it but differentiates them from others. Often the greater the commonality within one set of individuals, the more tangible their distinction from other such sets. With respect to certain aspects of Zambian society it is more helpful to speak of differences that underlie competition or differential change in political or economic spheres; in other instances commonalities are the important point.

Given this ambiguity as well as the specific circumstances of Zambia, it is more useful to speak of cleavages within Zambian society than of groups. Cleavages are potential lines of division; they may open up between populations under certain conditions or remain invisible when other issues evoke other alignments. For example, one individual may be considered a Lozi in Lusaka but an Mbunda tribesman in the Lozi town of Mongu and a member of a specific clan when among Luvale in Zambezi District. Some of these alternative identifications are subsumed one within another—all Lozi are Zambians—so that circumstances merely bring out a relevant level of generalization. In other cases the terms can become contradictory, imposing a choice in self-identification. Linguistic cleavages seldom correspond neatly with differences in kinship systems, nor do either of these necessarily reflect political relationships in the former "tribal authorities" based on historical chieftainships. The person is a Lozi in Lusaka thus might well not claim to be or be accepted by others as a Lozi in Mongu among other Lozi.

Zambia is at once a homogeneous and a heterogeneous country. Its borders were drawn with no regard to existing human organizations or logic; the Zaïre Pedicle (see Glossary), which almost cuts Zambia in half, is an eloquent witness to that. Yet in comparison with many other African nations, there are few sharp cultural boundaries in Zambia, and the various ethnic groups share cultural elements diffused throughout vast areas. Closely related Bantu languages, for example, were spoken throughout the nation. Thus the often-mentioned "seventy-three tribes of Zambia" are essentially artificial entities. Differences are real, but these units are defined by lines that the colonial government drew for administrative convenience. At times Zambians behave with great unity, with a commonality born of shared culture rather than merely adherence to an official ideology. At times Zambians fragment into myriad small communities, and leaders struggle to find ways to articulate them all in order to build a nation. At yet other times, a few broad groupings arise and exert strategic influence on Zambian national life.

The Physical Setting and Population

Zambia's landlocked 752,614 square kilometers were, on average, sparsely settled by an estimated population of 5.4 million in mid-1978—roughly seven persons per square kilometer. That density was, however, quite variable, the variation reflecting the country's substantial urbanization—more than 35 percent in 1974 —certain features of its transportation network and, in the rural areas, the carrying capacity of the land.

Terrain and Drainage

Most of Zambia lies on a portion of the great plateau that dominates central and southern Africa's landmass. Some of that plateau is undulating, some relatively flat, but most of it ranges between 900 and 1,500 meters, the higher sections (above 1,200 meters) occurring, for the most part, in the north. The few areas of still higher land (some of it above 2,000 meters) are found in the northeast, chiefly along the borders with Tanzania (the Mbala Highlands) and Malawi (the Mafingi Mountains) (see fig. 4). The significant areas of lower land are rift valleys in the east (the Luangwa River valley) and in the south (the middle Zambezi River valley), both bounded by escarpments.

Most of Zambia's streams—except for those in part of the eastern lobe—ultimately drain into the Indian Ocean via the Zambezi River and its main tributaries. In addition to those streams that enter the Zambezi directly, there are three main tributary systems—those of the Kafue, Luangwa, and Lusemfwa rivers.

The upper Zambezi, running roughly from north to south, has a low gradient, and the area through which it passes is marked by floodplains and swamps. After turning eastward, the Zambezi flows over Victoria Falls and through the middle Zambezi valley, much of it occupied by the great man-made Lake Kariba. Much of the upper Kafue River is also characterized by a low gradient, and extensive swamps are common. The Kafue Flats, through which the river passes after turning east, are too poorly drained to provide cultivable land but furnish good pasturage. The Lusemfwa drains that small portion of Zambia between the line of rail (see Glossary) and the Luangwa valley and joins the Luangwa River, more steeply graded than most of Zambia's streams.

The network of rivers and streams of northeastern Zambia drains via the Zaïre River to the Atlantic Ocean. The Chambeshi River collects most of the water in the region, its many channels then discharging into Lake Bangweulu or directly into the Luapula River. In either case the water finds its way via the Luapula to Lake Mweru and thence to a tributary of the Zaïre. Other streams enter Lake Mweru or Lake Tanganyika (whose waters also enter the Zaïre system) directly. A very small portion of the far northeast drains inland to Lake Rukwa in Tanzania.

Lake Bangweulu and several smaller bodies of water are part of the Bangweulu swamp complex. The main swamp is permanently flooded; the periphery (a belt about forty kilometers wide) is flooded during and immediately after the rainy season.

The flow of all watercourses in Zambia is affected by the clear demarcation between rainy and dry seasons. Most small streams dry up sometime between May and October, and even the larger rivers show a substantial difference between maximum (occurring variously between February and May) and minimum discharges.

Climate

A decisive element in the pattern of rural life is the cycle of wet and dry seasons. That cycle and associated variations in temperature govern Zambia's three seasons: the cool dry season runs from April to August (June and July are the coldest months); the hot dry season begins in August and runs through October or—particularly in the east—through November; the warm rainy season begins in early November in the northwest, later farther south and east, and continues until March or April. The longest rainy season and the heaviest annual rainfall occur in the northwest and in that part of the eastern lobe to the north of Lake Bangweulu (see fig. 5). Variability in annual rainfall occurs everywhere but is greatest in areas of lowest precipitation, i.e., in the south and low-lying

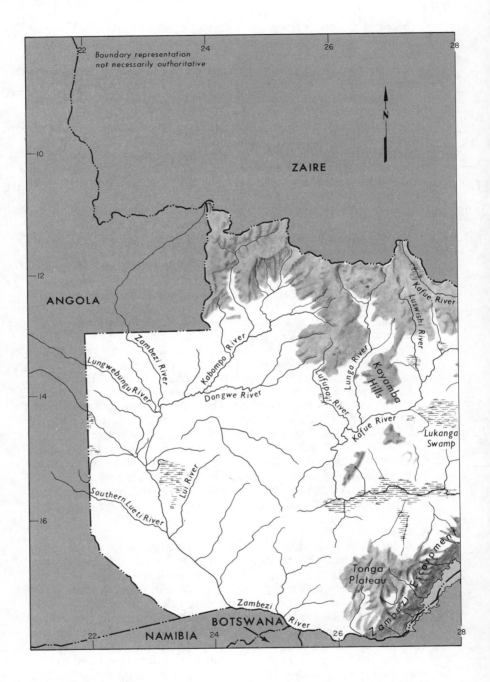

Source: Based on information from *Atlas for Zambia,* Glasgow, 1973, map 6.
Figure 4. Terrain and Drainage

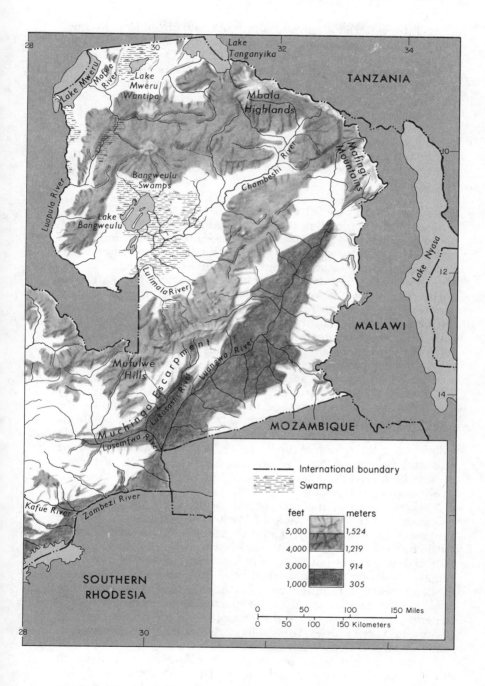

areas of the eastern lobe, where drought occurs from time to time.

Among the factors governing temperatures are distance from the equator, altitude, and cloud cover. Thus in October, when the highest mean daily maximums occur, the more northerly areas—although closer to the equator—are slightly cooler than the more southerly areas because they are higher and because the cloud cover presaging the onset of the rainy season has begun to move in. In general, the highest mean daily maximums in October occur in the low-lying Luangwa valley and in parts of the area along the Zambezi River in the south. Some of the lowest mean daily minimums in July also occur in parts of the south, however, reflecting the rapid loss of heat at night.

Ecological Zones and Settlement

Modes of rural life, densities of rural population, and settlement patterns are in good part governed by terrain gradients and drainage, soils, natural vegetation, and rainfall. Taken together these factors permit the establishment of a number of ecological zones. The first of these, covering much of the eastern lobe and the northern part of the western lobe, may be referred to as the northern zone of high rainfall. Where the heavy rainfall leaches the local soils of their nutrients—as it frequently does—traditional agriculture is characterized by one or another form of shifting cultivation involving one of several kinds of slash-and-burn techniques (locally called *citemene*) requiring substantial quantities of land for each household and limiting the density of population in the area (see Agriculture, ch. 4). Local communities are often small and may move from time to time as soils in the vicinity are temporarily exhausted. Exceptions to this pattern in the northern zone of high rainfall occur in the northern part of the Luapula valley and in the region of the Bangweulu swamps where different soils and vegetation have permitted the introduction of hoe or plow cultivation and where the availability of fish makes for relatively dense populations.

A second zone—sometimes called the western semiarid plains —is constituted by the whole of Western Province and parts of provinces (North-Western, Central, and Southern) immediately adjacent to it. The semiaridity referred to is not so much a question of low rainfall (although the southern section of the zone receives less rain than the north) as of the rapid loss of moisture by the Barotse (sometimes called Kalahari) Sands that cover the area and the comparatively wide spacing of rivers and tributary streams. The exceptions are the floodplains of the upper Zambezi River and its tributaries, their soils enriched by riverine deposits, which permit a denser population.

A third zone comprises the section of the Zambian plateau north of the Zambezi River and includes the Tonga Plateau, the Kafue Flats, and the Lukanga Swamp. Lusaka and more than half the line of rail lie with in it. Annual rainfall is less than 1,000 millimeters,

millimeters

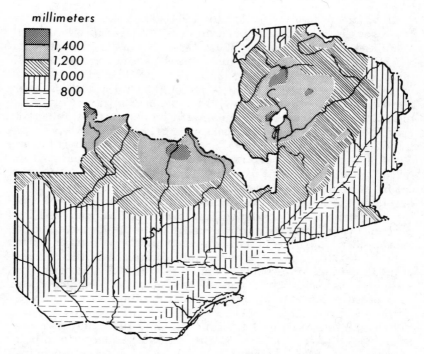

1,400
1,200
1,000
800

Source: Based on information from *Atlas for Zambia,* Glasgow, 1973, map 8.
Figure 5. Annual Rainfall

but the soils are among the most fertile in Zambia and, with the use of hoe and plow, can carry a fairly dense population (see Population, this ch.).

Separated from the central and southern plateau by the Luangwa valley is the small eastern plateau zone comprising the southeastern section of the eastern lobe of Zambia. The soil allows cultivation by ox- or tractor-drawn plow, and the area is characterized by a relatively dense population (see Population, this ch.; see Agriculture, ch. 4).

The last of the ecological zones includes the rift valley along the Luangwa and middle Zambezi (below Livingstone) rivers. Most of the Zambezi and Muchinga escarpments above these valleys have no value for agriculture, and the quality of the soil and the often low and erratic rainfall limit their carrying capacity. The lowlands are therefore sparsely populated except in the Gwembe Valley region of the middle Zambezi.

Population

The first complete census taken after independence, that of 1969, yielded a population of 4,056,995. The Central Statistical Office estimated an underenumeration of 2.1 percent, and the total was accordingly adjusted to 4,144,000. A sample census in 1974 was the basis for a population estimate of 4,695,000 in that year (see table 2, Appendix). *World Population 1977,* prepared by the United States Bureau of the Census, assumed an underenumeration of the same magnitude in 1974 as in 1969 and presented what it called an inflated figure of 4,793,000. On the basis of these figures, the annual rate of growth between 1969 and 1974 was a high 2.9 to 3.0 percent. Postulating a higher fertility rate and therefore a slightly higher annual rate of growth (up to 3.1 percent in 1976), the Bureau of the Census estimated a population of 5,224,000 in mid-1977. Assuming the same rate of annual growth in 1977, a mid-1978 estimate of 5,381,000 may be made.

The estimated annual rates of growth between 1969 and 1978 exceeded those between 1963, the year of the first complete census (just before independence), and 1969, which averaged 2.5 percent. That lower rate, however, reflects the departure of a substantial proportion of the European population (from 74,549 in 1961 to 43,390 in 1969), and the rate of growth of the African population in that interval has been estimated at 2.7 percent. The estimates for the 1969–78 period were essentially equivalent to rates of natural growth inasmuch as net migration across Zambia's borders had not been significant.

The high rate of natural growth to the late 1970s may give rise to an even higher rate in the 1980s and 1990s as larger numbers of women reach childbearing age and as the rates of mortality, particularly infant mortality, fall. On one projection, assuming constant fertility rates, the Zambian population, taken as 4.7 million in 1974, will double by 1994.

Other assumptions—that a 5- or 10-percent decline in fertility rates will take place after 1980—yield lower projections of population for the mid- and late 1990s, but such a lowering of fertility rates is unlikely given the attitudes toward population growth manifested by both people and government. Generally Zambians, urban dwellers with substantial education included, consider large families desirable. Government officials, in part because they share that value but also because they see a small population in a large territory and because they assume a decline in population growth as consequent upon economic development, have not stressed family planning. In fact, Zambia's low average population density implies a low carrying capacity of the land, a condition likely to continue unless a good deal of technological change and capital investment takes place. That kind of agricultural improvement is far enough off so that the rural areas are not likely to be able to absorb a rapidly increasing population even if the young saw rural life as desirable. Economic development too is a process barely begun and confronted by very substantial obstacles (see Migration and Urbanization, this ch; see ch. 4). Its impact on family size is in the distant future. In any case, family planning in Zambia is permitted but not actively encouraged. Facilities and information are available for those who take the trouble to seek them out, but it has been suggested that some of Zambia's policies, e.g., allowances for large families, are in fact pronatalist.

Density and Distribution

Zambia's population density of 5.5 per square kilometer in 1969 (based on the adjusted census figure) was roughly comparable to that of Angola but lower than that of other African states in southern Africa except for Botswana (and Namibia). Given an urban population of nearly 30 percent in that year, the average rural density was about 3.9 per square kilometer. The results of the 1974 sample census (inflated for underenumeration) yielded an average overall density of 6.4 per square kilometer. At that time the urban population constituted a little more than 35 percent of the total, and the average rural density has been calculated at a little more than four per square kilometer.

But rural densities are variable, ranging from fewer than two persons per square kilometer in substantial portions of Zambia to up to fifty (and in a few places, more) per square kilometer. The data published for the 1974 sample census did not permit the plotting of distribution for units smaller than provinces, but it may be assumed that the pattern ws essentially the same as that based on the 1969 census (just as that was, in general outline, similar to the pattern established on the basis of the 1963 census data).

There are two large areas that are sparsely populated (fewer than two persons per square kilometer): the first, the middle Kafue valley and its environs, encompasses small parts of the northern zone of high rainfall, sections of the central plateau, and the eastern section of the western semiarid plains; the second is the Luangwa valley and the adjacent escarpment (see fig. 6). The sparseness of the population in these areas is attributable in part to poor soils and in some sections to uncertain rainfall, but a salient characteristic of both areas is the presence of the tsetse fly, which makes those areas useless for herding and strongly discourages human habitation. Portions of the areas are, however, well stocked with game and have been set aside as major game reserves—Kafue National Park and Luangwa Valley Reserve. Several smaller areas —west of the upper Zambezi in the far northwest and far southwest, scattered places in the northern sections of the eastern lobe, and the middle Zambezi valley east of Lake Kariba—also are thinly populated, again largely a consequence of inadequate soils. These areas (fewer than two persons per square kilometer) together constitute roughly 57 percent of Zambia's territory but, in 1969, provided a habitat for only 9 percent of its population. Scattered throughut the eastern and western lobes of Zambia (but cumulatively a substantial area) are zones inhabited by roughly two to four persons per square kilometer.

Rural densities of from ten to more than fifty persons per square kilometer occur in four areas. The first of these is along the line

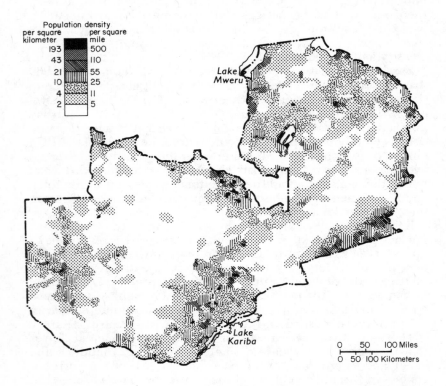

Population density
per square kilometer | per square mile
193 | 500
43 | 110
21 | 55
10 | 25
4 | 11
2 | 5

Lake Mweru

Lake Kariba

| 0 | 50 | 100 Miles |
| 0 | 50 | 100 Kilometers |

Source: D. Hywel Davies (ed.), *Zambia in Maps: Graphic Perspectives of a Developing Country,* New York, 1971, p. 43. Used by permission of Africana Publishing Company, a Division of Holmes & Meier Publishers, Inc., New York.

Figure 6. Population Density, 1969

of rail, a zone of relatively advanced agriculture developed in the colonial era on land alienated to Europeans but also including substantial numbers of African farmers and farm labor. In general these farms cater to the needs of the increasingly large urban centers, all of them located in the same area (see Agriculture, ch. 4).

A second area of dense rural population is in the far southeast, a region marked by good soils and advanced European and African cultivation. A third is the flood plain of the upper Zambezi and its western tributaries. The fourth area is somewhat more fragmented, but all of its sections are located in the northern portion of the eastern lobe. Most of them are adjacent to bodies of water or streams (Lake Bangweulu and its swamps, Lake Mweru, parts of the Luapula valley, Lake Mweru Wantipa, and the southeastern shores of Lake Tanganyika). A minor exception is the highland area at the border with Tanzania. A marked characteristic of most of these northeastern fragments and of the upper Zambezi flood-plain is the importance of fishing in addition to cultivation and, in many cases, herding. Except for the Luapula valley all of the densely settled areas of Zambia are free of tsetse fly. Fishing on the one hand and the historical fact of politically induced settlement (in the kingdom of the *mwata kazembe* of Luapula) on the other account for the Luapula valley's relatively dense settlement (see Peoples and Polities, ca. 1500–1800, ch. 1).

The distribution of the great bulk of the urban population falls along the line of rail. The major nodes are the copperbelt towns (containing roughly 62 percent of urban dwellers in 1969) and Lusaka and its environs. Other large towns on the line of rail include Kabwe and Livingstone. A number of smaller but still sizable towns, essentially agricultural and administrative centers, are also located in the area. Taking the urban and the relatively dense rural populations together, nearly 40 percent of Zambia's people live within forty kilometers of the line of rail.

Migration and Urbanization

The link between internal migration and urbanization in Zambia is clear. Although there is some migration from one rural area to another and some degree of counterflow of a temporary or permanent nature from town or city to rural area, the cumulative effect of migration has been to enlarge the cities and towns (see table 3, Appendix). The annual growth of the urban population, including those in towns under 20,000, averaged 8.9 percent between 1963 and 1969 and 6.8 percent between 1969 and 1974. In 1963 urban dwellers already constituted 20.5 percent of the total, a proportion exceeding that of a number of African states in the mid-1970s. That proportion rose to 29.4 percent in 1969 and to 35.4 percent in 1974. Although the rate of growth slowed in the 1969–74 interval and may have slowed even further thereafter, it is not unlikely that the urban population had reached roughly 40 percent of the total by early 1979.

All of Zambia's major towns (and a number of the smaller ones) are on the line of rail, and all but three—Lusaka, Kabwe, and Livingstone—are in the copperbelt. Ndola excepted, copperbelt towns are associated directly with mining. The larger ones, e.g., Kitwe, also have manufacturing, commercial, and service functions, whereas some of the smaller towns may be essentially mining camps. Ndola, a trading center in the precolonial era, became a commercial, manufacturing, and administrative center under British rule and has retained that character. Kabwe, outside the copperbelt, is located near a mine but, as the first major town south of the copperbelt on the line of rail, had developed as a commercial, transportation, and administrative center. The population of Lusaka (estimated at 415,000 in 1976) was roughly the same as that of Kitwe (just over 123,000) in 1963, but Lusaka grew more rapidly after independence than any other town. In part to keep Lusaka from becoming excessively large and in part to develop urban centers farther south, the government encouraged the growth of Kafue as a commercial and manufacturing center. Kafue, on the line of rail and near the newly developed hydroelectric dam on the Kafue River, was—at nearly 20,000 in 1974—the largest of the towns after the first ten. Livingstone, at the border with Southern Rhodesia (Zimbabwe), has been largely an administrative, commercial, and services center. In recent years emphasis has been placed on tourism (Livingstone is near Victoria Falls), and there is some processing of raw materials (e.g., a sawmill); but the closing of the border with Southern Rhodesia and the disuse of the rail line to the south led to a diminution of Livingstone's importance, a situation that may change with the reopening of the rail link in late 1978.

Although the largest towns attract the greatest number of migrants, some move to smaller towns, usually in response to economic opportunities. The growth of Kafue with its chemical fertilizer and textile plants has been noted.

The attraction of Mazabuka was, in part, agricultural, migrants responding to the establishment of a sugar estate and refinery. Special cases aside, the rural zone drawing most migrants (based on analyses of the 1963–69 intercensal period) was along the line of rail, particularly that part of it from Lusaka north where the farms served the large urban centers.

Migrants are generated by all rural areas but in different proportions; moreover people from specific rural areas tend to migrate to the same urban centers. With few exceptions the annual rates of growth of essentially rural districts in the 1963–69 interval reflected outmigration, and some districts, particularly in Northern and Luapula provinces, showed a negative rate.

Existing analyses of internal migration have certain flaws, however. For example, although it may be reasonably assumed that international immigration and emigration were roughly equivalent and may safely be ignored in the calculation of the national average annual growth rates, specific provinces and districts were probably affected in different ways. For example, in 1964 approximately 20,000 members of the Lumpa sect, chiefly from Northern Province, became exiles in Zaïre, accounting in part for the difference between anticipated and actual populations in some districts in 1969 (see Independence: The First Decade, 1964–74, ch. 1). Conversely, numbers of opponents or refugees from the Portuguese regime in Angola came to live in several districts of Western Province in the mid- and late 1960s. Differential fertility rates also affect estimates of migration from and to specific districts. In their estimates of anticipated populations for 1969, analysts added to each district's 1963 base the numbers obtained by calculations using the national average annual growth rate. Some districts or ethnic groups had lower fertility rates (and, therefore, lower natural growth rates) than others, however. Among these, apparently, are groups living in Western and North-Western provinces. Thus, the presence of Angolans on the one hand and a lower fertility rate on the other, rather than a lack of outmigration, may in part account for the small difference between anticipated and actual populations in those provinces. These caveats notwithstanding, it is worthwhile to survey the results of existing studies of rural-to-urban migration.

If the distribution of the population in 1963 is taken as a base, then Northern and Luapula provinces lost the largest numbers of persons to outmigration in the six years to 1969. Districts within these provinces generated outmigrants in different numbers and at varying rates, but only two, Mbala and Mpokoroso, did not show a negative rate of growth. Most parts of both provinces, characterized by *citemene* cultivation, have had difficulty in supporting an agricultural population (see Agriculture, ch. 4). Part of Luapula, once a prosperous fishing area, has for many of the years since independence suffered from a lack of fish, and the Zaïrian market around Lubumbashi has been cut off for some time.

Eastern and Southern provinces showed the next highest levels of net departures (Eastern, lacking a city as large as Livingstone in Southern Province, had a slightly greater number of net departures). It may be noted that, Livingstone aside, many of the local towns showed increases even when the predominantly rural districts in which they were located showed losses.

Least affected by outmigration were North-Western and Western provinces, although Kasempa District in North-Western Province showed heavy losses. One of North-Western's poorest districts and comparatively close to the copperbelt, it lost more than 19 percent of its potential population. Mongu, the center of what had been the Barotse Protectorate in Western (formerly Barotse) Province, showed a loss of more than 10 percent, very likely a consequence of the abolition of the special status of the protectorate after independence. Western Province's low rate of outmigration probably reflects the fact that the destination of most of its preindependence migrants had been South Africa, and this link had been cut after independence. As of 1969 the people of Western Province apparently had not reoriented themselves to a different pattern of migration.

The data derived from the 1974 sample census do not permit an analysis of migration patterns by district; yet it is noteworthy that, although most average annual provincial growth rates were less than the average national rates, they exceeded those for the 1963–69 period, a pattern consistent with the somewhat diminished rate of growth of urban centers in the 1969–74 interval. The growth rates for Central and Copperbelt provinces exceeded the national average, but these contained the major cities (Lusaka had not yet been made a province in 1974).

Analyses of the data from the 1963 and 1969 censuses show that the two most urbanized provinces had the greatest net gains from migration. In Copperbelt Province, all districts had an average annual growth exceeding the national average; in Central Province only Lusaka, Kabwe Urban and, to a small extent, Kabwe Rural showed such rates, other towns exhibiting the low and, in one case, negative rates characteristic of rural districts.

Historically migrants came to the towns as seekers of temporary jobs, a pattern that had considerable impact on the age and sex distribution in both urban and rural areas. The urban areas were inhabited by a preponderance of males in their prime working years—roughly from fifteen to fifty years of age, most perhaps in the narrower age range of twenty to forty. The outnumbered males in the rural areas tended to be children or old men.

By 1969 greater numbers of female migrants, coming as workers or as wives of the growing numbers of permanently established urban males, had led to a somewhat different age and sex distribution in town and country, although some features of the earlier pattern persisted. In the major urban areas the proportion of young women (between fifteen and thirty-five) was greater than in the country as a whole. Thereafter, unlike men, their proportion diminished. The presence of these younger women, many of them as part of relatively stable families, may account for the presence in urban centers of young children (up to age five) in roughly the same proportions as in Zambia as a whole. Data from the 1969 census showed that in urban centers the proportion of women older than thirty-five declined below that in the nation as a whole, whereas the proportion of men between thirty-five and forty-four remained higher. At the same time the proportion of children between five and fifteen in the urban centers was less than that in Zambia generally (and in the rural areas). This may reflect the relative youthfulness of urban mothers, but it may also reflect a tendency of urban parents to send their children to their rural home areas (and kin) to go to school and to acquire a background in a more traditional milieu.

Language

With the exception of a few scattered hunters in the extreme southwest and immigrant communities derived from Europe and Asia, all Zambians speak languages of the Bantu family as their mother tongues. Bantu languages, although spoken throughout central and southern Africa, began their process of differentiation a relatively short time ago. Further, all Zambian languages are near relatives within the large Bantu linguistic family, and even the least related ones stem from divergences of a few thousand years ago.

Despite this commonality of origin, there are many distinct Zambian languages. Linguists have no definitive rule as to when two dialects of one language become separate languages, but the process consists of a loss of mutual comprehensibility and a declining proportion of shared vocabulary. In much of the country simple geographic distance was the principal factor isolating developing dialects, and many Zambian languages fade from one into another, in such a way that individuals along the language border speak an intermediate form understandable by speakers of mutually incomprehensible languages on either side. Also a community speaking one language may come under such strong influence from a clearly distinct tongue that people borrow vocabulary, pronunciation, and grammar from the prestigious language. So-called Zambian English among individuals with limited formal education shows the influence of Bantu rules of pronunciation and grammar; similarly present-day Zambian languages contain large numbers of words derived from English, Swahili, Kabanga (the language of mining in Southern Africa), and Portuguese among others. Such borrowing can be so massive as to create a new language; Senga in eastern Zambia is the result of a Bisa dialect so influenced by Tumbuka as to become practically a dialect of the latter language.

Thus it is no simple task to identify and count the languages of Zambia. A recent study of them lists eighty Bantu languages or dialects that fall into sixteen groups within several larger blocks; further detailed analysis might show that the number of mutually incomprehensible languages is fewer than the eighty although certainly far more than the fourteen.

Maternal or First Languages

The scores of Zambian languages fall into larger subgroupings. The most important is the central block of related languages that occupies most of northeastern Zambia and extends along the line of rail to the Zambezi River; it in turn contains several language groups (see fig. 7). The Bemba group is the most widespread, accounting for 34.6 percent of black Zambians; it spreads through Northern, Luapula, Copperbelt, Central, and even a small portion of North-Western provinces. Bemba itself is by far the most commonly spoken maternal language in Zambia (18.6 percent of the population), and one of its dialects has become the lingua franca of the diverse urban population of the copperbelt. The initial spread of Bemba stems from the large precolonial Bemba kingdom in northeastern Zambia, and the Luunda dialect had become the vernacular of the *mwata kazembe's* Eastern Lunda kingdom by the beginning of the colonial period. Other important languages in the Bemba group include Lala, Aushi, Lamba, and Bisa. Languages of the Bemba group extend into southeastern Zaïre and are related to the large Luba language group there, to which Kaonde in Zambia directly belongs.

The remaining two language groups along the central axis of the country and related to the Bemba and Luba groups are those of Tonga and Nkoya. The Tonga languages are often called the Bantu Botatwe (three people) group after a shared myth expressing the

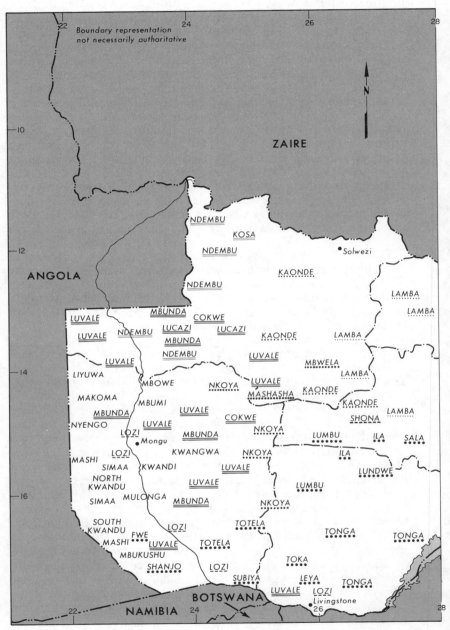

Source: Sirarpi Ohannessian and Mubanga E. Kashoki, *Language in Zambia,* London, 1978, map 8. Used by permission of the publisher, the International African Institute, London.

Figure 7. Languages of Zambia

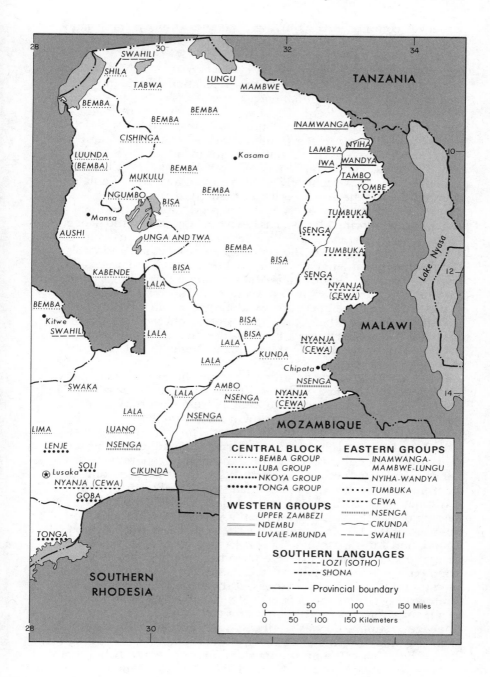

CENTRAL BLOCK
·········· BEMBA GROUP
·········· LUBA GROUP
·········· NKOYA GROUP
•••••• TONGA GROUP

WESTERN GROUPS
UPPER ZAMBEZI
══════ NDEMBU
═══════ LUVALE-MBUNDA

EASTERN GROUPS
────── INAMWANGA-
MAMBWE-LUNGU
────── NYIHA-WANDYA
·········· TUMBUKA
············ CEWA
ıııııııı NSENGA
─────── CIKUNDA
─ ─ ─ SWAHILI

SOUTHERN LANGUAGES
------ LOZI (SOTHO)
─ ─ ─ SHONA

───── Provincial boundary

0   50   100   150 Miles
0   50   100   150 Kilometers

perceived common origins of these peoples. Among these languages of Central and Southern provinces, only Lenje and Ila (aside from Tonga) are spoken by more than 1 percent of black Zambians. The final group in the central block, the Nkoya, accounts for less than 1 percent of the population, although it too consists of several distinct languages or dialects.

To the east of this central block, as to the west, are found a number of language groups and individual languages most closely related to languages in bordering countries. In eastern Zambia these include, from north to south, Inamwanga-Mambwe-Lungu, Nyiha-Wandya, Tumbuka, Nyanja (Cewa), Nsenga, and Cikunda. Although only 11 percent of Zambians speak forms of Nyanja as their mother tongue, its role is larger than mere numbers suggest. It has been adopted by one major group of Ngoni, is the lingua franca of neighboring Malawi, has been the language of the police and army since the days of British South Africa Company rule, is the dominant language of the central line-of-rail cities, and rivals Bemba in national language policy politics. Of the other eastern language groups, Inamwanga-Mabwe-Lungu, Tumbuka, and Nsenga each number about 5 percent of Zambians among their speakers. A few small pockets of Swahili speakers in the northeast are relics of nineteenth-century trade routes from the East African coast (see Vernacular Lingua Francas, this ch.; see The Commercial Revolution: The Late Eighteenth and Nineteenth Centuries, ch. 1).

Three separate language groups occupy the area west of the central block. The first includes Luvale, Mbunda, Lucazi, and Cokwe, all of which extend into Zambia from eastern Angola; at least the last three have been brought into Zambian territory by immigrants within the past two centuries. The Ndembu language farther north extends into southwestern Zaïre and forms a group of its own. Ndembu speakers in Zambia are generally called Lunda (Southern, Western, or North-Western Lunda according to different writers), but this is essentially a political term. Ndembu is distinct from both the Luunda dialect of Bemba spoken by Eastern or Northern Lunda of Luapula Province and the Ruund language of the Lunda imperial heartland in Zaïre; the Ndembu, Ruund, and Luvale-Mbunda-Lucazi-Cokwe groups do, however, form a related cluster. No single term has been acceptable to all Ndembu speakers and not created confusion with other groups having Lunda political structures but different linguistic and cultural heritages; the same language is thus commonly identified as Lunda for some areas and Ndembu for others. The third separate language group in the west centers on the upper Zambezi floodplain. Luyana, the original language of the rulers of the Lozi kingdom, is historically the most important but by the mid-twentieth century was almost extinct. None of the numerous languages in this group counts as many as 30,000 speakers today.

The remaining Zambian Bantu languages are recent imports

from the south (see The Commercial Revolution: The Late Eighteenth and Nineteenth Centuries, ch. 1). Lozi, a dialect of Sotho, was brought by the Kololo conquerors of the Lozi kingdom in the nineteenth century and is the dominant language of Western Province. The Nguni dialects of the other black South African military invaders of the previous century—the Ngoni bands of eastern Zambia—have become extinct as each group adopted the language of its indigenous neighbors. The Lozi and Ngoni thus illustrate within the documented recent past the independence of linguistic, political, and cultural factors. In the Zambezi valley the intrusive language was retained while other influences were deliberately weeded out, and in the eastern highlands the newcomers established permanent ethnic communities while freely adopting local languages. Shona is the third southern Bantu language in Zambia. Small numbers of Shona speakers may have long lived in the middle Zambezi valley along the border with Southern Rhodesia; others immigrated from the southern plateau to lands near the line of rail during the period of the Central African Federation of Rhodesia and Nyasaland in the 1950s as market farmers in search of land unavailable in their southern homeland under white settler domination.

The non-Bantu languages of Zambia fall into three groups, representing the very old and the very new. Khoisan or Click languages (so called after certain characteristic consonantal sounds) are used among a tiny number of nomadic hunters in the fringes of the Kalahari Desert in far southwestern Zambia. Such hunting bands once occupied all of Zambia and may have spoken other but now extinct Click languages (see The Stone Age, ch. 1). European languages arrived in Zambia with missionaries and colonizers; South Asian languages followed. English was the maternal language of over three-fourths of white residents in the 1969 census, and Gujarati accounted for almost as large a proportion of the Asian community. If the many temporary contract workers in each community were excluded and only Zambian citizens and permanent residents counted, the respective dominance of English and Gujarati would probably be even greater. The 1969 census did not calculate the number of Africans whose native tongue was English, but such individuals were assuredly few in the late 1970s.

The Role of English in Zambia

Maternal language is only one factor in an individual's choice of speech in specific situations. Most Zambians speak several languages, and a significant number have gained greater proficiency in a second or third language than in their first or mother tongue. Thus the actual use of languages in Zambia is as much the result of sociological forces as of the historical distribution of languages.

English has clearly been Zambia's language of prestige and power since independence. Government operations and official internal communications are exclusively in English. So is education from secondary school through university, although several vernaculars are offered as subjects for study. Many primary schools, especially in urban areas, conduct instruction in English from the start of the first grade, following the Zambia Primary Course introduced progressively since 1966. English is the sole language of Zambian television, whose audience is estimated at one quarter of the population (generally urban) within range of a transmitter. In the case of radio, two broadcasting channels and longer hours of operation offer greater air time, and programming is locally produced rather than purchased from overseas; nonetheless English-language offerings filled a large portion of Zambia Broadcast Services (ZBS) radio schedules in 1977. Besides being the home language of most white Zambians, English appears to be in the process of replacing Gujarati as the principal language of young Zambians of Asian descent.

Zambian language policy has been rooted in both practical and political factors. The former are exemplified by organizational inertia, industrial usage, and international flexibility. English was obviously the bureaucratic language inherited with the colonial state, and experience in such countries as Tanzania illustrates the great effort required to change over government materials and procedures. English is also the dominant language of the world copper industry and particularly of those multinational firms that have operated Zambia's mines. When Zambia moved to lessen its former dependence on South Africa, Southern Rhodesia, and the United Kingdom for educational and technical personnel, it could tap a diverse international pool of English speakers to fill the gap until a sufficient number of Zambian nationals were trained; the introduction of an indigenous official language would have almost eliminated such external assistance.

As for political reasons for continued reliance on English, it was the only language spoken in all areas of the country, and it is a politically neutral language. It is not identified with any of the competing political constituencies, nor has its association with the colonial past tarnished its image. This could, of course, change should bitter class conflict break out against the educated English-speaking elite, strong public revulsion develop toward white minority regimes farther south, or internal linguistic nationalisms gain significant political leverage. It is significant that such a major Zambian political figure as Simon Kapwepwe, then vice president, spoke out as early as 1969 against such reliance on a foreign language. It is also significant that ethnicity had, to an unusual degree, become a political issue in the 1968 elections and that Kapwepwe was a leader of the disaffected Bemba (see "Tribes" and "Tribalism," this ch.; see The Politics of Independence, ch. 1).

As such individuals as Kapwepwe point out, English carries strong disadvantages as well as advantages. Only a small proportion of the population has any facility in using English, a language radically different from their maternal tongues. A national radio audience survey in 1970–73 showed that only 27 percent of black Zambians over fifteen years of age claimed to listen to English-language radiobroadcasts, and only 26 percent said they could speak English; these figures are far lower than the 38 percent of air time given to English-language broadcasts. (In comparison, 37 percent listened to Bemba programming, and 56 percent claimed to speak it; 34 percent listened to broadcasts in Nyanja, and 42 percent spoke the language. Bemba and Nyanja were each used for about 15 percent of the broadcast week in 1977.) Such linguistic barriers will not disappear soon. It was estimated that in the late 1970s 45 percent of school-age children fail to find places entering primary school or drop out by the end of the fourth year before gaining the "critical mass" of modern education considered necessary for use and retention. While Zambia's reliance on English counters regionalism and favors a cosmopolitan outlook among the bureaucratic elite, the nation pays the price in the social exclusion of the majority of the population. It has thus been difficult for the central government to mobilize the masses for development projects, for even at the lowest echelons of the civil service or in the many new rural secondary schools the professional staff frequently cannot communicate with the local population.

Vernacular Lingua Francas

Since the masses do not speak English, Zambia has always used a small number of indigenous languages as official lingua francas. Bemba was the most common language of migrant workers to the copper mines, and a Bemba dialect (so-called Town Bemba) developed as the common speech of the copperbelt. Nyanja was the language of mission-educated clerks from Nyasaland (Malawi) and of the British South Africa Company's native troops in the territory originally administered from Nyasaland (see Company Rule, 1895–1924, ch. 1). Nyanja thus became the vernacular of the lower bureaucracy, of the army, and of Lusaka, the territorial capital. Lozi similarly came to be the lingua franca of the Livingstone urban area. Languages spoken by large populations were also more widely understood among rural people. The colonial government began broadcasting in Bemba and Nyanja during World War II and added Tonga and Lozi after the war. However, none of these languages has ever been widely used in North-Western Province, and Luvale and Ndembu (Lunda) were recognized by the government in 1954 and Kaonde somewhat later. Other languages, such as Tumbuka, Nsenga, and Mambwe, serve as vehicular languages in limited rural areas, but their proponents have not been able to win broadcast time or other official recognition. The proportion able to use the official vernacular of a province varies from 98 percent for regions where the lingua franca is also a major maternal language (Luapula Province for Bemba, Southern for Tonga) through the range from 80 to 90 percent in most provinces to less than 50 percent in North-Western Province, where there are three competing official languages.

In addition to radiobraodcasting, the official vernaculars are used in other contexts. All are utilized in adult literacy campaigns (to the exclusion of English), agricultural extension services, and government-sponsored biweekly newspapers. All seven are taught in primary schools in their respective regions, either as the medium of instruction or, in schools using the Zambia Primary Course, as a separate subject. The four principal vernaculars are taught as secondary-school and university subjects at all levels (see Education, this ch.). Bemba, Nyanja, Tonga, and Lozi have also been used in government-produced films for domestic audiences.

Nonetheless the status of vernaculars remains much lower than that of English. Little literature has been written in Zambian languages, and the most widely available materials in them are those produced by the various Christian churches. The impact of the vernacular newspapers is lessened by distribution problems and limited circulation within their largely rural constituencies. The use of Zambian languages in schools has suffered for other reasons. English is more prestigious; parents do not wish their children condemned to be second-class citizens. Second, teachers are under heavy pressure because of the triple-shift operation of most classroom facilities, and they often slight the vernaculars as the least important part of the program. Third, because the Ministry of Education assigns teachers from a national pool, instructors have frequently been charged with teaching languages that they do not themselves know and when they have little training and few materials for the task; since they may be posted elsewhere at any time or may leave teaching, there is limited incentive to learn a local language having little prestige or use in other areas of the country. Educational and political leaders are aware of these fundamental contradictions, and increasing efforts have been made during the 1970s to support the vernaculars as well as English; funding, however, has been limited because of the economic crisis brought on by declining copper prices.

One additional lingua franca, once widely used, has largely disappeared in contemporary Zambia. Kabanga, also known in Zambia as Chilapalapa and elsewhere as Fanagalo or Kitchen Kaffir, is a pidgin based on Bantu languages of South Africa, English, and Afrikaans; it was brought north as mines developed progressively inland from the Witwatersrand in the Republic of South Africa. Before independence Kabanga was the common form of communication between white supervisors and black laborers, especially in the mines; it was also used among the diverse copperbelt African population, between Asian shopkeeper and client, and between colonial householder and domestic servant. As a crude pidgin, Kabanga lacked the subtleties and nuances of other languages, and its usage was too limited to develop these. It was perceived as the language of racial domination and exploitation. With the assumption of political and social dominance by black Zambians since the 1960s, Bemba or other regional vernaculars have replaced Kabanga in many circumstances, while English has done so in others. Use of Kabanga today would be considered uncouth in most situations, as it expresses a degree of familiarity that is easily taken as scorn for another's inferiority.

Social Structure

Just as language is one major factor in perceptions of ethnic identity, so the ways in which individuals relate to one another in communities can serve to set some groups apart from others. All Zambians must interact with other people in multiple levels and forms of community. Even in the simplest rural area least affected by social and economic change, the individual is a member of a household, an extended family, a village, a neighborhood, perhaps a clan, a formal political system of chieftainship, an informal political system of prestige and influence, and a set of state administrative structures.

Each of these sorts of community makes its own demands on a person's behavior and offers him or her certain roles. In many cases several such levels of community correspond—for example, when the village is headed by a chief, who is also the most influential person there; societies develop various structures to accommodate differing roles or to contain the conflicts that arise between them. Even in the relatively simple case mentioned, individuals choose among conflicting norms—such as a village chief's obligation to his own family versus that to other village residents. Most Zambians, in fact, live not in such easily described communities but in conjunction with others of diverse background.

As expressed by one tradition of sociological thought well developed in Zambia, social structures often can be best seen through case histories of the resolution and accommodation of conflict. Social structures are regularities, or patterns or predictabilities, rather than static, permanent rules—structures cast in concrete, as it were. They are models that few individuals follow completely.

Family and Marriage

The word *family* for most Zambians refers not so much to the nuclear family of spouses and minor children but to an extended family that includes several generations. In rural areas this group, encompassing all the heirs of a living elder, may be the corporate property-holding unit, the cooperative work group, the sphere of shared cooking and eating, and so forth (see Lineage, Clan, and Descent System, this ch.). It may also consist of several relatively autonomous households that accept responsibility for a member who wishes to change his or her residence from one unit to the other; for example, a child frequently lives with aunts, uncles, or even cousins (in English usage) in order to gain access to education. Urban living arrangements made it more difficult for extended families to follow the pattern of contiguous households—adjacent dwellings are seldom immediately available—but siblings, nieces or nephews, parents, or even friends often live within a household. Even when no such relatives are resident, gifts and money may be regularly shared with members of the extended family having less access to cash. Such extended families are deeply embedded in Zambian languages. An individual generally has several "mothers," several "fathers," and perhaps a host of "sons" and "daughters"; the same languages, however, may differentiate relationships that European languages run together, so that mother's and father's kin or even full siblings may bear distinct terms.

Polygyny is traditionally permissible, but it has not been statistically common. Polygynous households were generally those of important chiefs. Chiefs often needed additional women because of their obligations of hospitality, for women's work traditionally included food preparation, beer brewing, and most crop cultivation. Chiefs also frequently used marriage as a way of building political alliances. In 1969 it was estimated that less than 8 percent of Zambian households were polygynous. Customs varied from ethnic group to ethnic group and even from one household to another, but a polygynous husband usually provided each wife with a house and fields. Each wife usually fed her own children and provided a share of the husband's food; each might keep her granaries and other goods individually or, for certain items, in a joint account for the entire household. Such polygynous households differed from the contemporary Zambian practice of keeping mistresses or "girlfriends" outside the marriage home, for co-wives were all recognized (though perhaps ranked by seniority or prestige) and lived in a common social unit, the household.

Zambian marriage rules are quite diverse. Zambian Africans may, since independence, marry under statutory law or under the numerous recognized varieties of customary law. In the former case, current British law prevails for marriage, divorce, and inheritance; statutory marriages can be dissolved only by the High Court. (Before 1964 statutory marriages were for whites and customary ones for blacks; there was no special form for Asians, as they usually sought eligible partners in India or Pakistan.) Very few Africans, however, have chosen to marry under statutory law. The prevailing British laws on divorce are no longer more restrictive than Zambian customary rules (formerly a disadvantage of marriage by ordinance), but statutory marriage still rules out polygyny, recognizes no rights for damages in adultery except as grounds for divorce, and specifies inheritance rules that differ from Zambian family patterns. Couples from dissimilar ethnic backgrounds generally marry under the customary law of the husband's group. Typical variations among Zambian systems of customary law include the amount and the recipients of bride-

Village housing: clustered (upper left) and linear
Courtesy ZIMCO

A rural homestead with outbuildings
Courtesy ZIMCO

wealth (gifts to the wife's parents or guardians), brideservice (labor provided to the bride's relatives, increasingly commuted to a cash payment), the definition of incest, and family allegiance of children and their custody after divorce or a parent's death.

Marriages have traditionally been based on practical rather than emotional grounds—on mutual advantage rather than love. Childbearing was considered a chief end of marriage, and the sexual division of labor left individual men and women in strongly dependent positions in traditional society. Women were expected to marry at puberty, and men remained dependent within some relative's household until they married. Divorce has never been uncommon in Zambia, although the rates varied by ethnic group. In general, marriages were most stable among patrilineal peoples and where large bridewealth was paid; they were very unstable among matrilineal communities where the marriage bond conflicted with inheritance patterns and where individuals often married nine or ten times during their lives. The most common grounds for divorce reflect this practical approach as well as certain universal difficulties in human relations: infertility, impotence, quarrelsomeness, long separation, and "uselessness," among others.

Such generalizations about the forms of marriage in the rural past describe only one aspect of contemporary Zambian marital mores. Zambians perceive that modern, urban life has brought increasing instability in the family and a higher divorce rate. With longer schooling for girls and the general fragmentation of urban life, many urban women seek to retain their social autonomy. Once called *kapenta* (painted women) or "champions" and more recently described as *toughu* (toughened), these women are by no means prostitutes and are often wage-earners themselves. At least until disillusioned they seek the customary goal of marriage but one arranged on their own terms; they observe certain aspects of traditional female etiquette (such as downcast eyes and servility around males) yet reject modest dress (any view of knees or thighs is thought an irresistible provocation). Zambian couples rarely share a common social life; together with a strong double standard, this means that the "movious" (in Zambian jargon) nightlife of urban elites and subelites is composed of married or single men and their single girlfriends.

Residence patterns vary across the country. In most areas a married couple was traditionally expected to spend most of their years together in the village of the groom's father. In some matrilineal areas, as among the Bemba, the man would reside with his wife's parents for a number of years while working within their household; only then was it permissible for him to take his family to his own village. Again, in some areas of Zambia, his own village might not be his father's home but that of his mother's brother. Considerable leeway remained within these rules to allow for the variables of a specific couple's situation.

Urban and industrial development have added new factors so that what has been customary practice may become the exception. In the mines it was always expected that the company would provide housing for its employees, and married quarters were increasingly constructed after the Great Depression and World War II. There seniority and rank in employment determined where a person lived, not ethnic and familial ties. Similarly the rotation policies of the Zambian civil service mean that state employees and their families, who live in government housing, do not reside according to any traditional rules of preference. Even after independence the Zambian government attempted to cope with the squatter settlements around the cities by building government housing; more recently the magnitude of the problem has brought a shift to aiding and facilitating self-help plans among new urban residents. Yet even in such revived forms of owner-initiated housing, residence patterns are largely ad hoc and do not reflect the specific rural background of the newly urbanized. Ethnic background, employment, site conditions, religious affiliation, and friendship—all are as apt to influence the settlement pattern as any customary residence rules.

Lineage, Clan, and Descent System

Beyond the level of the household or extended family, Zambian social structures frequently include two other modes of grouping persons: the lineage and the clan. A lineage is defined as all those who acknowledge a common ancestor through known links, through either men (a patrilineage) in some ethnic groups or women (a matrilineage) in others. Such lineages may consist of only a few generations (as among the Tonga) or as many as six or seven (as among the Luvale); the genealogies of chiefly families are frequently deeper than those of commoners. Lineages may function as corporate groups overseeing inheritance, settling disputes among their members, and acting as political entities in competition with other such units; this is especially true in those traditional societies with greater lineage depth or with less elaborate chiefly structures. In such cases, as among the Luvale and related groups, the lineages are generally segmentary ones: members of a branch at any level of the lineage unite whenever there is a conflict between one individual and someone in a "brother" or "sister" branch of the lineage, while they may oppose each other when the conflicting persons are in two subbranches. Powerful chiefs and powerful lineages, however, are not necessarily polar alternatives. For example, the Luvale link political office to leadership in the lineage. In contrast, the Tonga had neither chiefs nor significant lineages in the early twentieth century; in a sense they resolved tensions by escape—by living in dispersed homesteads rather than in villages grouping several families.

The form of lineage depends on the descent system of the ethnic group as well as on the social role of the lineage structure itself. Zambia lies astride the "matrilineal belt," an area spanning Central Africa from the Atlantic to the Indian Ocean where people trace their descent primarily through women. The occurrence of various descent systems correlates with economic factors, and the matrilineal belt corresponds with the savanna—its low population densities and ample, if relatively infertile, land for agriculture. In the present millennium Zambian populations have been composed primarily of subsistence farmers; in such situations the economy depended largely on the harvest from women's fields, while there was little conflict over land rights to mobilize male involvement in defending and seizing territory. Precolonial states in Central Africa were far more concerned to control people than territory, and women of childbearing age were crucial to a community's future. Matrilineal descent does not imply that women were dominant figures in social and political leadership; rather, the mother's oldest brother generally wielded family authority. Matrilineal societies generally had more fluid villages and often granted village headmen and chiefs less authority, for matrilineality poses certain contradictions. Households frequently resided in the village of the man's father, yet to inherit political offices or other social resources a man had to cultivate his relationship with his mother's kin, even at the expense of angering those on his father's side among whom he lived.

Those peoples who do not practice matrilineal descent further highlight the effects of economic conditions on social structure. Among the Lozi, with their more highly elaborated state and their intricate economic system based on the varied habitat of the Zambezi floodplain, individuals recognize all lines of descent. A person is thus a member of many sets of familial relationships at once, and the Lozi have no organized lineages. A unique Lozi social unit was the *makolo* (social regiment) under a chiefly title at the king's court; one additional new *makolo* was created by each king. Lozi society was more closely tied to the powerful king and much less to the family.

Several of the patrilineal ethnic groups of Zambia, such as the Shona-speaking Goba of the Zambezi valley or the Ngoni colonies of the eastern highlands, are derived from the cattle-keeping peoples of southern Africa. Because pastoral chores are male tasks throughout the area and cattle were the traditional bank for wealth, descent through males here corresponds to greater male dominance of economic assets.

Shifts in descent systems do occur. One example is the historic transition from a people that began as patrilineal Shona south of the Zambezi and became Goba, living without cattle on the Zambezi valley floor; some elements later became matrilineal Tonga, as groups gained rights to fertile soil on the northern plateau. One individual did not migrate through all phases in the transformation, but individuals did alter their values and life-styles as they made small moves along the larger line of change. Residence and marriage patterns had to change in the inhospitable valley where cattle for bridewealth could not live; the Goba thus married by brideservice as would the slaves and poor among the plateau Shona. Goba, who arrived on the plateau where they could reacquire cattle, retained the importance of links through women characteristic of their society in the valley, and they adopted the cultural model of their Tonga neighbors rather than reverting to plateau Shona patrilineality. The new plateau dwellers adopted the Tonga language and tried to lose their Goba and Shona past.

Another and perhaps far more important shift is that toward partilineal descent under the impact of urban society or, in the case of the Tonga, of the increasing cash value of agricultural assets along the line of rail. With men's participation in the money economy has come male control over cash expenditures, and men increasingly favor their own children over their sisters' children. One example of this trend concerns the importance of education in a child's chances for success in modern Zambia. Men were responsible for protecting and clothing their own young children in matrilineal as well as patrilineal societies, so school expenditures might easily be seen as customary expenses; at the same time school expenditures serve as capital investments that establish obligations for future generosity on the part of the students. The greater the man's resources to aid his male heirs, the more he seems to wish them to be his own sons.

Among Zambians in the north, central, and northwestern areas, the clan forms a grouping even larger than the lineage. Clan members accept their common descent, but the common ancestor may be unknown or largely mythical and beyond the depths of personal genealogies. Clans frequently extend beyond the limits of language groups, chieftainships, or other markers. For example, one complex of clans spreads among the Luvale, Cokwe, Mbunda, and Lucazi in northwestern and western Zambia; another system in the northeast extends among the Bemba, Eastern Lunda, Bisa, and Lamba among others. Clans have no recognized hierarchy of leadership, although they may be linked with significant offices and exert strong political influence. For example, all those in the northcentral area having chiefly dynasties of the Mushroom clan have become known as the Bisa ethnic group; those with chiefs of the Crocodile clan became united under the *citimukulu* (the Bemba paramount chief). Clans frequently played a role in determining permissible marriages either within or outside the clan; those inside the clan usually had to be outside the lineage. Among the Bemba and their neighbors, customary ties between pairs of clans provided for mutual assistance, such as in the ritually dangerous duties of burying the dead, and for exemptions from rules of appropriate behavior, as in exchange of mutual jests and satire expressing an unusual degree of familiarity.

Residual Precolonial Administrative/Political Structures

In addition to language and family structure, a third major factor in contemporary ethnic identification in Zambia is the heritage of precolonial state structures (see Peoples and Polities, ca. 1500–1800, ch. 1). Almost all Zambian groups had chiefs above the level of village headman, but the powers and possible higher organizations of these chiefs varied widely. In some cases, as among the Eastern Lunda and Bemba, modern ethnic differentiation is due primarily to their distinct precolonial states. The Lunda, for example, have spoken the Bemba language for most purposes for at least 150 years; the peoples of the former Lunda kingdom differ more socially and culturally among themselves than most of them do from the Bemba.

At one end of the organizational continuum were the groups organized in centralized kingdoms, such as the Lozi and the Eastern Lunda. Such states were characterized by elaborate political institutions that organized the population in complex ways; chiefly realms did not correspond with descent groups or, to a considerable extent, with residence. Thus the state could not easily segment along a single dominant line of cleavage. Both the Lozi and Eastern Lunda had multiethnic kingdoms; subjects differed in the languages they spoke, the descent systems they followed, and the social institutions they relied on. In each case one ethnic group came to be a political elite: the Luyi or Luyana among the Lozi, the Lunda proper (the heirs of the immigrants from the west) among the Eastern Lunda. At the same time chiefly polygyny and the descent system of the ruling elite prevented closed caste divisions between ethnic groups, and leaders of the subordinated peoples could achieve important posts. Even if political structures were not territorial, there was always a geographical differentiation in such African empires, for people living close to the capital were naturally much more closely integrated than those farther away who essentially only paid tribute. Thus a Lozi may also be something else, depending on how ethnic identity is defined at the moment; if, as is frequently the case, ancestors came from several groups within the state, the individual may adopt several ethnic identities during his or her life. This can also be seen in the career of Eastern Lunda aristocrats as they advance through titles associated respectively with different ethnic subgroups.

The Bemba are another example of an ethnic group defined by a former state, the paramountcy of the *citimukulu*. This was not so centralized a policy as those of the Lozi or Eastern Lunda, but the rotation of the royal office among a system of important Bemba regional lords gave a measure of cohesion to the whole. Even within the short documented history of precolonial Zambia, it is clear that the Bemba were expanding geographically as people conquered by Crocodile clan chiefs assimilated—"converted"—to Bemba culture and identity. In particular, it is well established that large areas, and presumably the majority of their previous populations, changed from Bisa to Bemba between 1800 and 1900.

Most sections of Zambia were not organized in governmental units that covered entire cultural areas. For example, there were several mutually independent Ndembu chiefs in North-Western Province, all respecting the suzerainty of the Lunda emperor, or *mwant yav,* to the north in Zaïre. There were many Bisa chieftaincies, although all were headed by members of the Mushroom clan. Not only were there multiple Kaonde polities, but at least some of them had established tributary relationships with Ndembu overlords to the northwest.

Such distinct political entities within a common cultural grouping were themselves potential cultural groups, for they could easily have evolved differing social institutions. For example, there is a sharp distinction in Western Province between Mbunda immigrant groups who migrated into the Lozi kingdom in the nineteenth century and those who entered the colonial protectorate more recently. The "Old Mbunda" retain their language and many cultural traits, such as reliance on diviners rather than judges to resolve social tension. The Old Mbunda, however, have undergone great assimilation to the Lozi in other respects, such as abandoning circumcision and the associated initiation schools. People in Western Province thus accept the Old Mbunda as Lozi, but the newer immigrants, speaking the same language and also calling themselves Mbunda, are lumped by other Western Province peoples with the Cokwe and Lucazi (who speak distinct languages) as Wiko (westerners).

The Tonga are the preeminent example at the other end of the organizational continuum. The Tonga recognized no political leaders as chiefs. They preferred to live in dispersed households rather than villages, although they were forced to group together in the nineteenth century under the continuing threat of Ndebele and Lozi raiding. The name *Tonga* was apparently a Shona term for *independent,* referring to the lack of formal political structures. Tonga identity is thus cultural rather than political, and it is originally a classification by non-Tonga rather than a self-identification. The Tonga shared closely related dialects, similar matrilineal descent systems, preferential patrilocal residence with dispersed homesteads, and the absence of any chiefly institutions to give them other and separate identities. It was the colonial government that appointed tribal officials, whom the Tonga significantly called government chiefs, for its own administrative convenience. British officials seized on prestigious persons—influential prophets or rain-shine priests—or simply more cooperative individuals and attempted to treat them as hereditary chiefs on the model of other areas. It was thus the colonial state that convinced the Tonga that they were a tribe—by calling them "the Tonga" and by arranging the government chiefs in a unified hierarchy.

Nonetheless the precolonial polities retained importance and developed new roles during the transformation brought by European rule.

British theories of indirect rule were embodied in the Native Authority system whereby the most important chiefs were recognized and encouraged to create a modernized, bureaucratic local government from the relevant features of their precolonial institutions. The Native Authorities created an institutional framework for African politics in rural areas, although the local British official retained ultimate authority. These local governments typically collected taxes, enforced conservation and agricultural controls, sponsored certain welfare and educational programs, and supported the recognized chiefs in partial replacement of old tribute systems.

Since Zambian independence the Native Authorities have been abolished. (In many areas nationalist activity was tied to resistance to the Native Authorities, for the chiefs were seen as dependent on the British.) Their place has been taken by the Rural Councils composed of some locally elected members and some appointed by the Zambian government. Traditional chieftainship remains but is outside the new official government structure, just as the Native Authority system never recognized all of the traditional political titles. Chiefs continue to wield great influence and are well represented on the current Rural Councils, belonging as either elected or appointed members; a few important chiefs have become members of parliament and Cabinet members. The Zambian Constitution also provides for a consultative House of Chiefs, but this is not a legislative body. (see Local Government, ch. 3).

"Tribes" and "Tribalism"

These two words, known to all and commonly used, are loaded with a wide range of meanings. A Zambian may speak freely of his own tribe and decry tribalism in politics; the same individual may also strongly resent use of the term *tribe* by non-Zambians, seeing an implication of African backwardness in it. Scholars are reluctant to use the two words unless they are precisely defined. It is important to note that the phenomena of "tribe" and "tribalism" are not unique to the parts of the world for which the terms are commonly used; they are forms of ethnic identity and competition related to familiar processes within the United States and other developed Western nations.

Tribes, then, are the convenient but artificial result of British attempts to tidy up colonial administration. Where precolonial states were based on control over people, European organizational concepts required boundaries and abhorred unattributed areas. The colonial government recognized one plane of ethnic identification in each area as the tribe, coterminous with one or more Native Authority, in order to construct a workable system of indirect rule. Thus small groups were amalgamated with more numerous neighbors; an autonomous chief with few subjects was often declared the subordinate of another with more followers, although both had formerly been equals. The complexity of ethnic divisions and the variety among Zambian societies meant that "workable systems" were not always easily built. The claim of Ndembu and Luvale speakers in the Balovale (present-day Zambezi) District for separation from the Barotseland Protectorate dragged on for decades; when the district was eventually transferred to North-Western Province, increased conflict between Luvale and Ndembu replaced their former united stance against the Lozi. Eventually, after decades of tinkering with the system, seventy-three units came to be officially recognized as tribes; understandably no single criterion lies behind all of the definitions and distinctions.

Tribalism, in common usage, is a somewhat different phenomenon. The word has such universally bad connotations that it is often a catchall denunciation. The ethnic and regional alignments called tribalism seldom involve the smaller ethnic groups among the seventy-three official tribes. Tribalism is rather the competition of broad coalitions within the relevant political arena; in the usual case—the Zambian nation-state—the blocks are frequently regional "supertribes" identified by the lingua franca of the area or the largest ethnic group within them. The case of the Balovale secession from Barotseland was an effort toward local autonomy, for the Lozi authorities had set up a new Lozi subcapital in the district in order to control the area more closely. The later Ndembu-Luvale tensions were in part a case of small-scale cultural nationalism, but they also represented a conflict of interest between the Ndembu, whose Lunda chiefs claimed authority over inhabitants of the area, and the Luvale, who were frequently more heavily involved in the modern cash economy than the Ndembu and resisted efforts at heavier local taxation. At the national level, the frequent accusations of Bemba tribalism conceal the complexities of coalition building in politics. The three Bemba-speaking provinces (Northern, Luapula, and Copperbelt) have diverse interests, which may even be directly opposed; e.g., in the commitment of capital either to urban development projects having higher immediate profit potential or to the cash-poor rural sector, such as the Bemba-speaking areas with their formerly poor transport links to the line of rail. Yet whenever two or more of these provinces take a common stand, tribalism is brought up as an important imputed motive. Tribalism is not the deeply rooted social structure so often depicted; rather, tribalism and charges of it are political phenomena in contemporary Zambian society (see The Politics of Independence, ch. 1).

Zambia is a heterogeneous society with little likelihood of becoming a homogeneous one in the forseeable future. Thus there will continue to be ethnic overrepresentation and underrepresentation in various spheres of the national life. Bemba are overrepresented among copper miners, Tonga among commercial farmers, Asians, among wholesalers, and so forth. It is not ethnic conflict that is so remarkable, but its relative unimportance. This is partly through historical accident—all groups and even the major ethnic blocs are minorities inside the nation's boundaries and, furthermore, relatively evenly matched—and partly because the Kaunda regime has striven continuously to remain above tribe and has apportioned power among all constituencies, even those politically hostile (see Ethnicity in Politics, ch. 3).

The Dual Society: From Race to Class and Urbanization

Zambia has been strongly marked by dual social structures since the imposition of company rule in the late nineteenth century. Until the mid 1960s the two societies were separated by race, with class and rural or urban permanent residence associated. Since independence the dualism has become an internal matter among Zambian Africans. To some extent it is now a division by class—between the privileged elite and the masses—but it can also pit the urban poor along with their wealthy fellow townsmen against the rural poor. Stark differences in social stratification have become, in a sense, traditional over the past century, although the groups in the respective strata have changed.

Zambia began to move away from a racially dual society toward a heterogeneous one during the late colonial period. Africans advanced into a few jobs formerly reserved for whites in the mines and in administration, and the policy of equal pay for equal work was established. White salaries were high, based on the companies' need to attract qualified workers on a world market. African wages had been very low, initially pegged at only the cost of maintaining the worker himself while actually employed; tax pressure supplied his motive for seeking work, while rural areas were expected to support families and those unsuitable for mine labor. The result of Africans working at better jobs and receiving salaries was the development of a well-paid bureaucratic middle class in the mines, in parastatal corporations, and in government. (At the same time the conditions and wages of ordinary miners also improved dramatically; with decolonialization came concessions to the African Mineworkers' Union, converting the miners into what has often been called a labor aristocracy owing to their high wages and benefits in comparison with those of the average Zambian.) The mining companies have continued to rely on expatriates in certain highly technical positions, and the government has done so for teachers in the rapidly expanded secondary and postsecondary schools; but their supplementary benefits have aroused less resentment than before because such temporary contract employees are perceived as politically impotent. Racial tensions have thus been very limited in postindependence Zambia, despite the continuing aggravation of racial confrontation in neighboring

Southern Rhodesia and government rhetoric during the prolonged economic decline of the late 1970s attacking the neocolonialism of white Western nations. Rhodesian military raids inside Zambia in late 1978 provoked racial attacks against expatriate whites, but these must also be seen in the nationalistic context of the numerous roundups of black noncitizens in the late 1960s and 1970s.

Class formation was one of the most important social processes operating in Zambia beginning in the mid- and late 1960s. When all Africans were excluded from participation in official politics and administration, when no black could own property in an urban area and each thus needed to retain the option of return to his ancestral rural area, then the relatively high status within African communities of a teacher or clergyman had few consequences on the way the individual actually lived. The progressive zambianization of formerly white sectors of the economy brought to Africans the benefits whites had taken for granted: housing in so-called low-density neighborhoods, automobile ownership, access to bank credit, the consumption of imported foods and goods, and economic leverage through administrative responsibilities and access to inside knowledge and personal contacts. Unlike the situation in some other developing nations, the new propertied class has not acquired its wealth through outright diversion of state assets; the frequent attacks on corruption in the Zambian press and the United National Independence Party (UNIP) releases are more a symbol of the regime's strenuous efforts to avoid graft than of any significant rate of failure in that policy. Nonetheless the government and party are closely tied to this emerging economic interest group, for individuals move back and forth during their careers, and the government and the parastatal companies are often invaluable training centers for would-be businessmen.

Much of the elite's social behavior is a direct outgrowth of new economic status. Members of the elite, frequently having risen to their positions from poor families, are conscious of the benefits of schools and hospitals; understandably they have used their increased economic resources to gain access for their children to better education and medical care by using private or foreign rather than public institutions when available. Prestige still leads to the retention of certain characteristics of the colonial white upper class or to the spread of international fads and fashions among the elite; Zambians are no more immune to such pressures than any other nationality.

It is too early to predict whether Zambia's emerging classes will become self-perpetuating strata: the children of the elite are for the most part only beginning their careers. President Kenneth Kaunda's regime has taken certain steps to equalize opportunities, such as the 1976 abolition of the more prestigious fee-paying, government-aided schools and medical facilities. Moreover the elite retain family connections with the nonelite.

Housing in a squatter community in Lusaka
Courtesy WORLD BANK PHOTO (Edwin G. Huffman)

Upgrading squatter housing in Lusaka
Courtesy WORLD BANK PHOTO (Edwin G. Huffman)

High-density (middle-class and skilled workers) housing
Courtesy ZIMCO

Low-density (elite) housing
Courtesy ZIMCO

Urban elite and urban masses do not appreciably differ in family structure; individuals in both classes continue to help educate and raise children from their extended families in addition to their own.

Urbanization itself also exerts a strong impact in differentiating Zambian society into two sectors. Zambia has the highest percentage of urbanization in black-ruled Africa, second on the continent only to South Africa. The proportion rose from 29 to 35 percent between the 1969 and 1974 censuses and is estimated to reach 46 percent by 1980 (see Population, this ch.). Zambia similarly has the continent's second-highest percentage of population in wage employment, again following South Africa. Despite formal assertions of government policy, investment continues to be restricted in practice to the urban areas, increasingly so in recent years (see Income Distribution, Wages, and Prices, ch. 4). Although the opening of the Tanzania-Zambia Railway Authority (TAZARA) line may lead to a large expansion of the periurban line of rail, most rural Zambians remain subsistence farmers with limited cash incomes. A major part of urban growth since independence may consist of working poor in squatter settlements, but they are participants within the modern economy.

Moreover sociological shifts make the reality even more dramatic than these figures indicate. With the stabilization of mine labor in the 1950s through family housing and the gaining by Africans of permanent residence and property rights in urban areas during the 1960s, new generations born and raised in the urban areas assume they will always live there. Unlike their predecessors among the so-called permanent target workers who came to town to achieve some monetary goal or the temporary target workers who stayed on in town as long as practical, such new urban workers retain no real rural roots. In a sense, then, new ethnic groups of townspeople are beginning to emerge, sharing variant social structures differing from those in rural areas and relying increasingly on urban lingua francas as home languages. So long as new immigrants continue to move into the cities, cultural connections with the rural areas are maintained. However, with urban families able to saturate the labor market and reproducing ample numbers for future replacement, any successful moves by the government to restrict migration to the cities could increase the urban-rural social divisions.

Major Ethnic Groups

Certain ethnic groups are more important than others in Zambian national life. Some owe their prominent roles to their numbers, others to their concentration in specific industries, still others to their wealth. Some are typified or defined by rural societies; others are essentially urban ethnic groups.

Bemba

The Bemba occupy much of northeastern Zambia. Bemba is also the most widely spoken maternal language in the country, although Bemba proper constitute only a small portion of all Zambians—less than 19 percent. The language and culture of the Bemba are very similar to those of the Bisa to the south, the Tabwa to the northwest, and various groups in Luapula Province to the west. The Bemba proper were loosely united in an expansive state under the *citimukulu* and related chiefs of the Crocodile clan. The Bemba social system is based on the matrilineage, with men working in their wives' villages for a number of years—frequently until several children are born—and then returning to the village of their own maternal uncle where they may inherit political responsibilities. The agricultural system was based on *citemene* (see Glossary).

The Bemba were thus a characteristic matrilineal society. Bemba agricultural technology, which was simple and well adapted to the poor, sandy soils, encouraged small and impermanent villages. Although males were heavily involved in clearing new fields, men were preoccupied primarily with political affairs and trade; agriculture was not a significant male concern, for neither was land scarce nor did agriculture contribute more than local subsistence goods. Reproductive potential was important to the group's prosperity, so ties among men through (and control of) women were very important. The role of women was symbolized by the highly developed puberty ritual *(cisungu)* for girls, contrasting with the absence of any male initiation cult. At the same time fathers did play an important role for their children, and Bemba society recognized the relevance of family relationships through males.

The Bemba, farthest from earlier wage opportunities in mines farther south, soon became the dominant source of manpower for the Northern Rhodesian (Zambian) copperbelt, and their language became the urban lingua franca there. As a result of heavy labor migration during the colonial period, the rural areas contained a large proportion of women; agriculture stagnated because of the lack of male labor to clear trees. The cycle of migration to the cities thus fed on itself, for it caused greater deprivation in the rural areas. In 1969 Bemba rural areas were second only to Eastern Province in their shortage of men, and the situation had worsened since independence in 1964.

Nyanja

The "supertribe" of eastern Zambia is the broad group known in Zambia as Nyanja but in Malawi as Chewa. The many autonomous chieftainships claim derivation from a former Maravi kingdom or confederation that perhaps reached its peak about the seventeenth century (see Peoples and Polities, ca. 1500–1800, ch. 1). These alleged common political origins, the closely related dialects of the area, the common economic base in subsistence agriculture, and the shared matrilineal social structures furnished the foundation for the development of a Nyanja ethnic identity under colonial rule. Associated with these Nyanja/Chewa proper are the Nsenga and some of the Ngoni. The Nsenga are a distinct group linguistically, politically, and culturally from the Nyanja cluster, but they are commonly lumped in with their more numerous neighbors when considered within an urban or national context. (The "Town Nyanja" vernacular of Lusaka correspondingly includes a considerable amount that is Nsenga rather than Nyanja.) The Ngoni are the heirs to nineteenth-century bands that fled north from revolutions in southern Africa. The groups that eventually settled in modern Zambia and Malawi absorbed large numbers of local people and eventually adopted the dialects of their neighbors—Nyanja or Nsenga for the Zambian groups. Thus the Ngoni speak one of these two politically linked languages, but they retain other cultural features—patrilineal descent, political structures, folklore, costumes—brought with the immigrants from the south.

The Nyanja, among the major ethnic blocks of Zambia, are especially associated with Lusaka and the government bureaucracy in the way the Bemba are with the copper mines. This is the result of geographical and historical factors. Lusaka is the major urban area most easily reached from Eastern Province; other regions are all closer to one of the other urban centers. The early availability of education in the east also played a part. The Scots Presbyterians of the Livingstonia mission along Lake Malawi were one of the first groups to open schools in Central Africa and sought to create a Christian vanguard trained in the arts and sciences. Furthermore the British South Africa Company originally based its government for Northern Rhodesia in Nyasaland (Malawi) and recruited troops there. Thus Nyanja speakers spread out throughout Northern Rhodesia to seize opportunities created by European penetration and the new age. Nyanja became the lingua franca of the army. The mines and the administration recruited educated Nyanja clerks and artisans. President Kaunda's father was a Presbyterian pastor from Nyasaland who went as a missionary to Chinsali in Northern Province. The educational advantage of Nyanja speakers disappeared as schools became available elsewhere; migration from Malawi stopped completely with the breakup of the federation and with the Zambian government's desire to favor its own citizens.

Tonga

The unusual features of traditional Tonga social structure have been noted: shallow lineages, dispersed homesteads rather than villages, and the lack of chiefs. Coupled with their location along the line of rail on soils having better than average fertility, these qualities promoted the early and dramatic participation of the

Tonga in commercial agriculture. Although much Tonga land along the railroad was alienated by the British South Africa Company for white farmers, the Tonga responded to new colonial markets by increasing their own production of maize. Tonga competition was sufficiently threatening to the European farmers that they sought to exclude or severely limit Tonga participation in the mine market. The colonial government also became concerned about the effects on the soil of intensive cultivation by traditional methods, and funds from the price differential between European- and Tonga-produced maize were invested in extension services and soil conservation works. The Tonga adopted ox-drawn plows and implements after the model of their white neighbors and acquired fertilizers and hybrid seed as these demonstrated their potential to improve yields. Not all Tonga were able to make the transition at the same rate, however, and in the 1970s the majority remained subsistence farmers who produced only a small surplus for sale. Nonetheless others were full-fledged commercial farmers; many more were in what has been called the emergent farmer category. The Tonga are the major ethnic or regional group with the least inclination to migrate and the only one of the four "supertribes" whose power and wealth are rurally based.

Lozi

The Lozi of Western Province are constituted by diverse groups identified by their inclusion in a precolonial kingdom. The Lozi proper—those most closely involved with the former state and inhabiting the floodplain—are neither patrilineal nor matrilineal. Rather, their kinship system is bilateral, the product of past need to mobilize diverse economic resources in the exceptionally varied Lozi habitat and of the nonhereditary and nongeographical system of political organization in the kingdom. Much of the precolonial history of the Lozi state recounts the kings' struggle to keep the political and social systems in flux so that they could dominate the kingdom without creating rival power centers. Major groups around the fringes (such as the Nkoya) and relatively recent immigrants (such as the Mbunda and the so-called Wiko) are generally matrilineal. As a result of Lozi overrule, however, their distinctive large-scale political and social institutions (chiefs, lineage structures, et cetera) have atrophied or evolved toward Lozi models.

The role of the Lozi in Zambia is perhaps less clear than that of other broad groupings, such as the Bemba or the Nyanja. The Lozi kingdom's precolonial wealth attracted missionaries at an early date, and political developments within the kingdom encouraged the spread of schools. With the economic decline that accompanied suppression of the Lozi system of forced labor, the population turned to migrant labor. Given their location near the rail link to the south and their speaking a Southern Bantu language, the Lozi established a tradition of traveling to the South African Witwatersrand rather than to the Northern Rhodesian copperbelt. Since independence these former migration patterns have been stopped, because Zambian economic nationalism and sanctions against the Ian Smith regime in Southern Rhodesia have blocked the route to the south. The same economic reorientation of Zambia away from the white south has also limited the economy of Livingstone itself, the one Zambian urban area dominated historically by Lozi workers. The political struggles leading to the constitutional transformation of the Barotseland Protectorate into an ordinary province have also shaken the position of the Lozi in Zambia (see The Politics of Independence, ch. 1).

Peoples of North-Western Province

The matrilineal peoples of central and northwestern Zambia include no single supertribe. The indigenous groups of Central and Copperbelt provinces in the eastern part of this area are culturally and linguistically similar to the Bemba, although lacking the structures of large kingdoms. The small groups who had lived in what became urban areas were quickly overwhelmed in numbers by the immigrants, and many immigrant workers married local women when family life became possible. Thus these two provinces are dominated culturally by the urban centers. Tensions persist, as when village schools teach the local Lamba dialect rather than the official Bemba vernacular of Copperbelt Province, but the disproportion of numbers diminishes the danger of serious strife between immigrants and those native to the area.

West of the copperbelt, however, there are no urban centers and thus no recently imposed dominant language or culture. In the eastern portion of North-Western Province, just west of the mining centers, live the Kaonde, a matrilineal extension of the Luba of Shaba Province in Zaïre. Like their neighbors to the east, the Kaonde lack large social units. Matrilineages are grouped in clans shared with other ethnic groups to the east, and there were several mutually autonomous chiefdoms, some of which were tributary to Lunda chiefs to the northwest. The western portions of the province are occupied by the Ndembu (Lunda) and Luvale; these two distinct peoples live in close proximity, especially in Zambezi District. The Ndembu tend to be subsistence farmers, the Luvale fishermen or traders; most of the former live east of the Zambezi, the latter to the west. Both speak western languages not belonging to the broad Luba-Bemba family that accounts for most Zambian tongues. Both have chiefs tracing their titles to the Lunda heartland to the north. However, Luvale social structure is essentially acephalous—based on segmenting matrilineages, the chiefs having little or no authority independent of the lineages. The Ndembu proudly identify themselves as Lunda, and Lunda political institutions coexist with and cut across the lineage divisions among the Ndembu. Several Lunda chiefs, the *kanongesha* and the *ishindi* in particular, retained tributary relationships over large parts of the Ndembu-speaking area. Smaller numbers of Cokwe, Lucazi, and other immigrants from Angola are associated with the Luvale within Zambian borders. Three languages of North-Western Province—Ndembu (Lunda), Luvale, and Kaonde —have been recognized as official national languages, but none of the three is spoken or understood by a sufficient number to gain significant government emphasis. Among all the rural provinces with few local cash resources, North-Western Province has the lowest rate of labor migration, a fact that underlines the marginal position of its internally divided population within the wider social and political life of Zambia.

Urban Africans

The urban working class corresponds roughly with those living in high-density housing. The oldest such townships are the mine- or other company-managed housing built for African employees; although standardized and lacking the variety of other areas, such housing has not fallen into disrepute, for it shows one's salaried employment and thus stable economic position.

Other urban dwellers with limited incomes rent or own dwellings in parallel municipally sponsored townships or in unauthorized squatter settlements. The rapid growth of major urban centers since independence is largely accounted for by new squatter settlements, although government policy in the 1960s was to add new municipal townships. During the 1970s official policy turned toward improving the unofficial settlements by regularizing property rights and by helping individuals improve their dwellings.

While those living in company housing must be employed by the firm or agency, the other kinds of high-density neighborhoods show a large range in occupations. Squatters generally are actively participating in the modern economy, and their unrecognized settlements show occupation distributions very similar to those of municipal townships. This refutes the widely held notion that the squatter camps house the unemployed or the marginally self-employed who have wrongly poured into the overcrowded urban areas. Working-class women have been reluctant to work outside the home, and social pressure encourages this attitude. Their chief means of earning money has been the illicit brewing of African beer for sale; others have worked in the markets as petty traders.

In the 1970s the Zambian elite and subelite were more easily distinguished from the working class by education and occupation than by housing. The elite occupy bureaucratic positions formerly filled by whites and live in low-density neighborhoods. The subelite work at skilled jobs—also originally white positions—in education, nursing, officework, and so forth. The subelite consider themselves a part of modern Zambia with the elite although lacking the financial resources, spacious houses, and international exposure of the more privileged. Few elite black Zambians are self-employed. Women are employed by the government and by companies in professional and white-collar positions, and women as well as men are educated and speak English.

Urban life has profoundly influenced social structures for all groups. The urban family tends to be more egalitarian than rural families. Neither father nor mother emphasize their authority over children, and child-rearing practices are more permissive. This reflects the consciousness of urban dwellers that life is rapidly changing; past experience is always subject to question. The length of urban residence has relatively little effect, and migrants seem to adapt to urban social patterns quickly.

In the urban areas, ethnicity is but little more important than education and socioeconomic status in determining social relationships. Unlike the experience of many African countries (or of the United States and its immigrant communities), formal ethnic organizations have never developed in the cities. Ethnic conflict has also been discouraged by the integrating nature of mine employment (historically the most important economic sector), by the colonial government's policy of discouraging urbanization, and by the popular linkage of ethnicity to the mine management and colonial rule through the failed institution of "tribal elders" at the mine. Further, none of the major ethnic blocks has acquired the kind of real or apparent social and economic advantage that has elsewhere, and briefly in Zambia, led to conflict. It remains true that individuals at all status levels tend to associate more with those of their own ethnic group or those from groups stemming from neighboring rural areas. The degree of such ethnic association varies inversely with the size of the group; members of large groups are much less likely to seek fellow Bemba, Nyanja, or whatever than are individuals from smaller communities.

Status groups, however, are becoming increasingly important. The highest and lowest levels of the urban population act as more coherent status groups or classes than do the middle ranges, maintaining social boundaries more effectively. The sociologist Howard Garrison found that the most important change over the 1967–73 period was increasing inwardness of the groups having the highest educational achievement.

Whites

The majority of Northern Rhodesia's white population left independent Zambia, but a sizable white minority remains. The largest portion are contract workers with the mines or government and are only temporary residents of Zambia. An important minority of permanent residents remains in industry, commerce, and agriculture and has a disproportionate impact on the economy. The remaining white farmers of Southern and Central provinces (estimated at between 300 and 350) continue to produce 40 percent of Zambia's staple maize crop and 60 to 70 percent of total marketed agricultural produce. Government zambianization policies have required entrepreneurs to operate in partnership with

Urban bus service
Courtesy ZIMCO

Traditional dancing in a squatter community in Lusaka
Courtesy WORLD BANK PHOTO (Edwin G. Huffman)

Zambians, but those white settlers who opted for Zambian citizenship have not been affected. Most Zambian whites retain social and family ties with the white communities of southern Africa. As elsewhere in this region, white women have preferred not to work outside the home.

Asians

Zambians of Asian descent are overwhelmingly an urban ethnic group. The community traces its roots to immigrants from the Gujarati-speaking region of British India who came to dominate retail commerce in African communities during the colonial period. At that time a large portion of the community operated shops in rural areas; the copperbelt was only opened to Asian merchants in the late 1950s, however. More Asians were Hindu than Muslim; the latter predominated in Eastern Province near Nyasaland, where they were the majority.

Southern Rhodesian restrictions on Asian immigration were extended to Northern Rhodesia in 1954 with federation, so the permanent resident community in Zambia has been a self-sustaining and stable one for over twenty-five years. The economic evolution of the country and the independent government's policy of zambianization have led to the progressive replacement of Asians by blacks in petty trade in the rural areas, but many members of the community still operate retail or wholesale stores in the cities. Others have invested in new industries promoted by the government to replace suppliers in southern Africa; Asians have been particularly prominent in the clothing industry. Parents have also invested heavily in professional training for their children (a very portable form of assets), and many young Zambian Asians are engaged in medicine, law, education, and civil service.

Zambian Asians appear to be moving toward a common anglophone Zambian elite culture. A larger portion of Asians than whites opted for Zambian citizenship at independence, and others sought nationalization after the United Kingdom began restricting entry of Asians with British passports. The Hindu and Muslim communities maintain Gujarati and Quranic supplementary schools to socialize their offspring, but children no longer attend segregated academic schools and do not need to go abroad (frequently to India or Pakistan in earlier periods) for university training. Zambian Asians are increasingly marrying within the country, further diminishing the influence of the homeland, and many young couples are setting up nuclear households rather than living jointly with their extended families.

Other Forms of Social Differentiation

In addition to language, ethnicity, race, and class, two other lines of cleavage are profoundly important in Zambian society. They are gender and age.

Sex Roles

Men and women are subject to quite distinct role expectations in most sections of Zambian society. In precolonial Zambian cultures, women were typically responsible for child care, cultivation of fields, and food preparation. Men cleared fields, hunted, and occupied themselves with social and political matters. Such blanket descriptions are not exact, of course. Women might participate in the male domain of hunting by "gathering" small rodents in drives, and men might do significant work in the fields at specific times or for certain crops. A number of influential political positions within kingdoms and chieftaincies were frequently reserved for females, and women exerted unofficial political influence individually and as a group. Nonetheless male and female roles were clearly distinct.

The relative position of men and women changed considerably in Zambia during the twentieth century. In a subsistence economy, the roles were relatively clear but balanced each other. A man could not live in isolation for lack of someone to prepare his food; a woman needed a male to provide new fields, to supply meat, and to gain a voice in formal political institutions. The colonial regime replaced indigenous political structures and increased the power of a few chiefs (generally male) as Native Authority administrative officers. Large portions of the active men were away from the community selling their labor at any given time. When employers paid only the living expenses of the laborers themselves, women in the rural areas bore the brunt of supporting the young and old. As the sociologist Godfrey Wilson remarked in the 1940s, the Bemba, whose men went to the mines, "bought clothes with hunger."

With the stabilization of urban families, new situations developed. First, there was a differential effect among rural areas. Urban women tended to come from the areas close to the cities, for men from distant districts often met their new wives in town. Thus sex distribution imbalances persisted in some areas, despite the flow of dependents to the cities in the 1960s. Second, urban labor was well established by independence as a male domain. Even those jobs considered female in the introduced European culture—domestic service, nursing, primary teaching, and clerical work—had been filled in Central Africa by men. Women kept largely to their customary activities, minus responsibility for producing the family food supply. The balance thus shifted in the cities toward the male breadwinner, who controlled the money.

Women also lagged behind men in education. Schooling was linked to the new economic roles occupied by men. Second, expectations of early marriage conflicted with education—in earlier periods because students began school at older ages and could attend only sporadically and more recently because of the increased number of years devoted to formal study. Nonetheless mission churches often emphasized education for girls in spite of the obstacles, and the government is officially pledged to the equality of women in all fields.

Women will clearly not gain proportional prominence in affairs in the near future. Fewer girls than boys continue to enter primary school, and they drop out at a much faster rate. Their competitive position is limited by the common practice of using girls to care for small children or to aid with housework. As increasing numbers of girls have been educated, there has been an increasing tendency to concentrate them in certain jobs according to European patterns of women's work. Once they have become wage earners, elite women face salary and benefit discrimination when married, and widely accepted double standards place control of money in the hands of husbands and frequently make the woman responsible for the cost of feeding and clothing the family while the husband retains discretionary income. Men expect deference from women, and wives do not share a social life with their husbands except for a few highly formal occasions (see Family and Marriage, this ch.).

The Generation Gap

Zambia is demographically a very young country; about half the population is under the age of fifteen. Given the rapid social change during the past several decades and the confrontation of multiple cultures and economies, it is not surprising that there are great social distinctions between Zambians of different ages.

Social structures often vary greatly from one age cohort to another. Older people are much more closely tied to rural homelands, for African residential and property rights in urban areas were never secure during their economic careers under colonial rule. (The same is true within the Asian community, where many of the old have retired back to Asia to spend their last days; the young may leave the country but not for India and Pakistan.) The youth have lived all their lives in a society under secure black control, while the oldest generation may still remember the last years of precolonial chiefly states. Life experiences and hence priorities and expectations are certainly diverse.

The governing elite is also young. President Kaunda, having governed the country for fifteen years, is only fifty-five. Most officials in government and industry are even younger. This implies, of course, the absence of older Zambians from influential positions in the modern sector. Moreover, because zambianization is largely a fact, it also implies a shrinking job market at the same time that ever-larger numbers of educated youths leave school. The exceptional copper prices of the 1960s and the wide scope for advancement allowed career expectations to rise dramatically and thus diminished the competition among Zambians that might have opened up social cleavages. The present challenge of the school-leavers is a major one to the social institutions of the society as well as to whatever government is in power.

Religion

Shared religious beliefs and practices are a basis for potential social groupings in Zambia, but religious divisions have played no significant role in recent Zambian history. The religion of most Zambians would fall along a transition from traditional systems to Christianity; only portions of minority racial groups (Hindu and Muslim Asians and Jewish whites) belong to other religious traditions. Christian missionaries of various denominations entered what is present-day Zambia from the late nineteenth century; various African-spread Christian movements came into the area from South Africa or originated within the country, mostly during the twentieth century. Few Zambians have totally abandoned all aspects of traditional belief systems, and few traditionalists are totally uninfluenced by Christianity or its trappings. Since Christianity and indigenous religions differ greatly in their overt manifestations, many Zambians find little contradiction between them; a traditional doctor may also be a staunch churchgoer.

Traditional Religious Beliefs

Traditional religious systems throughout Zambia had much in common. They were not institutionalized religions in the sense of fixed doctrines, scriptures, or rites. People typically thought there was a single high god, the Creator, who was removed from everyday life. Often known as Nzambi or Nyambi in the west and Mungu or Leza in the east, this high god tended to receive more attention in centralized kingdoms and at times of exceptional stress in society. Ancestors were much more immediate preternatural agents, because the family included the dead as well as the living. The senior dead, like living elders, demanded respect but were also concerned that their social group prosper and increase; thus the ancestors could be called to aid the living. Similarly, just as the dead had supernatural power over the members of their families, so did the living; witchcraft is the belief that jealous relatives can harm and thwart through supernatural means. Witchcraft beliefs were thus a powerful force in preserving social order within traditional communities, ensuring conformity with common norms and the sharing of wealth. In addition to the remote high god and the immediate family of the living and the dead, indigenous Zambian religious beliefs identified other powers or spirits in the world that could affect human lives. Such spirits had names and might in myth be said to have had human progeny, but they were not close kin of any individual as all relevant ancestors were. Spirits were often linked with areas of land, the forces of nature (such as rain), specific shrines, or certain objects (such as trees, rocks, or statues).

For most Zambians the focus of traditional religion was the alleviation of affliction. It thus differed from Western Christianity with its stronger emphasis on salvation and eternal life. Various forms of religious practice coexisted as alternative strategies for dealing with a problem. One might begin, for example, with herbal remedies—to Western observers a nonreligious response. Frequently diagnosis required the identification of a hidden agent provoking the affliction. A traditional doctor or "witch doctor" (really a witch finder) might divine to determine the cause and the appropriate therapy. The instruments of divination varied, most commonly including throwing bones, reading mirrors or animal entrails, or testing by ordeal. The prescription might be wearing a protective charm, avoiding certain foods or actions in order to purify and strengthen the sufferer, giving gifts to appease ancestors or spirits, being inducted into a curing cult, or simply neutralizing a relative's witchcraft by identifying him or her. (Witches were typically considered to be unaware of their harmful acts.) Witchcraft accusations increased in frequency at times of social stress when the community did not agree on common aims; those identified as witches were frequently marginal people, such as the elderly or the eccentric.

Individual curing cults spread over wide areas and might come and go without significant change in the underlying religious system. Once a person was cured by a cult, he or she became an adept and could in turn cure others through the same ritual initiation. Such rites frequently included spirit possession, in which the adept would speak or act in the name of some spirit. Certain individuals in an area, however, gained reputations for greater curative skill and became recognized specialists; they might have been inducted into numerous cults or they might have acquired greater pharmaceutical and psychological understanding useful for a practitioner.

Individual populations within Zambia, while sharing the same traditional religious heritage, yet gave differing emphases to various aspects of it. For example, religious activity was the key social institution for the resolution of conflict in many ethnic groups without significant chiefs. Among the Tonga of Southern Province, for example, prophets and rain priests were the only persons having significant influence beyond the homestead. Significantly, the British seized on these regional prophets as so-called Tonga chiefs and made the most important, Monze, into the eventual Tonga paramount Native Authority. Among the Luvale, Mbunda, and related groups of western Zambia, the key religious figures were not prophets or priests but professional diviners. In more centralized societies, chiefs coordinated social life in ways Westerners would more likely call political than religious; yet the sacred and magical powers of chieftainship were important bases for their role. In the most centralized states, religious belief and practice were even more tied to kingship: among the Lozi the king was considered the direct descendant of the high god, who was invoked frequently. Within the Lozi kingdom, nineteenth-century events show the close connection between religious and political systems and the differences between those of distinct peoples.

Lwena hut with charm to ward off malicious spirits
Courtesy J. Jeffrey Hoover

Lozi religion had come to center on the royal graves and on the kings as descendants of the high god. Mbunda immigrants from the northwest brought their professional diviners to the Zambezi valley, and they began to identify evildoers in place of chiefly judges. The Lozi kings found the independent authority of the diviners a grave danger to the state, and the nineteenth-century Lozi king Lewanika had to break their power to keep his throne.

Christianity

Christianity spread in Zambia slowly but progressively. The European missionaries brought literacy, crafts, and skills in high demand by the new colonial government and mines. In most cases, and especially outside the urban areas, whatever education existed until the 1960s was provided by the missions, and Christianity was associated with the new opportunities opened to the Africans by education. Furthermore Christianity furnished a way out of traditional social constraints for those who sought to escape them; since Christianity condemned certain customs and beliefs perceived by Westerners as immoral and superstitious, Christians could more easily dissociate themselves from group norms. Petty rural merchants, for example, frequently belong to the Watch Tower Bible and Tract Society (Jehovah's Witnesses or Kitawala), for church rules allow them to escape certain customs of redistributing wealth among kin and also motivate them to lead exemplary lives and trust one another. The majority of Tonga commercial farmers are of Seventh-Day Adventist background. Besides opening a door to education and an escape from existing social constraints, Christianity associated itself with progress in a third way. During the colonial period the positions of catechist and teacher were two of the most prestigious available to Africans in Northern Rhodesia. Even those members of the Westernized elite who might be termed post-Christian illustrate the missionary impact, for in their secular way they may stand closer to the actual belief systems of the Western missionaries than do many staunch Zambian Christians.

Developments in the Late 1970s

Indigenous religion in Zambia is not a fixed and unchanged tradition; sometimes it has evolved into forms quite different from those of a century ago. Those aspects associated with former centralized states have disappeared along with the autonomy of chieftaincies; outward forms remain as part of folklore or in the ceremonial trappings of such chiefs as the Lozi *litunga*. At the other end of the traditional political scale were the lengthy initiation camps for boys among the Ndembu, Luvale, and other northwestern peoples that have fallen victim to the school calendar; the *makishi* (costumed spirit dancers) have become well-known folklore performers. The most widely practiced aspects of traditional religious systems are those that deal with physical and psychological affliction (see Health, this ch.).

Within Zambian Christianity there has long been a tension between the foreign ties of the missionary and the desires of Zambian churchmen for equal opportunity and autonomy. The earliest missionaries often sought to train responsible African pastors to carry on their work should the few missionaries die or be forced to leave, and some Protestant pioneers at the beginning of the 1900s were convinced of the need to evangelize the world in one generation before Christ's second coming. In practice, then, catechists bore great responsibility despite their limited formal training. During the colonial period the growing sense of security and greater white numbers (among missionaries as well as in colonial society in general) led to rising standards within churches and a hesitancy among many missionaries to turn control over to less qualified African disciples. New denominations, such as the African Methodist Episcopal (AME) church (a main-line black body from the United States) and Jehovah's Witnesses were introduced by Africans. Independent bodies having no international ties were also widely established; some, such as the Apostolic church (or Apostolos), spread from South Africa as did the AME, while others formed around a local prophet or pastor in Northern Rhodesia.

Many of the sects created favorable impressions among Africans before independence through their tenets of noncooperation with the British state. (Colonial officials, meanwhile, fretted about their role in fomenting nationalist sedition and rebellion.) The Lumpa church of Alice Lenshina, a movement centered in Northern Province, was at first applauded by UNIP as an ally. After independence, however, a bitter struggle ensued between the Zambian government and the Lumpas, and most of the latter took refuge in Zaïre. The sect found a black Zambian government no more godly than the former colonial one; the nationalists, for their part, could not tolerate nonsupport.

The churches have had to adapt to a changed Zambian society resulting from independence. With the elimination of the color bar and the zambianization of managerial and technical positions in government and industry, the church no longer offers the only or the most prestigious careers open to educated youth. As a result the churches have struggled to recruit clergy and upgrade their educational standards. The experience of the AME church illustrates the dramatically changing roles of the churches during the period. As an international church, but one operating in practice without overseas support or control, the AME denomination included many of the nationalist political elite among its membership during the 1950s, and the body grew rapidly. Since independence, however, most elite members have become preoccupied with responsibilities outside the church, young people no longer join, and those who do become members are typically constituents with long ties to the church. The AME church's independence

Roman Catholic church built out of local materials by villagers

from white control ceased being significant to Zambians with the end of white domination. The lack of institutionalized AME educational and social outreach—because of the very poverty of the larger denomination that had allowed the African conferences so much autonomy—have made the church seem irrelevant to contemporary Zambian society.

The Zambian government has been able to assume control of all primary education, thus taking over the mission school systems, and mission-related denominations have moved into new forms of social witness. Given the rudimentary state of secondary education inside Zambia in 1964, the government challenged the churches to replace their primary-school programs with new secondary institutions. High schools have been far more capital intensive, especially since official policy has favored boarding schools so that children might study outside their home area. A major cooperative program, the Mindolo Ecumenical Centre outside Kitwe, sponsors varied training programs for government and industry; institutes for church literature, art, and music; and conferences for regional as well as Zambian audiences.

The mission-related denominations have also sought greater ecclesiastical self-reliance. Official segregation within church structures was eliminated before independence, although white membership remains concentrated in certain urban churches because of cultural differences. The United Church of Zambia is the result of successive mergers between churches founded by British Congregationalist, Scots Presbyterian, French Reformed, and British Methodist missions and black and white interdenominational movements on the copperbelt. The United Church of Zambia and the three Anglican dioceses of the nation discussed merger during the 1960s and 1970s, but no agreement had been reached by the late 1970s. Although the parish pastorate and the denominational agencies of the Protestant churches were staffed by Zambians, the mission-related churches continued to rely on subventions from overseas to support much of the cost of administration and specialized programs (such as secondary schools); by early 1979 missionary personnel were found primarily in technical support positions. In the larger Roman Catholic Church, still heavily dependent on expatriate priests and (to a much lesser extent) nuns, the bishops of the eight dioceses are Zambians, and married catechists have come to serve as de facto pastors in many local churches where Zambian priests are unavailable. There is growing sentiment among the leaders and members of the various mission-related churches for financial autonomy, even though this may mean a short-range cut in clergy salaries and in the educational and social efforts of the churches.

Size of Religious Constituencies

For both practical and theoretical reasons it is not possible to give comprehensive, standardized figures for the relative size of religious communities. Although mission-related churches make an effort to keep internal membership statistics, the accuracy and availability of such figures were lower in the 1970s than when hierarchies were under expatriate control. Criteria for formal membership vary widely—baptism in the Roman Catholic Church and confirmation in most Protestant groups—yet the constituency of each denomination is much larger than its rolls. Churches and congregations vary in their attitudes toward the compatibility of church membership with community activities having traditional religious overtones: beer drinking, funerals, initiations, dancing, and wife inheritance. Just as the definition of Christian blurs at the edges, so does that of the adherent of traditional religion. One cannot subtract Christian membership from the total Zambian population and identify the rest as traditionalist. Thus accurate statistics are not available for all groups, and they would not necessarily be comparable if they existed.

In the light of these caveats, it was estimated that approximately half of the Zambian population considered itself Christian by 1976. Between 55 and 66 percent of these belonged to the Roman Catholic constituency; the remainder included both orthodox mission-related Protestant churches and independent sects. Where statistics were available, most groups more than doubled in membership over the 1960s, thus growing faster than the Zambian population as a whole and enlarging the percentage of Zambians who were Christian. Roman Catholic figures for 1976 indicated 1,357,000 Catholics, and Jehovah's Witnesss claimed over 200,-000 attending services in 1977. On the basis of earlier data, the constituencies of the African Reformed (South African Dutch Reformed mission), Anglican, and United Church of Zambia bodies were probably each on the order of 100,000 in the late 1970s.

Other Voluntary Associations

In addition to religious denominations, a variety of other forms of voluntary associations play important roles in Zambian society. Some correspond with familiar organizations in Western nations, but their ways of operating may differ in the Zambian context.

Many groups form around economic interests. The African Mineworkers' Union developed during the colonial period as an independent body under African control to seek higher wages and opportunities more equal to those of white miners. Since independence the Zambian government has sought to use the union to diffuse official economic policy among workers—as an instrument for labor peace and greater productivity rather than as an adversary advocate of workers' interests. The government has been largely successful in co-opting national union leadership but much less so with individual union branches; as a result the union has become less coordinated and more decentralized (see Industrial Workers and Labor Unions, ch. 3).

Another sort of association includes the national umbrella organizations, such as the Zambia Congress of Trade Unions, the Zambian Farmers Union, or the Zambian Christian Council. These groups aid coordination and communication among their constituent members, lobby with the government for their interests, and cooperate with international agencies and associations in their fields.

The Zambian government has also promoted the creation of certain local economic interest groups. Particular emphasis has been placed on the organization of cooperatives and of the Radio Farm Forum groups, where local farmers meet to hear and discuss broadcasts on modernized methods. The successful implantation of such local associations has been variable, of course, and less effective than planners wished (see Agriculture, ch. 4).

Political associations flourished during the late colonial period, and UNIP and the African National Congress continued as political parties during the First Republic. Since 1974 UNIP has been the only authorized party, and all other political organizing has been unofficial and informal (see The Decade of Federation, 1953–63; Independence: The First Decade, 1964–74, ch. 1; see Political Dynamics, ch. 3).

Social, service, and charitable associations are widespread. Athletic clubs, particularly the ubiquitous football (i.e., soccer) teams, are found in small rural centers as well as in urban areas. Youth groups include branches of the international boy scout and girl guide movements, and the government has talked at times of establishing a national mass youth organization. Schools, especially the majority that are boarding schools, encourage a wide variety of voluntary groups: debate teams, athletic clubs, Bible study groups, and so forth. Service organizations (Rotary, Professional Women's Clubs, Zambia Helpers Society, the Young Men's Christian Association, and the Young Women's Christian Association), cultural clubs (music, theater, and cinema), and hobby groups (stamp collecting, chess, and private aviation) are predominantly urban and elite in membership. Most such groups are the outgrowths of colonial-era white organizations.

Education

The educational system at independence was rudimentary and its standards low, perhaps the least developed of all of Great Britain's former colonies. Missionaries had been largely responsible for the education of Africans in the colonial period with but little help from government funds (most of which went to schools for the children of European settlers). During the period of federation a university college was established at Salisbury in Southern Rhodesia, but Zambian graduates of that school and other institutions of higher education elsewhere numbered no more than 100 in 1965. In that year roughly 1,500 students had completed senior secondary school (Form V), and another 6,000 had a junior secondary (Form II) education, that is, nine to ten years of schooling.

Estimates of the proportion of the entire population that had completed primary school (eight years of schooling before independence, seven years since 1965) vary from 1 to 3 percent.

Since independence the government has devoted substantial operating and capital funds in an effort to construct a system that would meet the needs for skilled manpower and for a population with a general level of education adequate to the tasks of development. The government and party were also concerned to use the schools, as all countries do, to inculcate certain values, although this task became more salient with the reform of the educational system proposed in 1976.

In the mid-1970s and, on the basis of information available, in the late 1970s, Zambia's system of education comprised several levels of academic and vocational institutions beginning with primary schools and culminating, for a relatively small number, in the University of Zambia (see fig. 8). The formal structure notwithstanding, only 65 percent of pupils reaching grade four of primary school in some rural areas had the chance to go on to the last three years of primary school. The Second National Development Plan (ending in 1976) provided for an average national progression rate from grade four to grade five of 80 percent, but it was not clear that this had been achieved. Some observers expected that the Third National Development Plan (1979–83) would include provisions for universal education to the end of the seventh grade, but that plan had not yet been published in early 1979.

In 1976 the Ministry of Education presented for discussion a plan calling for radical revision of the structure and substance of the school system; among the elements in the plan was the expansion of universal compulsory education to include ten years of schooling, that is, the equivalent of primary (seven grades) and lower secondary grades (Forms I, II, and III) combined; the entire program would be a single continuous one, however. No date was then set for the realization of that goal, but the necessary funding and the reuqirement for a staff trained to teach the kind of curriculum contemplated are such that it is unlikely that the program could be fully instituted before the mid-1980s.

Because fees were not charged at any level of the education system, lack of personal or family wealth was not an obstacle to education. Residence—particularly in rural rather than in urban areas—was an obstacle, as the lack of opportunity for full primary schooling in some rural areas indicates. Specific postsecondary institutions ranging from the University of Zambia (established in 1966) to the majority of technical colleges and institutions were also more accessible to urban dwellers, but it is not clear that this was a significant obstacle to students of rural origin who had managed to pass their examinations at the end of upper secondary school (Form V). There were differences in secondary school enrollment ratios from province to province (Copperbelt and Southern provinces were easily the highest, Eastern the lowest), but this

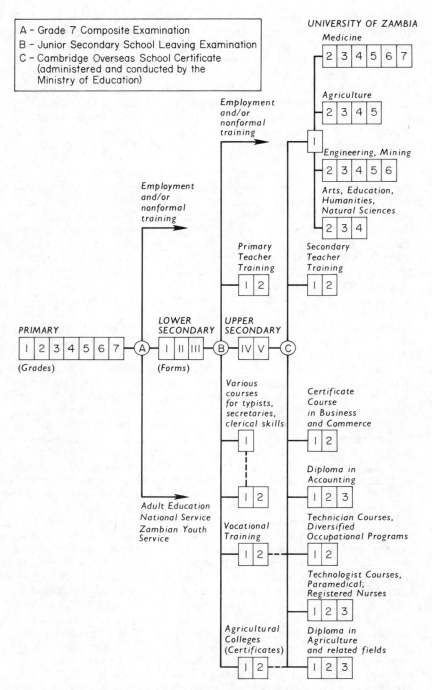

Figure 8. Structure of the School System, 1975

may not have been a consequence of differences in opportunity imposed by the availability of such schools. The status of Copperbelt Province may reflect an awareness of education more characteristic of urban than of rural populations, but the status of Southern Province cannot be accounted for in this way. Most secondary schools were boarding schools, a number of them constructed in thinly populated rural areas, and most students had to leave home to go to them. Distance alone does not seem to have made for differences in enrollment ratios. It is possible that variations in the values and aptitudes of local populations do, but that has not yet been established.

All levels in the educational system of the 1970s showed varying but on the whole substantial increases in enrollment (see table 4, Appendix). The decline in enrollment in adult education from 1975 to 1976 is not explained in available sources, but economic difficulties, including a rise in unemployment that was strongly felt in the mid-1970s, may account for it in part. Despite the general growth in enrollment Zambia was still some distance from providing the managerial, professional, and technically proficient manpower that it needed. Broadly speaking, there were too many unskilled persons (including most of those with complete or partial primary schooling and many who had completed junior secondary school) seeking too few jobs and a lack of persons for the jobs requiring more advanced education or training. This situation obtained in part because of the expansion of government and government services and of certain sectors of the economy. Much of that expansion was capital intensive, requiring fewer unskilled and semiskilled workers and greater numbers of persons having technical skills. Interestingly this demand for reasonably well-educated or skilled persons had a deleterious impact on the schools. Because jobs elsewhere often paid better than the school system, good students either did not become teachers at all or, if they did, left the school system after a time to take other jobs. This was particularly true of secondary-school teachers, whose post-secondary education made them highly eligible for good positions outside the school system. An average increase of roughly 20 percent in the salaries of civil servants (including teachers) approved in the mid-1970s may have an effect on the rate of attrition; however, that remained to be seen. Among other things, secondary-school teachers, like other educated Zambians, preferred urban positions to postings to remote rural schools, frequently not in or near their home territories.

The inability of those with less than a full secondary education to make use of the education they had was a consequence not only of the limited number of years of schooling they had undergone, but of curriculum content and the quality of instruction as well. Those who had not gone beyond grade four had rarely achieved a level of literacy in English or any of the major vernaculars that would stay with them (see Language, this ch.).

Important changes in the structure and content of education in the primary and junior secondary grades have occurred since independence. Textbooks oriented to the Zambian environment and experience have been introduced, and some attention has been given to teaching practical skills at these levels. Beginning in 1970 laboratories and workshops, most of them adequately equipped, were established in the junior secondary schools. There have been too few teachers who were able to impart these skills, however, again in part because the well-trained could find more remunerative work elsewhere. With the assistance of the Swedish International Development Agency, a technical teachers' college was established in the mid-1970s to provide adequate numbers of teachers, and it was to graduate its first class in 1977. Whether such teachers will remain in the system is another matter.

The curriculum of the senior secondary school has tended to remain heavily academic and oriented to the successful completion of examinations set by the Cambridge Examination Syndicate. Even its academic content has been only gradually adapted to Zambian conditions. A document issued by UNIP on national policies for the decade 1974 to 1984, which apparently inspired the Ministry of Education's plan for overhauling the educational system, called for the preparation of the Senior School Certificate internally and the abolition of the Cambridge School Certificate.

Those who complete the seven years of primary school but do not enter junior secondary school can obtain further education or training either in the adult education system (which has both primary and secondary components) or on the job wherever there is an opportunity for some kind of apprenticeship. Those holding a junior secondary school-leaving certificate but who have not done well enough to go to senior secondary school may enter a variety of vocational schools, the successful graduates of which have usually had little difficulty in finding work. Given the limitations in the quality of their preparation, however, many junior secondary leavers have not been ready to take full advantage of the vocational courses available. The lack of adequate practical training has already been noted, as has the inadequate English of those who might like to acquire clerical skills.

If a student manages to complete senior secondary school but is unable (or does not choose) to enter the University of Zambia, he or she may turn to a number of vocational or technical schools supplying courses ranging from those for industrial workers to those for managerial or administrative personnel (e.g., accounting or bookkeeping). Again, successful completion of such courses almost invariably led to reasonably good jobs. The output of industrial schools had been supplemented by training programs developed by various industries (e.g., mining). Such programs were not readily available to develop managerial or administrative workers, and the output of schools for such persons continued to fall far short of need in the mid- and late 1970s.

Roughly two-thirds of the Zambian population was rural in the mid-1970s, and even some Zambians in urban areas were engaged in cultivation. A good deal of attention has therefore been given to producing agricultural specialists and to training for working farmers. The need for education of both kinds is underscored by Zambia's continuing problems with food production. Moreover it is possible that a more prosperous agriculture would help to stem the flow of unskilled and often unemployable persons to the urban areas.

Aspects of agriculture were taught in the secondary schools, but qualified instructors were relatively few until the mid-1970s, at which time roughly twenty teachers—enough to meet the need—were being turned out annually by the National Resources Development College. But once having fulfilled their obligation to teach for two years, these teachers—like other secondary teachers—have tended to leave for more highly paid work, a pattern that may change when the higher salary scale is fully in effect.

There are two agriculture schools open to students who have completed junior secondary school, each offering a two-year course that prepares students for lower level jobs in extension work and other tasks. One, the Zambia College of Agriculture, also offers the first year in a course for veterinary assistants, the second year of which is taken at the Veterinary College at Mazabuka.

In addition to preparing teachers of agriculture, the National Resources Development College also offers programs to senior secondary-school graduates in agriculture, agricultural engineering, management of agricultural business, livestock science and production, water development, and home economics (nutrition). Persons thus trained become mid-level agricultural technicians, and they have been in short supply (in the mid-1970s many at this level were expatriates). The college had not trained enough graduates to meet the country's needs, owing largely to inadequate facilities. Proposals to establish the rural-oriented schools (those of forestry and technology, veterinary sciences, and agricultural sciences) of the University of Zambia and the development college to a rural campus at Solwezi may change that picture.

In addition to the formal training of agricultural technicians, there have a number of programs for the instruction of farmers, but these have had only limited success owing to the inadequacy of facilities and, often, of instructors. In addition, the sheer task of covering often large territories without motor vehicles has proved to be an obstacle to extension workers. The government, aided by the World Bank (see Glossary), undertook to improve and expand these facilities in the mid-1970s, but information on the success of that effort was not available.

By the mid-1970s the University of Zambia had roughly 2,500 to 2,600 students enrolled and had granted nearly 900 degrees, the first of them in 1968. The kinds of degree programs and the range of degrees had gradually broadened, and the university, whose first graduates had received the degree of bachelor of arts, granted fourteen different degrees in the 1970s, including masters' degrees in arts and in science. (Following the British pattern, the medical school granted bachelor's degrees in medicine or surgery after a seven-year program of study.)

The demand for students degreed in subjects directly relevant to Zambia's economy may be met more readily if the governments intention to establish two new campuses is carried out. The proposal to establish a campus at Solwezi has already been noted. Also proposed in the late 1970s was a campus at Ndola in the copperbelt for a school of industrial sciences and a school of environmental science.

Until the mid-1970s fewer than 15 percent of the university staff of more than 300 were Zambians. It was hoped, however, that the program of staff fellowships for study at home and abroad instituted at that time would gradually lead to an increasing number of Zambians on the faculty.

In addition to its intent to provide a full ten years of education to all Zambians, the revision of the educational system proposed by the Ministry of Education suggested a number of other changes. The chief goals of the revised system were to develop the potential of the Zambian people and to eliminate illiteracy. The implementation of ten years of universal education would, of course, go a long way to achieving the latter goal. Among the elements in the program directed to the potential of the people were greater stress on the connection between study and work and on Kaunda's philosophy of Humanism (see Humanism, ch. 3).

The emphasis on the link between work and study may be seen in the proposal for the last three years of the ten-year basic education program. Each of these years was to have four quarters, but students were to attend classes in only two of them and to engage in work contributing to the community and to development in the other two. The four-quarter system would, in addition, permit the enrollment of larger numbers of students using the same facilities and teachers while decreasing the size of classes.

Renewed and enhanced attention to Humanism in the curriculum and to work and study is directed at what President Kaunda sees as a tendency toward the development of great differences in status and outlook between the elite and subelite (middle class) on the one hand and the great mass of Zambians, urban and rural, on the other. The drift toward such differentiation has in fact been substantial, and the educational system has contributed to it (see The Dual Society: From Race to Class and Urbanization; Urban Africans, this ch.).

Whether the growth of the system of education in any form, radically revised or as an extension of the existing structure, will take place remained open to doubt in early 1979. Although the World Bank and other sources of aid might be willing to continue to contribute specific projects, the development of the system contemplated by Zambians required substantial investment and allocation of operating funds from the Zambian government itself. When the revision was first proposed, Zambia had already begun to feel the effects of the economic downturn that has persisted into the late 1970s and that may be checked but is not likely to be reversed in the early 1980s (see ch. 4). In these circumstances the capital investment and operating budget necessary to achieve the goals of the proposed revision will probably not be made. Which elements will receive support and which will not cannot be foretold.

Health

Zambia, like most sub-Saharan African countries, is marked by a range of tropical diseases; some are lethal, others are less so but certainly debilitating. Perhaps the most common of these debilitating diseases is malaria. Efforts to control the anopheles mosquito that transmits it have had only limited success, chiefly in line-of-rail urban areas. Another debilitating illness is bilharzia (schistosomiasis), transmitted by parasite-carrying waterborne snails. It occurs less frequently than malaria but is geographically quite widespread.

More lethal but geographically more limited in its incidence is sleeping sickness, caused by trypanosomes carried by the tsetse fly of which several varieties are found in Zambia. Most areas where tsetse fly was present in the 1970s and carried trypanosomes dangerous to man (some afflict only cattle) were sparsely settled (the burning of cover as prelude to cultivation deprives tsetse fly of breeding places). Many of the areas had been declared game reserves: examples are parts of the Luangwa Valley and a large area west of the great bend of the Kafue River.

Other verminborne diseases of lesser importance are typhoid and paratyphoid fever. Cholera made an appearance in 1978 in the northernmost districts of the eastern lobe of Zambia. Neither yellow fever nor smallpox was present in the 1970s.

The number of reported cases of bacillary and amoebic dysentery was not very great, but it is likely that these diseases were responsible for a good deal of infant illness and mortality, so common that only those Zambians strongly oriented to Western medicines and close to sources of help would report it. Another common childhood disease (apparently more often reported) is measles. Despite some inoculation efforts more than 14,000 cases of measles and over 1,100 deaths were noted in 1975.

Other tropical diseases were leprosy and hookworm. Neither appeared in the data submitted to the World Health Organization (WHO) for its statistical annual appearing in 1977, but other sources indicated that these diseases were still endemic in the early 1970s, and there was no reason to think that they had been eliminated by the late 1970s. Leprosariums were, however, giving way to outpatient treatment in clinics and rural health centers.

113

The treatment of individuals for hookworm has little long-range effect either for them or for the population to which they belong if patterns of living and sanitation are not dealt with.

Zambians also suffer from a range of so-called temperate diseases, such as tuberculosis, gastroenteritis, pneumonia, bronchitis, and influenza. Here again tuberculosis was not reported to WHO, and it is likely that mass vaccination of children in the mid- to late 1960s has had an effect. Pneumonia and influenza were reported, but it is not known what proportion of all cases came to the attention of the health authorities.

Malnutrition is itself a threat to health and underlies susceptibility to or exacerbates the effects of a number of diseases. Several varieties occur in Zambia: kwashiorkor (protein deficiency), avitaminosis, marasmus (caloric deficiency), and iron-deficiency anemia. These deficiencies are particularly dangerous to infants, young children, and pregnant women.

The chief medical goals of the government since independence have been to make health care more widely available, particularly in the rural areas, at little or no direct cost to the people, and to institute preventative health measures. There has been some progress toward these goals, but the lack of funds and personnel were significant obstacles to rapid realization of the program and were likely to remain so given the economic difficulties confronting Zambia in the mid- and late 1970s.

In 1975, according to data supplied to WHO, general hospitals were operated under government auspices, but more than half of the smaller hospitals were run either by the urban mining industry for its employees or by rural missions. Most medical centers, largely but not exclusively rural and intended chiefly for outpatient services, were government-operated, but a number were missionary-run. These facilities offered maternity and under-five clinics, among other programs. Also government-supported was the Flying Doctor Service, based in Ndola and serving otherwise inaccessible areas.

The large general hospitals (twelve in 1975), including the teaching hospital of the medical school of the University of Zambia in Lusaka, were to be found in the cities and towns along the line of rail, but most provinces had smaller hospitals (sixty-four in 1975) staffed by one or more physicians, registered nurses, medical assistants, and auxiliaries. Only some of these had or were regularly visited by specialists, however. Medical centers were typically staffed by nurses, medical assistants, and others but were in principal under the supervision of physicians at nearby hospitals.

By the mid-1970s well over 90 percent of paramedical personnel (laboratory and other technicians) and medical auxiliaries were Zambians, some of whom worked or trained in hospitals but constituted the regular staff of medical centers. Of the physicians, registered nurses, and midwives, however, less than 10 percent were Zambian, and the percentage was much smaller for dentists and pharmacists. The University of Zambia medical school graduated its first fourteen physicians in 1972 and continued to produce between fifteen and twenty annually thereafter, but it will be some time before Zambia can manage to do without expatriates. Even with them there was only one physician for every 10,000 Zambians in 1975. No specific ratio of doctors to population has been set as a goal, but it is clear that the Zambian ratio is fairly low and that it will take some time to improve it—let alone to replace non-Zambians, even if the number of physicians produced annually by the university medical school were to be doubled. The demand for dentists was not yet great in the 1970s, and the few Zambians among them were trained outside the country. Pharmacists also were educated elsewhere.

Despite the funds spent on medical facilities and training, there has been a good deal of criticism of the Zambian health maintenance and prevention systems. The issue came to a head in July 1978 at a meeting of the National Council of UNIP at Mulungushi when, according to an article in the *Zambia Daily Mail,* "President Kaunda expressed his concern over the deteriorating standards and critical problems affecting health services in the country." The article went on to say:

> Every indigenous citizen is well aware of the sad and dubious activities that have been taking place in the Government hospitals and clinics. . . .
> It is, therefore, right and proper to mention here that . . . our health services have been crippled by malpractices, corruption and incompetence on the part of the top management as well as ordinary workers.
> These evil activities have brought about unnecessary deaths in the medical centers as well as an alarming shortage of drugs on which the Government spends millions of Kwacha every year by importing them from abroad.

At the same meeting Kaunda announced that a new man had been appointed as minister of health to deal with the problems besetting the system. Less than six months later, after the general elections of December 1978, the Cabinet was reorganized, and still another individual was appointed to head the ministry. Given the prevalent pattern of shifting Cabinet personnel, no inference as to the personal efforts of the preceding minister can be made, however. It should perhaps be noted that criticism by citizens and public officials has been directed to government-run health facilities. There is no indication of similar criticism of facilities under other auspices.

The official government position and that of many in the largely urbanized educated elite look to Western (or, as some have called it, cosmopolitan) medicine to deal with health matters. As the work of the anthropologist Anita Spring (among others) has shown, the world view of most Zambians, rural and urban (including, in some degree, the elite) is such, however, that they rely in certain contexts on the local, more or less traditional, notions of the causes of and cures for illness (see Religion, this ch.). In some cases aspects of Western medicine are for practical purposes assimilated to the traditional view. Thus each community has a repertory of treatments for the range of illnesses it identifies. If a given illness does not respond to the therapy first tried, another is looked for. One kind of therapy, often the first resorted to, consists of herbal medicines; some are known and readily available to ordinary Zambians (i.e., laymen); others are prepared by herbalists. From the point of view of many Zambians the pharmaceuticals dispensed at hospitals and medical centers are simply additions to the herbal remedies in their own traditions.

Officials in the Ministry of Health have from time to time referred to the desirability of the systematic study of local herbal remedies to determine their effectiveness with a view to their integration into the repertory of modern medicine. A few studies that in fact have been made indicate that they can be effective in the treatment of some illnesses. Moreover Western pharmaceutical houses have also shown an interest in the possibilities of traditional herbal medicines.

If the herbal remedies fail, or if the illness is defined as untreatable solely by such remedies, the next step is to consult a diviner —usually done by the kin and neighbors (the therapy managing group, as some scholars have called it) of the sick person. A ritual of some kind is then prescribed. Such a ritual assumes that a spirit of some kind (or a witch) is ultimately responsible for the illness. Because diagnosis and treatment are embedded in indigenous religious systems, the participation of Christians in the relevant rituals is often prohibited or at least discouraged by churches. Where the church is adamant, Christians may in fact rely almost wholly on western medicine, particularly if the church offers reasonably effective medical services. In many cases, however, Christians do resort to ritual if Western medicine seems to fail them. Non-Christians usually have no difficulty in turning to modern medical facilities if they have clearly proved effective. Spring, referring to the Luvale, notes that the success of the maternity and infant care provided by the Plymouth Brethren attracted many non-Christian women.

One study of urban Zambians suggests that they have recourse to modern medicine when they think of their illness as having physiological roots but turn to a traditional doctor *(nganga)* when they consider their illness to have other causes. Spring suggests that so simple a distinction does not necessarily apply to the people she studied or to other Zambians who do turn to traditional specialists even in the case of an illness having a clearly physical basis.

*   *   *

Zambia has been fortunate in its sound and continuing tradition of social research. The Rhodes-Livingstone Institute (the present-day Institute for Social Research of the University of Zambia) was long an exceptional center within Africa for anthropologists and sociologists conducting and analyzing field research. Many of its staff and affiliates had been trained by the University of Manchester, and "Manchester school" hallmarks are evident in the literature: analysis of social networks, narrative description of events as "social drama," interest in conflict and in social change emerging during its resolution. The ethnographic literature includes works considered classics in African anthropology: Max Gluckman on the Lozi, Elizabeth Colson on the Tonga, Audrey I. Richards on the Bemba, Ian Cunnison on the Eastern (Luapula Province) Lunda, and Victor W. Turner on the Ndembu or Southern Lunda of North-Western Province. There has also been a heritage of sociological work within the evolving African urban communities, beginning with Godfrey Wilson and J. Clyde Mitchell and with Bruce Kapferer and Michael Burawoy among the many current researchers. Robert H. Bates has stimulated great debate on the relationship of the seemingly stagnant rural areas to the dynamism of the urban sectors, arguing that the actions of the country dwellers reflect rational economic responses by individuals well aware of national development processes.

No single adequate work is available as a guide to Zambian ethnicity. *Language in Zambia,* edited by Sirarpi Ohannessian and Mubanga E. Kashoki, brings together much recent work on Zambian languages and language use. William Vernon Brelsford's *The Tribes of Zambia* is still the only compendium giving background on the entire spectrum of Zambian peoples. It, however, is far out of date, based on assumptions of "tribe" current in the 1930s with the text unchanged in the recent second edition; one is much better advised to turn to the excellent ethnographic monographs available on most of the major ethnic groups of Zambia. A new census is scheduled for 1979, so updated demographic data and analyses will emerge during the next several years to replace those based on information now a decade old. (For further information see Bibliography.)

Chapter 3. Government and Politics

Bemba drum

BY THE END of 1978 ethnic, regional, religious, and social conflicts, exacerbated by Zambia's desperate economic situation and the consequences of the escalating struggle against the white-ruled neighboring countries, had raised the possibility that the government would face a large opposition vote in December. Contrary to some predictions, however, the results proved that after three terms in office President Kenneth Kaunda still enjoyed the support of better than half the electorate. In the copperbelt, one traditional locus of strong opposition, he actually did better than the national average.

Shortly before the elections President Kaunda undercut his opponents by doing at least part of what they had advised. He opened the border with Southern Rhodesia to some degree, bringing in needed goods and making possible the export of foreign exchange earning minerals. Further, he denationalized certain state-owned industries. The manner in which he dealt with the challenges facing him testified to his flexibility, his willingness to experiment, and his ability to temper principle with practicability, if need be.

In 1979 he remained the strongest force for unity. Buttressed by the legal provisions of the 1973 constitution, he controlled the two separate hierarchies of government and party. The United National Independence Party (UNIP) is meant to be the main political institution. It legitimates the government, and legally the Central Committee of UNIP is more important than the Cabinet. But the Constitution does not spell out exactly how the principle of party primacy is to be implemented; in fact the real decisionmaking power lies with the president and his advisers.

Kaunda opted for a one-party system to counter the centrifugal forces operating within the nation. He considers a multiparty system a heritage from the West inapplicable to African conditions. He sees the single party as the main tool for nationbuilding, for economic development, and for political integration; in his view all differences and conflicting internal interests should be resolved by discussion and accommodation. However, with the end of legal organized opposition in 1973 interparty competition became simply intraparty conflict. Moreover, insofar as the high expectations raised during the struggle for independence remained largely unfulfilled, the party lost its mobilizing force. Participatory democracy, envisioned by the president, remained illusory because decisions were made at the center and not at the grass roots.

The stresses and strains within society had remained largely latent as long as the national coffers were full. Difficult policy choices confronted the leadership only with the economic crisis of the mid-1970s, in which the fall of copper prices and the disruption of transportation routes played a considerable part (see ch. 4). What became startlingly evident at that time was the wide gap that had developed between the newly formed upper class and the rest of the population. A tiny minority—composed of leading officials in UNIP, government, and parastatal organizations, as well as a few businessmen—had moved into positions vacated by whites. Many of them developed a capitalist and consumer ethic at variance with the official ideology of Humanism, which expressed Kaunda's vision of an egalitarian man-centered society. Its imperatives run counter to the personal ambitions of the new upper class, and the philosophy was probably understood only dimly by the ordinary Zambians who might have been expected to support it. Consequently a debate developed, muted at first but becoming more and more vocal, over the place of private enterprise between the supporters of a mixed economy and the advocates of doctrinaire socialism. Kaunda, whose unostentatious lifestyle bespeaks his preferences, needs the bureaucrats, technocrats, and managers, and his attempts at constraining the new elite by means of a strict leadership code have failed.

Kaunda attributes many of Zambia's troubles to forces beyond his control—the fall of copper prices, the civil war in Angola that closed the transport links to the Atlantic, and the turmoil caused by the Zimbabwean and Namibian liberation struggles. Some of them, however, have been exacerbated by his commitment to the establishment of majority rule in southern Africa, which led him to become deeply involved in the explosive affairs of Zambia's white-ruled neighbors, such as the fighting that began in Mozambique in 1963 and in Namibia (South-West Africa) in 1964. Similarly, after Southern Rhodesia's Unilateral Declaration of Independence (UDI) in 1965 he closed the border at an enormous cost to Zambia's security and internal stability. The low turnout of voters in Southern Province in December 1978 may in part have reflected resentment over the presence of guerrilla fighters, the number of dead caused by land mines, and the general disruption caused by the liberation struggle.

In his foreign policy Kaunda has been torn all along by the conflict between his moral convictions and necessity—i.e., between his support of the struggle for majority rule and Zambia's close link to the southern African economic system. He has alternated between attempts at a peaceful settlement and support of military action that would bring about an end to white rule—"at horrendous human cost," in his words. His decision to open the border with Southern Rhodesia in 1978 was dictated by dire necessity. It deeply strained relations with Mozambique and Tanzania, his closest allies, who saw this action as tantamount to an accommodation with the Ian Smith regime. The military attacks on Zambian territory by Rhodesian and South African forces demonstrated the vulnerability of his position and led Kaunda, hitherto considered a friend of the West, to threaten rapprochement with the Soviet bloc.

Political Geography

Clockwise from the north, landlocked Zambia shares frontiers with Zaïre, Tanzania, Malawi, Mozambique, Southern Rhodesia, Namibia along the Caprivi Strip, and Angola (see fig. 1). It also presumably touches Botswana at the quadripoint between Southern Rhodesia and the Caprivi Strip. Several of these borders were arbitrarily drawn during the nineteenth century and reflected agreements between colonial powers; many showed little regard for ethnic boundaries. They have, however, remained stable. Others follow streams or watershed ridgelines. The latter are usually not rugged or high enough to provide clear physiographic demarcation.

In the northeast the border goes through the Luapula River, Lake Mweru, and Lake Tanganyika, although the actual location in the lake or river may be subject to discussion or technical adjustment. The 336-kilometer border with Tanzania extends from an informally accepted tripoint in Lake Tanganyika to the Malawi tripoint southeast of Tunduma; the line follows drainage divides and streams and is marked where appropriate with pillars.

The Zambia-Malawi border is primarily a watershed ridgeline. There has been considerable movement across this line, as Malawi citizens passed to and from jobs in Zambia's copperbelt or South Africa. Farther south the Mozambique border is partly a low ridgeline, intersecting the Luangwa River and following it to Luangwa. The Zambezi River and Lake Kariba, created by a new dam, form a clearly defined border with Southern Rhodesia for 792 kilometers. Parts of this river and associated gorges, above and below Victoria Falls, may have been a barrier to migration in the past, but crossing it in other areas is not difficult.

West of Victoria Falls and Livingstone the Zambezi forms part of the border with Namibia's Caprivi Strip. Farther west this border and much of the border with Angola are arbitrary lines that reflect administrative agreements. In other places this border follows minor ridgelines. From Angola to the copperbelt and the southeastern end of the Zaïre Pedicle, the border with Zaïre follows a series of ridgelines. The Pedicle itself is a holdover from the empire-building era before 1900 when the Belgians were able to arrange a territorial agreement with a local chief; its eastern end is simply an arbitrary longitudinal line.

Administratively the country has been divided into nine provinces since January 1976. At that time creation of a ninth province was announced, comprising the city of Lusaka and its surrounding area, a total of 360 square kilometers.

Provinces are subdivided into a number of urban and rural districts that differ substantially in area and population. These discrepancies are vestiges of the British colonial officials' creation of political subdivisions on a tribal area basis in accordance with Great Britain's philosophy of "indirect rule," in which tribes were the basic units of colonial administration (see The Colonial Interlude, ca. 1890–1964, ch. 1).

Political Developments, 1975–79

By 1975 Kaunda realized that a disastrous economic situation was rapidly undermining his political base and curtailing his freedom of action. Plummeting copper prices and skyrocketing oil prices coupled with disruption of transport routes had led to a balance-of-payment crisis and sharply reduced government revenues. Kaunda had hoped that the decolonization of Angola and Mozambique that followed the coup in Portugal in April 1974 would ease the tensions along his borders; he tried, with South Africa, Tanzania, and Botswana, to achieve a peaceful transfer to majority rule in Southern Rhodesia. However, these efforts came to an abrupt end when South Africa interfered in the civil war that was breaking out in Angola among the three liberation movements toward the end of 1975. The war dealt a further blow to the Zambian economy because it blocked the Benguela railroad, which had transported half of Zambia's copper exports since the closing of the Rhodesian border.

Repeated efforts to achieve majority rule in Southern Rhodesia through mediation had come to nothing, and Kaunda was forced to accept the prospect of full-scale armed conflict. The political turmoil in neighboring countries reverberated inside Zambia, where offices and followers of various liberation movements were repeatedly attacked. Thousands of refugees from Angola flooded the country.

In June 1975, at a meeting of the National Council, the party's highest deliberative body, Kaunda gave a major (seven-hour) policy address that came to be known as a watershed speech. He urged reliance on agricultural production rather than mining for economic security and announced a set of new measures designed to prevent undue accumulation of wealth. Freehold land titles would be transformed at once into 100-year leases; land belonging to urban owners would be nationalized within five years; subsidies to parastatal bodies would be rigorously reduced; and the *Times of Zambia,* owned by Lonhro, which had extensive business interests in both Zambia and Southern Rhodesia as well as elsewhere in Africa, would be taken over by UNIP.

Increased controls on Zambia's economy failed to make it function more efficiently, however. Food and import prices continued to soar, and crime and unemployment increased. There was widespread discontent and a growing demand for the resumption of trade with Southern Rhodesia and for less emphasis on socialism and egalitarianism. At the end of the year, in yet another speech to the National Council, Kaunda declared that the crisis against which he had repeatedly warned was finally upon the country and that all Zambians would be called on to make personal sacrifices.

In January 1976, fearful that internal unrest might be politically exploited by outside forces, Kaunda fully activated the state of emergency that had existed since the UDI in Southern Rhodesia. He also tried—unsuccessfully—to effect a reconciliation with Simon Kapwepwe and other members of the banned United Progressive Party (UPP) (see The Politics of Independence, ch. 1). A former opposition leader won a by-election in February and was given a Cabinet post.

Also in February Kaunda met with the presidents of Tanzania, Botswana, and Mozambique. The four officially endorsed the necessity for armed struggle to achieve majority rule in Southern Rhodesia. Addressing a February party meeting, Kaunda said that a bloodbath in Southern Rhodesia was inevitable and that Zambia had to be prepared for the resultant turmoil. In April Kaunda officially committed Zambia to support the armed struggle against Southern Rhodesia, and guerrillas were given permission to operate staging areas inside the country. On May 16 the president announced a "state of war" with Southern Rhodesia after receiving a warning from Great Britain that the Smith regime might order preemptive strikes against guerrilla bases in Zambia.

The economic and political difficulties brought latent social divisions into sharp relief. There was discontent among the top-ranking leaders in government, party, and business; student protests (the University of Zambia was actually closed from February 9 until April 8); shortages and unemployment in the cities; and widespread misery in rural areas. There were public discussions of various issues, such as the place of private enterprise, workers' participation, and the relative roles of the Central Committee and the Cabinet. It became apparent that the introduction of a single-party regime had not put an end to organized opposition and that members of outlawed parties were not ready to work within UNIP.

Kaunda tried to deal with the internal unrest by pressing for reforms that would realize his vision of a "communocracy," which he defined as a people's economy under humanism. He tackled corruption, and he encouraged workers' participation in industry. After a number of scandals during the year the National Assembly introduced, in December, an amendment to the Penal Code designed to fight corruption among government and party officials that Kaunda called the most serious internal problem facing Zambia.

In October 1976 three Zimbabwean guerrillas—who had been brought to trial for the car bomb killing in March 1975 of Herbert Chitepo, a former leader of the Zimbabwe African National Union (ZANU)—were released on the prompting of Robert Mugabe, who demanded that the case be withdrawn before he would attend the Geneva Conference on Southern Rhodesia. The government reluctantly agreed to interfere in the process of justice.

In the spring of 1977—in response to continuing reports of corruption and in preparation for the 1978 elections—Kaunda reshuffled his Cabinet including the senior personnel of the Zambia National Defense Force, the leaders of five provinces, and a number of ambassadors and high commissioners. Two cabinet ministers and one minister of state were dismissed, one for abuse of power, the other two for "anti-party activities."

During 1977 the hazards of being host to thousands of guerrillas became starkly evident when Zambia was repeatedly drawn into the critical affairs of neighboring countries. In January Jason Moyo, a leader of the Zimbabwe African People's Union (ZAPU), was killed by a parcel post bomb, and in July a rocket attack on ZAPU headquarters occurred. Zambia blamed both incidents on the Rhodesian government.

In August Rhodesian jet bombers attacked the town of Feira (present-day Luangwa) about 225 kilometers east of Lusaka after an exchange of fire between Zambian and Rhodesian forces. That attack led the government to order a curfew and blackout in Lusaka and three other cities. These were lifted on September 20 with a warning that they might be reimposed on short notice and that maximum vigilance was needed by all citizens during what amounted to conditions of war.

Responding to a call for unity, former opposition leader Kapwepwe, whose breakaway UPP had been banned five years earlier, agreed to rejoin UNIP with four of his aides, and he appealed to other former UPP members to do the same. On September 25 Prime Minister Smith held talks with President Kaunda in Lusaka—unsuccessfully as it turned out—during which they discussed the Anglo-American proposals in yet another attempt at solving the Rhodesian impasse. Presumably Smith also met with Joshua Nkomo, leader of ZAPU, although this was denied by Kaunda.

In October Kaunda called for a "drastic reduction of personnel in over-employed government ministries and other public services." He asked that civil servants be put to work on the land as part of a crash program for increased agricultural production.

The forthcoming elections and increasing warfare with Southern Rhodesia dominated 1978. In February more than fifty ZAPU guerrillas were killed in a helicopter raid—the largest up to that point—in camps in the Gwembe Valley near Lake Kariba. The invaders were reported to have briefly occupied some twenty villages.

On March 3 Prime Minister Smith signed an internal agreement with three moderate black nationalist leaders. According to Smith, the agreement was to bring majority rule at the end of the year. Dismissing the agreement as "irrelevant" unless Smith stepped down, Kaunda promised continued Zambian support for the Patriotic Front (consisting of ZANU and ZAPU). Another Rhodesian raid by jet and helicopter on Luangwa in Southeast

Zambia in March was condemned by the United Nations Security Council.

Preparations for the general elections got under way during April and May 1978 when UNIP Secretary General Grey Zulu urged everyone sixteen years and older to get registration cards. At a meeting in Mulungushi Hall, President Kaunda warned ex-UPP members against holding illegal secret meetings and plotting against UNIP. Both activities were reportedly taking place, particularly in the copperbelt.

Although Zambia continued to give unequivocal support to ZAPU, there was a growing concern over the sheer size of guerrilla forces building up inside Zambia. Moreover the number of refugees—13,000 from Angola alone according to the *Times of Zambia* of April 17—was becoming more and more of a burden on Zambia's already strained economy.

In May Zaïrian exiles, in their attack on the Zaïrian mining town of Kolwezi, crossed a strip of Zambian territory on their way from Angola, presumably without either Zambian knowledge or encouragement. Shortly thereafter President Kaunda met with Zaïrian President Mobutu Sese Seko, apologized and assured him of the friendship between the two countries. Subsequently more than seventy of the invaders were rounded up by Zambian armed forces and paramilitary police, disarmed, and driven back over the frontier.

In July Kapwepwe challenged Kaunda's socialist policies and his commitment to the war with Southern Rhodesia. He announced on August 1 that he would dispute President Kaunda's candidacy as head of UNIP during the party's General Conference, which was slated to begin on September 9. Two others also were contesting Kaunda's candidacy, although the UNIP National Council meeting (in an unprecedented proceeding) had already nominated Kaunda as the only candidate for party president. One was Harry Nkumbula, former leader of the African National Congress, an independence movement founded in 1951, and a member of the Zambian National Assembly for Bengwa, who had his base of support in Southern Province; another was Robert Chiluwe, a Lusaka businessman. A massive television, radio, and newspaper campaign got under way supporting Kaunda's candidacy while his critics were reduced to surreptitiously passing circulars. Local newspapers, which had repeatedly affirmed the right of all Zambians to criticize and oppose the president, at once condemned those whom they considered "plotting against the government."

All chances of challenging Kaunda legally at the polls were dashed when the party's General Conference, meeting in conjunction with the National Council, approved by a show of hands a change in the party constitution that prohibited the nomination of anyone who had not been a member of UNIP for at least five years. This automatically removed Kapwepwe, who had rejoined the party only one year earlier. Subsequently sporadic violence, including numerous bomb scares, flared up here and there, and seven former top officials of the banned UPP were arrested. Both Kapwepwe and Nkumbula announced that they would take their case to the High Court, inasmuch as members of the National Council had not been given the required one month's notice of the constitutional amendment, and no proper voting had taken place as required by the constitution. The court dismissed the case on November 16.

In a complete reversal of his former stand, Kaunda announced in mid-October 1978 what he labeled "the politics of survival," namely the partial opening of the border with Southern Rhodesia to allow the transit of Zambian imports and exports. Tons of fertilizer desperately needed for the maize planting season in November had been stranded at the Mozambican ports of Beira and Maputo for several months. Kaunda also said that there would be no direct trade route with Southern Rhodesia and that the border would remain closed to all other traffic. Thus Zambia's southern route to the Indian Ocean through Southern Rhodesia and South Africa was opened after nearly six years. The move isolated the Zambian leader since both President Samora Machel of Mozambique and President Julius K. Nyerere of Tanzania declared after an all-night emergency meeting that they would have nothing to do with Kaunda's "sanction-busting."

Inside the country the policy seemed to have gained Kaunda additional votes in the elections that took place on December 12. He was reelected for a fourth term by 1,024,954 votes as against 248,539 negative votes. There was, however, a marked disparity in provincial support. The highest percentage of affirmative votes, 96 percent, was recorded in North-Western Province, and the next highest was 93.8 percent in Eastern Province; this compared with only 51.2 percent in Southern Province.

Lusaka Province had the highest turnout of voters (72.7 percent), a tribute to the highly effective election campaign that focused on the "yes" to such a degree that some people may have been unaware of their right to say "no." This high percentage contrasted with only 44.6 percent turnout in Western Province. In Southern Province 59.8 percent of all potential voters went to the polls, but almost half of them voted "no."

The Structure of Government

In May 1971 Kaunda announced the establishment of two separate but parallel structures of government and party, condemning an earlier system integrating the two. UNIP's Central Committee would be the policymaking body; implementation of these policies would be the domain of the Cabinet. Only the president, the prime minister, and the secretary general of UNIP would be permitted to belong both to the Cabinet and to the party's Central Committee.

The Constitution

The Constitution in force in early 1979 was proposed in December 1972 and promulgated in August 1973, establishing the Second Republic. It transformed the Zambian political system by giving UNIP the sole right to roganize and to act as a political party. From then on—at least theoretically—the party's Central Committee had more powers than the Cabinet. Indeed, the prime purpose of the structural changes was to ensure the supremacy of the sole party vis-à-vis the government while observing an efficient division of labor in carrying out functions. The secretary general of UNIP became the second personage of the state after the president, taking precedence over the prime minister.

A two-tiered executive-cum-parliament replaced the previous presidential-parliamentary system. The office of vice president was abolished, and the position of prime minister was added: this official was to serve as head of government administration and chief spokesman on government matters. The prime minister was to be appointed by the president, subject to parliament's approval, and was to serve at the pleasure of the president and/or parliament. No cabinet minister could belong to UNIP's Central Committee, except for the prime minister, who was to be an ex officio member. A thorough intermingling of governmental and party roles, however, was to obtain at the very top of the political system. The president of the party, on being elected by the General Conference of UNIP, became ipso facto the sole candidate for election as president of the republic.

The preamble to the Constitution established a "One Party Participatory Democracy under the Philosophy of Humanism" without, however, spelling out how this was to be implemented. The Constitution also guaranteed fundamental freedoms and rights subject, however, to the limitations of Article 4, which decrees that there "shall be one and only one political party or organization in Zambia, namely the United National Independence Party. Nothing contained in this Constitution shall be so construed as to entitle any person lawfully to form or attempt to form any political party or organization other than the Party, or to belong to, assemble or associate with, or express opinion or do any other thing in sympathy with, such political party or organ." The Constitution acknowledged the right to form and belong to nonpolitical associations. This right, however, was qualified by the rather broad provision that such associations must not be prejudicial to the national interest. The Constitution also guaranteed that a person accused of any crime must be heard by an impartial court within a reasonable time; had the right to be informed as quickly as practicable of the specific charges against him; be given the time and facilities to conduct his defense; and be presumed innocent until proven guilty. The Constitution also guaranteed protection from double jeopardy, from the effect of ex post facto legislation, and from self-incrimination.

It was hoped that the Code of Leadership set out in the Constitution would be a major contribution to unity. The code applies to virtually all citizens holding an official position; it covers not only government and party officers of senior status but also civil servants, members of the police and defense forces, academic and administrative staff of educational institutions, and labor officials. The code holds those so designated responsible for exemplary behavior in performing their duties and in rejecting temptation to turn public service into an avenue of enrichment.

The aim of the code is to forestall the development, or redress such tendencies already in evidence, of a society consisting of a few rich and a mass of poor. Specifically an official who wished to continue to run a business would have to forfeit his state or party salary. If he chose not to forfeit such salary, he would be obliged to give up his business. Even where the two activities were ruled compatible—and that could be decided by the president—the business could employ no more than ten people or, alternatively, would have to be run on a cooperative basis. Similarly an official who was living in a house owned by any public body, including UNIP, or by anyone receiving public funds would be barred from leasing to others any house that he owned.

There were further injunctions against obtaining material benefit other than salary from public service, including reneging on personal debt responsibilities. In addition the Code of Leadership prohibited legally unsanctioned behavior and seditious acts. Finally the sanctions were stipulated: an official who committed a breach of the code would be expelled from office and be liable to expulsion or suspension from the party.

The President

With the establishment of the Second Republic the powers of the president were vastly increased. He acts, according to the Constitution, on "his own deliberate judgement and shall not be obligated to follow advice rendered by any other person or authority." He completely dominates the government and the party, and no limitations are placed on his number of terms in office. He is head of state, head of UNIP, and commander in chief of the armed forces. He appoints UNIP's secretary general and the prime minister. He can initiate laws and has the right to dissolve the National Assembly. To help him with his many duties, he has a large staff of experts at the State House.

The president is elected by popular vote every five years, after being chosen as president of UNIP at its General Conference. Voters have a choice of voting "yes" or "no" for the party nominee. A constitutional amendment adopted at the General Conference in October 1978 provided that a candidate had to be supported by twenty delegates from each of the country's nine provinces to ensure ethnic balance. A further change required that a presidential candidate had to be a paid-up party member

View of Lusaka, Zambia's capital
Courtesy WORLD BANK PHOTO (Edwin G. Huffman)

View of the Lusaka High Court building
Courtesy WORLD BANK PHOTO (Edwin G. Huffman)

for five years. The official reason given was that proof was needed of consistent faithfulness to the party. However, adoption of this change at that time seemed clearly directed at Kapwepwe and Nkumbula, who were challenging Kaunda (see Political Developments, 1975–79, this ch.).

Should the sole candidate receive less than a majority of the votes cast, the General Conference of the party has to meet again to choose another person as president of the party. In accordance with these provisions, Kaunda was elected candidate for reelection as president of the republic in the popular election on December 12, 1978.

Parliament

Legislative functions of the government are vested in a parliament, defined as the president and the National Assembly. The National Assembly consists of 125 members—one from each constituency—elected for five-year periods under party auspices and ten members who are nominated by the president. After the elections in December 1978 the nominated members included five members of the Central Committee whose primary function was to explain party policies to the National Assembly.

Bills introduced either by members of the National Assembly or by the president require presidential assent to become law. The president can dissolve the parliament, necessitating a new election, but he himself is not subject to a vote of no-confidence.

The constitution of the Second Republic continued the previous practice of contested elections to the National Assembly on a constituency basis. All candidates had to be members of UNIP as must all voters. This meant that any Zambian citizen who met the specified age and other common procedural requirements could offer his or her candidacy. Civil servants must take leave from their posts to seek election to the National Assembly; if they are defeated, they may return to their posts without loss of civil service benefits.

UNIP's control of elections is maintained insofar as all leading party officials from branch to constituency level constitute the electorate in primaries for National Assembly nominees. The number of votes received by each nominee is then forwarded to the Central Committee. Unless this body rejects a particular nominee, the three with the highest numbers of votes then become candidates for election to the National Assembly. In the late 1970s the National Assembly contained a fair number of educated men with professional and administrative experience. Over 40 percent were businessmen or small traders. As under the First Republic workers and small farmers were underrepresented.

The National Assembly has not been an effective body, especially during the Second Republic. It had been progressively stripped of its real power by early 1979; yet it continued to have what William Tordoff, an expert on African politics, calls "residual powers." It still held the executive accountable for policies and performance, and it continued to constitute an arena for vigorous debate and a forum for contact among elected politicians and between the people and their government.

Kaunda seems to be of two minds about the role of the National Assembly. On the one hand he has said that "party and government will not stomach any indiscipline among members of parliament masquerading under parliamentary privilege" and has warned members to desist from "anti-party and anti-government mouthings." On the other hand he seems anxious to preserve the assembly's voice in his participatory democracy and has urged members to promote the interests of their constituents and to strengthen their links with them.

House of Chiefs

A second national representative body is the House of Chiefs, intended to provide a voice at the national level for the country's traditional leaders, most of whom continue to exert influence in local affairs. Members of the house do not make law, nor do they decide policies. They are a purely advisory group without legislative powers but with the right to be heard by the government and the National Assembly on all matters affecting traditional leaders and their people. They meet only a few days each year, when and where the president asks them.

The House of Chiefs consists of twenty-seven members, four each from Northern, Western, Southern, and Eastern provinces; three each from North-Western, Luapula, and Central provinces; and two from Copperbelt Province. Except for Western Province, where members are nominated, all are elected for three-year periods by chiefs in the provinces.

The Cabinet

Cabinet ministers, appointed by the president after consultation with the prime minister, are solely responsible to him and can be dismissed by him at will. Although not responsible to it, all Cabinet members must be chosen from among members (either elected or appointed) of the National Assembly; the purpose of this requirement is to establish a close relationship between the executive and legislative branches.

In December 1978 ministries were reorganized in an effort to streamline the government. Some were abolished, others were merged, and new ones were created. The number of ministries was reduced from twenty-seven to seventeen. In a major move nine ministries, each dealing with a province, were abolished. Also abolished were the Ministry of Local Government and Housing and the Ministry of Development and Planning. Three offices—decentralization (i.e., local government), development planning, and civil service—were established under the prime minister. Each was headed by a secretary of state.

In addition the Ministry of Defense, headed by Kaunda, had been dissolved in September and the post of Secretary of State for Defense and Security created. Its incumbent was a member of parliament and of the party's Central Committee but not of the cabinet. Kaunda termed it the fourth most important office in the country—after the president, the secretary general, and the prime minister. Three new ministries were created. They were the Ministry of Youth and Sports, the Ministry of Tourism, and the Ministry of National Guidance.

The Civil Service

In the December 1978 reorganization a civil service office was created by unifying four separate commissions (civil service, teaching service, police and prisons service, and local government service). It was headed by a secretary of state and located in the prime minister's office.

Civil servants, who must pass strict examinations, are recruited by a Civil Service commission whose members are appointed by the president. The chief civil servant in each ministry is the permanent secretary.

Known for its high turnover rate, the Zambian civil service has been chronically short of personnel. Government officials cannot hold party executive positions while in the civil service, and they are banned from holding outside jobs under the Leadership Code, but cases of corruption and abuse of state power have led to the establishment of the office of investigator general, a sort of ombudsman.

Regional Administration

Until the reorganization of the government in December 1978 provinces were headed by provincial ministers who had both political and administrative functions. This structure had been set up in 1969, at which time it was described as "decentralization in centralism" and was intended to spur rural development. It had been hoped that having officers of greater status and awareness of national activities would facilitate local decisionmaking. It turned out, however, that the advantage of access to central government deliberations afforded the provincial executive was offset by the need to spend much time in Lusaka. What "decentralization" did was to politicize the regional governments, for one of the ministers' special tasks had been to exercise strict control over local party affairs. In December 1978 the political functions were assigned to members of the party's Central Committee. The purely administrative functions continued, as before, to be the responsibility of a permanent secretary who is the senior civil servant in each province.

At the district level the former system remained in force. Districts continued to be headed by governors who coordinated the operations of the central government's technical departments and of the local government units in their districts to ensure implementation of policies. Like the former provincial ministers, they are also the political heads of the district and are appointed and may be dismissed by the president. They supervised rather than controlled. In this capacity they chaired the district development committees and supervised village productivity and ward development committees. They were automatically members of UNIP's National Council, and a number of them were also members of the National Assembly. When things went wrong, the official press frequently blamed them for being government workers first and party workers second.

Local Government

Local government consisted of a single tier of urban and rural councils having both executive and legislative functions. There were city councils in Lusaka, Kitwe, and Ndola; municipal councils in five smaller cities; and township councils in fourteen very small towns. All the councils met monthly and had elected councillors, although the government had the power to appoint additional councillors. Government in this context meant an office called decentralization, which was in the office of the prime minister. Headed by a minister of state, it was set up in December 1978 to replace the Ministry of Local Government and Housing, which was abolished.

Each administrative district outside urban areas had a rural council. The councils evolved from the traditional Native Authorities set up by the British colonial government and had a majority of elected members and a minority of nominated members, mainly chiefs, appointed by the government (see Colonial Office Protectorate, 1924–53, ch. 1; see Residual Precolonial Administrative/Political Structures, ch. 2).

Councils maintained law and order, provided welfare and recreational services, maintained roads, and assisted the national health authorities. In cities they provided sanitation and sewage facilities, established building codes, and performed other tasks.

In the late 1970s the large urban councils had their own revenues because they collected certain taxes, such as personal and real estate levies, and had their own employees who were not part of the civil service. The central government, which closely controlled all councils, also subsidized the small ones, providing up to 90 percent of their revenues.

One councillor was chosen from each of the wards into which the area under a council was divided. Councillors were chosen on the same day all over Zambia for three-year periods in elections organized by an electoral commission under UNIP auspices. Candidates must live within the council area but not necessarily within the ward area. The central government appointed (and could dismiss) the mayors and deputy mayors of municipal councils and the chairmen and vice chairmen of other councils. Apparently fairly often the government chose traditional chiefs for the rural posts.

Every councillor was required to form a ward development committee, which met every three months. The ward develop-' ment and the productivity committees in villages and in sections of rural areas were supposed to be the link between the government and the people at the lowest level. They were to promote economic development by implementing government directives as well as by formulating policies. They were to promote grass roots participation and yet ensure party control over local decisions. Their political function was to ensure what Kaunda calls participatory democracy. Yet the usual picture has been one of apathy, lack of coordination, and lack of communication.

The Judicial System

The court system comprised the Supreme Court, the High Court, subordinate magistrates' courts, and local courts, all of which—with the exception of the Supreme Court—have both criminal and civil jurisdiction. The basis of jurisprudence in all courts aside from the local courts consisted of English common law, those statutes still in force that originated in the colonial and federation periods, and the acts of the Zambian legislature. The local courts dealt mainly with customary law, though they had certain statutory powers in addition.

The highest court was the Supreme Court, which heard only appeals from the High Court. It had a chief justice, a deputy justice, and two Supreme Court judges, all appointed by the president. When sitting as a court of appeal it was required to be composed of an uneven number of judges—no fewer than three.

The High Court served as an appellate court for the review of the actions of subordinate courts and as a court of first instance in serious offenses, including all cases in which the death penalty might be imposed. The magistrates' courts were divided into four classes, reflecting the differences in the training of the court officers, the geographic extent of their jurisdiction, and the severity of the sentences they might impose. The local courts, of which there were several in each district, had very limited jurisdiction.

Judges and magistrates, except Supreme Court judges, were appointed by an independent judicial service commission and were removable only by that commission for proven misbehavior or inability to perform duties. The commission consisted of the chief justice as chairman, one judge of the High Court, the chairman of the Public Service Commission, and one presidential appointee who must be either a judge or a former judge. Although the courts continued to be formally independent, they had no real power to protect the Constitution from legislative or executive interference. Over the years they have become responsive to the values of the political system of which they were a part.

The gradual zambianization of the courts began in 1969. By

early 1979 most judges and magistrates were African. Judges had to be either trained lawyers or magistrates who have had five years' experience in addition to some training in law. The presidents and justices of the local courts had to be conversant with local customary law.

The attorney general, nominated by the president, was the judicial adviser to the government and supervised the director of public prosecution (see Zambia Police Force, ch. 5). He was not a member of the Cabinet. The office, however, was usually occupied by the minister of legal affairs, who was, of course, a member.

The government had the right to detain persons without trial in time of a state emergency, but the detained person was to be given the reason for the detention, and public notice of the detention and the reasons for it were required. After a year a detainee had the right of review of his condition by an independent tribunal presided over by a judge of the High Court. If the independent tribunal approved, detention without trial apparently could be perpetuated indefinitely. Zambia has been under a state of emergency since independence, and detention of political opponents is not unknown.

The Party

The constitution of UNIP was published as an annex to the 1973 Constitution of the Republic of Zambia when the new one-party system became fully operative. Whereas the previous party constitutions of 1967 and 1971 had given Zambia's president successively more formal power within the party, this power became total in 1973. Up to that time Kaunda had been the party's secretary general, and his tenure as president of the republic had been constitutionally separate from his party position. In 1973 he became president of the party as well. As such he appointed—subject to approval by the National Council—a secretary general from among members of the UNIP Central Committee. The secretary general, according to the party constitution, was to "carry out all party duties as directed by the President of the Party." The three national bodies of UNIP are the Central Committee, the smallest and operationally the most significant; the larger National Council, which has advisory functions; and the General Conference, a gathering of about 6,000 delegates who meet every five years (and occasionally for extraordinary sessions).

The Central Committee

Party activities were coordinated by the Central Committee, which was the highest executive body of the party and was meant to be its driving force. According to the Constitution the committee devises policies, and the Cabinet executes them; the two bodies meet in joint sessions when the need arises. In reality, however, there has been comparatively little to do for the Central Committee, and there have even been suggestions to abolish it, which have led to angry controversies within UNIP ranks. Official documents always emphasize the priority of UNIP, referring routinely to "the party and its government," and some measures taken in the government reorganization of December 1978 seemed designed to ensure the party's preeminence.

The twenty-five members of the Central Committee include— aside from the president—the prime minister as ex officio member, three members nominated by the president, and twenty others elected by the party's General Conference. Aspirants must be backed by ten delegates to the conference, and they must prove that they have national support.

Members of the Central Committee chaired a number of subcommittees. Six of these dealt with different government activities, each of which was the domain of one or several ministries (see fig. 9). The staffs of these subcommittees were chosen from members of the National Council, the Cabinet, the civil service, and in some cases from nongovernment personnel; ordinary party members acted as advisers. The political affairs of each of the provinces were dealt with by a subcommittee that had responsibilities including strict control of local party affairs.

The National Council

Policies initiated by the Central Committee are brought before the National Council, the party's supreme deliberative body, for approval, rejection, or modification. Once agreed on, proposals are sent to parliament to become law, if legislation is required. Once a law is adopted, all party members, including those initially opposed, must abide by it.

The National Council has the power to amend the party constitution and may suspend, discharge, dismiss, or expel party members who have violated provisions of the constitution or rules made under it. Its members, meeting at least twice a year, include all the members of the Central Committee and of parliament, district governors and regional party officials, ten representatives of the security forces, six representatives from each affiliated organization, heads of diplomatic missions abroad, the administrative secretary, some executive officers at the headquarters of the party, and members of the executive committees of the women's and youth leagues.

The General Conference

General party policies are defined and modified by the General Conference, which has the power to "consider, review, or change any policy of the Party." Included are up to 600 delegates from each province, all members of the National Council, and representatives of the party's affiliated organizations and the Zambia Congress of Trade Unions (ZCTU). The conference elects the president of the party, who thus automatically becomes the sole candi-

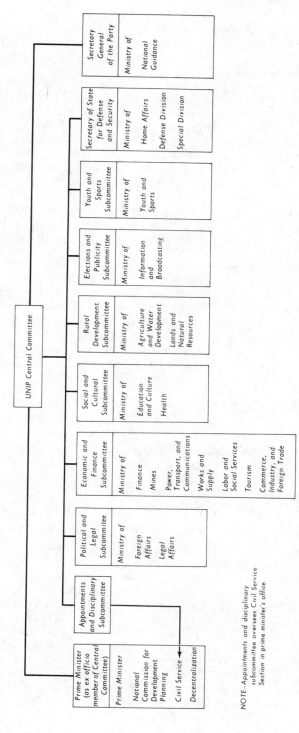

Figure 9. Relationship of UNIP to Ministries and Other Major Government Offices

date for presidental elections. It also elects most members of the Central Committee.

Local Organization

In early 1979 the party was organized into fifty-three regions (more or less congruent with administrative districts), several hundred constituencies, an unknown number of branches in villages and town sections (comprising roughly twenty houses), besides committees (in places of work). The Central Committee appoints the party's regional officials—namely the regional secretary, the regional women's secretary, and the regional youth and publicity secretary—despite a move within the party to have such officials locally elected.

There have been frequent complaints in the press over party members' apathy and the lack of party organization at the lower levels. Posts remained unfilled, and meetings often were poorly attended or not called.

Some officials worked their way up through the party hierarchy by starting out in the UNIP Youth League, whose members were between the ages of fourteen and thirty. In June 1978 the Youth League published the Five-Year Program of Action in which it advocated forming several groups within the league, such as the Young Pioneers (for those below the age of fourteen) and other groups for students in higher institutions of learning, working youth, peasant youth, and unemployed youth. The latter two were to be organized in socialist-oriented cooperatives.

Political Dynamics

In early 1979 Zambia stood out among the countries of Africa as one of the small minority still maintaining elements of a democratic society. Although legal opposition had been banned by the establishment of a one-party system in 1973, the courts maintained a measure of independence, members of the National Assembly spoke out against the government and party, and the press continued to report opinions of the opposition, if in a highly critical tone.

Dissent, comparatively peaceful, had its roots in a number of underlying problems and conflicts. Some protest had ethnic overtones, some religious, and some generational. More important, however, was the gap that had developed between a small elite, who had moved into the positions vacated by whites or those created by the establishment of an independent state, and the majority, whose position had not improved and had actually deteriorated. This gap became more acute with the economic decline brought about in major part by a number of external causes—including involvement in the liberation struggle of neighboring countries. The gap also reflected the tendency of the essentially urban educated elite to stress investment in industry rather than in agriculture and the rural areas, despite an official ideological emphasis on rural development (see Agriculture, ch. 4).

The Impact of the Party

With elected positions dominated by a single party, the most important political relations, conflicts, and alliances take place within UNIP, which originally became strong because it led the way to independence, bringing an end to federation, white racism, and colonial rule (see The Decade of Federation, 1953–63, ch. 1). In the drive for independence it created an efficient, permanent organizational structure throughout the country. An aura of success and organizational depth attracted the progressive, younger African leaders from all the country's regional, ethnic, and economic sectors. This attraction was reinforced by the realization that only through united effort could they make their demands heard in London. Even the more conservative leaders supported UNIP's demand for an end to federation.

After independence UNIP remained the main focus of power in the country because of its ability during the first years to maintain its preindependence unity. Few of the political tensions that later emerged were then evident, largely because all interests were represented in high government and party positions. Political energies that might have developed into political intrigues were to a large degree absorbed by the nationbuilding projects at hand.

The establishment of a one-party system—or, as it was officially designated, a one-party participatory democracy—in 1973 was the culmination of a gradual process. President Kaunda and most members of UNIP had long felt that a multiparty system constituted a threat to national unity and an administrative burden that the new state, which had a limited number of trained public officials, could not afford. It also signified an attempt to deal with highly divisive tendencies in Zambian public life that had, since the late 1960s, produced extensive opposition to the existing leadership (see Independence: The First Decade, 1964–74, ch. 1).

UNIP claimed to be a mass party, but it clearly did not have a mass following. In 1978 only 5 percent of the population of voting age was estimated to belong. People wishing to join had to submit an application at party offices either orally or in writing with recommendations by two party members. An individual's application was examined by the branch executive committee that gathered information on the applicant's integrity both from within and from without the party. Strong-arm methods apparently were sometimes used by overzealous officials to enroll people in the party. In early 1978 the president and the secretary general warned against forcing people to join by such actions as preventing them from going to their offices, entering a bus, or drawing water from a well unless they applied for membership.

Support for UNIP varied from region to region. Southern and Western provinces and Mumbwa District of Central Province were considered "weak" regions, whereas support in Northern and Luapula provinces and in parts of Eastern and Central provinces was fairly strong.

In the early years after independence, with a favorable economic situation and easy access to government resources, officials were able to make good on promises and easily won support at the local level. People joined UNIP because they expected such benefits as jobs, government loans, and trade and liquor licenses. In fact many party officials, who sat on local councils and cooperative credit advisory boards, were able to exert pressure on civil servants and private employers to establish themselves in business. According to Ian Scott, who made a thorough study of UNIP's base of support, there was a definite correlation between the amount of government help going into an area and the size of party membership. The "criterion for access to many resources became party service."

According to Scott this system of intermingled patronage and party loyalty led to a convergence of interests between the emerging middle class and party leaders. When the economic situation worsened in the early 1970s, less patronage became available, leading to a decline in support for the party and an increase of factionalism. More important was the split that had developed between the educated middle class, who by then thought they could rule the country without mass support and wanted to strengthen the national political leadership, and those among the party rank and file who felt that their involvement in the drive for independence entitled them to some control over the national and local leadership.

This populist attitude was especially noticeable among the Bemba who had been very active in the independence struggle. According to Scott this factor was at least as important as ethnic separatism in the formation of the UPP in August 1971. It was this growth of opposition parties that in turn led UNIP's leaders to create a one-party system in 1973.

Humanism

Humanism was adopted as UNIP's official ideology at the National Council meeting on April 27, 1967. Essentially it is an articulation of Kaunda's philosophical position. Although the ideology is frequently referred to by government and party elites and has in some way been communicated to all Zambians, it is not at all certain that a significant number of the elite or of the ordinary people share Kaunda's views.

Humanism's central tenet is a commitment to increase the dignity and capabilities of the common man. It is also Kaunda's prescription for averting the further development of what he sees as emergent social classes and their growing occupational and educational differences. He wants to salvage what he views as the traditional egalitarian principles of African society. The preamble of the constitution states, "the party shall bolster up and maintain this noble and worthy way of life."

Underlying Kaunda's views is his conception of the worth of the individual: society must ultimately serve men and their well-being. Men do not exist for the state. This perspective is linked to Kaunda's rejection of communist doctrine and underlies what he considers to be Africa's special brand of socialism. He calls for overall guidance of the economy by the state, but he rejects Marxist socialism for its dehumanization of man.

Humanism relies for inspiration on Kaunda's understanding of specific Christian concepts of man and society. It demands a classless society, conceived of as the natural state of Africa before the arrival of colonialism, and an avoidance of the concentration of wealth in the hands of a racial or numerical minority. Society is to be redesigned in order to be man-centered rather than wealth- or philosophy-centered. The new society, described as a return to the values of traditional African society, is an attempt to create an order based on mutual assistance and to satisfy the basic needs of all individuals.

Humanism is expounded—usually in moralizing terms—in Kaunda's writings, various official documents, and the mass media, as well as in all formal educational institutions. In practice it has meant the nationalization of businesses, the enactment of the Leadership Code that restricts the economic activities of public servants, the establishment of cooperatives in rural areas, and worker participation in enterprises.

> One has got to understand [Kaunda wrote] and appreciate that the powerful forces from the West which have been aggressively shattering in their individualist, competitive and possessive approach, have had serious and grave consequences on the African society. . . . If the distribution of wealth is not done properly, it might lead to the creation of classes in society and the much-valued humanist approach that is traditional and inherent in our African society would have suffered a final blow. . . . The way we plan our villages, towns, and cities will have a lot to do with the way our nation is going to develop . . . whether we shall have high-, middle-, and low-class citizens. . . . Such divisions of human beings [are] ungodly and contrary to the philosophy of Humanism in Zambia.

National development is UNIP's practical aim but is considered important only insofar as it benefits each person in the country individually and not just collectively. "Humanism is a description of society we are striving to achieve. For this reason we must be pragmatic and eclectic." The economic program therefore calls for an industrial and agricultural development policy under state direction with mixed private, cooperative, and public ownership.

Ethnicity in Politics

Several circumstances have tended to minimize the impact of ethnic issues on Zambian politics. In the first place, during the 1970s President Kaunda had been extremely careful in balancing representation in the highest and most visible government and party positions. In fact his repeated reshuffling of ministerial posts in attempts to achieve a sectional balance at times frustrated his goal to mold an efficient administration.

At lower levels also, from district governors down, officials were routinely posted to areas other than their own. Beyond this, overt manifestations of what is called tribalism have been considered reprehensible. The president himself, whose parents were African missionaries from Nyasaland (now Malawi), was considered "above tribe." Another factor was that historically no group had been able to obtain a lasting significant advantage in access to educational, economic, and other opportunities (see "Tribes" and "Tribalism," ch. 2).

Nevertheless there was always the danger that politicians would appeal for support to ethnic or regional loyalties as happened in 1968. At that time politicians capitalized on the resentment against real or perceived Bemba dominance, which then led to widespread defection from UNIP and support for the African National Council (ANC) (see Independence: The First Decade, 1964–74, ch. 1). Even after the establishment of a one-party system regional and ethnic considerations were bound to play a role in the elections for the National Assembly because of the way candidates were nominated locally. The ethnic factor was injected in the general elections of 1978 when Kapwepwe, a Bemba, and Nkumbula, of the Tonga-speaking Ila group, attempted to challenge Kaunda for his candidacy to the presidency. They were not allowed to run, but at the time it was predicted that each one's support would come largely from his own ethnic group and that this would awaken animosities that had been dormant.

Class Differences

For years after independence the largest party appeal was generated not by nationalism but by the concept of economic development. To most Zambians this meant government programs designed to provide better educational and economic opportunities for themselves and their children. Coupled with this was an expectation, encouraged by President Kaunda's philosophy of Humanism, that improvements in the national economy would benefit all and not just a small minority.

In fact social change, economic development, and the proliferation of government and party posts have provided an opportunity for a fair number of Zambians, especially those with particular skills, to replace a white with a black upper class. Kaunda had hoped that the Leadership Code and the process that he labeled "establishing a communocracy" would prevent the formation of a privileged class. He was wrong. In fact the economic reforms designed in the late 1960s to implement Humanism and to benefit the poor swelled the numbers of the new upper class. The parastatal sector expanded, and large numbers of foreign-owned businesses were taken over, thereby creating key positions for young educated Zambians. The very people who thus profited from the reforms then resisted further Humanist measures. They frequently flouted the Leadership Code, and some began demanding more and more openly a return to a free economy. The appeal of the UPP and the ANC, the two parties that had been bannedin 1972, was based in part on demands for the relinquishing of socialist and egalitarian objectives.

Not only at the national level but also in rural areas a local elite composed of government and party officials, prosperous commercial farmers, and officials of cooperatives and businesses amounting to no more than 10 percent of the rural population profited the most from government efforts to alleviate rural poverty. "It is estimated," says Patrick Ollawa, who made a study of rural development policies and strategies in Zambia, "that this ten percent of the rural population absorb most of the distributive outputs of the districts." President Kaunda has frequently commented on the inherent contradiction of "sowing" Humanism and "reaping" capitalism. "I have been shocked," he said in April 1976 at a National Council meeting, "that only individual business men have been able to borrow so much money to expand their capitalist enterprises at the expense of peasants and workers."

Actually in early 1979 no clear-cut boundaries had as yet developed between classes. Nor were political attitudes simply related to social position. Among party leaders, who were members of the new elite, the titles of "extremist" and "moderate" were applied to the same persons more than once, varying with the issues involved. Ideological divisions between those advocating strict adherence to humanist principles and those advocating fewer controls and more private initiative have primarily reflected temporary political alliances between leaders' ambitious for greater political power.

Industrial Workers and Labor Unions

Although unionized wage workers represented only a very small percent of the population, strikes in support of union demands could threaten the nation's economic and political stability. This was especially true for the copper miners, who expressed their demands through an aggressive union. Even during the colonial period miners were fighting management for higher wages. After independence they did not hesitate to express their displeasure when the government tried to keep wages down in the interest of national economy.

Labor unions have been fairly autonomous, and their participation in the political process has been oriented mainly toward seeking maximum benefits for their members. In particular, the mine workers have for some time constituted a kind of labor aristocracy and are prepared to defend their economic status, if necessary, in the political arena. Although labor leaders belong to UNIP, they are not part of the top hierarchy, and whatever control the party exerts has been indirect.

An indication that there is some competition between the party and the unions for the allegiance of the young surfaced in September 1978 when a group of young workers formed a union on their own initiative specifically to defend the rights of working youth. They called it the Union of Working Youth in Zambia. It was to cooperate but not to affiliate with the ZCTU. It would, however, accept the guidance of UNIP's Youth League. ZCTU leaders immediately denounced the establishment of the new union. They were assured by UNIP that the new organization did not represent a threat to the trade unions and that the group would not engage in collective bargaining but was rather an attempt to mobilize youth for political participation.

Students

The students at the University of Zambia represented a rebellious element, although they were still able in the 1970s to look forward to lucrative jobs after graduation in a country short of skilled manpower, and thus they could be assumed to have a stake in the existing regime (see Education, ch. 2). A poll taken in 1971 showed 81 percent being opposed to a single-party system. Nearly 75 percent were against the establishment of a UNIP branch within the university. There have been indications that their attitudes had not changed in the intervening years. Reportedly they were also critical of Humanism and its glorification of traditional African life, which they equated with backwardness. They have openly expressed their displeasure with internal and external policies. In early 1976 they demonstrated against Kaunda's support for a coalition government in Angola, preferring instead the Soviet-backed Popular Movement for the Liberation of Angola (Movimento Popular de Libertação de Angola—MPLA). They also demanded the dismissal of two African lecturers with whose political views they disagreed. The antigovernment turmoil and strikes led to the official closing of the university on February 9, 1976. Four foreign lecturers, described in the press as socialists, were arrested and detained under the state of emergency, which had come fully into force on January 28. Three of them were subsequently deported to their countries of origin. The university was reopened at the end of May, but students and staff were warned against submitting to foreign interference and subversive elements. Tensions between the students and UNIP persisted into the fall. The government radio reported in October that the newly elected executive of the National Union of Zambian Students refused to affiliate with the party.

In May 1978 the University of Zambia Students Union (UNZASU) declared that it would not affiliate with UNIP because its "objectives were at variance with the union's aspirations." They would, however, not prevent individual students from being party members.

Religious Groups

Strains and tensions have persisted between the state and some of the Christian sects, particularly Jehovah's Witnesses and the Lumpa church, both of which concentrate on salvation and a life hereafter and preach noninvolvement in political activities. Members of both sects tend to withdraw from public affairs and to form societies of their own that may appear potentially dangerous for a government or a party anxious to gain total allegiance (see Colonial Office Protectorate, 1924–53, ch. 1).

The Lumpa church was banned in 1964 and its founder, Alice Lenshina, jailed after repeated bloody clashes between church members and government troops. She was freed in December 1975 when she promised to join the United Church of Zambia. By 1977, however, about 4,000 of her followers had fled to Zaïre, where they hoped to revive the sect. In August 1977 Lenshina and forty-seven of her followers were charged with attending an illegal meeting, but they were acquitted shortly thereafter by a Lusaka court for insufficient evidence. It was not clear in 1979 whether Lenshina's death in December 1978 would mean the end of the sect.

In the mid-1970s members of the banned ANC were said to be joining Jehovah's Witnesses in protest against UNIP. Sporadic clashes between the government and Jehovah's Witnesses have not been as serious as those with Lumpa church members, however. Jehovah's Witnesses apparently were joining labor unions and other organizations that they had previously shunned. Party leaders complained, however, in the spring of 1978 that Jehovah's Witnesses did not like to register for the coming elections.

Reports circulated in 1978 of churches being organized in the copperbelt. They were said to be in reality a facade for antiparty and antigovernment activities.

The Press

In early 1979 there were two national dailies—the UNIP-owned *Times of Zambia* and the government-owned *Zambia Daily Mail*. Although they were controlled by the regime, they seemed to have a fair measure of independence, and criticism of official policies was fairly frequent. At times they attacked high and low party officials and members of the Cabinet and had questioned the usefulness of the Central Committee. They reported parliamentary debates, which were often highly critical of government and party. Usually they did it by publishing the adverse criticism faithfully and then condemning it editorially. Nevertheless this meant that opposition views got publicized. For example, when Kapwepwe declared his candidacy for the presidential election, he was able to publish an eight-page election manifesto totally at variance with Kaunda's policies. It was printed on the front page of both daily newspapers and reported on radio and television.

Public Participation

Despite the exhortations of government and party, press and radio, the prevailing mood in the late 1970s seemed one of frustration. The official goal of a participatory democracy notwithstanding, the leaders had progressively eliminated various forms of self-expression. Tight party control over the nomination of candidates, and even more so the veto power of the Central Committee over candidates nominated in primaries by local party officials (the Central Committee excluded twenty-eight contenders for parliament who had been locally chosen), threats, intimidation, the banning of opposition groups and individuals, and finally a constitutional amendment in 1978 preventing candidates from running against Kaunda had contributed to discourage participation in the political process. Only 62 percent voted in the general election on December 12, 1978, and more than half of the party posts at village and section levels were uncontested and unfilled. The regime's practice of making major policy decisions first and trying to stir up public approval afterward has been unproductive. The rural masses in particular were said to feel that their interests were not represented by anyone.

In recognition of this widespread apathy, a suggestion was made in 1978 that the truly dedicated and militant members of UNIP should form a vanguard within the party. However, opponents of the proposal pointed out that this might discourage people from joining UNIP because they would then be only second-class party members.

The Role of the President

President Kaunda's career has closely paralleled the political development of Zambia. When UNIP was founded, he was so popular that the party presidency was held open pending his release from imprisonment. As president of independent Zambia he has played the key role in balancing the various interests in the Cabinet, UNIP, and the nation. Kaunda's reelection in December 1978 showed that he remained popular, possibly because of his proven ability to contain the fissiparous tendencies in the country, possibly because no one had emerged who was considered capable of replacing him.

Foreign Relations

In the late 1970s the major concern of Zambia's foreign policy continued to be opposition to white domination in Southern Africa, particularly Southern Rhodesia, although the pursuit of the goal of ending that domination was tempered by practical considerations. Zambia had been totally dependent on Great Britain at independence, and its economic ties were predominantly with Western countries, including its white-ruled neighbors. This forced President Kaunda to become the foremost advocate of détente and peaceful transition to majority rule, a policy that agreed with his religious scruples and pacifist leanings. In 1976, however, he came reluctantly and regretfully to the conclusion that armed struggle was inevitable and from then on openly allowed guerrillas from Southern Rhodesia and Namibia to maintain training and staging camps on Zambian territory. By late 1978 economic necessity and military vulnerability forced him to try a more conciliatory route.

The basic tenets of foreign policy were spelled out in the Party constitution: "Declaring that the Party recognizes the inalienable rights of a people to self-determination and national independence and that they have a right to wage liberation struggles to this end; and further that the Party pledges its support for all people waging a just struggle for national liberation from colonialism, neo-colonialism, imperialism and racism; and that the Party shall work to enhance the development of Pan-Africanism, African Unity and Non-Alignment." Kaunda has defined nonalignment as the right of his government to examine international problems in the light of Africa's interests and to decide Zambia's position without reference to external ideologies.

Although pledged to a policy of Pan-Africanism and to support of the decisions of the Organization of African Unity (OAU), Zambia challenged the OAU's hard-line stand on the territorial integrity of Nigeria and was one of only four states to recognize and support Biafran secession from Nigeria. President Kaunda stated that Zambia in this and other cases would decide foreign policy issues on moral grounds even if such decisions go against the country's usual interests. Such moral considerations also underlie Zambia's adverse reaction to the Israeli seizure of Arab territories in the 1967 war despite the significant assistance provided to the country by the Israeli government. In late 1978 Kaunda condemned Ugandan President Idi Amin's invasion of Tanzania, which the OAU failed to censure.

President Kaunda has continually voiced strong support for the United Nations (UN) while often viewing its decisions as ineffectual. Although the UN's economic sanctions against Southern Rhodesia were both highly damaging to the Zambian economy and believed by Kaunda to be inadequate, he adhered to the ruling and supported its sanctions.

Kaunda has been chairman of the OAU and of the group of nonaligned nations. He has been especially interested in a north-south dialogue with the aim of a more equitable worldwide distribution of economic benefits between developed and underdeveloped countries.

The president dominates foreign policymaking, although the Ministry of Foreign Affairs has always been held by one of the country's strong political figures and has not, as in many developing countries, been subordinated to formal presidential control.

Decisions are generally reached collegially by the Cabinet or by the National Council, both of which Kaunda chairs. The president undoubtedly exerts the strongest influence over foreign policy within the Cabinet, not only as its chairman but because of his access to information and his prestige on the international scene, where he is generally admired for his high principles and moral courage. He conducts much of the country's diplomacy personally, on a president-to-president level.

Relations with Neighboring States

Zambia has tried as much as possible to change its trade and transport ties from a southward orientation in order to break the economic links formed with Southern Rhodesia and South Africa during the colonial era (see The Colonial Interlude, ca. 1890–1964; The Decade of Federation, 1953–63, ch. 1; see Transportation, ch. 4). In this and other matters Kaunda maintains close ties with the leaders of the so-called front-line states that include, in addition to Zambia, Tanzania, Mozambique, Angola, and Botswana.

Southern Rhodesia

President Kaunda has often pointed out that the people of no other country have suffered as much as for the freedom of Zimbabwe (as South Africans call Southern Rhodesia) as Zambians with the exception of the Zimbabweans themselves. Certainly no other African leader has tried harder to find a peaceful solution, has paid a bigger price in maintaining sanctions, or has been more generous in providing sanctuary to thousands of guerrillas.

Interaction with the Rhodesian regime has required communication with that of South Africa. In his quest for a peaceful settlement, Kaunda tried to get South Africa to put pressure on the Smith regime. He met Balthazar Johannes Vorster for the first time in a railroad carriage on the Victoria Falls bridge across the Zambezi River on August 25, 1975, at a conference that brought together all the parties in the Rhodesian dispute. The meeting was a fiasco, and on February 15, 1976, after earlier consultation with the presidents of Mozambique, Tanzania, and Botswana, Kaunda declared that full armed struggle was inevitable. In a published interview he said, "Due to Smith's intransigence, Zambia has reached the end of the road regarding negotiations as an instrument of change. We have discharged our obligations under the OAU manifesto on southern Africa. The Western countries have refused to extend a hand of friendship to us by responding positively in Rhodesia." He also raised for the first time the specter of Soviet-bloc involvement.

The meeting on the Victoria Falls bridge and a subsequent unsuccessful conference in Geneva brought out the deep rift existing between Zimbabwean liberation groups—ZANU, led by Mugabe and based in Mozambique, and ZAPU, led by Nkomo and based in Zambia. The two, in an attempt to reconcile their differences, formed the Patriotic Front. Zambia supported the front but identified itself more specifically with the cause of ZAPU. Southern Rhodesia warned Kaunda that preemptive attacks might be made on ZAPU bases inside Zambia, and such attacks began to occur in the fall of 1977.

On March 3, 1978, an internal settlement was signed by Prime Minister Smith and Bishop Abel Muzorewa, Ndabaningi Sithole, and Jeremiah Chirau, three African leaders working for majority rule inside the country. It was immediately denounced not only by Mugabe and Nkomo but also by Kaunda, who dismissed it as "irrelevant and lacking in substance," warning the United States and Great Britain against recognizing it. He argued that the agreement would not stop guerrilla warfare.

Zambia continued to be drawn into the quarrel between ZAPU and ZANU that persisted despite attempts to fuse the two wings of the Patriotic Front. Mugabe insisted on first merging the two armies; Nkomo wanted a prior political union, which he thought would prevent clashes between the troops.

Meanwhile Kaunda, hard pressed by a rapidly deteriorating economy, which he blamed mainly on the sanctions against Southern Rhodesia, continued his efforts for a settlement that would constitute a genuine transfer to majority rule and be acceptable to the Patriotic Front. But when he was told again—this time indirectly by Great Britain—that Southern Rhodesia would seriously strike at guerrilla bases in Zambia if they were used for attacks, Kaunda declared Zambia to be in a "state of war" with Southern Rhodesia. He promptly received messages of support from the OAU and a number of African countries and offers of aid from outside the continent.

Despite these martial declarations Kaunda kept pressing Great Britain to call an all-parties conference. He also sent envoys to Botswana, Angola, Tanzania, and other key African states to revive the stalled peace efforts and conferred with President Machel of Mozambique. On October 6, in a complete reversal of his previous stand, he suddenly announced a partial lifting of the economic blockade imposed on Southern Rhodesia five years earlier. He specifically opened the southern rail route that links Zambia to South Africa via Southern Rhodesia and was desperately needed to export copper and import fertilizers for the coming season's crop.

Meanwhile British and United States representatives consulted with representatives of South Africa and of the front-line states, as well as with members of the Patriotic Front and the other Southern Rhodesian parties concerning the British-American proposals that were published September 1, 1977. During those discussions the various parties suggested possible modifications of the proposals. These included granting independence to Southern Rhodesia by Great Britain either before or after the free election of a new government and defining the relative powers during a transition

151

period of a British-appointed resident commissioner vis-à-vis a governing council made up of the parties to the conflict. The suggestions were subsequently incorporated into a summary document on the history of the negotiations on the British-American proposals, which was presented to the parties on October 20, 1978. The document incorporated the parties' suggestions into a series of options concerning the transition process. However, none of these options was accepted, and further discussions—including secret meetings between Kaunda and Smith and between Smith and Nkomo—also proved fruitless.

On October 19, 1978, while Smith was in Washington, Rhodesian aircraft struck at ZAPU camps 130 kilometers inside Zambia, killing and wounding hundreds of guerrillas and a number of refugees and Zambians. This attack, which continued on the following days, seriously sabotaged plans for the proposed all-parties conference (see The State of Emergency, ch. 5). The only alternatives left at that moment were either a secret deal between participants in the internal settlement and members of the Patriotic Front or a fight to the finish. In early 1979 it seemed that the Rhodesian attacks had had the effect of hardening the attitude of the guerrilla fighters and angering their Zambian hosts.

The raids also demonstrated how little room Kaunda had to maneuver. He played his remaining card, which was to threaten a shift toward the Soviet Union and Cuba. He declared that he would no longer support the British-American initiative for an all-parties conference unless tough preconditions were met, and he condemned the Western response to the Rhodesian raids as lukewarm. At the same time he turned to the People's Republic of China (China) and Great Britain for increased military assistance and announced that he would divert money from economic development to arms.

Angola

Landlocked Zambia finds itself in a difficult and ambiguous position with respect to Angola. In 1975 just before the Benguela railroad was closed by the civil war, the line carried nearly 40 percent of Zambia's exports, including one-third of its copper exports. Dependence on the railroad led Kaunda to give unofficial support to the National Union for the Total Independence of Angola (União Nacional para a Independência Total de Angola— UNITA). The smallest of the three liberation movements fighting for supremacy in Angola, it controlled some of the territory traversed by the railroad.

The seizure by MPLA forces of the strategic port of Lobito in August 1975 and the collapse of the coalition between UNITA and the National Front for the Liberation of Angola (Frente Nacional de Libertação de Angola—FNLA) forced Kuanda to come to terms with Agostinho Neto, the leader of the MPLA. He procrastinated, however, which led to trouble with university students (see Political Dynamics, this ch.). Zambia recognized Angola's independence on November 11, 1975, but refused to acknowledge the existence of a legal government. Even after the OAU recognized the MPLA government in February 1976, formal approval was withheld because the MPLA had won its victory with the help of the Soviet Union and the Cubans, a "tiger and its cubs," as Kaunda referred to them, and he advised Neto to reconcile his differences with UNITA and to form a coalition government.

An Angolan delegation arrived in Lusaka on March 16 to discuss the normalization of relations between the two countries. One of the issues at stake was the fate of Angolan refugees, thousands of whom had fled to Zambia during the struggle against the Portuguese and the subsequent civil war. Shortly after this visit Zambia forbade UNITA and FNLA to use bases in the country; on April 15 Zambia finally recognized the MPLA regime, long after it had been recognized by the rest of the continent. Kaunda and Neto met for the first time during a conference of nonaligned nations in Sri Lanka on August 17, and Neto subsequently joined the group of presidents of front-line states. Repatriation of the Angolan refugees in Zambia was being discussed again in 1978, at which time their number was estimated at about 18,000.

Tanzania

Zambia's strongest fraternal ties in the past have been with Tanzania. Kaunda and President Nyerere shared similar social philosophies and a common outlook on many African problems, and they have been personally compatible. Tanzania became closely involved in Zambia's efforts to reorient its trade and transport ties when China built a rail line for the Tanzania-Zambia Railway Authority (TAZARA) from Kapiri Mposhi to Dar es Salaam. But the common hostility to the existing system of white rule in southern Africa and the physical possibilities for joint actions against that rule gave the relationship its dynamic quality.

The spirit of collaboration between Kaunda and Nyerere involved Zambia more deeply than might otherwise have happened in the bitter quarrel between Nyerere and Amin. This quarrel arose after Amin's military coup in January 1971 overthrew the civilian regime led by another friend of Nyerere, President Milton Obote. The Ugandan situation did not affect Zambia simply by virtue of Kaunda's personal ties with Nyerere, however. Kaunda was too fervently committed to a civilian philosophy of government to take kindly to a government installed in any country by a military coup. The sudden violent seizure of power by the commanding officer of the Ugandan army was as disturbing an event in Lusaka as it was in Dar es Salaam. During a major border clash in 1972 between Uganda and Tanzania, Kaunda had stood openly with Nyerere, and he did so again during the Ugandan invasion of Tanzania in the fall of 1978.

In 1975, however, Kaunda and Nyerere took totally opposite

positions over Angola, Kaunda promoting a coalition government that would include representatives of the three liberation movements competing for power and Nyerere supporting the MPLA. Strains also developed between the two countries over delays of Zambian traffic on the TAZARA railroad and the Tanzanian decision to raise port charges at Dar es Salaam.

In 1978 the two presidents began to differ over the Rhodesian issue, Nyerere supporting Mugabe and Kaunda, Nkomo. The growing rift between the two guerrilla leaders, fueled by Mugabe's anger over Nkomo's reported secret meetings with Smith, affected relations between Nyerere and Kaunda. In late 1978, when Kaunda decided that Zambia's economic survival required the opening of the railroad through Southern Rhodesia to South African ports, Nyerere was unsympathetic, further exacerbating Zambian-Tanzanian tensions.

South Africa

Relations with South Africa were dominated by two factors: economic dependence and the bitter dispute over Namibia, which, as in the case of Southern Rhodesia, pulled Kaunda in two directions. He was, on the one hand, foremost among the frontline presidents in exploring a peaceful solution through direct discussions with South African leaders. On the other hand he gave aid and asylum to the South-West African People's Organization (SWAPO). Consequently there were frequent border incidents between South African forces and SWAPO guerrillas, including a serious clash on August 24, 1978, near the eastern Caprivi area. South Africa accused Zambia of allowing SWAPO to use its country as a guerrilla base. Zambia bitterly complained of South African attacks on civilian targets.

In discussions with Vorster Kaunda never wavered in his belief that the people of Namibia were entitled to immediate independence under majority rule. However, internal rifts within SWAPO and a shift in alliances began affecting the relationship with Zambia in 1976. Dissidents among SWAPO members who were disenchanted with the leadership of President Sam Nujoma included Andreas Shipanga, SWAPO information officer. He and ten others petitioned the government in Lusaka for a SWAPO conference to elect a new executive because they believed that military and other supplies were being withheld from camps in southern areas of Zambia. They were detained and subsequently brought a habeas corpus action against the Zambian government. The lower court dismissed the case, saying that Shipanga and the others had been put in protective custody only at the request of SWAPO. The case was taken to a higher court, but it could not proceed because Shipanga flew to Tanzania on June 18, 1976 (or was kidnapped by Tanzanian officials, according to Shipanga), where he was imprisoned on August 25. Nujoma demanded that Shipanga be handed over to him for trial on charges of having conspired with whites in Namibia. In early 1979, however, Shipanga was back in Namibia, actively involved in politics.

Temporary strains developed also over SWAPO's changing alliances in Angola. At first it had had a firm relationship with UNITA, the liberation movement closest to Kaunda. However, in December 1976, after South Africa's attack on SWAPO camps within Angola and its presumed collaboration with UNITA, Nujoma shifted his ties to the MPLA.

The presence not only of guerrillas and their quarrels but also of thousands of refugees created difficulties for Zambia. To reduce friction, in the mid-1970s SWAPO camps were moved from near Lusaka closer to the border. This in turn led to frequent border violations and clashes between South African troops and SWAPO guerrillas, involving Zambian military forces at times. In the summer of 1978 Vorster called on Zambia to use its influence with SWAPO to agree to a UN plan for a peaceful transition, which called for elections under UN auspices and independence. In a sudden change of policy, however, South Africa conducted elections in Namibia in November 1978 without SWAPO or UN participation.

Relations with Western Countries

Zambia at independence was tied into the southern African economic zone and therefore to the Western world. Kaunda has tried to diversify his links. Zambia is associated with the European Economic Community and has increased its trade with Eastern countries. Its main partners, however, remained Western—notably, as formerly, Great Britain—an economic fact that inevitably limits President Kaunda's political options. Despite very strong dissatisfaction over the failure of the British government to take what he considered effective action, President Kaunda therefore looked primarily to Great Britain for support. In October 1978, after Rhodesia's attack on guerrilla camps inside Zambia, Great Britain agreed to supply Zambia with weaponry and other matériel (see Foreign Influences, ch. 5).

Association with the United States has been of long standing because of the early and continued American involvement in the copper industry. Diplomatic relations have been carried out at the ambassadorial level since independence. During Kaunda's second visit to the United States in May 1978 a close personal friendship developed between him and President Carter, who pledged US$100 million in economic aid for Zambia during the next two years. Kaunda, however, contrary to expectations, refused to condemn the Soviet and Cuban role in Africa.

Other Western countries with embassies in Lusaka include Belgium, France, the Federal Republic of Germany (West Germany), Italy, and the Netherlands. Denmark, Greece, and Austria maintain cousulates. Zambia, in common with most other sub-Saharan African states, has broken diplomatic relations with Israel. Relations with Japan, an increasingly important trade partner, were primarily economic.

Relations with Communist Countries

Kaunda implied in 1978 that he might turn to the Soviet Union and Cuba for help if Western countries did not protect him against Rhodesian attacks, and there were some Central Committee members who advocated closer association with the Soviet bloc. His relations with communist countries, however, were limited mostly to contacts with China.

Such relations dated back to 1965 when the first envoy came from Peking to Lusaka at a time when China became a champion of so-called Third World causes in its growing rivalry with the Soviet Union. In 1967 President Kaunda went to China, and shortly thereafter he announced that China would build the railroad to Dar es Salaam for which he had unsuccessfully pleaded with Western powers.

In February 1974 Kaunda visited China again, this time bringing a large retinue of officials. Some of them stayed behind to study Chinese institutions, especially the interaction between party and civil service. Ever since this visit the president has repeatedly praised China's self-sufficiency and its stand on international affairs.

Relations with the Soviet Union were warming in late 1978 and early 1979 after a long period of frost. In February 1976 after the MPLA had won the civil war in Angola with Soviet and Cuban help, Kuanda considered these two countries a threat to Africa. Relations became worse when Kaunda suspected Soviet involvement in the university troubles of that year. Kaunda's disappointment at what he perceived to be Western insensitivity to his troubles with Southern Rhodesia made him consider closer ties to Moscow as a last resort. There were reports that the number of Cubans training ZAPU guerrillas in Zambian camps was increasing in 1978.

*   *   *

Two long-time observers, Douglas G. Anglin and Timothy M. Shaw, deal comprehensively with Zambia's foreign policy in *Studies in Diplomacy and Dependence.* The two authors point up the conflict between a firm commitment to the liberation struggle and an inherited dependence on the white-dominated southern African economic system. For the political impact of the predominance of the copper industry see Richard L. Sklar, *Corporate Power in an African State: The Political Impact of Multinational Mining Companies in Zambia.* Sklar examines the constraints this predominance places on Zambia's foreign policy options. He characterizes the new elite as a managerial bourgeoisie whose outlook and interest are at variance with the official ideology of Humanism and possibly with the long-term interests of Zambia's people.

Henry S. Meebelo, editor of a volume entitled *Main Currents of*

Zambian Humanist Thought, examines the influences of western philosophy and Zambian traditions on Zambia's official ideology. For the working of UNIP at the local level and the interaction of the party and the middle class, see Ian Scott's articles "Party Functions and Capabilities: The Local-Level UNIP Organisation during the first Zambian Republic" and "Middle-Class Politics in Zambia."

Although dealing mainly with Lusaka, Nigel R. Hawkesworth's *Local Government in Zambia* provides a detailed look at the workings of local government. He describes the increasing dependence of local government on the central government despite Kaunda's professed goal of decentralization. For a sympathetic portrait of Kaunda, see Fergus MacPherson's *Kenneth Kaunda of Zambia; The Times and the Man,* in which he describes the influences (Ghandi among others) that shaped Kaunda's thinking and their conflict with the harsh measures he sometimes adopted as a statesman.

For an excellent study of Zambian politics and government, see *Politics in Zambia,* written by a group of professors from the University of Zambia and edited by William Tordoff. It describes, among other things, the administrative hierarchy and the relationship between civil servants and the ruling party. The book also gives a useful analysis of Humanism. (For further information see Bibliography.)

Chapter 4. The Economy

*Ila wooden comb depicting a trader astride a bullock,
a traditional symbol of wealth*

PERHAPS THE MOST promising aspect of the Zambian economy at the end of the 1970s was the potential for growth offered
by the country's relatively immense mineral resources, primarily
copper, and the large quantity of land suited for agricultural production and cattle raising. The setting was a dual economic system
consisting of a modern sector that was largely confined to the line
of rail (see Glossary) and urban-oriented and a rural agricultural
sector that was basically of subsistence character and encompassed some three-fifths of the population and the major portion
of the national territory.

The modern sector was dominated by parastatals (state-owned
or -controlled enterprises) that operated in all economic sectors
from manufacturing, mining, power, and transport to agricultural
marketing and services, finance, wholesale and retail trade, and
the hotel and restaurant trade. Only in construction and agricultural production was the private sector still supreme in 1979.
Parastatals employed over one-third of all wage earners and accounted for more than one-half of gross domestic product (GDP
—see Glossary). At independence the economy was basically pri-
vate-sector oriented, although some public enterprises existed,
principally public services. Underlying the change in direction has
been President Kenneth Kaunda's concept of group ownership
and participation and his opposition to the development in
Zambia of what he characterized as Western-style private capitalism. The first major step in the transformation was taken in 1968
through the Mulungushi Reforms, which established the policy,
and began acquisition, of government majority holdings in existing large-scale private firms; the policy of government control of
new enterprises was also enunciated. The next year state participation was vastly strengthened when control was secured of the
two economically dominant copper mining operations. Expansion
of state holdings continued in the 1970s. In 1979 the giant su-
praholding company, Zambia Industrial and Mining Corporation
(ZIMCO), created in 1970, was the state's principal agency of
control; with minor exceptions, all components of the state sector
were under the direct control of ZIMCO or of its subholding
companies, the Industrial Development Corporation of Zambia
(INDECO) and the National Import and Export Corporation
(NIEC). A number of other such companies were abolished in
December 1978, and control of their subsidiaries was transferred
directly to ZIMCO in a move to streamline state participation in
the economy and improve performance, with which rather widespread dissatisfaction had been voiced.

At the time of the Mulungushi Reforms the private sector seems
to have been considered essentially a necessary evil, an area for

the development of small enterprise. This attitude persisted into the mid-1970s without the limits for the sector's activities ever being clearly defined. During this time some private investment went into the formal sector, and an unknown but relatively small amount also was put into the informal sector. The latter was labor intensive, generally paid considerably lower wages, and required more limited skills. It produced, however, a large number of items and was important in the social context of the urban areas by providing employment that accounted for an estimated one-fifth of the urban labor force in the mid-1970s. The general economic situation from the mid-1970s on and the frequently superior performance of private enterprise in the formal sector led finally to government acceptance of the importance of private undertakings to the development effort. This position was confirmed by the provisions of the Industrial Development Act of 1977, which clarified the government's stand and in fact proclaimed the economy to be a mixed one in which private investment would be welcomed.

The government's economic goals and the hoped-for social gains were stated in the first two of its national development plans (1966–70 and 1972–76). Basically these goals were: improvement of the general level of well-being; reduction of the disparity between urban and rural incomes; diversification of economic activity to lessen dependence on the copper industry; and training of Zambians to manage and operate the economy. The situation at independence offered the hope of substantial progress toward these aims. Through 1978, however, real progress had been slow. This was related in part to external factors, both political and economic, and also in no small way to domestic decisions. At independence the country's rich mineral resources were already well developed. For the rest of the 1960s world market conditions generally favored Zambia. Relatively high steady export earnings from copper during those years apparently led to the illusion of constant wealth, which was reflected in economic policies that continued into the mid-1970s. Diversification, instead of promoting greater expansion of the use of local materials and development of industries using them, was slanted, largely by tariff and quota policies, toward the processing of imported primary and intermediate materials. Funds were used to subsidize imported agricultural products and hold down domestic food prices, principally to the benefit of the urban population, thereby discouraging domestic agricultural production; the latter was further affected by a failure to increase producer prices. The cost of capital was kept low, while moderately substantial increases in wages were permitted. The result was that modern larger scale industry developed along capital-intensive lines, to the detriment of urban employment. At the same time, however, efforts to train Zambians to assume positions in the modern sector were generally satisfactory, and substantial progress was made in establishing the transport and power infrastructure needed for economic expansion.

Zambia's implementation of United Nations (UN) sanctions against Southern Rhodesia after that country's Unilateral Declaration of Independence (UDI) in 1965 cost the economy dearly. In addition there were sharply fluctuating copper prices beginning in the early 1970s—including a major downturn in 1974—which showed signs of being alleviated only in late 1978, and overwhelming transport problems, especially from 1973 on. Development under the Second National Development Plan; 1972–76, could not be carried out as programmed because substantial funds had to be committed to ad hoc projects, and the start of the Third National Development Plan had to be postponed until 1979. Although international assistance was furnished in greater measure to help out, it fell far short of the extraordinary costs to Zambia's economy, which were estimated by the UN in 1977 to have reached the equivalent of almost US$750 million and which had forced the government to pursue policies aimed at economic survival rather than development.

The possibility of continued instability in export earnings apparent during the 1970s, aside from transport problems that were presumably resolvable, has compelled the government to reassess the pattern for future economic development. Under the Third National Development Plan investment priorities were to be accorded the directly productive sectors with emphasis on agriculture and manufacturing, including the development of agro-based and labor-intensive industries using local raw materials for import substitution and for export products. Investment in transport was to be reduced in view of the essential completion of the main transport network, and there was to be a reduction in investment in social infrastructure. An important feature of the plan was the projected creation of the Budget Stabilization Fund, which would be used during periods of low copper prices to maintain development expenditures on an even level.

Agriculture

Although about 60 percent of the population is dependent on agriculture for its livelihood, the contribution of the sector to GDP has been extremely low since independence, annually accounting for only an estimated 13 to 14 percent. From 1965 to 1975 government policy was to restrain agricultural producer prices as a means of keeping food prices low. Tariffs on imported consumer goods resulted in decidedly unfavorable terms of trade for the agricultural sector, and at the same time relatively high urban wages encouraged migration from the rural areas. In combination these factors acted as a strong disincentive to increased agricultural production and were largely responsible for the general stagnation that characterized the subsistence subsector in particular during this time. Between 1965 and 1976 value added by agriculture grew at an average rate of only about 2.7 percent, which matched roughly the population growth rate and was about equal to the rate of growth of total GDP in real terms (see Population, ch. 2).

Government efforts to increase agricultural output—and at the same time improve the lot of people in the rural areas outside the line of rail—were centered initially in producer cooperatives in which groups of farmers banded together to clear and cultivate land on a collective basis. Liberally financed from copper revenues acquired by the newly independent government, the program began in early 1965, and by 1968 somewhat over 600 cooperatives had been formed. At the start enthusiasm was high, but by 1970 or 1971 most of these groups had become inactive or disappeared. Among the principal causes were that many cooperatives had been set up primarily to obtain the government subsidy for clearing land; trained government personnel were inadequate for the task; and markets for the crops produced and sources for needed inputs were lacking in the rural areas. In 1970 the government began promoting so-called family farming as a way to increase production and improve rural welfare. Some success was achieved in the production of tobacco and maize, but the effect did not appear highly significant overall in 1979 (see Crops, this ch.). At the same time encouragement was given to maintaining private large-scale farms. Through the late 1970s, however, the most effective step to encourage increased output had been the raising of agricultural producer prices. This began during the 1974–75 growing season and continued into 1978–79; the desirability of further increases was reportedly to be considered on a regular basis. Largely attributed to the result of these increases—aided by favorable weather—value added by agriculture between 1975 and 1977 grew by an estimated 4.6 percent annually.

Zambian agriculture, as in neighboring Angola, Zaïre, Tanzania, and Mozambique, during colonial rule developed a pronounced dichotomy between commercial and subsistence subsectors. The principal aim of much of Zambian commercial farming (unlike that in these neighboring states) was not the production of primary materials for export, but the supplying of foodstuffs to the work force employed in mining operations—mostly in the copperbelt (see Glossary) but to some extent also in Katanga (present-day Shaba) region in Zaïre—and to the growing urban population, which together constituted a relatively constantly expanding market for the domestic output.

Commercial farming began around Fort Jameson (present-day Chipata) in the early 1900s when that town was headquarters for the British South Africa Company. The center of European farming gravitated to the line of rail after extension of the railroad from Livingstone to the mining center of Broken Hill (present-day Kabwe) in 1906 and the Zaïre border in 1909, but commercial farming did not grow rapidly until large-scale development of copper mining in the copperbelt in the early 1930s. At independence the commercial sector consisted of an estimated 1,200 farms, all operated by expatriates. The number of operations declined substantially through the late 1960s as European owners left. The total area farmed did not decline materially, however, since many of the operators who remained increased the size of their holdings, and other farms were acquired by Zambians. In the late 1970s the subsector had roughly 800 units occupied under leasehold from the state. Of these about 500 to 600, or roughly two-thirds, were farmed by expatriates; the remainder comprised state farms and commercial operations of Zambian farmers. Together they accounted by value for more than half of the domestic agricultural production that was marketed, including half of the locally produced milk, pork, and tobacco and more than three-fifths of the maize.

The subsistence subsector consisted of more than 600,000 households in the rural areas, which generally practiced some form of shifting cultivation. This so-called traditional sector chiefly produced such staples as maize, millet, sorghum, cassava, beans, and peanuts, and in tsetse-free areas also raised open-range cattle. Output was intended primarily to meet the subsistence needs of the family, but in years of surplus a portion of the harvest might be sold. Some subsistence farmers also intentionally grew somewhat larger crops for marketing, an activity that appeared to have increased after the improvement in agricultural producer prices in the mid-1970s. More than two-fifths of subsistence farmers cultivated 2.5 hectares or less, about one-quarter had between 2.5 and 4.5 hectares, and about one-fifth farmed from 4.5 to 9.5 hectares.

Within the traditional subsistence subsector a small number of farmers, principally Tonga in Southern Province, had long carried on small-scale commercial operations (see Tonga, ch. 2). Stimulated by the changed economic situation after independence, however, a large group of agricultural households, variously estimated at between 20,000 and 30,000, has emerged that carries on farming essentially for commercial marketing. Although found in all parts of the country, most of these households are located in Southern and Central provinces along the line of rail and to a lesser extent in Copperbelt and Eastern provinces. Generally this group of emergent farmers (see Glossary) operates on a small scale, although some medium-size farms have been developed; they produce a wide range of crops approximating those grown by the officially designated commercial subsector, as well as beef cattle and pigs.

Land Use, Soils, and Land-Use Systems

The UN Food and Agriculture Organization (FAO) has estimated that of Zambia's close to 75.3 million hectares, about 35 million hectares, or 46.5 percent, was used for temporary and permanent cropland, including land in fallow, and temporary and permanent pastureland. Of the remainder, forest and woodland occupied over 37.3 million hectares (49.6 percent); miscellaneous uses—roads, urban structures, and the like—accounted for almost 3 million hectares, or 3.9 percent. From the standpoint of human impact, other sources have estimated that somewhat less than a quarter of the country's total area had been affected significantly by human activity, mainly in the form of agricultural pursuits such as crop cultivation, cattle raising, fishing, and harvesting of forest products. Minor agricultural activities impinged on slightly more than one-quarter of the total area, but the effect on the natural environment in this case was relatively small. The remaining half of the total area generally was affected by human activity only in the form of scattered gathering and hunting.

The amount of land used, including land in fallow, differed greatly in different regions. For instance, in the Luangwa River Valley, where up to 20 percent of the area was considered suitable for cropping, usage did not exceed 5 percent. In some parts of the Eastern Plateau utilization was estimated at over 60 percent, approximating the percentage of suitable land in those areas. In much of Northern and Luapula provinces utilization ranged from 40 to 60 percent, also close to the potential. In sharp contrast, in the western half of the country—excluding the intensively cultivated belt along the line of rail—land used for agricultural purposes was only between 5 and 20 percent. For much of this vast area the potential was in this same range, but major exceptions were found in the southwest and in areas of southeastern Southern and Central provinces where land suited to agriculture constituted over 60 percent of the region.

Soil types and rainfall amounts, in combination with local conditions, such as the presence or absence of the tsetse fly, have played important roles in the development of a number of distinct traditional systems of land use (see The Physical Setting and Population, ch. 2). Sandy soils cover much of the northeastern and northwestern parts of the country. Rainfall that is usually above 1,000 millimeters a year has caused extensive leaching and loss of soil fertility. This situation has given rise to a form of slash-and-burn cultivation known as *citemene* (often written as *chitemene*)—derived from a Bemba word meaning "to cut"—that is generally unique to the Congo-Zambezi watershed, including that part of the watershed that lies in southern Zaïre (see fig. 10). The principal aim of the several *citemene* variations is to increase soil fertility, in contrast to the removal of vegetation to permit cultivation, which is the usual goal of other slash-and-burn or bush fallow systems. In so-called large-circle *citemene,* found in the northeast and the characteristic system of the Bemba, large trees are lopped and small ones are pollarded a few feet above the ground over an area of a hectare or more. A single low pile of branches and trunks, often covering an area of a half-hectare or more, is then made in the center of the clearing. At the appropriate time the pile is burned, cassava roots are planted when the rains come, and finger millet is broadcast over the ash-fertilized ground shortly thereafter. In the second year peanuts are planted, and in the third year beans. During this time the cassava continues to be harvested, the last of it in the fourth year, when another millet crop may be sown. After this the land is usually abandoned to regenerate. New fields are ordinarily prepared each year, with the result that a variety of crops is available at any one time.

So-called small-circle *citemene* is also found in northeast Zambia, where it is practiced mainly by the Bisa and Lala. In this system all but the largest trees are cut off several feet above the ground, and the debris is arranged throughout the cleared area in a considerable number of small stacks, roughly seven to ten meters across. The system is extremely wasteful; after a first crop of finger millet only a few of the circles may be used for a second crop consisting of peanuts or beans. After this the area is abandoned. In northwest Zambia a block *citemene* system is practiced, especially by the Lamba and Kaonde, in which the branches are piled together in the form of a rough square. In this system the cleared land outside the ash zone is also more extensively used for hoe cultivation of crops, especially sorghum, than in the large-circle and small-circle systems. Users of the large-circle *citemene* method, as well as those practicing other *citemene* forms, also grow a variety of crops in small fields or gardens near their houses, which they cultivate on a relatively permanent basis. In all areas, also, maize had become an important crop in the 1970s, in some places achieving dominance as a staple and in others attaining equality with millet and sorghum.

The *citemene* method is practiced as the principal form of cultivation over almost two-fifths of Zambia (see fig. 10). Next in extent are variations of a semipermanent system based mainly on hoe culture and the use of oxen for plowing. This form is prevalent in about a quarter of the country, including all of Western and part of North-Western provinces and the Zambezi Escarpment area of southern Zambia, where absence of the tsetse fly permits raising cattle. Rainfall is below 1,000 millimeters annually throughout these areas. The Western area is overlain by poor soils formed on the Barotse (sometimes called Kalahari) Sands, part of the widespread sand deposits found from southwestern Africa northward to Zaïre. This western area includes the extensive floodplains of the Zambezi. The main crops on the sands are cassava and bulrush millet, and maize is the principal crop on the alluvial floodplains. Cattle raising is widespread, and seasonal migrations occur to the plains in the dry period from about June to December, when the grasses there are of high quality, and back to the higher woodlands when the plains flood again during the wet season.

The farming population of the Luangwa River Valley, which encompasses about a tenth of the country's total area, practices a

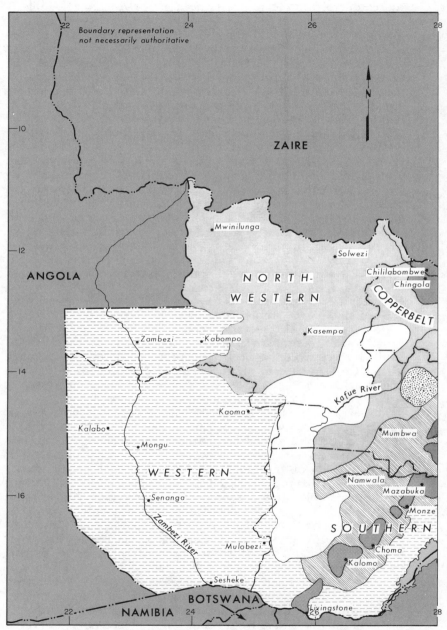

Source: Based on map compiled by Jürgen Schultz in his *Land Use in Zambia*,
Munich, 1976, fig. 11. Used by permission of the publisher, Weltforum
Verlag, Munich.

Figure 10. Land-Use Systems

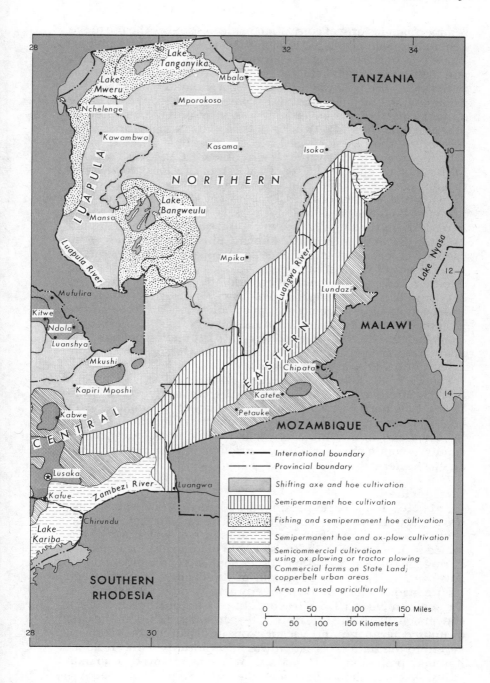

International boundary
Provincial boundary
Shifting axe and hoe cultivation
Semipermanent hoe cultivation
Fishing and semipermanent hoe cultivation
Semipermanent hoe and ox-plow cultivation
Semicommercial cultivation
using ox plowing or tractor plowing
Commercial farms on State Land;
copperbelt urban areas
Area not used agriculturally

0   50   100   150 Miles
0   50   100   150 Kilometers

semipermanent form of cultivation made possible by the use of the generally fertile alluvial soils along the river and its tributaries. These rich soils may be used continuously for as long as ten years, and the time required in fallow is comparatively short. Other soils in the valley are poor and little used. Sorghum has long been the traditional staple, but maize has become the dominant crop in the southern part of the valley and was increasingly cultivated in other sections in the 1970s. The tsetse fly infests the entire valley, preventing the raising of cattle.

Semipermanent cultivation is also practiced, in areas covering in all about an additional fifteenth of Zambia, by local populations that engage in fishing as a major economic activity. The groups are found in the vicinity of lakes Tanganyika, Mweru, Mweru Wantipa, and Bangweulu, as well as the large swamp adjacent to the latter lake; in the lower valley of the Luapula River; and around Lukanga Swamp in central Zambia. Cultivation activities in all cases are of secondary importance and—apparently because of the general lack of interest in farming—cassava, which requires little attention and can be grown for considerable periods of time even in poor soils, is the principal staple. However, maize is also grown, and peanuts have become an important secondary crop in the Luapula River Valley and around Lake Bangweulu. In these areas *citemene* cultivation is practiced by the surrounding peoples, and many fishermen-farmers also make use of this system to some extent, utilizing nearby woodlands.

Zambia's best soils are the reddish sandy clay loams found in a belt that stretches generally along the present-day line of rail from Livingstone northeastward toward the copperbelt. Similar soils of good quality occur in the area of Petauke and Chipata in Eastern Province and in a number of other isolated areas. Most of the country's commercial farming is carried on in the line-of-rail belt and in Eastern Province.

Land Tenure

As of 1979 tenure of approximately 93 percent of Zambian land was regulated by customary practice. The remaining 6 to 7 percent was classified as State Land, the tenure of which was determined in accordance with British law as modified by local statutes during the colonial period and subsequent acts of the independent government. The most important of the changes in State Land tenure made by the Zambian government through 1978 had been the abolishment in 1975 of freehold titles, rural and urban, and the conversion of existing titles into 100-year leases, except in the case of unused farmland and vacant plots in urban areas, which reverted to the state. This action was in conformity with President Kaunda's philosophy of Humanism, which maintains that no individual or group should have absolute ownership of land (see Humanism, ch. 3).

The area encompassed by State Land was generally delineated

in 1928. As in other of its African territories, the British government set aside certain areas of land for the non-African population, primarily for agricultural development. This land, designated Crown Land, was made available to individuals on either a freehold or a leasehold basis. In Zambia Crown Land was located mostly along the line of rail, where coincidentally some of the country's best soils were situated. A few other widely separated areas—around Chipata in the east, Mbala in the northeast, Mwinilunga in the northwest, and Mumbwa in the west central part of the country—all favored with good agricultural land—were also made Crown Land. At independence this category, which was redesignated State Land and was vested in the president, comprised some 4.7 million hectares, or between 6 and 7 percent of Zambia's total area. About half of State Land was then held under freehold or leasehold, mainly by European farmers, and another one-sixth remained unalienated; roughly an eighth of the total was still occupied by indigenous groups. The remainder encompassed townships, forest reserves and protected areas, and a small inundated area.

In 1928 the British government also set aside certain areas that were classified as Native Reserves. These were vested in the Secretary of State for the Colonies and were intended solely for use by indigenous peoples. At the time the reserves were considered adequate—based on plans to improve African methods of land use and soil conservation—for the needs of the African population. The plans were not implemented, however, and there had been a failure to take into consideration the land requirements of shifting cultivation. As a result high population growth in some reserves adjacent to Crown Land, which ordinarily would have been available to absorb the excess, led to soil depletion and growing discontent among indigenous groups. In 1947 all remaining nondesignated land—except Barotseland (present-day Western Province), where landrights had been retained by the paramount chief —was made into Native Trust Lands, also to be held in trust for the African population. A provision was made for alienation to Europeans, but little appears actually to have occurred. Before independence the Native Trust Lands were used mainly for large-scale resettlement of African villages, particularly in Central and Eastern provinces. Resettlement by individuals and groups after independence appears to have involved chiefly the takeover of unalienated former Crown Land and land abandoned by former European holders.

At independence the Native Reserves and Native Trust Lands were simply redesignated Reserves and Trust Lands; in 1969 Barotseland was reclassified as Reserves. Since then both Reserves and Trust Lands have been statutorily vested in the president, who is authorized to grant leases in the former and occupancy rights in the latter to either Africans or non-Africans. Very few such leases and rights have been issued, however; the government in effect has made no effort to regulate or intervene in customary practices under which Africans occupy and use such land.

Traditional tenure practices vary, but certain broad principles are discernible. Arable land and the land on which the family house is located, together with the land comprising associated garden plots, are individually rather than communally held in almost all cases. Only infrequently is a lineage (see Glossary) found acting as the holding unit. Grazing rights, however, are communal, and all members of the community have equal access to any vacant land, including land temporarily in fallow over which individuals hold rights. Although the surrounding land is felt to belong to the community or village, in areas where population pressure is negligible the individual has virtually complete freedom to acquire free land and establish a direct claim by clearing and using it. Question might arise only if another person had a prior claim. The chief or village headman is usually consulted before new land is acquired concerning such possibility and to all intents grants permission for use of the land, although neither statutory nor customary law makes this a requirement for land acquisition. The situation is different in areas where permanent cultivation is practiced and in heavily populated regions. In such cases the right to use a piece of land usually must be acquired from the individual having acknowledged tenure.

In most ethnic groups the individual has secure tenure rights over land directly acquired, and these are lost only through abandonment of the land or by transfer to someone else. Since independence, however, the state might set aside such land for public use in the Reserves without compensation, and the land continued to be classified as Reserves. The government could also purchase land, by payment of compensation, in the Trust Lands, which then became State Land. Ordinary transfer and inheritance practices vary considerably, but in the country's chiefly matrilineal systems a man's heirs were usually his sister's sons. In present-day Zambia, this arrangement may give rise to conflict, particularly in areas of relatively permanent cultivation where the emergent farmer who has developed the land has a strong interest in passing on his holdings and improvement to his own sons. Among various ethnic groups, however, during his own lifetime the cultivator may freely transfer rights to a holding he has cleared. Sale is usually not permitted under customary law, but where land had acquired substantial economic value, disguised forms—such as the sale of improvements—were already common by independence.

The direct acquisition of land in the Reserves and Trust Lands theoretically is open to all Zambians on the basis that under Article 24 of the 1973 Constitution of the Republic of Zambia every Zambian has the right to reside freely anywhere in the state. In practice, however, to establish residence in areas governed by customary law, individuals who are not members of the group must first secure permission from the local chief or headman. Failure to receive permission effectively denies the individual the right to land. This chiefly power was considered a matter of course during the colonial period but supposedly lapsed under the provisions of the republican constitution. In reality, however, according to foreign observers in the mid-1970s it seemed still to be exercised and quietly accepted by the public.

Crops

Maize, cassava, sorghum, finger and bulrush millet, peanuts, and beans are the principal staples grown in Zambia. The spread of maize and cassava cultivation in the colonial period, and especially of maize after independence, has brought a major change in the relative importance of individual crops. Originally sorghum and millet were the predominant food crops in many areas. By the 1970s, however, although sorghum cultivation remained widespread, significant acreage was devoted to this crop only by farmers using the block *citemene* syste of cultivation in northwestern Zambia and by some settled agriculturists farming along the Zambezi River in a stretch extending from lower Western Province to Lake Kariba. In other areas smaller quantities of the grain were also regularly grown, not so much for food as for brewing beer. Finger millet remained an important crop in northeast Zambia—chiefly among cultivators using the circle *citemene* systems. The main areas of continuing bulrush millet cultivation included the western part of the country overlain by the poor soils of the Barotse Sands, in which this crop grew relatively well, and the comparatively dry Gwembe Valley region of Southern Province.

Maize, introduced by early European settlers, has become the dominant staple and the major subsistence and cash crop. Although most marketed maize is grown in Central and Southern provinces, it is cultivated to some extent by half or more of the farmers in almost all parts of the country. Its importance in the agricultural sector, not only as a food crop but also as basic feed in the production of poultry, beef cattle, and hogs, has led some observers to label maize cultivation Zambian agriculture. White varieties of maize are preferred, and most of the crop used domestically is ground into meal, although fresh maize is also eaten in many places as a vegetable.

Maize production (marketed quantity) increased from some 204,000 tons in 1964 to 677,000 tons in 1977, but substantial fluctuations in output occurred during this time. (The low was 135,000 tons in 1970 and the high 746,000 tons in 1976.) The government's goal after independence was national self-sufficiency in maize production. At the same time it had little interest in seeing the production of surplus maize for export continued by the predominantly European commercial sector, since much of this grain had to be sold abroad often at a loss to the government. As a countermeasure the official price for maize was reduced. The expected disincentive effect on commercial growers was not realized, however. The price reduction was more than offset by a concurrent shift of land by many expatriate farmers to maize growing—brought on by uncertainties among these farmers concerning their future and a desire for short-term gains with little investment, which maize production offered. This and the promotion of maize cultivation by Zambian farmers led by 1967 to a large national surplus that increased the following year. The government thereupon undertook a nationwide campaign to get farmers to grow other crops. In 1970 the harvest, which was affected by poor weather conditions as well as by government policy. was disastrously small, and a food crisis resulted that forced the import of large amounts of grain. In late 1970 the producer price for maize was increased, and further incentives to raise production were offered through subsidies for inputs such as fertilizer. Beginning in the 1974–75 growing season additional price raises were made, although in 1978 the price was still considered unrealistic by some producers. Production met domestic demand from 1972 through 1978, and in some years there were surpluses that were sold on an ad hoc basis to Angola, Tanzania, and Zaïre. Maize offers the opportunity to diversify Zambia's export trade, but as of early 1979 the government had failed to take steps to establish firm markets abroad to which production planning could be geared.

Cassava cultivation is largely restricted to northeastern Zambia, a belt across the northern part of the country below Zaïre, and the far western area. Where it is found, it is a major staple but often complementary to maize. The principal cultivators in northeastern and northern Zambia are traditional farmers practicing some form of *citemene* culture. Cassava is also a major crop among the fishing populations around lakes Bangweulu, Mweru, and Mweru Wantipa (see Land Use, Soils, and Land-Use Systems, this ch.). In western Zambia, where cultivation extends as far south as Sesheke District, cassava and maize are grown in roughly equal proportions. Cassava is usually consumed locally in the form of starch from the roots and as a leaf salad; commercialization is relatively minor.

Peanuts of local varieties are grown throughout the country primarily as a subsistence crop. In Eastern Province, however, a high-grade nut used in making confectionery is raised commercially—a substantial portion of this crop is exported—and improved varieties are available to farmers elsewhere for cash cropping for sale in the production of cooking oil. Cultivation is labor intensive, sown plots are usually small, and production is entirely a smallholder operation. Total output in the late 1970s did not meet the domestic requirement for processing into oil, and large amounts of peanuts had to be imported for that purpose. Government pricing policies had long discouraged increased production, but a significant raise in the purchase price was made in 1976, and another increase was made in 1977. Substantial increases in output

—aided in the 1976–77 season by favorable weather—were reported for 1977 and 1978.

A government agricultural census made in the crop year ended September 1970 reported output in shelled weight at 70,180 tons grown on approximately 161,000 hectares. In general, however, information was available only for sales made through official marketing agencies. These reached a high of almost 15,000 tons in 1967 but fluctuated markedly thereafter; sales in 1975 amounted only to some 3,600 tons. In 1978 the quantity marketed through government channels was about 7,500 tons.

Cotton cultivation was begun by European farmers in the 1920s and was taken up by African growers in the 1950s, but during the latter decade production practically ceased because of continuing pest problems. With the introduction of improved pesticides in the 1960s interest was renewed, especially among African smallholders. European commercial farmers, attracted by better returns from maize, stopped growing cotton in 1970, and smallholder output also declined. By 1974 the total marketed quantity was down to less than 2,200 tons of seed cotton, after having reached almost 12,700 tons in 1971. Price increases made by the government in 1975, 1976, and 1977 stimulated output, which reached almost 9,000 tons in the 1977–78 marketing season. More and more farmers were reported to be growing cotton, and production in 1978–79 was originally estimated to reach 12,000 tons. It was expected as of late 1978 to be only about 10,000 tons because of unfavorable weather, which had reduced the planted acreage. This would be somewhat short of the needs of Kafue Textiles, opened in 1970, and would apparently require some imports. Cotton ginneries were located at Lusaka and Chipata. Their total capacity of over 21,000 tons was adequate to meet Zambia's estimated seed cotton requirements through the mid-1980s. Cotton growing is carried on mainly on the plateau areas of Central, Eastern, and Southern provinces and to some extent in the Luangwa River Valley, where rainfall (which ordinarily does not exceed 1,000 millimeters annually), soil conditions, and adequate hours of sunlight are well suited to cotton cultivation.

At independence tobacco was the most important agricultural export. Flue-cured Virginia tobacco was the leading variety, but some Burley and Turkish (Oriental) tobaccos were also produced. Tobacco cultivation in Zambia has experienced wide fluctuations. In Eastern Province European settlers established a number of farms growing Virginia tobacco after World War II. In the early 1950s the price dropped drastically, and most of these farms had been given up by 1960. Virginia tobacco also became a major commercial crop on the line of rail in Southern and Central provinces, where it was completely in the hands of European growers, many of them from Rhodesia and South Africa. In 1964 production of the Virginia variety reached a high of almost 11 million kilograms. Line-of-rail tobacco had been sold through the market at

A small Tonga farm near the highway
Courtesy J. Jeffrey Hoover

Commercial farming
Courtesy ZIMCO

Irrigation at the Mazabuka Sugar Estates
Courtesy ZIMCO

Salisbury in Southern Rhodesia, but on the assumption that output would continue to increase, the newly independent Zambian government invested a substantial sum to construct a modern auction floor, warehouse, and processing plant in Lusaka. Expectations were not fulfilled, primarily because labor shortages and wage problems led many growers to shift to less labor-intensive crops. In 1970 marketed Virginia tobacco declined to a low of 4.8 million kilograms, and annual output through 1977 ranged mostly between about 5.5 million and 6.2 million kilograms. Excessive rainfall affected the 1978 crop, as did a further reported decline in the number of large-scale growers, and only 3.7 million kilograms were marketed during that year.

Soils and climatic conditions are favorable for the production of Virginia tobacco, and the government has endeavored to arouse African interest in growing this crop. The Tobacco Board of Zambia (TBZ)—a parastatal corporation set up in 1967 to manage the auction floor, warehouse, and processing plant and subsequently further charged with government development, extension, and training programs—has carried on a number of promotional schemes since the late 1960s. These included the so-called Tenant Scheme, under which leases were granted for relatively large-scale farms and substantial subsidies and other support provided, and the Assisted Tenant Scheme (aided by a 1970 loan from the World Bank—see Glossary), through which persons with experience were given extensive training and then were helped to grow tobacco—and maize—on their own farms on a commercial scale. In 1973 a further loan from the World Bank was granted for an integrated smallholder family farming project for tobacco and maize cultivation. TBZ also produced Virginia tobacco at its two training colleges at Mukonchi in Central Province and Popota in Southern Province. In 1974 these programs were reported to have accounted for almost two-thirds of total production.

Burley tobacco grows well in the red sandy clay loams of Eastern Province, where its cultivation first began about 1938; in the late 1970s the province remained the principal production center, accounting for an estimated over 95 percent of the total marketed crop. Burley is air cured and requires only simple handling facilities, so it is an excellent crop for smallholder cultivation. Burley output reached a peak of over 1.7 million kilograms in 1964, but declining prices, which hit a low in the 1966–67 marketing season, left only a few small-scale growers active. Since the end of the decade improved prices and government efforts through TBZ have brought renewed interest, but marketed output amounted to only 500,000 kilograms in 1975 and only 312,000 kilograms in 1977.

Turkish tobacco was an important source of cash income for many African smallholders in Central, Southern, Eastern, Northern, and Luapula provinces until the mid-1960s when world competition forced prices to decline and made production in Zambia uneconomic. Output, which totaled almost 300,000 kilograms in 1964, had practically ceased by the beginning of the 1970s.

Sugarcane is grown at the Nakambala Sugar Estate at Mazabuka in Southern Province. Located near the Kafue River, the estate is completely irrigated—a necessity because the area's average annual rainfall of 750 millimeters is far short of the requirement (2,000 millimeters a year) for growing sugarcane. The first experimental planting of cane was made in 1964, and the area had been expanded to some 2,000 hectares by 1968 when the associated raw sugar mill was opened. This mill furnished materials for a refinery at Ndola that had opened in 1960 using imported supplies. The estate has gradually been expanded further; in 1976 a loan was secured from the Commonwealth Development Corporation that permitted an increase in the area under sugarcane to over 11,000 hectares. Through the same loan the mill at Nakambala was to be expanded to produce 150,000 tons of raw sugar annually by about 1980. In the late 1970s Zambia was self-sufficient in sugar production, and there were suggestions that sugar might be exported; but domestic demand was continuing to rise at a rapid rate, and the government appeared hesitant to sell sugar abroad for the time being.

Bread and other products made from wheat flour have become staples for a large sector of the urban population, and the number of people using them has continued to grow. In the late 1970s domestic production of wheat was only a fraction of the requirement, and mounting foreign exchange expenditures were being made for importation. In 1977 some 125,000 tons of wheat, a quantity still short of the demand, were imported; domestic production totaled only 4,700 tons. Production reached 6,000 tons in 1978, but through July 1978 the import total had already reached 133,000 tons. The imported wheat long was sold to millers in the domestic market at a cost that would allow the sale of bread at a comparatively low price, in effect providing a substantial consumer subsidy that benefited only the already better off urban wage earner, essentially at the expense of the rural population. Economic problems after the mid-1970s, however, led to reduced subsidies, and substantial increases in the price of both flour and bread were made in the late 1970s.

Until the mid-1970s the wheat grown in Zambia was entirely under irrigation, successful cultivation having been found possible only during the dry season. At independence production amounted to about 2,500 tons annually, which met about one-seventh of the requirement. Low output per hectare and low fixed prices made cultivation uneconomical, and by 1968—when imports reached 60,000 tons—production had to all intents ceased. In 1969 government research services began successful experiments with higher-yield improved wheat varieties, and beginning in 1975 producer prices were also increased. In 1976 the Canadian International Development Agency began a three-year project near Livingstone—other areas were encompassed later—to grow rain-fed wheat. Yields were expected to be considerably lower than for irrigated wheat, but costs were also expected to be substantially less. The agency expressed confidence that with proper government support, given Zambia's abundance of land, self-sufficiency in wheat could be reached in fifteen or twenty years.

Rapidly rising demands for vegetable oils led to a drive in the 1970s for increased production of sunflower seeds. The response by both commercial and smallholder farmers was impressive; and marketed output rose from almost nil in 1970 to 16,000 tons in 1976 (about 13,300 tons in 1977). By 1977 production had reached such a point that the country's two major processors were unable to handle all available quantities, and during 1978 the National Agricultural Marketing Board (NAMBOARD), the official government purchasing agency, asked permission from the Ministry of Lands and Agriculture to export part of its sunflower seed holdings.

Tea and coffee have been produced for some time but both in relatively small quantities. In early 1979 the principal tea project was at Kawambwa in Luapula Province. It was run by the Rural Development Corporation, which also operated a tea factory opened at Kawambwa in October 1976. Plans existed for the gradual expansion of plantings, and it was hoped to meet the country's total requirement for tea by about the mid-1980s, but little information was available on progress toward that goal. Parts of northern Zambia are also suitable for arabica coffee cultivation, and some coffee has been produced there since the 1920s, but not enough to meet domestic demand. In December 1978 the International Development Association (IDA)—part of the World Bank Group (see Glossary)—provided a US$6 million credit to rehabilitate and develop coffee production at estates at Ngoli and Kateshi and to aid production by several hundred smallholders in Northern and North-Western provinces. Coffee processing, roasting, and packing facilities were also to be set up.

Livestock Raising and Dairy Farming

Although Zambia is considered to have the potential for self-sufficiency in beef production on the basis of its land resources and the size of the traditional herd, the availability of domestic beef in the commercial market fell far short of a demand that has increased steadily as the relative affluence of the urban areas has grown. Through 1975 beef imports made up between a third and a half of the beef supply. In early 1976, however, further imports were banned to save foreign exchange and also statedly to encourage domestic production. Since then what commercial producers have called unrealistic prices appear to have had an adverse effect; although some growth has occurred in the commercial sector, which in 1978 was said to have furnished 55 percent of the beef supply on the market, it has been relatively small. The situation has been compounded by failure to get the traditional sector to provide more animals for slaughtering. Much of this sector, which owns most of the country's cattle, has a relatively negative attitude toward any substantial animal offtake. This attitude was related to social considerations of status in part, but practical factors also played a significant role in the retention of cattle. Milk was an important food and possible source of cash. The family herd, in a sense, was also like a bank account that could be called on to make marriage payments and to pay school fees and possible debts. Cattle were also needed on occasion for slaughtering at wedding festivals and funeral ceremonies. Weighed against these advantages, the cost of maintaining the herd was comparatively slight. Thus there was an added disincentive to disposing of capital holdings solely for money unless, it has been suggested, other worthwhile investments could be secured in return—such as better housing, transportation equipment, and durable consumer goods —an alternative not yet available in early 1979.

The traditional herd was estimated roughly at between 1.6 and 1.9 million head in the mid-1970s—later data were unavailable. The offtake for the regular commercial market was believed to run about 4 percent a year. In addition somewhere between 40,-000 and 100,000 animals were slaughtered for local use. Commercial farmers had about 220,000 to 230,000 head. Estimated offtake annually ran about 15 to 17 percent—the Zambian Commercial Farmers Bureau set the figure at close to 25 percent in 1978. State ranches held about 45,000 head from thich the offtake approached that of the commercial operators. The first state farm was started in 1967, and eventually thirteen were set up, about half of them with assistance from a World Bank loan. In about 1975 ten were operational, but financial and management problems were reported. Little further information on their situation was available in early 1979.

Commercial slaughtering was carried out by the parastatal Cold Storage Board of Zambia (CSBZ), which bought animals on its own account and also processed animals for private buyers and butchers who sold their meat through private shops. CSBZ secured most of its animals from commercial producers, whereas private buyers obtained them mostly from the traditional sector. Until late 1976 when the government imposed controls on wholesale animal buying prices, private buyers had often offered higher prices to producers. Sales to private buyers by traditional farmers were also stimulated by immediate payment and better shipping arrangements than those offered by CSBZ, which was frequently accused of inefficiency and whose purchasing system appeared to have lost the confidence of traditional farmers.

Cattle raising is restricted to certain parts of the country by infestations of the tsetse fly. In some areas, for instance Northern Province, it is practiced only in a limited way because of the absence of a cattle-raising tradition. The largest numbers of cattle are found along the line of rail; the greatest concentration is in the southern part, where roughly two-fifths of the traditional herd is located. This southern section also has some commercial farms producing beef and dairy products. About a sixth of the traditional herd is in the central part of the line-of-rail zone, as are about half of the commercial producers of beef and most of the dairy farmers. The cattle population of the copperbelt is small. It was owned predominantly by commercial operators and provided products primarily to people engaged in the mining industry. In early 1979 Zambia's largest dairy—the Kafubu State Dairy—was located in the copperbelt.

A strong pastoral tradition associated with farming pursuits exists in the western tsetse-free areas of Zambia, where about one-quarter of the national herd is located. Feeding conditions in the region are unsatisfactory during the rainy season and—coupled with poor reproductive rates that were associated in part with large-scale use of milk for home consumption or for sale—resulted in a comparatively low animal offtake for commercial purposes. About one-tenth of the traditional cattle are in Eastern Province, but much of the province is infested with tsetse fly. Because of the tsetse fly cattle raising is quite restricted in northeastern Zambia as well, except in an area along the Tanzanian border. In the late 1970s few animals from the eastern and northeastern regions were slaughtered for the commercial market.

Dairy farming for the commercial market was concentrated along the line of rail, where production was largely in the hands of expatriate farmers. Growth of the demand for milk and milk products after independence has been estimated at almost 400 percent in the decade beginning in 1964. At the same time, however, low producer prices paid by the parastatal Dairy Produce Board (DPB), which had a virtual monopoly on the collection and distribution of milk, coupled with restrictions on the repatriation of earnings that led to reduced investment in the industry, resulted in a substantial drop in production. To make up the shortage, dried milk was imported and reconstituted. In the early 1970s reconstituted milk made up close to two-thirds of the annual milk sales of well over 30 million liters. In 1976 milk reconstituted from imported materials alone amounted to over 28 million liters, or some 74 percent of sales, compared with fresh milk sales of 9.6 million liters.

Information on the situation in the late 1970s was meager, but newspaper reports in late 1978 indicated that despite increases in milk prices in 1976 and 1977, low producer return with respect to increasingly costly input remained a major disincentive. The result was that more and more dairy farmers were giving up the business. In November 1978 the general manager of the DPB stated that an acute shortage of foreign exchange had prevented the importation of adequate packaging supplies and spare parts, thereby greatly reducing milk availability. He also noted that the country's farmers were providing less than a quarter of the total demand. The DPB hoped to establish eight regional collection depots during the Third National Development Plan period to improve local marketing of milk by producers. However, domestic observers remained of the opinion that price incentives were much more important if output was to be increased.

The traditional sector and the emergent farmer offered the potential for substantial increases in production. Milk collection from traditional farmers had been carried out experimentally by the DPB for a short period, but operations had apparently not been handled in such a way as to create trust among the farmers, and the outcome had been unsatisfactory. The proposed rural collection depots could help to establish a sound system and evoke better farmer response. In the case of the emergent farmer, the provision of adequate credit and extension and other services to those interested in entering the dairy business was believed by foreign analysts to offer good possibilities for raising milk output.

Forestry

The Zambian Forest Department has classified almost 55 percent of the country as forested. In the late 1970s some 67,000 square kilometers of this area, or about 9 percent, was contained in state forest reserves; a small additional amount was encompassed by communal reserved forests. Most of the country's forest is actually savanna woodland, more than half of which is of the kind known in eastern and southern Africa as miombo. Just about all woodlands have been cut over in the course of shifting cultivation and at present consist largely of secondary growth chiefly of value for firewood and poles. However, a large area of the miombo in northwestern Zambia has been exploited to provide timbers and rough lumber to the mines of the copperbelt. In late 1977 extensive deforestation because of steadily mounting demands for fuel was reported around Lusaka and Mongu (capital of Western Province), and a government source stated that by 1980 there would be insufficient trees in the vicinities of these urban centers to meet fuel needs if the current rate of cutting continued. A replanting program had reportedly begun at Lusaka.

A large area in southwestern Zambia has dry deciduous forest that is dominated by the commercially valuable Zambian teak and *mukwa* (a species of Pterocarpus). Exploitation of this area began in 1911 when a sawmill was established at Livingstone, in part to meet demands for railroad ties. In the late 1970s operations were centered on Mulobezi, northwest of Livingstone—the two connected by rail—and in the area of Sesheke. *Mukwa* forest is also found in parts of Eastern Province; some exploitation was reported in the mid-1970s, but later information was unavailable. Information on the low evergreen forest in western North-Western Province was also unavailable in early 1979.

Large plantations of exotic species for industrial use have been established in Copperbelt Province, where growing conditions are very favorable. The colonial government began plantings in 1962, and the program was continued by the independent government. By 1969 approximately 7,000 hectares of fast-growing pine and eucalyptus had been planted in the area of Kitwe and Ndola. Between 1969 and 1975 another 16,000 hectares were established in the same area, with substantial assistance through a loan from the World Bank. A second loan was given in 1977 that will aid in planting a further 17,500 hectares between 1978 and 1982; this program also includes replanting 2,000 hectares to be clearfelled during the five-year period for processing by local sawmills. By 1982 the area of industrial forest should reach about 40,000 hectares, and government plans call for the total to rise to 80,000 hectares or more before the end of the 1990s.

The annual wood requirement was estimated in the mid-1970s at about 5 million cubic meters of roundwood equivalent; the requirement was expected to rise to close to 5.7 million cubic meters by 1980. About 90 percent was produced locally and mostly used for fuel, and a relatively small amount was employed for poles. A large part of the remaining requirement (500,000 cubic meters) was imported, including about half of the needed sawtimber, all paper, and almost all panels. All phases of the domestic industry were in a very early stage of development in 1979. From domestic sources about a dozen sawmills produced support timbers and rough lumber for mines, powerline and similar poles (from planted tree stands), fenceposts, and the like. From Zambian teak and *mukwa* some railroad ties, wood for furniture, and materials for crates and packing boxes were also fabricated, but as of 1979 most of the materials for this group of products had to be imported. Woodworking was carried on by perhaps fifty enterprises making furniture, doors, prefabricated housing, and other wood products. As the plantation stands begin to mature, the establishment of a forest industrial complex, including a pulp and paper mill, would appear desirable. The government reportedly has plans for this, but full implementation will presumably depend in part on securing some measure of external financing.

Fisheries

Although Zambia is landlocked, fishing is an important industry engaged in by roughly 50,000 persons. About half of these are regular commercial fishermen, another quarter carry on fishing as a part-time commercial activity, and the remainder fish for subsistence only. The main sources of fish are a number of large lakes, including Tanganyika, Mweru, Mweru Wantipa, Bangweulu, and Kariba; the Luapula, Chambeshi, Luangwa, Kafue, and Zambezi rivers; the extensive floodplains of those rivers, except the Luangwa; and major swamps around Lake Mweru Wantipa, Lake Bangweulu—the latter swamp complex may be the largest in the world—and the Lukanga Swamp in central Zambia. In all these

A women's basket-fishing group, Lake Bangweulu
Courtesy ZIMCO

Lusaka market scene
Courtesy WORLD BANK PHOTO (Edwin G. Huffman)

185

areas provide about 152,000 hectares of fishing grounds. It was estimated that there were close to 2,000 fish ponds, but information on these was lacking.

Estimates of annual fish production varied. The Department of Fisheries, established as a separate entity in 1974, has estimated the total fish catch at between 29,000 and 32,000 tons in the late 1960s and at 35,000 to 38,000 tons from 1970 to 1974. Employing a new collection method, the total for 1975 was established at close to 57,500 tons. This figure excluded the catch at Lake Kariba (which has usually been under 2,000 tons), where fishing was disturbed by the hostilities with Southern Rhodesia (see The State of Emergency, ch. 5). The potential fish catch in Zambia from natural resources has been estimated at up to 100,000 tons a year, but experts have questioned the feasibility of attaining that figure and were of the opinion that considerable reliance on fish culture would be necessary to meet future production goals. Lake Tanganyika possessed good possibilities for a substantially increased catch through extension of fishing into deep water. The lake had, in addition to the usual small fishing boats, a number of steel-hulled, covered-deck craft up to about fifteen meters in length that were equipped with industrial gear and capable of operating in all kinds of weather. In practice, however, these vessels ordinarily fished only in the shallower waters along the lakeshore.

Only limited facilities existed for the handling and distribution of fresh and frozen fish, which accounted for about one-fifth of the marketed output. Commercial firms engaged in this activity included a private company located on Lake Tanganyika and Lake Fisheries of Zambia. The latter from 1974 to 1977 was a subsidiary of Zambia Industrial and Mining Corporation (ZIMCO). In 1977 the United National Independence Party (UNIP) arranged for its holding company, Zambia National Holdings Limited, to take over operations. (Legal transfer had not been completed by late 1978, however, because of failure to agree on the sale price.) The remaining four-fifths of the catch, dried either by sun or by smoke, was sold mainly by small traders. Fish were distributed mostly to the more affluent communities along the line of rail, and rural residents except in the vicinity of the fishing areas were able to secure fish only infrequently. A considerable amount of fish from the Luapula River and islands at the southern end of Lake Mweru was sold to neighboring Zaïre.

Problems faced by the industry in the late 1970s related to the remoteness of the fisheries from major markets and to the poorness of transportation and storage facilities, which resulted in spoilage of about a fifth of the catch. The government's pricing policy also needed reconsideration; maximum consumer prices for particular kinds of fish applied equally throughout the country without regard to transport costs, and producer prices continued to be held at a low level to benefit consumers. Efforts were also needed to provide suitable equipment and effective extension services to fishermen.

Mining

Mining has been the country's most important economic activity since the 1930s. Since 1964 the sector has been the chief source of foreign exchange for independent Zambia, and until the economic crisis that began in the mid-1970s it was the provider of a large part of the funds required for general economic development. The industry was the largest employer of wage labor; its roughly 64,600 employees in the quarter ended December 1976 constituted about 17.5 percent of all wage earners (see table 5, Appendix). Copper is by far the most important mineral, but there is also significant production of zinc, lead, cobalt, and coal (see table 6, Appendix). Other metallic minerals include gold and silver produced as by-products of copper (as is cobalt). Industrial minerals including gypsum, feldspar, fluorspar, kaolin, magnetite, and tin ore are mined in small quantities. Somewhat more important is the production of limestone and sulphur from pyrite. Extensive deposits of phosphates and of uranium ore have been reported. Iron ore deposits of various grades also exist, but the economic viability of mining this ore was still in question in the late 1970s. Emeralds are mined in the copperbelt region. A mixed company (government, 70 percent, foreign corporations, 30 percent) was formed in 1978 to expand exploitation of this gem by means that would include the training abroad of Zambians in cutting and polishing the stones.

Surface deposits of copper ores were found at the beginning of the 1900s in north-central Zambia. They were leached and unattractive by comparison with the rich copper ore deposits in the adjacent Katanga (present-day Shaba) region of Zaïre, and exploitation was on a small scale. In 1906 an important lead and zinc mine was opened at Kabwe (Broken Hill), about 160 kilometers south of the copperbelt, but mining remained relatively unimportant until the discovery in the late 1920s of huge subsurface copper ore deposits in the copperbelt. The discoveries were made in concessions granted by the British South Africa Company, holder of the mineral rights, to the highly capitalized Anglo American Corporation (AAC) of South Africa and to Roan Selection Trust (RST), a subsidiary of American Metal Climax of the United States. Development followed immediately, and the first major mines— Luanshya and Mufulira controlled by RST and Rhokana by AAC —opened in the early 1930s. Additional deposits were developed later (notably AAC's Nchanga mine, the country's largest) by operating companies under the domination of the two financial holding corporations, which at independence controlled all producing copper mines in Zambia. Beyond the economic effect, the opening of the mines brought a major change in the demography of Zambia by attracting large numbers of African workers from the rural areas and an accompanying influx of Europeans. Both groups settled near the mines and became the nuclei for new towns. Services multiplied, as did the number of new in-migrants, and by the 1950s the entire copperbelt had acquired much of its present-day broad urban character (see Population, ch. 2).

After independence the holdings of both AAC and RST were incorporated under Zambian law, those of AAC as Zambian Anglo American Limited (ZAMANGLO), while the holdings of RST retained their earlier name. Neither was affected by the Mulungushi Reforms of 1968—the government had rather regularly given assurances that the copper industry would not be nationalized. However, in August 1969 the government expressed its interest in acquiring 51 percent of the shares of both, which was effected in January 1970 through ZIMCO. RST was redesignated Roan Consolidated Mines (RCM), and ZAMANGLO became Nchanga Consolidated Copper Mines (NCCM); the government holding in NCCM was increased to 60 percent in 1978. Payment for the shares was at book value (US$296.5 million) in bonds—issued by ZIMCO and fully backed by the state—that were to be repaid (AAC in twelve years, RST in eight years) from dividends accruing to the government. Ten-year management and sales agreements with the two companies gave the minority shareholders continuing substantial control. In 1973 the government, arguing that the arrangements had worked financially against national interests, announced cancellation of the agreements, for which compensation was to be paid, and plans for immediate redemption of outstanding bonds. These actions were carried out in late 1974 and in 1975. Zambian managers took over control, although a considerable part of the expatriate staff engaged in financial and technical activities was kept on. To replace the marketing arrangement, the government established the Metal Marketing Corporation of Zambia (MEMACO) in September 1973 as the sole agent for all metals and minerals.

The preeminent position of mining, particularly of copper, in the economy is apparent in the sector's contribution to GDP, export earnings, and government revenue. In 1965 copper alone accounted for about 45 percent of GDP and 93 percent of the country's exports, and it provided 60 percent of government revenue. Over the longer period from independence to 1975 mining's average contribution in current prices to GDP was about 35 percent; it accounted for 95 percent of export earnings, and it furnished the government with 45 percent of its revenue. This situation was sharply altered by the drastic decline in world copper prices in late 1974 and 1975 and continuing low prices through 1977. (Some improvement in prices began in 1978.) During the 1974–78 period copper mining operations failed to increase output materially, and production costs rose steadily. In 1975 mining's contribution to GDP dropped to under 13 percent in current prices and in 1977 was only 12.6 percent. Mineral and metal

Plant area at Luanshya mine
Courtesy ZIMCO

Jackhammer drilling underground at Mufulira mine
Courtesy ZIMCO

exports continued to account for well over 90 percent of exports (close to 97 percent in 1977), but government revenue from this source dropped from 39 percent in 1974 to 13.3 percent in 1975, 2.6 percent in 1976, and zero in 1977, forcing recourse to deficit financing.

Copper production in the decade before independence rose from close to 346,000 tons in 1955 to 685,000 tons in 1965. Ups and downs have occurred since then, but in general output has stagnated at below the 700,000-ton level—1977 production was 660,-000 tons—whereas the Second National Development Plan had called for an increase to 900,000 tons in 1976. A number of factors helped to contribute to the disappointing performance. In September 1970 a major disaster at the Mufulira mine of RCM, then the world's second largest underground copper mine, resulted in a drop in production in 1971 to 80,000 tons, less than half the 1969 output of almost 174,000 tons. Although extensive efforts were made to restore production, it remained about 20 percent below the predisaster level in the late 1970s. The closing of the border with Southern Rhodesia in 1973, loss of use of the Benguela railroad, and difficulties associated with the Tanzania-Zambia Railway Authority (TAZARA) rail line to Dar es Salaam port also seriously affected the import of essential materials and spare parts, which was reflected in a loss in productivity because of equipment downtime. Further declines in productivity have occurred because of the increasing depth of operations. One of the principal causes of production stagnation, however, was a lack of foreign exchange to carry out expansion projects, which resulted from the inability to export copper rapidly. This factor was reflected in attainment of only about 85 percent of planned expenditures set by the second development plan.

Manufacturing

Zambia began its independent existence in 1964 with a very limited manufacturing establishment consisting of roughly 260 enterprises, mostly quite small, having a total work force of under 18,500. During Zambia's earlier membership in the Central African Federation of Rhodesia and Nyasaland most investment in the manufacturing sector had gone into Southern Rhodesia, and Zambia had been treated essentially as a primary market for Rhodesian manufactured goods. As independence approached, Zambia's own production met only about one-third of its domestic demand for manufactured goods. Consumer and intermediate products accounted for about three-quarters of the value added by the sector; the manufacture and processing of foods, beverages, textiles, wearing apparel, and tobacco made up half of the total.

Industrial development during the period 1965–70 was rapid, stimulated in part by the government's promotion of import-substitution enterprises and a growing consumer market and in part by efforts to reduce Rhodesian imports after the UDI. Some of the new manufacturing establishments were undertaken independently by foreign or local firms to take advantage of the more favorable domestic situation. Others were joint efforts of foreign concerns and the government; the latter also carried out a number of projects on its own. During the five-year period manufacturing production annually grew at a high rate of over 11 percent. The pace slowed thereafter to an average rate of under 5 percent a year. During the 1975–77 period manufacturing output declined by 11 percent. Various reasons for the decline have been suggested, the most likely being the detrimental effect of recurrent foreign exchange shortages on the import of primary and intermediate materials, equipment, and spare parts and a variety of problems arising from changes in Zambia's principal transportation routes. Both factors still seriously reduced the level of manufacturing production in early 1979.

At independence, aside from metal smelters and refineries, few large enterprises existed in the manufacturing sector. These enterprises included a sugar refinery that processed imported raw sugar, two breweries, a cement plant, and several metal products fabricating plants. Major installations since added to the sector include an oil refinery; glass, fertilizer, and mining explosives plants; a textile mill; plants making batteries, automobile tires, plastics, soap and toiletries, and pharmaceuticals; automobile and truck assembly plants; and several large food processing factories. In mid-1976 the sector had a total of 44,560 employees including 2,730 non-Zambians. Despite the diversification that has occurred, structural changes in value added by the manufacturing subsectors have not been particularly marked except for chemicals, petroleum, rubber, and plastic products, all of which grew almost threefold between 1965 and 1976, affected especially by the output of the petroleum refinery and the fertilizer and explosives plants. Food, beverages, tobacco, and textiles and wearing apparel continued to account for about one-half of value added in 1976, little different from 1965.

Direct government participation in the manufacturing sector is substantial. In 1979 the government had majority holdings in, or complete ownership of, almost all large manufacturing establishments. The primary vehicle through which this had been effected was the wholly government-owned Industrial Development Corporation of Zambia (INDECO), which was in 1979 a subholding company of ZIMCO. Large-scale government participation in manufacturing began essentially with the Mulungushi Reforms of 1968 when INDECO acquired, among other enterprises, a 51-percent interest in five manufacturing firms that were nationalized "by invitation" at that time. The government's takeover appeared based largely on the conclusion that the then almost entirely foreign- or expatriate-owned enterprises were concerned primarily with maximizing and repatriating profits and capital rather than with Zambia's economic development and the indigenization of staff.

In 1968 President Kaunda welcomed non-Zambian private industry, provided it was carried on for the good of the country. However, limits imposed on profit repatriation and restriction on areas of activity, as well as the rapid extension of state participation to the point of practically complete control of all large operations by the mid-1970s, raised a question concerning the actual scope and possibilities of foreign-sponsored private enterprise. The issue was largely clarified by the Industrial Development Act of 1977 (effective in October 1977). Aimed at attracting foreign investment, this act in effect affirms that Zambia has a mixed economy. It offered a ten-year guarantee of immunity from nationalization and provided for preferential treatment for investors who started so-called priority industries. These included enterprises manufacturing for export and using a maximum of domestic raw materials or fabricating such materials or intermediate goods for use by other Zambia-based industries; enterprises creating substantial permanent employment or fostering the development of domestic technology; and industries established in rural areas using local raw materials. The government also offered various tax incentives and more attractive terms with respect to profit and dividend repatriation.

Power Sources and Production

Electric Power

In early 1979 Zambia was self-sufficient in electrical power production, a situation that was expected to continue at least to the mid-1980s. In addition it possessed excellent sites on the Kafue, Luapula, and Zambezi rivers having hydroelectric potential that could meet anticipated national power needs well into the future. This favorable situation resulted largely from the government's continued determination after independence—and concern after Southern Rhodesia's UDI in 1965—to create domestic power facilities that would adequately meet the needs of an expanding economy and would at the same time eliminate dependency on the Kariba I (South) hydroelectric plant located in Southern Rhodesia. This facility, built during the period of the Central African Federation, provided about 70 percent of Zambian needs in the mid- and late 1960s. After dissolution of the federation in 1963 Zambia retained 50-percent ownership of the facility through the joint Zambia-Southern Rhodesia Central African Power Corporation (CAPC), newly established as the operational organization, but the Zambian economy was left largely at the mercy of future developments inside Southern Rhodesia.

At independence domestic power production facilities consisted principally of a number of small plants built in the 1920s and 1930s to supply the immediate needs of the mining industry; a small hydroelectric generating station serving the Victoria Falls area (from 1938); and a number of thermal units in a few other towns. After federation in 1953 a decision had been made to dam the Zambezi River and construct two major power facilities, one each on the south (Rhodesian) and the north (Zambian) banks of the new lake. The Kariba I plant on the south bank went into operation in 1960 with an installed capacity of 600,000 kilowatts (later increased to 705,000 kilowatts). From there transmission lines carried power to Lusaka and along the line of rail to the copperbelt. However, the breakup of the federation in 1963 delayed the proposed north bank facility, and the Rhodesian UDI in 1965 posed further difficulties.

In 1966 the Zambian government initiated a project to construct two additional plants at Victoria Falls, one of 60,000 kilowatts installed capacity (completed in 1969) and one of 40,000 kilowatts (completed in 1973). In 1967 a decision was reached to construct a major generating facility on the Kafue River that would have four turbines with a total installed capacity of 600,000 kilowatts. There had been strong support in Zambia for this project going back to the federation period, but federal authorities had overruled it in favor of Kariba. Financing for the Kafue scheme was sought from the World Bank but was turned down because the bank favored construction of a second plant at Lake Kariba, located on the north bank as called for in the original Kariba scheme. Funding was eventually secured from Yugoslavia, and a Yugoslav firm began construction in 1968; the facility was completed in late 1972. In 1973, in a change of position, the World Bank furnished a loan of US$115 million to cover foreign exchange costs for construction of a retaining dam upstream on the Kafue River and expansion of the Kafue generating facility through the addition of two more 150,000-kilowatt units; the latter were commissioned in mid-1977, raising installed capacity to 900,000 kilowatts.

The final major undertaking in power development to 1979 was the 600,000-kilowatt Kariba II (North) generating plant in 1970, assisted by a US$40 million loan from the World Bank; this was increased to US$82.1 million in 1974. The project had been scheduled for completion in 1974, but unexpected delays caused by geological problems and cost overruns led to withdrawal of the contractor in 1973 and takeover by a Yugoslav concern, which brought the power station into full operation in early 1977.

In 1979 the total installed capacity of the main hydroelectric generating facilities was over 1.6 million kilowatts. Another roughly 100,000 kilowatts was provided by gas turbine and thermal installations in the copperbelt. In addition there was an unknown amount of local capacity consisting of units in various provincial capitals and towns in other parts of Zambia. The main facilities were connected in a grid that was tied in to the power systems of Southern Rhodesia and Zaïre, to both of which countries surplus power was being exported in the late 1970s. Production in 1977 was almost 8.7 billion kilowatt-hours, of which 95.6 percent was generated by the units at Victoria Falls, Kariba II, and Kafue. Consumption estimates vary, but about three-quarters of total domestic consumption was in the copperbelt, mostly for the production of copper. In all, industry was believed to account for about 90 percent of total domestic use, commercial and home consumption for the remaining roughly 10 percent. A substantial amount of power was also exported (reported in the quarter April-June 1978 at 328 million kilowatt-hours).

Ownership of the Kafue and Victoria Falls generating plants was vested in the parastatal Zambia Electricity Supply Corporation (ZESCO) and of the Kariba II installation in the governmental Kariba North Bank Company (KNBC). However, the main transmission lines interconnecting these plants and the major distribution centers belonged to CAPC. ZESCO sold its entire output to CAPC, which then resold power to ZESCO and the Copperbelt Power Company for retail distribution over their own lines. In mid-1977 ZESCO took over complete distribution of its own power production and began paying CAPC a charge for transmission costs. Power from Kariba II passed over the same CAPC lines, but further information on relations between KNBC and CAPC was unavailable.

Self-sufficiency on a large scale in electric power production has not been accompanied by wide electrification. Most power services were concentrated in a zone roughly eighty kilometers wide along the line of rail from Livingstone to the upper copperbelt. Various towns outside the line of rail also had local power systems, some of them interconnected. In the late 1970s ZESCO carried out a major program, still under way in 1979, to extend several of these systems, construct additional power lines to nearby towns, and where feasible bring the systems into the central power grid. Over large areas, however, rural electrification was inhibited by the lack of permanence of many villages and settlements whose occupants practiced shifting cultivation and moved from time to time to new sites as soil fertility declined, erosion set in, or other factors stimulated a move. The low per capita income of subsistence farmers cultivating land on a semi-permanent basis and the potentially only slight demand for electricity among such groups were also deterrents to investment in service facilities. ZESCO has also pointed out another important factor inhibiting rural electrification: people who had retired and who had funds that would enable them to start small-scale power-using industries tended to settle along the line of rail rather than return to the rural areas, where available power supply was not fully used. In contrast, ZESCO had been unable through 1978 to provide connections to the power system for numerous potential users—especially emergent farmers along the line of rail—because of a great shortage of such materials as transformers and insulators, which ZESCO could not import because of difficulties in obtaining foreign exchange.

Petroleum

In early 1979 Zambia had no known petroleum or natural gas deposits. Until the Rhodesian UDI all petroleum products were secured from Southern Rhodesia, amounting in the year before the declaration to 146,000 tons. In conformity with UN-voted sanctions Zambia cut off oil imports from Southern Rhodesia after the UDI, introducing fuel rationing at the same time and turning to other transportation routes for supplies. Initially about two-thirds of the requirement, which had risen to 225,000 tons by 1968, was brought in over the then largely unpaved Great North Road, one-quarter over the Great East Road, and the remainder by the Benguela railroad from Lobito in Angola and an emergency airlift from Dar es Salaam (see Roads, this ch.). Meanwhile construction of a 1,710-kilometer pipeline from Dar es Salaam to Ndola—having a capacity of 760,000 tons a year—began in 1967 under a joint Zambia-Tanzania project financed by Italy. The first oil products reached Ndola in August 1968. In 1970 construction of a refinery at Ndola having a rated capacity of 1.1 million tons got under way; it went into operation in mid-1973. The capacity of the pipeline, which was switched to pumping crude oil, was raised to about 1.1 million tons during 1972 and 1973 through installation of an additional 780 kilometers of parallel pipe and some new pumping stations. Construction of part of the pipeline in Zambia appears to have been faulty; a considerable number of leaks were reported in 1978. TAZAMA Pipelines, the joint government owner (Zambia 67 percent, Tanzania 33 percent), stated that it intended to take legal action against the Italian builder. There was no indication to what extent the problem would affect oil supply to Zambia; information on demand in the late 1970s was also unavailable.

Coal

In the late 1970s Zambia appeared able to meet its annual coal requirements (estimated in 1977 at about 780,000 tons) through domestic production. The major problem, of some duration according to industry sources, was the inability of Zambia Railways to move supplies to consumers on time. The chief user of coal was the mining industry, but substantial amounts were also consumed in such industries as brewing, cement, and fertilizers. Zambia was long known to have large coal deposits, but until the mid-1960s all coal requirements were met by imports from mines at Wankie in Southern Rhodesia located not far south of Livingstone on the through rail line to the Zambian copperbelt. After the UDI exploitation of the hitherto ignored deposits was begun. A mine was opened in 1966 at Nkandabwe close to Lake Kariba in Southern Province. The coal was of poor quality, however, and production was gradually phased out after the start of a nearby second mine at Maamba in early 1968; this mine continued to be the prime producer in 1979. Coal from this wholly government-owned colliery was of considerably better grade but still required installation of a washing plant to raise its quality to the level needed in smelting copper. A screening plant was also built to size the coal.

Coal requirements through the late 1960s had been between 1 and 1.2 million tons annually, supplied almost entirely by the Wankie colliery. In 1972 domestic production reached 936,500 tons, and imports declined to about 10,000 tons. Since then the demand for coal has dropped, in part because of the conversion of some copper-smelting operations to oil. The expanding manufacturing sector has increased its use of coal, but this has only partially offset the decline in use by the mining industry. Lower overall economic activity after the mid-1970s had also probably contributed to reduced use. Information on the country's coal reserves was unavailable in early 1979. A survey of Maamba published in 1967 showed reserves in excess of 50 million tons at that time. In 1978 another deposit of about 21 million tons of good-grade coal was located in the same general area. Also in 1978 several very large deposits of good-quality coal, including coking coal, were found by a Romanian team in other parts of the country.

Transportation

Zambia since independence has been plagued in varying degrees by transportation problems. These problems have widely been attributed chiefly to the basic structure of the transportation system left by the colonial administration. The country's rail facilities at independence and its only major asphalted road—from the copperbelt to the border with Southern Rhodesia—were in fact extensions of the transportation system of Southern Rhodesia. At the time, however, the combined system rather adequately met the needs of the modern sector of the Zambian economy, which consisted predominantly of the copper mining industry in the northern part of the country and the commercial farming interests located along the line of rail. Supplementing this system was the export-import route, used chiefly by the copper industry, provided by a connecting rail line through Zaïre and Angola that ran to the Atlantic Ocean port of Lobito (see fig. 11).

Zambia's new leaders were understandably desirous of establishing alternative routes for the country's exports and imports as part of plans to develop an independent economy. The evolutionary development of new routes, however, was almost immediately interrupted by Southern Rhodesia's UDI and Zambia's political decision to comply with UN sanctions against that country. Although Zambia applied sanctions progressively and the Lobito rail route took up part of the new transportation requirements, immediate suspension of petroleum imports through Southern Rhodesia made it necessary to use—at much higher cost—the Great North Road to Tanzania and the Great East Road to Chipata and the Malawi border as import routes until 1968 when transportation of petroleum by pipeline from Dar es Salaam began (see Petroleum, this ch.). Substantial shipments of goods other than petroleum continued through Southern Rhodesia, however; during the 1970–72 period an average of one-half of all Zambian exports passed through Southern Rhodesia, and almost 70 percent of imports came from or through that country.

In early January 1973 the transportation situation became critical when Southern Rhodesia closed its border with Zambia to all Zambian goods traffic for reasons of security. A few days later it was announced that the shipment of Zambian copper to the Mozambique port of Beira would still be allowed, and at the end of January the blockade was lifted. However, the Zambian government, in large part for ideological reasons, decided to institute a permanent ban on use of Rhodesian transportation facilities. This ban held until October 1978 when the deterioration of the country's economic position and the immediate concern—that vital fertilizer would not arrive in time for the fall 1978 planting period —brought a rescinding of the ban with respect to specific items. In early 1979 there was no indication how long the renewed use of the Rhodesian transportation system might continue. However, there appeared to be pressure from various elements in the Zambian economy not only for continuation but also for a widening of the list of goods permitted to transit Southern Rhodesia.

At the time of reopening of the southern route in October 1978 the only available major transportation route was through Tanzania via the Chinese-financed and -constructed TAZARA rail line from Dar es Salaam—which began operating in late 1975—and the Tanzania-Zambia (TANZAM) highway, of which the Great North Road formed the Zambian section. In 1975 civil strife in Angola had closed the rail line to Lobito, and reopening of that line did not appear in the immediate offing in early 1979. The link to Malawi through the Great East Road was only of small help, and the same situation prevailed for the road links with Mozambique and Botswana.

The TAZARA line when opened had been expected to carry 1 million tons a year in each direction, a quantity that would have met most of Zambia's transportation needs. In 1977 and 1978 actual cargo movement was well below that target; exports in 1977 totaled 524,000 tons and imports 413,000 tons. The problem stemmed in part from the insufficient capacity of Dar es Salaam port. The major underlying factors, however, appeared to be a lack of spare parts, inadequate maintenance because of inexperienced personnel, and inadequate offloading storage space; the line's construction and its equipment entered little if at all into the problem. By 1978 a large number of freight cars and locomotives were laid up for repairs, and freight car turnaround time and

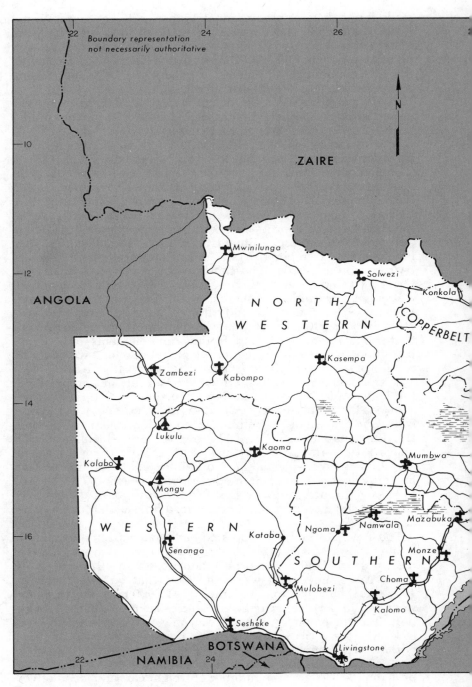

Figure 11. Transportation System

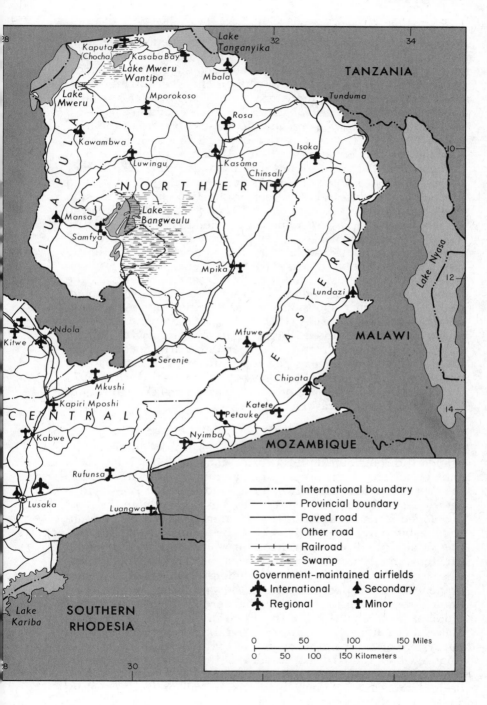

locomotive availability were far below planned performance. A regular training program for new staff was carried on, but many individuals in Zambia—soon after they had completed the course at the line's workshops at Mpika and acquired some practical experience—left for jobs in the copperbelt, where living conditions were considerably more attractive. This situation, as well as problems of goods security, had reached such a point in early 1978 that Chinese crews were recalled to assist in operating the line.

The TANZAM Highway carried between 25 and 30 percent of Zambian exports between 1970 and 1972 and roughly 15 to 18 percent of imports. The totals increased after the 1973 border closing to about a third of exports and a quarter of imports and reached highs of 45 and 35 percent respectively in 1975 as additional efforts were made to offset the closing of the railroad to Lobito. When the TAZARA line was opened to full traffic in 1976, a planned reduction in the use of the road took place, and by 1977 goods transported had declined to about one-fifth of exports and less than a quarter of imports. TAZARA's failure to meet expectations was followed by an attempt to increase shipments by the highway, but this had been relatively unsuccessful at least through mid-1978. Largely responsible was the condition of the vehicles of Zambia-Tanzania Road Services (ZTRS), whose operational fleet had dropped to only about 180 trucks from an original 520. Efforts to use private subcontractors had been only partly successful because of the difficulties experienced by many of the contractors, who were non-Zambians, in repatriating earnings. In mid-1978 ZTRS was reported to have ordered an additional 200 trucks, but further information was unavailable.

Railroads

The rail system consists of two main lines of 1.067-meter guage (standard throughout southern Africa) totaling about 1,960 route kilometers. The original trunkline running from Livingstone to the copperbelt was built between 1905 and 1909 (see The Colonial Interlude, ca. 1890–1964, ch. 1). This line runs through the most developed agricultural, industrial, and mining section of the country, inhabited by a substantial part of the population and the location of almost all of the principal urban centers, most of them situated directly on the railroad. This main rail segment totals close to 1,100 route kilometers, including a number of spurs and branches in the copperbelt serving the various mining centers, a branch from Livingstone northward to forest logging areas around Mulobezi and Kataba, and a spur built in the 1970s to serve the Maamba coal mine. At its northern end the line connects with the rail system of Zaïre and through that to the Benguela railroad in Angola, which affords direct access in normal times to the Atlantic Ocean. The southern terminus at Livingstone is connected by a bridge across the Zambezi River to the rail network covering Southern Rhodesia, South Africa, and Mozambique and giving access to the major ports of Beira and Maputo in Mozambique and East London and other ports in South Africa.

The second major segment of the rail system, approximately 860 kilometers long, is known as the TAZARA line and runs from Kapiri Mposhi in Central Province on the main north-south trunk-line to Tunduma in Northern Province on the Tanzanian border. From there the line continues for roughly another 1,000 kilometers through Tanzania to Dar es Salaam. After Zambian independence Zambia and Tanzania had sought external aid to construct a rail line linking the two countries. For various reasons, including a belief abroad that existing facilities were adequate, aid was not forthcoming. In 1967, however, the People's Republic of China (China)—apparently as part of an effort to expand its influence in Africa—agreed to finance, equip, and furnish substantial technical assistance for the undertaking. Work began in late 1970 in Tanzania and was generally completed on the system during 1975, although full-scale traffic did not commence until mid-1976. China also supplied locomotives and rolling stock and provided training for Zambian (and Tanzanian) operating staff.

The two systems are operated separately. The Livingstone-copperbelt line constitutes Zambia Railways, established in 1967 by separation from Rhodesia Railways. Subsequent operational and management problems led in 1970 to an agreement with Canadian National Railways to run the railroad. In 1975 control was returned to Zambian personnel, who in late 1978 constituted almost 98 percent of Zambia Railways staff. The country's overall foreign exchange shortage of the late 1970s has affected operations; a report in 1978 stated that only between forty and fifty of a total of seventy-five locomotives were in use, primarily because of the lack of spare parts. Lubricating oil shortages were also laying up locomotives, and at one time during the year eleven engines were inoperable because of oil unavailability. The railroad was also seriously in need of additional rolling stock. The TAZARA line, owned equally by the Zambian and Tanzanian governments, is operated by TAZARA and has its headquarters in Lusaka.

Roads

At independence the road system was oriented toward the south; the main asphalted road ran from the copperbelt through Lusaka to Livingstone, where it tied into the Rhodesian network. Elsewhere, from Kapiri Mposhi the Great North Road ran northeast roughly 820 kilometers to the Tanzanian border, but much of this road had never been permanently surfaced. Its poor condition was apparent from the description "hell run" given to it after the UDI in 1965 made it a major import route from Dar es Salaam. The other through road was the Great East Road, close to 600 kilometers in length, from Lusaka to Chipata. A connection ran from Chipata to a road in Malawi that continued on to Salima, terminus of the Malawi railroad system. This road was of some economic significance and was in better shape, being partly asphalted and partly gravel-surfaced. Otherwise, outside the line of rail in 1964 roads connecting the country's widely scattered towns were generally poor. Probably no more than 20 percent of them had any kind of semipermanent surface, and the remainder were unsurfaced and in many cases little more than trails.

After the UDI an emergency program, aided by international help that included loans in 1966 and 1968 totaling US$23.7 million from the World Bank, resulted in the upgrading and asphalting of the Great North Road (similar work being carried out in Tanzania) and the Great East Road. Both projects were generally completed by the end of 1970. Major improvements to the internal network included upgrading and asphalting of the 550-kilometer road from Lusaka to Mongu, capital of Western Province, financed by China and completed in 1973. The road from Livingstone to Sesheke was also paved. This road connected at Kazungula with an improved road in Botswana leading to Francistown, thereby permitting bypassing Southern Rhodesia for imports from South Africa. In 1978 work was started on a replacement all-weather road from Katete on the Great East Road to the Mozambique border. In 1977 Zambia had given Mozambique a loan to improve the dirt road, passable only in dry weather, that ran from the railhead at Tete to the border connection. Elsewhere the paving and improvement program had connected seven of the eight provincial capitals by asphalted roads to Lusaka, and work was under way in 1978 on the final road to Mansa.

The latest available report on roads showed 4,456 kilometers asphalted at the end of 1974. Reports of substantial progress on paving since then indicated that asphalted roads probably totaled 5,000 kilometers or more by the end of 1978. These constituted roughly one-seventh of the road system of about 35,500 kilometers (1974). Gravel roads at the end of 1974 amounted to about 7,500 kilometers, and unimproved roads totaled another 23,500 kilometers; maintenance of 16,500 kilometers of the latter was the responsibility of rural local authorities.

The size of the transport fleet was unknown in early 1979. It was reported at almost 133,000 in 1974, of which about three-fifths were passenger vehicles and the remainder commercial vehicles including trucks. New registrations during the first half of the 1970s were averaging about 14,000 a year (13,500 in 1975), but this dropped sharply in 1976 and again in 1977 as foreign exchange shortages developed; in 1977 new vehicles totaled less than 5,400, of which roughly half were commercial vehicles and trucks or construction and work equipment. Complaints of shortages were widespread in the late 1970s. In early 1978 a member of the government stated that of approximately 12,570 vehicles in the government fleet some 4,650 were laid up awaiting repairs. In part this was due to age, but the chief reason was that delays in foreign exchange allocations had held up procurement of spare

A typical Zambian National Bus Company vehicle
Courtesy J. Jeffrey Hoover

Oxcart at rest stop
Courtesy J. Jeffrey Hoover

parts. A considerable number of vehicles were said to be beyond repair, and government shops were cannibalizing these to keep other transport on the road. A locally serious and apparently typical case was the report from Mwinilunga District in North-Western Province of the layup of the local government's entire fleet of eight vehicles primarily because of a lack of repair parts. These vehicles constituted the transport system of the district, and their inoperability had caused considerable hardship for the area's rural community.

Civil Aviation

Air transport, both domestic and international, was furnished by the government-owned Zambia Airways. Several major international and African national airlines also had flights to Zambia. The national airline was formed in December 1967 when Southern Rhodesia-based Central African Airways, which provided air services to the three former members of the federation, split up. The new airline was managed under contract by Alitalia until December 1974 when Zambia Airways took full control. Zambianization of personnel has been pushed, and about 80 percent of operational staff were reported to be Zambian in 1978, including three internationally qualified pilots. However, the airline remained dependent on expatriate senior staff, and in 1978 the resignations of a number of expatriate pilots because of low take-home pay and poor conditions of service forced arrangements for secondment of pilots and first officers—obtained from Qantas and Air India—to prevent a major cutback in operations. The airline's international operations, which included flights in Africa to adjacent Botswana, Mozambique, Malawi, and Tanzania and to Kenya, Mauritius, and Swaziland as well as flights to Cyprus, Belgrade, Rome, Moscow, Frankfurt, and London in Europe were reported to be financially profitable in the late 1970s. In contrast, domestic operations suffered substantial losses as the result of government policy to furnish services to the rural areas at low cost to the consumer; substantial increases in domestic fares were introduced in January 1979, however. Losses had been made up in part through government subsidy, but this practice was discontinued in 1978 in a general withdrawal of subsidies to parastatal corporations.

There were some 120 to 130 airfields widely distributed throughout the country. About fifty of these were maintained by the government, the remainder by the private sector. In 1979 the sole international airport was at Lusaka. Commissioned in 1967, this airport had facilities to handle all modern aircraft and accounted for the bulk of passenger and plane movements. Regional airports of some significance were located at Ndola and Livingstone, and there were about ten airfields classified as secondary at more important towns. Zambia Airway's domestic service was reported to cover nineteen population centers in the mid-1970s. In addition various charter services, based principally in Lusaka and in the copperbelt, were furnished by light planes operated by a number of private companies. Zambia also had a Flying Doctor Service that operated out of Ndola, and there were a number of flying clubs. All nonscheduled flights were banned in October 1978 after raids on camps of the Zimbabwe African People's Union (ZAPU) in Zambia by aircraft from Southern Rhodesia. There was no indication in early 1979 how long this ban would last.

Balance of Payments and Foreign Trade

Balance of Payments

Copper dominated Zambia's export trade from independence through 1978, in every year accounting for more than 90 percent of exports by value, and there was little in early 1979 to indicate that this situation would not continue in the foreseeable future. Notably, however, during this time the annual production of copper and copper sales remained roughly the same. The result was that world copper prices became the major determining factor in the country's foreign exchange earnings.

From 1965 to 1970 copper prices were generally good, and trade surpluses annually exceeded K100 million (for value of the kwacha—see Glossary), except in 1967; the terms of trade also remained favorable during this period. The erratic nature of copper prices after 1971, however, resulted in fluctuating trade balances that, except in 1973 and 1974, were on average considerably less satisfactory. Through 1978 these factors—coupled with deteriorating terms of trade and growing services payments and private transfers—had an unfavorable effect on current account balances that was reflected in a deterioration of the overall balance-of-payments position (see table 7, Appendix).

The worldwide economic recession of 1971 and 1972 was reflected in greatly reduced trade balances as receipts declined, whereas import expenditures continued to rise. The removal of restrictions in early 1970 on the repatriation of profits contributed to high net transfers during the two years, and the current account balance registered large deficits. Net capital inflow was insufficient to cover these deficits, and a major drawdown on foreign exchange holdings was necessary. Copper prices rose again by 1973 and held at a high level until mid-1974. Foreign exchange receipts increased dramatically and, accompanied by restraints on imports, resulted in positive trade balances (above K395 million in both years). However, closure of the border with Southern Rhodesia in 1973 and efforts to use other transportation routes greatly increased freight and insurance costs, and net transfers continued high. A UN mission, assessing the economic situation in 1978, noted that few developing countries had services and transfer payments constituting such a high proportion of foreign exchange earnings.

Beginning in 1975 the country's financial situation deteriorated rapidly. Closure of the Benguela railroad, congestion at the port of Dar es Salaam, and some cutback in copper exports in agreement with other members of the Intergovernmental Council of Copper Exporting Countries (usually known as Conseil Inter-gouvernemental des Pays Exportateurs de Cuivre—CIPEC)—in addition to the low price of copper—resulted in a large drop in sales and receipts. At the same time the effects of the world oil crisis were reflected in higher overall import costs, and in 1975 the trade balance was negative for the first time since 1964. The current account balance was in deficit by K438.3 million and the overall balance of payments by K250 million. Although foreign exchange receipts improved in 1976 (aided by larger sales and a 20-percent devaluation of the kwacha) and 1977 and the trade balance registered surpluses, the deficit on net invisibles rose. Preliminary current account balance figures show further deficits of over K148 million in 1976 and almost K258 million in 1977; balance-of-payments deficits were K136.2 million and K223.5 million respectively. Net capital inflows were insufficient to cover these, and most of the deficits have been met by a drawdown on foreign exchange reserves (which stood at K56 million at the end of 1977, or the equivalent of approximately one month's imports), by the accumulation of arrears in private remittances, and by a large accumulation of arrears in payments for imports (totaling K363 million at the end of 1977). The severe foreign exchange shortage was felt in heavy cutbacks in the import of needed spare parts, raw materials, and intermediate goods. These cutbacks resulted in idle capacity in the productive sectors and contributed to a decline of an estimated 2 percent in real GDP in the three-year period.

Foreign Trade

Excluding copper, exports consisted of very small quantities by value of zinc, lead, and cobalt and equally small amounts of maize, tobacco, and miscellaneous goods. No significant change in composition had occurred between 1965, when copper accounted for 91.5 percent of the value of domestic exports and maize and tobacco together for 1.8 percent, and 1977, when the proportions were 91.4 percent and 1.3 percent respectively (see table 8, Appendix).

Dependence on imports for many essential consumer goods, machinery and equipment, and raw and intermediate goods for production use continued high in 1978; there had been only a few changes in composition since independence. By value machinery and transport equipment were the largest category, followed by manufactured goods classified by materials, electricity and mineral fuels, and chemicals (see table 9, Appendix). Some changes in percentage shares of the categories in real terms occurred during this time. Increased domestic production of beverages and tobacco products utilizing local materials resulted in a considerable proportional decline in imports. Likewise, although absolute expenditure for petroleum and petroleum products increased markedly from 1974 after world prices for petroleum rose, operation of the Kariba II and Kafue hydroelectric plants and self-sufficiency in the production of coal brought a decline in real terms in the percentage share of electricity and mineral fuel imports. Only chemicals registered a significant growth, from an average annual percentage share of 7.3 percent during the 1966–70 period to 11.1 percent during 1971–75.

At independence the principal countries of destination for exports, basically copper, were the United Kingdom, members of the European Economic Community (EEC—also known as the Common Market), and Japan. South Africa took important quantities of copper, and that country and Southern Rhodesia were the main destinations for Zambia's other exports. By the late 1970s Japan had become the largest market, and Great Britain and the Federal Republic of Germany (West Germany) were purchasing only slightly less (see table 10, Appendix). China had also been the destination for sizable amounts of copper since the end of the 1960s. The United States has usually made only relatively small purchases from Zambia but in both 1976 and 1977 bought large amounts of copper. Exports to Southern Rhodesia declined drastically after Zambia opened its own tobacco auction facilities in the mid-1960s. Exports to South Africa also declined as efforts to reduce trade with that country gradually became effective; the amount dropped substantially further after Zambia's decision in 1973 not to use the southern rail route through Southern Rhodesia.

Southern Rhodesia was the principal supplier at independence, accounting for about two-fifths of total imports. South Africa was next, furnishing about 21 percent, and the United Kingdom provided 17 percent. After the UDI in 1965 and the gradual application of sanctions by Zambia, South Africa took over as principal supplier, in part because of connections during the colonial period of Zambian firms with Rhodesian businesses that had been subsidiaries of South African enterprises. Zambia actively sought to diversify its sources of supply, and by 1967 important quantities of imports came from the EEC, United States, and Japan. South Africa, however, remained a major supplier, although a significant drop in imports from that country occurred after closure of the Zambia-Southern Rhodesia border in 1973. Reopening of the rail line through Southern Rhodesia to South Africa in October 1978 was followed by additional imports of South African goods that, if Zambian newspaper accounts were an indication, could result gradually in an increase in the South Africa total. After the UDI imports from Southern Rhodesia continued to consist largely of coal and electric power, but they were cut off completely after closure of the border in 1973.

By 1970 the United Kingdom had assumed first place as supplier, a position it continued to hold in 1977. South Africa was second, and the EEC was third; West Germany provided the largest country share of the EEC total. The United States was fourth and Japan fifth. The EEC moved into second place in the early 1970s and remained Zambia's second largest supplier in 1977. During this time the European Free Trade Association also became an increasingly important source of imports (see table 11, Appendix). Imports from China grew in the mid-1970s as the result of an agreement whereby proceeds in Zambian currency were used to defray local costs in the construction of the TAZARA rail line. They had reached a high in 1974 but tapered off by 1976, although it appeared very likely that Chinese consumer goods would continue to be imported in important quantities, since many items had been found quite competitive in price and were reportedly of better quality than goods from some other sources.

External Aid and Debt

More than a dozen countries had provided loans or made grants to Zambia on a bilateral basis through 1978. The largest amount had been furnished by China chiefly in connection with its funding of the construction and equipping of the TAZARA railroad. Significant assistance in loans had also been given by Canada, Japan, the Scandinavian countries (including Finland), the United Kingdom, the United States, and West Germany. Loans from the East European communist states had been furnished mainly by the Soviet Union and Romania. A large amount of multilateral funds had also been secured, mostly from the World Bank and the IDA.

At the end of 1977 the total disbursed debt outstanding amounted to US$1,379.7 million, which was equal to 59 percent of the estimated gross national product (GNP—see Glossary) that year. In 1965 the total debt had been under US$155 million. In the next several years surpluses generated by copper receipts met a considerable part of fund requirements for development, and external borrowing increased only moderately; the external debt reached US$246.6 million in 1969. The debt more than doubled to almost US$548 in 1970, largely stemming from the Chinese funding of the TAZARA rail line, but then it continued relatively stable until 1974 when it reached US$762.2 million, partly due to a large loan obtained in Eurodollars to redeem outstanding bonds issued earlier in the acquisition of the country's two major copper operations (see Mining, this ch.). However, between 1975 and 1977 the external debt grew rapidly as measures were taken to meet the effects of the financial crisis, including external borrowing from both bilateral and multilateral sources and a large increase in debt to private creditors.

Bilateral loans outstanding at the end of 1977 were US$480.9 million, or close to 35 percent of total external debt, and loans owed multilateral bodies were an additional US$309.8 million, somewhat over 22 percent of the total. The largest amount was due private creditors—US$589 million, or close to 43 percent—of which supplier credits accounted for one-third and private financial institutions most of the remainder. Total debt service in 1976 was US$112.7 million, and the debt service ratio to exports was 8.9 percent. Debt service payments in 1977 amounted to US$180.7 million, equivalent to more than one-quarter of export earnings.

National Budget

A marked shift in the sources of government recurrent revenue occurred in the mid-1970s as the government took positive steps to offset the loss of mining revenues through substantially higher personal and company income taxes, increases in the taxes on wages of expatriates, and increases in customs duties and excise and sales taxes (sales taxes were raised chiefly on luxury goods). In fiscal year (FY—see Glossary) 1965–66 mining revenues had made up over three-fifths of government recurrent revenue, whereas income taxes accounted for only about one-tenth. Customs duties and excise and sales taxes combined provided less than 12 percent of revenue. Based on the recommendations of the 1964 UN survey mission, the government gradually introduced increases in nonmining taxes that raised the share of income taxes in particular in total revenue. Through 1970 the amount provided by mining revenues continued only slightly reduced, but it declined substantially between 1971 and 1973 during a period of low copper prices. They recovered in 1974, furnishing over one-half of government recurrent revenue, only to drop drastically thereafter to virtually nil in 1977 (see table 12, Appendix). No contribution to revenue was anticipated in 1978. As mining revenues declined, income tax, customs duties, and excise and sales taxes increased their shares proportionally—income taxes from 18 percent in 1974 to 38 percent in 1977 and custom duties and excise and sales taxes from under 23 percent to over 48 percent. Significantly, both grew substantially in absolute terms, thereby maintaining recurrent revenue at or close to earlier levels and preventing a possibly serious impairment of public sector operations.

Recurrent expenditure from FY 1965–66 to FY 1975 grew at an average annual rate of between 15 and 16 percent. From 1975 the restraints imposed by the economic crisis—which included stricter control of ministerial outlays to prevent overspending, reductions in subsidy payments for basic foods and fertilizer, and the freezing of government wages—resulted in a decrease in the rate to slightly over 4 percent between 1975 and 1977. This comparatively moderate expansion was necessitated by increases in debt service payments, larger expenditure on defense, and the higher prices paid by the government for goods and materials. The rate of growth was below that of prices and represented a decline in recurrent expenditure in real terms. The decline was reflected in cutbacks in government services—including those for education and health—and in services related to the productive sectors, such as agricultural extension and the upkeep of the road system. The budget for 1978, which was characterized by the minister of finance as the toughest since independence, projected an overall decrease in recurrent expenditure of 2 percent during the year. Measures to bring about the decrease included further cuts in subsidies; postponement of all new projects not directly productive; and a freeze on government jobs, including vacant positions in the administrative and professional categories.

Rising revenue between FY 1965–66 and FY 1970 outpaced the increase in recurrent expenditure and furnished the government with substantial savings that were applied to capital expenditure. The erratic nature of copper prices from 1971, however—largely on the downside while recurrent expenditure continued to climb —resulted in recurrent budget deficits from 1971 through 1977 (with the exception of 1974) and lower levels of government capital expenditure, which declined in real terms as a percentage of gross fixed capital formation from roughly one-half in the five-year period immediately after independence to somewhat more than one-third between 1971 and 1976. Since 1975 the government has made an effort to relate the size of recurrent expenditure chiefly to receipts from income, excise, and sales taxes and customs duties. A continuation of this policy would hold the promise of a return to relatively sustained government savings as copper prices improved.

Income Distribution, Wages, and Prices

In the late 1970s urban average annual per capita incomes were estimated to be well over three times those in the rural sector. Late detailed data were unavailable, but some indication of the large disparities in income between the urban and rural sectors and between groups within urban and rural areas was provided by a government survey in the early 1970s. At the time the average annual income of urban households was over K1,400, whereas rural households averaged under K350; more than 70 percent of rural households had incomes under K360, compared with 14 percent of urban households. In the rural sector close to 8 percent, which presumably consisted mostly of emergent farmers, had average incomes of almost K1,370, more than ten times the average income of the some 24 percent in the lowest rural group (K0.0 to K180 per year). In urban areas the disparity between the top and bottom groups was even more pronounced, average incomes of the more than 17 percent of urban households in the high-income category (K1,800 and over) being nineteen times those in the bottom income group.

The annual average earnings of Zambian employees in the monetized economy varied substantially by industrial sector, and similar variations were found for non-Zambians, although the differences were generally less. The most pronounced disparities were those between Zambian and non-Zambian employees, and the latter were still numerous in 1978 (see table 13, Appendix). Since independence zambianization has brought greater equalization in pay for comparable positions, but average Zambian earnings continued to be substantially smaller because Zambian personnel mainly occupied jobs that were paid less, whereas non-Zambian staff usually held higher-level positions involving administrative, managerial, and professional and technical duties. This situation stemmed initially from the extreme shortage of trained Zambians at independence, attributed to the failure of the colonial administration to promote secondary and higher education for the indigenous population. The growth of the economy since independence, including the emphasis on industrialization and expansion of the transport infrastructure, has greatly increased the requirement for skilled personnel. Heavy expenditure on the educational system had increased the number of trained individuals by the mid-1970s, but lack of experience remained a constraining factor in their effectiveness, and there was continued heavy reliance on expatriates in the late 1970s (see Education, ch. 2).

Pressures for wage increases were strong after independence, backed by the well-entrenched trade unions spearheaded by the Zambia Mine Workers' Union, whose origins went back to 1949 (see Colonial Office Protectorate, 1924–53, ch. 1). Through 1969 the wages of indigenous workers grew at a rate of about 15 percent a year and those of expatriates at about 8 percent. In both cases the rises were greater than productivity gains. During this time prices rose on average only about 5 percent a year, resulting in increased consumption and pressure for greater imports. The 1964 Seers Report, based on a survey by a combined UN, Economic Commission for Africa, and FAO mission, had warned that independent Zambia would have a choice between higher wages and higher employment but that the economy could not support both. In 1969, concerned over rapidly growing wages, the government took steps to hold wage increases to productivity gains with a maximum allowable rise of 5 percent in any case. From 1970 to 1975 wages of indigenous workers grew at somewhat under that figure and those of expatriates slightly above it. Prices rose at a higher rate, however, averaging between 7.2 and 7.4 percent for low- and high-income groups respectively and in 1975 reached an average of 10 percent for both groups. Government wages were increased in 1975 on a sliding scale for an average of 20 percent; they remained frozen from 1975 to 1978. Those of mining workers were raised by 7 to 20 percent, and a further increase of 12 percent was made in 1976.

After 1975 government budgetary deficits, domestic borrowing, and reductions in consumer goods subsidies (resulting in higher consumer goods prices) increased inflation, and prices grew by 19 percent in 1976 and by close to 20 percent in 1977. In 1978 the government permitted a new wage increase of 5 percent for all employees except those in the public sector, whose wages remained frozen. This policy of wage restraint and the subsidy cuts planned for 1978–80—which would effectively increase prices for consumer items and, it was hoped, discourage buying—were expected to reduce inflationary pressures materially. These measures primarily affect the urban population, which the government had long tended to favor because of its political importance. The magnitude of the economic crisis of the mid- and late 1970s, however, finally forced a coming to grips with this problem, which, if left unresolved, had the potential to weaken seriously the entire recovery effort.

*   *   *

A wide range of recent statistical data on the economy is available in the *Monthly Digest of Statistics* published regularly by Zambia's Central Statistical Office. Another useful source of data is the annual report of the Bank of Zambia. Some ministries and departments of the government also issue annual reports, but in the late 1970s the information presented appeared mostly to cover periods from some time before the publication date. Of particular sectoral interest is *Land Use in Zambia* by Jürgen Schultz, which presents a highly informative analysis of the traditional land use systems found in different parts of the country. Robert H. Bates offers a thoughtful but provocative discussion of the interplay of rural and urban economic and political forces in his *Rural Responses to Industrialization: A Study of Village Zambia.* Richard L. Sklar in *Corporate Power in an African State: The Impact of Multinational Mining Companies in Zambia* examines the political impact that multinational mining companies have had on the Zambian economy and the actions of the Zambian leadership (to 1974) to direct the operation of the mining industry toward benefiting Zambians. An account of the takeover of that industry by the government is tellingly described in Anthony Martin's *Minding Their Own Business: Zambia's Struggle Against Western Control.* The UN Economic and Social Council offers a brief but highly informative overview of the economic situation in 1978 in *Assistance to Zambia,* published in late 1978. (For further information see Bibliography.)

Chapter 5. National Security

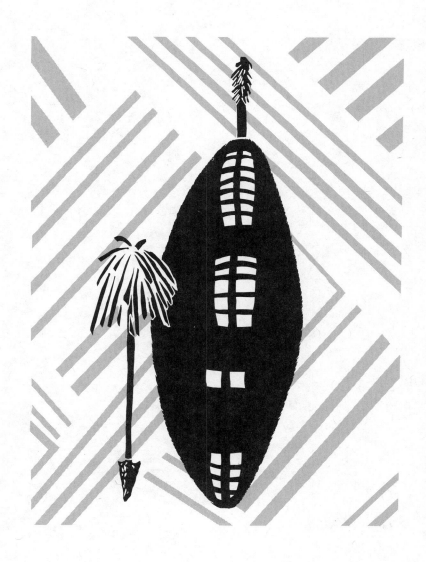

Ngoni shield and spear

NATIONAL SECURITY HAS been one of President Kenneth Kaunda's foremost concerns since his country gained its independence in 1964. Landlocked Zambia is bordered by Angola, Zaïre, Tanzania, Malawi, Mozambique, Southern Rhodesia, Botswana, and Namibia (South-West Africa). At the time of independence Zambian authorities considered that four neighboring countries were at best unfriendly and at worst hostile. The four were Angola and Mozambique, then under Portuguese rule; Namibia, under the control of South Africa; and Southern Rhodesia, whose white regime issued its Unilateral Declaration of Independence (UDI) from the United Kingdom in 1965.

The departure of Portugal from Africa in the mid-1970s eased tensions on the Mozambique border, but trouble on the Angola border continued until after the end of the civil war in that country. In the meantime Zambia had allowed Joshua Nkomo to establish training camps and staging areas for guerrilla forces from which they could attack Southern Rhodesia. Nkomo was the leader of the Zimbabwe African People's Union (ZAPU), one of the factions trying to free Southern Rhodesia from the Ian Smith regime. Other guerrilla forces, those of the South-West African People's Organization (SWAPO), in trying to wrest control of Namibia, freely used sanctuaries in southern Zambia, bringing confrontations between South African and Zambian forces. The greatest danger, however, came from Rhodesian attacks against Nkomo's camps.

Kaunda is the constitutional commander in chief of the Zambia National Defense Force (ZNDF), which consists of the Zambia Army and the Zambia Air Force. He is also titular head of the Zambia Police Force, which in early 1979 included two paramilitary organizations. The mission of the ZNDF is the defense of the national territory and the preservation of the country's sovereignty. The police preserve the peace and maintain public order. The military forces are expected to reinforce the police in the event of a major internal threat; the police, particularly the paramilitary units, assist the military against external threats. In early 1978 the International Institute of Strategic Studies estimated ZNDF strength at 14,300—12,800 in the army and 1,500 in the air force.

Kaunda has not made himself a military chieftain either in title or in fact. He relies on his top military commanders for day-to-day operations of the forces and is assisted and advised by the top military command in addition to a civilian defense staff. The president, of course, retains operational control of the military; that is, he is the ultimate decisionmaker who would order the armed forces into combat if that became necessary. At times Kaunda has acted as his own minister of defense, e.g., in 1978, but because of the pressures of what was almost a state of war between Zambia and Southern Rhodesia, the post of secretary of state for defense and security was created in September 1978 to absorb some of the burden borne by the president.

The state of readiness of the ZNDF at the beginning of 1979 was difficult to ascertain because little is published about the military or about defense matters in general. In 1970 Kaunda's government pushed through the National Assembly a constitutional amendment that prohibited the publication of information concerning defense expenditures. In the interim that official policy of secrecy has carried over into all aspects of the military, and references to defense affairs in the country's news media have been infrequent. Early in 1978 when Rhodesian forces attacked Luangwa, about 225 kilometers east of Lusaka, newspapers in the capital gave only brief reports of the raids, stating that the enemy had been repulsed by the ZNDF and that some enemy aircraft had been shot down. In the October and November raids the targets were only twelve kilometers from the capital, and the Zambians could conclude for themselves from the Rhodesian aircraft overhead and from the stream of wounded guerrillas being brought to the city's hospitals that their armed forces had not responded to the attacks. The president stated that he had held back the ZNDF to prevent the spread of war; nevertheless some people grumbled, and some military officers complained that they should have been allowed to meet the enemy.

Aside from the scattered complaints about holding back the military, there was no significant dissident movement in the country in the late 1970s (see Political Developments, 1975–79; Political Dynamics, ch. 3). Kaunda continued as president after a victory at the polls in December 1978 and, although the country was beset with problems of various kinds, there was no apparent threat to the regime. Serious crime had been a growing problem for several years, and it was exacerbated by rising unemployment and the disruption of society brought about by the continuing national emergency. The police, needing more personnel and better equipment, were sorely tested, but the situation was not out of control.

The Zambia Police Force was a national organization under the supervision of the Ministry of Home Affairs. The force was commanded by a presidential appointee who had the title of inspector general of police. Overall strength of the force in early 1979 was estimated at about 10,000; the two police paramilitary units had between 800 and 900 men each.

Armed Forces

Constitutional Provisions

Article 54 of the 1973 Constitution of the Republic of Zambia provides that "supreme command of the armed forces of the Republic shall vest in the President and he shall hold the office of Commander-in-Chief." The same article states that the president has the power to "determine the operational use of the armed forces" and authorizes him to appoint, dismiss, and promote military personnel. The president, as commander in chief, may delegate any of his powers to a member of the armed forces provided he does so in writing. Explicit restrictions on the exercise of powers by the president or by an officer to whom he has delegated authority are contained in the final clause of Article 54, which states that "Parliament may regulate the exercise of the powers conferred by or under this Article." Under the Zambian system, however, the president is also the leading member of parliament (see The Structure of Government, ch. 3).

According to the Constitution the authority to declare war is vested in parliament, which consists of the president and the National Assembly. Short of a declaration of war, the president has the authority to declare a state of emergency, which must be proclaimed in the official Government Gazette. To remain in force, such a declaration must be approved by a two-thirds vote of the National Assembly.

In September 1978—as the confrontation with Southern Rhodesia worsened—President Kaunda, who also held the defense portfolio at that time, announced the creation of a high-level party post that would aid him in handling the increasing defense burdens of his office. Gray Zulu, who was appointed to the new post of secretary of state for defense and security, had been minister of defense in the early 1970s and more recently had been secretary general of the United National Independence Party (UNIP). The president told the party conference meeting in September at Mulungushi that the new post would rank fourth in the country's political hierarchy, preceded only by the president, the secretary general of UNIP, and the prime minister, in that order.

The Office of the Secretary of State for Defense and Security would encompass the Defense Division, the Ministry of Home Affairs, and the Special Division. The Defense Division—evidently a replacement for the abolished Ministry of Defense—was to be headed by Ian Sikazwe, who was named permanent secretary. The newly appointed commander of the ZNDF, Lieutenant General Benjamin Mibenge, and the deputy commander, Major General Malimba Masheke, by virtue of their positions, were also assigned to the Defense Division. Wilted Phiri, the incumbent minister of home affairs, was reappointed. The Special Division, which was assumed to be a high-level investigative agency concerned with national security, continued under the direction of A.K. Mbewe, permanent secretary and director general.

Observers believed that one of Zulu's most important tasks in his new post would be that of maintaining close liaison with the guerrilla forces of Nkomo. Zulu will also be required to keep the Cabinet and the National Assembly as well as the Central Committee of UNIP informed on all important defense matters. Before his appointment Zulu had been listed as the chairman of the Defense and Security Subcommittee of the Central Committee, but that subcommittee probably was abolished in a reorganization after the elections of December 1978 (see The Party, ch. 3).

Military Tradition

Zambia's military tradition combines a long African legacy with the more recent British influences inherited from the period of colonial rule. The African heritage was one in which bands of young warriors fought to defend their home territory or to conquer someone else's or in which some groups raided others for cattle or slaves, particularly in the nineteenth century when demands from both European and Arab slave traders had effects far inland. Although such bands were not professional forces organized exclusively for combat, their existence earned for some ethnic groups a reputation for militarism (see Peoples and Polities, ca. 1500–1800; The Commercial Revolution: The Late Eighteenth and Nineteenth Centuries, ch. 1). The British military legacy was of order and discipline, pomp and ceremony. Even though the colonial period lasted only seventy-four years—and during the first thirty-four Northern Rhodesia, as Zambia was then called, was ruled by a private company—the main influence on the development of the armed forces after independence was British.

British interest in the area began in the late nineteenth century with the first penetration by the British South Africa Company under the direction of Cecil Rhodes (see The Colonial Interlude, ca. 1890–1964, ch. 1). In exchange for mineral exploitation rights and permission to colonize, agents of the company guaranteed armed protection against external threats to the area's chiefs. In order to fulfill that guarantee the company formed a small constabulary, which was the forerunner of British armed force in that region and the ancestor of the present-day Zambia Army.

From the beginning of the British period part of the constabulary (which eventually became the Northern Rhodesia Police) was in fact an army whose mission was purely military. In the early 1890s this army was made up of Sikhs from India, Makua from Mozambique, and Zanzibaris. The Sikhs were permitted by the British authorities in India to leave their regiments for voluntary tours in Africa; the Portuguese raised no objections to British recruiters operating in Mozambique; and the Zanzibaris were recruited through arrangements made with the reigning sultan of Zanzibar. The principal activities of the Military Branch of the

President Kenneth Kaunda and aides
visit a Zambian Army unit
Courtesy Zambia Information Services

Northern Rhodesia Police were fighting Arab slave traders and protecting the commercial operations of the British South Africa Company.

Until 1912 Northern Rhodesia was policed by two organizations: the North-Eastern Rhodesian Constabulary in the eastern half of the territory and the Barotse Native Police (in the Barotse Protectorate) in the western half. Both units were organized and trained primarily as infantry, but both also had small contingents that performed civil police functions. In a general reorganization in 1912 the two were combined to form the Northern Rhodesia Police, which had a strength of nineteen British officers, eight British noncommissioned officers (NCOs), and 750 enlisted Africans. Although a few of its members were designated to perform civil police duties, the unit was primarily a military organization.

During World War I the police, still under the nominal control of the British South Africa Company, provided the defense for Northern Rhodesia and also engaged in campaigns in neighboring German East Africa (present-day Tanzania) and German Southwest Africa (present-day Namibia). The military branch of the Northern Rhodesia Police was organized as an infantry battalion, operating four to six infantry companies supported by heavy weapons, communications, engineer, and medical units. About 40 percent of the adult males of Northern Rhodesia served on active duty during World War I, some in Europe but the majority in the African campaigns.

After the war the Northern Rhodesia Police was reduced in size and returned to its dual function of providing military and police protection to the territory. The British South Africa Company continued to administer Northern Rhodesia until 1924 when the British government took control, placing the administration under the Colonial Office; however, the police status and title of the security force were retained. In 1933 the military branch of the Northern Rhodesia Police was separated and designated the Northern Rhodesia Regiment.

Just before the outbreak of World War II in 1939 regimental strength numbered about 400 Africans and twenty British officers and NCOs. In 1940 military service was made compulsory for British males between the ages of eighteen and forty-five, but Africans were exempt from the draft because of their designation as "British Protected Persons." Recruiters had no trouble filling the ranks with African volunteers, however, and during the course of the war the Northern Rhodesia Regiment attained brigade strength and was designated the 27th Infantry Brigade (Northern Rhodesia). Because of the danger of a unit from a small area suffering very heavy casualties in a single engagement or a series of engagements, the brigade was not committed to battle as a unit. Instead its elements were scattered and campaigned in British Somaliland, Ethiopia, Palestine, Ceylon, and Madagascar. In Burma units of the brigade engaged in fighting that was equal in severity to any combat faced by British troops during the entire war. The officers and soldiers from Northern Rhodesia acquitted themselves well—sometimes heroically—and many were decorated for valor during their long campaigns away from their homeland.

For the African soldiers of Northern Rhodesia the World War II experience differed from that of their countrymen who served in the earlier war in that they received more technical training and traveled more broadly. Primarily the African troops were still infantrymen; but their weapons and equipment were more complicated, necessitating longer and better training. For example, there had been no school for training African Rhodesians as truck drivers and mechanics until May 1940. Deployment of the Northern Rhodesians to far-flung battlefields in Africa and Asia also enriched their experience in comparison with that of their predecessors in World War I, who went no farther afield than Tanzania or Mozambique.

In 1953 the two Rhodesias and Nyasaland (present-day Malawi) were drawn together in the Central African Federation of Rhodesia and Nyasaland over the objections of the Africans of Northern Rhodesia and Nyasaland, who feared domination by the whites of Southern Rhodesia (see Colonial Office Protectorate, 1924–53, ch. 1). The military units of all three territories were combined under the federal government and became part of the King's African Rifles (KAR). The KAR at that time also had units in Kenya, Tanganyika, and Uganda, all officered by Europeans. During the period of federation, which lasted until December 1963, the 7,000-man federal army included five infantry battalions —one of which was all white—an armored reconnaissance squadron, and a paratroop unit. All officers were white, but in 1963 africanization of the officer corps began by upgrading NCOs and by providing scholarships for black youths to be trained as officers. In addition to the federal army there was also a parttime, well-trained territorial force of European reservists known as the Royal Rhodesia Regiment that had 7,000 men on its roster. The federation also had an emergency register of 46,000 unorganized whites who were subject to mobilization. All ablebodied European youths underwent compulsory military training, after which they were assigned to local army units for periodic drills.

Under the federation the Royal Rhodesian Air Force attained a strength of 1,100 men and approximately ninety aircraft. About 900 of the airmen were African ground personnel. In addition to their role in the defense of the federation the air units were also designated to participate in joint operations with other Commonwealth countries, and their airfields were used by British military aircraft on training missions. When the federation was dissolved, the Royal Rhodesian Air Force was transferred almost intact to Southern Rhodesia over the objections of Northern Rhodesia and Nyasaland, whose spokesmen stated that so much strength in the hands of the Southern Rhodesians would constitute a threat to international peace. Almost half of the federation's regular army was also transferred to Southern Rhodesia. When the split came, Northern Rhodesia acquired two infantry battalions—the 1st Northern Rhodesia Rifles and the 2nd King's Rifles—and an armored car squadron. To support this ground force, a transport and reconnaissance air wing consisting of four C-47s and two Pembrokes and sufficient personnel to fly and maintain them was also given to Northern Rhodesia.

The colonial forces acquired at the time of the breakup of the federation became national forces a few months later when Zambia was granted independence. Maintenance of internal peace and security was absolutely essential for the attainment of the new state's development goals, and for this purpose President Kaunda secured the support of the military. Kaunda and his government desired a truly integrated national military force; the colonial policy of having African troops commanded by white officers was discarded. Under the policy of zambianization the legacies of Zambia's African and colonial backgrounds were to be combined with new educational and professional programs to develop an independent, nonracial military force dedicated to serving the new nation.

Development of National Armed Forces

After independence and for the remainder of the 1960s the British colonial heritage was the strongest influence on the development of the Zambia Armed Forces, and all command positions were held by British officers. In 1964 there was only one Zambian commissioned officer. Under those conditions it was only natural that the British would be relied on to provide military leaders, technicians, and instructors as well as weapons and equipment. During this period Zambians were being trained in Great Britain and in their own country for the eventual zambianization of the forces. By the end of the 1960s all NCO positions had been filled by Zambians, and by the early 1970s all British army officers had been discharged and replaced by Zambians.

In 1973 the army, which had reached a strength of 5,000 men, was primarily an infantry organization, as it had been during colonial times. Its four battalions were supported by two artillery batteries and an armored car unit. A battery of Rapier surface-to-air missiles (SAMs) had also been activated. The government had earlier terminated its agreement with Great Britain through which British pilots flew Zambia Air Force planes while Zambian youths were undergoing flight training there. In 1969 Kaunda asked the Italian government for help in developing the air force, and by mid-1971 eight Zambians had earned their pilot's wings in Italy. In that year Zambia also purchased several training planes from Yugoslavia. Through these arrangements

Kaunda was drawing away from the almost complete reliance on the British.

In 1970 twenty-seven-year-old Colonel Kingsley G. Chinkuli—a graduate of the Royal Military Academy at Sandhurst, England, who two years earlier had been a lieutenant—became the first Zambian to command the army; two years later Wing Commander Peter Zuze, also a native Zambian, was similarly honored by appointment to the top post in the air force. After that time each promotion for Chinkuli in the army and Zuze in the air force was a first for a Zambian in either service. By 1973 President Kaunda had promoted Chinkuli to major general and Zuze to air commodore. In June 1976 Kaunda announced that the army, the air force, and various civilian components including the Home Guard and the Zambia National Service (ZNS) would be united under the ZNDF. Chinkuli was named commander and Zuze, deputy commander. Before leaving the service in April 1977 to become minister of mines, Chinkuli commanded the ZNDF as a full general. Zuze replaced Chinkuli as commander of the ZNDF and was promoted to lieutenant general. On January 2, 1979, Kaunda announced that Lieutanant General Benjamin Mibenge would take over command of the forces and that Zuze would leave military service to take a diplomatic post.

For the troops in the developing Zambian forces, life entailed more than guard duty and parades. During the late 1960s and early 1970s army patrols sometimes engaged in cross-border firefights. At times the exchanges were with Portuguese soldiers firing from their sides of the Angolan or Mozambican borders, but more often the opposition came from Rhodesian troops on the far side of the Zambezi River. In May 1973, assertedly to prevent a feared attack on a power station, Zambian soldiers opened fire on a group of tourists visiting the Rhodesian side of Victoria Falls. Two Canadian women were killed, and an American man was wounded. The government eventually apologized to the Canadian and American governments and offered compensation to the families of the victims, but there was no indication that any military personnel had been punished or censured for bad judgment or irresponsibility.

After the Portuguese gave up their colonies and withdrew their forces from Angola and Mozambique, tensions along those frontiers eased. However, as Kaunda allowed more guerrilla forces to establish training bases and staging areas on Zambian territory, hostile actions increased along the borders with Southern Rhodesia and Namibia, which was occupied by South Africa under a mandate of the defunct League of Nations. In the years from 1975 through 1978 border incidents became numerous, and incursions by Rhodesian and South African forces into Zambia became common. In late 1978 Rhodesian raids against Nkomo's guerrilla camps in Zambia challenged Zambian sovereignty.

Missions and Manpower

As is the case with the military services in several other African countries, the ZNDF has a dual mission—that is, to assist the police in the maintenance of public order if necessary and to defend national territory from outside attack. It is common in Zambia to see references to "the security forces," a term that includes the army, the air force, and the police. During fourteen years of independence the near-wartime conditions that have existed in southern Africa have generally necessitated deployment of the ZNDF along the country's borders. The mission of the small Zambia Air Force has been to provide support and air transport for the ground forces.

Service in the armed forces has been voluntary ever since independence, and the government had no trouble maintaining the relatively small army and air force. In 1978 there were approximately 1.2 million males between the ages of fifteen and forty-nine, and of that number about 52 percent were considered fit for military service. Even with the expansion of army strength from 7,000 to 12,800 in late 1977 and early 1978, there was no indication of recruiting difficulties. The chief problems were those of recruiting technicians for modern armed forces and of retaining those who had received technical training for which there was a demand in civilian enterprises. Because of its small size the 1,500-man air force made no adverse impact on the country's manpower resources, but its need for technically trained personnel was even greater than the army's.

Women also served in the ZNDF, but no information was available concerning their service other than that they served voluntarily. It was not known nor did observers speculate on whether women received combat training or whether they were enlisted solely for administrative tasks. Nor was it known if women served in those units in the southern part of the country that have engaged in firefights or if they were assigned only to interior units. No statistics were available on the number of women in service in early 1979, but observers guessed that the number was very small.

In the late 1960s and early 1970s delegates to the National Assembly frequently complained that their particular ethnic group or their particular region of the country was being discriminated against by military recruiters who sought to make other groups or other regions more powerful within the armed forces. If in fact those complaints had validity at the time, the personnel situation in the late 1970s appeared to be in balance, and similar complaints have not been publicized. President Kaunda has certainly been the most vocal advocate of zambianism as well as the most vocal foe of tribalism and sectionalism. As commander in chief he has striven to keep those dangerous ailments out of the armed forces in the same manner as he has tried to purge them from society in general.

Information is woefully deficient on the recruitment and

training of both officers and enlisted men for the ZNDF. Some Zambians earned commissions at Sandhurst, but their numbers were not sufficient to maintain the strength of the officer corps. In all likelihood more officer candidates have been commissioned from the Army's School of Military Training in Lusaka and, because more NCOs had finished secondary school since independence, it is possible that more officers have come up through the ranks. Candidates for commissions in both services must be citizens between the ages of eighteen and twenty-six, must be physically fit, and must have completed secondary school. Physical requirements were more stringent for those applicants entering pilot training. Some Zambia Air Force pilots have been trained in Yugoslavia in addition to those trained in Italy and at home. Volunteers for enlisted service must be citizens of eighteen years or older and must have completed nine years of schooling. Basic training is given during the first thirteen weeks of service, usually at the Army's School of Military Training.

The armed forces of landlocked Zambia consisted only of ground and air elements: the Zambia Army and the Zambia Air Force. The army in 1978 was primarily an infantry organization and had been since independence, but ten old Soviet T-54 tanks had been acquired to give the foot soldiers additional support. It was not known how the tanks would be distributed or where they would be deployed. Presumably a tank company would be formed, but no publicity had been given to the newly acquired armor. The bulk of army strength was assigned to eight infantry battalions, which probably had as many as 1,000 men in each. In addition to the tanks the army was supported by two batteries of field artillery, a unit of armored cars, and a unit of antiaircraft artillery. Integral to each infantry battalion were engineer, signal, supply, medical, and maintenance support units. At the beginning of the year overall equipment inventories showed twenty-eight Ferret scout cars, eight 105-mm howitzers, and twenty-four 20-mm antiaircraft guns. Several additional 20-mm guns were among the arms and equipment airlifted to Zambia by the British after the Southern Rhodesian raids of October 1978 (see Foreign Influences, this ch.).

As late as 1970 the Zambia Air Force remained a tiny organization of about 400 men, a few old transports, and some helicopters. Much of the flying was still being done by European pilots; however, about that time a decision was made to create an air combat capability and to train more Zambians as pilots. By the terms of an agreement between Zambia and Great Britain, British pilots were not permitted to fly combat missions; therefore they were to be released as combat aircraft were acquired and Zambians became qualified to fly them. Some Italian armed jet trainers were purchased, and an agreement was signed whereby Italians would train Zambians and assist in the long process of building a modern air force. By 1978 the air force had six squadrons: two combat, two transport, one liaison, and one helicopter. The aircraft inventory showed a wide variety of planes from several different countries (see table 14, Appendix).

Ranks, Uniforms, and Insignia

Rank structures in the army and the air force after fourteen years of independence continued to be similar to those of the British forces. Army officer ranks were the same as or similar to those in most Western armies; that is, second lieutenant, lieutenant, captain, major, lieutenant colonel, colonel, brigadier, major general, lieutenant general, and general. Rank structure in the air force was the same as in the army, although titles corresponded to those used in the British air force: flying officer, flight lieutenant, squadron leader, wing commander, group captain, and air commodore. The small Zambia Air Force had not instituted ranks above air commodore.

Army officers and enlisted men wear forest green uniforms for garrison duty and some ceremonial occasions. The officers' jacket is safari-style and is worn with a black or dark brown wide leather belt. Enlisted duty jackets are also safari-style but are tucked in at the waist like a shirt. Trousers for both officers and enlisted men are of the same forest green material and have a bright red, three-quarter-inch stripe running the entire length of the outer seam. Enlisted men wear their trousers tucked into combat boots; officers wear low-quarter shoes. All ranks wear visored forest green caps that are circled by a bright red band. Cap ornaments are miniature representations of the Zambian coat of arms. Berets are sometimes worn in place of the service caps. The common duty uniform, which is sometimes worn on ceremonial parade, is the familiar camouflage fatigue uniform with combat boots, web belt, and steel helmet.

Officers' rank insignia are worn on forest green epaulets that are rimmed in red piping. The British pips and crowns that formerly designated ranks have been replaced by stars and eagles. One star designates a second lieutenant, two a lieutenant, and three a captain. A major wears an eagle, a lieutenant colonel an eagle and a star, and a colonel an eagle and two stars. The insignia of a brigadier is an eagle above two crossed swords. The mix of swords, eagles, and stars worn by generals above the grade of brigadier was not known. Enlisted ranks are depicted by bright red, V-shaped chevrons worn on both upper sleeves of outer garments. Privates wear no insignia. Lance corporals, corporals, and sergeants wear one, two, and three stripes respectively. The three stripes of a staff sergeant's chevrons have an eagle in the opening of the V. The rank insignia of a sergeant major is an embroidered eagle that is sewn on both sleeves near the wrist or worn on shoulder tabs of short-sleeve shirts.

The State of Emergency

Actually Zambians have lived under some kind of a state of emergency almost since independence, and the country's armed forces have been perennially under varying degrees of alert. During the last half of the 1960s and the early 1970s leaders of the new Republic of Zambia perceived threats to their sovereignty emanating from four neighboring countries: Angola and Mozambique (both ruled by the Portuguese until 1974) and Southern Rhodesia and South Africa. As Zambia played host to an ever-larger number of guerrilla forces, Portuguese, South African, and Rhodesian troops increasingly violated Zambia's borders. The decline in tensions along the Angola and Mozambique borders after the Portuguese withdrawal and after the Angolan civil war was more than offset by the increased hostilities along the 640-kilometer Southern Rhodesia border and to a lesser degree along the Caprivi Strip. By 1978 no area in Zambia was immune from Rhodesian attacks.

When the Ian Smith regime issued the UDI, Zambia entered a state of emergency that has never been lifted. At times that condition has been formalized, as in January 1976 when Kaunda said in a nationwide broadcast, "We are at war. We must respond in a warlike manner. With the application of the full powers of the State of Emergency we will deal without mercy with people who commit crimes against the State." That particular reiteration of the condition of emergency was Kaunda's reaction to the rapid Soviet-Cuban buildup in neighboring Angola. At other times the state of emergency has been more a general condition under which the country has existed because of the unrest and discontent in the whole of southern Africa.

During the remainder of 1976 the situation in Angola was resolved in favor of Agostinho Neto and his Popular Movement for the Liberation of Angola, and Kaunda seemed less concerned with the Soviet-Cuban presence; but the emergency situation vis-à-vis Southern Rhodesia had worsened. In May 1977 Kaunda again announced that "a state of war" existed. This statement was issued in response to a declaration by Southern Rhodesia to the effect that its forces would make preemptive strikes against guerrilla bases in Zambia. Two days later Zambian and Rhodesian troops faced each other across the Zambezi River after the Zambians had delivered a twenty-five-minute mortar and rocket barrage across the Victoria Falls bridge. The Rhodesians, claiming that the action was unprovoked, held their fire but issued a stern warning against any recurrence. The tension at Victoria Falls subsided, but within a week Zambian troops were involved in an exchange of fire with South African forces in the Caprivi Strip, and in a separate incident Zambian soldiers reportedly fired on a South African civilian plane in the same area.

In the fall of 1977, as Zambia celebrated its thirteenth year of independence, a brief news item in the UNIP-owned *Times of Zambia*—despite the official secrecy law—stated that supplemental funds for national defense had been approved. "Parliament last night overwhelmingly approved proposals for K44,530,162 supplementary estimates for the Government to finance the defense and security of the nation in the face of mounting tension with rebel Rhodesia." Perhaps the supplementary funding financed the increase in army strength that was reflected in the estimates for the 1978–79 period, which showed 5,800 more men in the army at the beginning of 1978 than had been estimated one year earlier.

The increased strength of the Zambian Army did not deter the Rhodesian army in its incursions into Zambian territory. In March 1978 Rhodesian troops supported by jets and helicopters attacked the Luangwa District southeast of Lusaka. Zambian spokesmen said that it was an unprovoked attack, but Rhodesians claimed that the raid was against "terrorists" in a ZAPU camp. Zambia later acknowledged that ten of its soldiers were among the twenty-two Zambians killed in the attack. Later in the month Rhodesians attacked targets up to forty-eight kilometers inside the border, thus serving notice to ZAPU guerrillas that there would be no sanctuaries and alerting the Zambians to the fact that their entire country was open to attack.

The most serious attacks that Zambia had endured occurred just as the country prepared to celebrate its fourteenth anniversary in October 1978. Rhodesian jets bombed a guerrilla camp at Chikumbi, only nineteen kilometers north of Lusaka, beginning a three-day attack that included helicopter-borne troops who conducted mop-up operations after the bombing ceased. The raids against Chikumbi and other targets alarmed and angered the people of Lusaka, many of whom complained about the lack of response by the ZDNF. The Rhodesians claimed that Chikumbi had been the main military headquarters for Nkomo's black nationalist army. Nkomo and Kaunda claimed that Chikumbi housed only a camp for unarmed refugees. Witnesses watching the procession of wounded into Lusaka said that many of them were young men of military age, but the dispute remained unsettled. Eventually the University Teaching Hospital of Lusaka released casualty figures showing that more than 600 wounded had been treated in that facility and that 337 had died. Among the dead were fifteen Zambian policemen and six Zambian soldiers.

The raids emphasized the fact that Rhodesian forces could strike into Zambia with impunity. Not only were no Rhodesian planes shot down, but the Rapier antiaircraft missile system that had been acquired from Great Britain some years earlier proved inoperable, probably because of lack of maintenance and spare parts. No Zambian fighter planes scrambled to meet the intruders in air combat but, in fairness to the Zambia Air Force, it should be noted that distances are so short that Rhodesian jets were able to penetrate as far as Lusaka before Zambian pilots could get their planes off the ground. Kaunda later stated that he had purposely restrained his forces rather than ignite a general war that would have engulfed much of southern Africa. He also said that he would not order retaliation raids because "I would be committing suicide for Zambia." Many Zambians, however, expressed anger and dismay over the nonparticipation of their armed forces in the face of enemy incursions. In letters to newspapers and in public gatherings people questioned the expenditure of large sums on military forces that did nothing during a national emergency. Fearing political repercussions in the elections scheduled for December, UNIP spokesmen quickly responded to those critics who called for armed action as well as to others who called for the expulsion of the guerrillas.

An editorial in the *Times of Zambia* after the Rhodesian raids of October 1978 used the expression "we are at war" in describing the situation of Zambia and the white-ruled countries of southern Africa. Actually there was no declared state of war, nor were Zambian soldiers regularly engaged in combat with Rhodesians or South Africans. Nevertheless the language of the editorial was not entirely rhetoric. Rhodesian planes and troops had attacked ZAPU guerrilla camps deep inside Zambia. Some members of Zambia's security forces had been killed fighting in these incursions. Along the Caprivi Strip there were exchanges of fire with South African troops who often pursued SWAPO guerrillas across Zambia's border; again, some Zambians had been killed. In the early months of 1979 such intermittent hostilities continued.

Home Guard

The Home Guard, established by an act of Parliament in 1971, was intended to give military training to citizens who would then constitute a reserve that would reinforce security forces in defending the country and in maintaining public order and public safety. Citizens between the ages of eighteen and forty-five were eligible for enlistment in the Home Guard; incentives for enlistment were the satisfaction of performing a patriotic duty and the possibility that training as drivers, mechanics, and clerks or in other specialties could help personal advancement in civilian life. By law the president was made commander in chief of the Home Guard and given authority to call the entire organization or any part of it to active duty. If mobilized, Home Guardsmen are considered to be members of the armed forces and become subject to military law.

The state of training of the Home Guard and its readiness for mobilization in early 1979 were not known. References to the guard have been infrequent, and it is possible that after its creation in 1971 it never really took hold except in and around Lusaka and perhaps a few of the other major population centers. In late 1972 a nationwide alert was declared when the government feared that Southern Rhodesia might attack. During the alert the Lusaka elements of the Home Guard were called to duty, but there was no mobilization of other guard units if in fact any existed. Since that one publicized occasion there has been no indication that the guard has figured in any of the alerts or states of emergency that have occurred with increasing frequency. In a speech to party leaders at the end of November 1978 in Kitwe Kaunda said that weaknesses still existed in the country's defense and security systems and that the remedy for those weaknesses would be the formation of local defense units in all Zambian villages, institutions, and places of work. Units such as those mentioned by the president would seem to coincide directly with the basic premises that fostered the creation of the Home Guard; yet he made no reference to that organization.

Zambia National Service (ZNS)

The ZNS evolved from the Zambia Youth Service, which until 1971 was an organization for the training of Zambians between the ages of sixteen and twenty-five who were unemployed and generally lacked basic skills. Youth service camps were established in various parts of the country shortly after independence to house young people while they were undergoing training courses. The program, which originally lasted only three or four months, was intended to benefit the country as well as the individuals because the skills were in demand in the economy. Young men were taught rural skills including basic agricultural practices, animal husbandry, farm mechanics, brickmaking, and various handicrafts. Young women received instruction in domestic sciences, nutrition, poultry-raising, and the organization of village cooperatives. Courses in government, geography, and history were added, and in 1966 military training was incorporated into the curriculum. For the remainder of the 1960s and into the early 1970s graduates of the youth service and the follow-on ZNS were readily absorbed into the economy.

At first the youth service was administered by the then-existing Ministry of Cooperatives, Youth, and Social Development. Later the Ministry of Home Affairs took over; however, the service was eventually transferred to the Ministry of Defense in January 1971, and when ZNS started it too was placed under defense. During the 1970s, as crisis followed crisis between Zambia and its neighbors, the military aspects of the training given to young people in ZNS took on greater importance. At times there were reports that after completion of their ZNS tours trainees would be required to enroll in the Home Guard. In this manner the country would be able to build a large reserve of trained citizens who would be available for military service when needed. The number of ZNS graduates assigned to Home Guard units was not known.

In the mid-1970s military training had become of primary importance, although basic skills and handicrafts were still in the curriculum. In January 1976 a twenty-month tour in ZNS was made compulsory for all young Zambians. According to law no student may enter an institution of higher learning or enter the job market without first satisfying the ZNS requirement. Students aspiring toward a university education must serve ten months in the ZNS before matriculation; they then complete the total of twenty months in segments during several long university vacations. School dropouts and those who have completed secondary school but do not intend to continue their education are kept out of the labor pool by ZNS service for almost two years, an important consideration because of the continuing high unemployment rate. In addition ZNS graduates constitute a military reserve that could be mobilized to augment the regular armed forces. The uniform worn by ZNS trainees in 1978 was barely distinguishable from the field uniform of the Zambia Army; that is, camouflage fatigues, combat boots, web belts, and berets. Members received training in small arms and in light crew-served weapons.

In a commencement speech to "hundreds" of trainees at the Kafue ZNS camp, Prime Minister Daniel Lisulo said that enemies of Zambia had unleashed a propaganda attack against the organization. Lisulo did not say why such an attack had occurred but said only that ridiculous rumors had been spread throughout the country and that some Zambians had been taken in by those falsehoods. He mentioned stories that referred to service in the ZNS as being dangerous and other claims that some young Zambians had lost their lives in ZNS camps. Duped by such rumors, some Zambians tried to avoid serving, and some parents tried to have their children medically disqualified or else had them sent abroad to study rather than have them enter the ZNS. Lisulo did not mention what steps the government was taking to counteract the propaganda. One of the problems that hindered Zambian acceptance of the ZNS was the veil of secrecy that covered the organization because of its military subordination. Many of the 20,000 youths who had served in the ZNS complained about poor food, poor living conditions, and time wasted on useless training, but none corroborated the exaggerated rumors that had been circulated.

Foreign Influences

Other than the changes in names at the time of independence, to all outward appearances the Zambia Army and Zambia Air Force remained British colonial forces. Totally dependent on Great Britain for arms and equipment, the new government continued to rely heavily on the former colonial power and on some other Commonwealth countries for military assistance. In addition to the weapons and matériel that gave a colonial atmosphere to Zambian military bases during the 1960s, the officer corps remained almost entirely British, ensuring that the customs and practices of the services would retain a decidedly British air.

Although not formally committed to any military alliances, Kaunda has explored the possibilities of such commitments on several occasions since independence, particularly when seeking outside assistance. After the formal training agreements with Great Britain ended in 1969, assistance was sought from Italy, and through the ensuing years many Zambian airmen have been trained at Italian bases. Yugoslavia also lent its support by selling aircraft and training pilots. Opposition to colonialism and white minority regimes, and Kaunda's participation as a leader of the so-called front-line states (Zambia, Tanzania, Mozambique, Botswana, and Angola), have at times led to discussions of joint military ventures by these states, but no formal agreements have been publicized.

After the Rhodesian raids of October 1978 against guerrilla camps in Zambia, the British government for the first time gave military aid free of charge to the Zambians. David Owen, the foreign secretary, emphasized to the British Parliament that the weapons and equipment were for defense purposes only and stated that he had assurances from Kaunda that the matériel would not be passed on to the guerrillas. British transport planes were immediately assigned to airlift about 100 tons of weapons and equipment including Tiger Cat SAMs, 20-mm antiaircraft guns, mortars, landmines, and radar sets. It was also reported that spare parts for the Zambian Rapier missiles had been included in the shipments. The Tiger Cat is a more advanced and more effective weapon than the obsolescent Rapier, but the inclusion of the newer missiles in the aid shipment seemed to be a political rather than a military gesture because there was no one in Zambia trained to operate the system, and it would take several months for Zambians to receive Tiger Cat training in Great Britain.

Public Order

The state of emergency that has existed in Zambia since the Unilateral Declaration of Independence (UDI) by the white minority government of neighboring Southern Rhodesia has had a major effect on the maintenance of public order in Zambia (see Foreign Relations, ch. 3). Zambians have not lived in chaos or anarchy, and the government has maintained order during very difficult times; but conditions of near-warfare have contributed to the increase in crimes, the incidence of terrorism, and the atmosphere of lawlessness that has sometimes prevailed. Attacks by Rhodesian forces deep into Zambia, even though they were against guerrilla camps, added to the tension and the generally unsettled conditions. The amount of money needed for military and police forces was a drain on the treasury, which desperately needed developmental rather than defense spending.

Social Controls

Before European colonization of the area respect for group authority, expressed in unwritten norms, was characteristic of tribal society (see Social Structure, ch. 2). The changes brought about by the colonizers radically affected the attitudes of the indigenous peoples toward authority but did not lessen their basic appreciation of the need for public order. New standards of behavior and concepts of crime and punishment were brought about by Christian teaching, Western forms of education, and British law at the same time that traditional patterns of living were being altered by urbanization, economic development, and efforts by the government to diminish the powers of the chiefs.

The roles of family, lineage, and local organization continued to be important factors in the control of individual behavior, but a greater respect for the authority of the state was also fostered by independence and nurtured by the new leaders. The rapid growth of a money economy, however, and the increasing mobility of the population provided opportunities for and inducements to new varieties of criminal activities.

After independence the government, under the strong personal leadership of Kaunda, made a determined effort to strengthen institutional and group controls over public conduct in order to increase the pace of national development. In its development programs and through the schools and the mass media, the government called for personal industry, service to society, honesty in public and private affairs, self-improvement, and determination to enhance the good name of Zambia. The programs have met with some success since independence, but corruption in public life continues to be a problem (although much less of a problem than in most newly independent nations), and sectionalism and tribalism still detracted from the goal inherent in the national motto, "One Zambia—One Nation."

Zambia Police Force

Like the military services, the police force is similar in organization and training to the British colonial force from which it evolved. In the rural areas before independence the Native Authorities were responsible for the maintenance of law and order within their areas. The forces and means available to them for those purposes, however, were limited and consisted only of unarmed rural policemen who usually were little more than messengers enforcing Native Authority edicts and serving court summonses. They lacked any enforcement capability, but the Native Authorities could call on the Northern Rhodesian Police through the district commissioners if assistance were needed in police operations. The Northern Rhodesian Police had reached a strength of 6,000 at the time of independence, and it was considered a well-organized and well-trained force capable of maintaining public order in the country.

In 1964 the Northern Rhodesia Police was transferred intact to the government of the new republic, assuming police responsibility throughout the country. Most European and Asian officers remained with the force for a period of years after independence, ensuring continuity and allowing an orderly transfer of police functions to Zambians as they gained experience and received training for positions in the police hierarchy. Zambianization proceeded at a much more rapid pace in the police force than in the army and air force (see Development of National Armed Forces, this ch.).

The first Zambian constitution established the Zambia Police Force as one of the public (civil) services and established the Public Service Commission to advise and assist the president in the administration of the public services. The Constitution of 1973 did not alter the police establishment in any fundamental way, but it did remove the police and prison functions from the Public Service Commission and established the Police and Prison Service Commission, which consisted of "a chairman and not less than three nor more than six other members," all of whom were to be appointed by the president. In early January 1979 the *Times of Zambia* reported that the Police and Prison Service Commission would be combined with three other commissions under the heading of Civil Service, and the functioning of that single institution would be supervised by a minister of state in the office of the prime minister. The commission members serve two-year terms during which they advise the president on operations and assist him in the exercise of his appointment and dismissal powers. The president also exercised disciplinary control over the police and prison services; but actual command of the Zambia Police Force was vested in the inspector general of police, whose top staff included a commissioner, a deputy commissioner, and a senior assistant commissioner. Administrative control of the police was a function of the Ministry of Home Affairs.

The Zambia Police Force is a national police, charged with the preservation of peace, the prevention and detection of crime, and the apprehension of offenders throughout the entire republic. The police were also responsible for the supervision of parolees from the country's prisons. The police force was considered the primary element in the preservation of peace within the country, and the Zambia Army was a reserve that was prepared to augment police units in the event of major internal disturbances. In a reversal of these roles, police units on the borders have been used as reserve forces to augment regular army troops involved in hostilities. At the beginning of 1975 the strength of the force was officially reported by the inspector general of police at 9,727 (men and women), which was thirty-eight under the number authorized. As far as was known at the beginning of 1979, the authorized strength remained slightly below 10,000, and actual strength was estimated at near that figure. The Zambia Police Reserve, which paralleled the structure of the regular force, had an estimated strength of between 2,000 and 3,000 and was located in major population centers throughout the country.

The main police headquarters in Lusaka established policy, supervised operations, and directed the activities of all subordinate units. In 1975 headquarters had five functional departments: Administration, Staff, Criminal Investigation, Communications, and

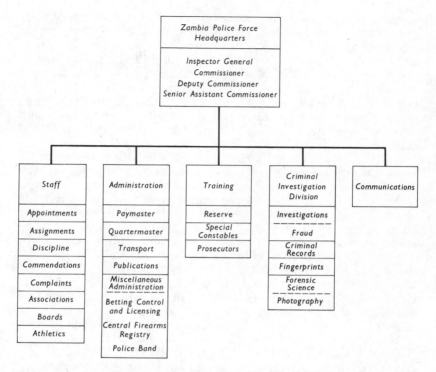

Source: Based on information from Zambia Police Force, *Zambia Police Annual Report*, Lusaka, 1976.

Figure 12. Zambia Police Force Headquarters, 1975

Training (see fig. 12). From 1975 until early 1979 there had been no indication of any fundamental reorganization of police headquarters. The operational breakdown of the force was both territorial and functional. There were nine territorial divisions having responsibilities that were generally delineated by provincial boundaries and having headquarters in the provincial capitals. There were also four special divisions: the Mobile Unit, headquartered at Kamfinsa (near Ndola); the Para-Military Battalion, headquartered at Lilayi (near Lusaka); the Police Training School, located at Lilayi; and the Tazara Police, headquartered at Lusaka. The latter is a special security force that was organized and trained specifically for the protection of the railroad operated by the Tanzania-Zambia Railway Authority (TAZARA).

Subordinate units in the police divisions varied in size, strength, and capability generally depending on population density and urbanization. Subordinate to the divisions were police districts corresponding to governmental districts, and on the lowest level were police posts established in towns and villages. Grade structure conformed to the British pattern and was grouped in three basic categories—superior police officers, subordinate police officers, and other ranks (see table 15, Appendix). Police were generally confronted with tasks that were the same as in any other country. In the larger Zambian towns subordinate police officers supervised the activities of sergeants and constables and managed so-called charge offices where complaints from the public were received and police records were maintained. Subordinate officers, sergeants, and constables all participated in beat duty and operated motorized patrols in the towns, villages, and countryside.

Zambian police are authorized to carry weapons in the performance of their duties, but the law places explicit restrictions on the use of firearms. Police may use firearms only to prevent the escape of persons in custody who have been charged with or convicted of felonies, against a person who frees or attempts to free someone being held in lawful custody, or in self-defense. In any case a police officer would be expected to shoot to disable rather than to kill.

Although routine law enforcement was generally handled by the regular police establishment, a major threat to public order would often bring out one of the paramilitary units—the Mobile Unit or the Para-Military Battalion. The Mobile Unit, which had a strength of 881 in 1975 and was estimated to be about the same in early 1979, was divided into four operational companies each of which consisted of four platoons. According to the *Zambia Police Annual Report, 1974,* "The main objective of the Unit is to give a striking force in areas under disturbance. Its secondary objective is to reinforce Police stations experiencing outbreaks of crime beyond the capacity of normal formation strength." The Mobile Unit is a flexible organization, designed to operate as a unit if necessary but also designed to allow companies or platoons to be detached for separate operations, which was the usual case.

"The main tasks of the Para-Military Battalion," according to the police report, "are to guard vital installations throughout Zambia and to provide a force to assist in the maintenance of law and order, particularly along the borders of the Republic of Zambia." Like the Mobile Unit, the Para-Military Battalion had four operational companies in addition to various headquarters elements. It had a total of 833 men in 1975. Each of the companies had four operational platoons consisting of forty men and, again like the Mobile Unit, the companies and platoons of the Para-Military Battalion were designed to operate separately when called on to do so. The basic training and ongoing training of paramilitary personnel is much more like that of infantrymen than of police.

Another special activity of the Zambia Police Force was the dog training center, a small facility at the Police Training School in Lilayi that had kennels for twenty-six dogs. A small staff at the school was assigned duties as dog trainers and dog-handler trainers. In the mid-1970s there were about forty trained German shepherds and trained handlers assigned to nine different urban police posts around the country. Although relatively few in number, the dog patrols had established a reputation for efficient anti-crime work.

The Mounted Section was best known for its appearances on ceremonial occasions when it often escorted the president. In 1975 the section numbered twenty-four men and twenty-nine horses, and its strength was estimated to be about the same in 1979. In addition to its ceremonial assignments the section also handled routine patrols and crowd-control duties. The home station of the Mounted Section was Lusaka, but it was frequently employed outside the capital in areas along the line of rail (see Glossary), where it has appeared in ceremonies and parades in various cities and where it has also been used in police work in the countryside, particularly in pursuit of cattle rustlers.

The Marine Section in 1975 had a strength of fifty-two men who operated a variety of launches and small motor boats. The major activities of the Marine Section were antismuggling patrols on Lake Tanganyika and Lake Mweru in the northeastern part of the country and anti-infiltration patrols on Lake Kariba in the south. Although the section was too small for its assigned duties, higher priorities of other police sections had precluded a buildup of the Marine Section, and it was believed to be about the same size in the late 1970s.

A rather unusual feature of the Zambia Police Force is the Prosecutions Branch. Almost all criminal prosecutions in magistrates' courts are conducted by police prosecutors under the general supervision of the Director of Public Prosecutions (DPP). Police officers above the rank of subinspector are appointed by the DPP to become public prosecutors, and after a lengthy period of training they prosecute most criminal cases in the lower courts. Unless they have become fully qualified lawyers, however, they do not take cases to the High Court. Members of the branch are selected from the ranks and must successfully complete a nine-month course taught by experienced prosecutors and lawyers. After passing examinations in criminal law and procedures, rules of evidence, and English, inter alia, they are then assigned court duties.

The Prosecutions Branch is headed by a senior superintendent of police who is assigned to headquarters in Lusaka. The head of the branch is responsible to the inspector general through the assistant commissioner and is designated senior prosecutions officer. In addition to directing the day-to-day operations of the branch, his major responsibilities include maintaining liaison between the police force and the office of the DPP. The number of police officers assigned to the Prosecutions Branch in 1979 was not known.

The Police Training School provided initial training for new police recruits and also offers promotion courses, refresher training, motor vehicle and motorcycle courses, traffic courses, and instructor training for all ranks. The school, located at Lilayi a few kilometers south of Lusaka, was commanded by a senior superintendent who had a uniformed staff of seventy-two plus a staff of forty-eight civilians including clerks, craftsmen, kitchen help, and laborers. Basic training for recruits lasted twenty-six weeks and, in addition to weapons training and physical fitness training, the curriculum included courses in basic law, police subjects, first aid, self-defense, English, civics, current affairs, and Kaunda's philosophy of Humanism. To be accepted as a police recruit, a candidate must be a citizen between the ages of eighteen and twenty-five, at least five feet six inches tall (five feet two inches for women), physically fit, and have a Form III school certificate (see Education, ch. 2).

One of the high priority items on the police agenda during the 1970s was traffic conrol. Police and government officials have continually expressed concern over the growing number of traffic accidents and more particularly over the growing number of fatalities. Operating primarily on trunk roads but also in the towns and cities, the Traffic Section of the Zambia Police Force struggled against great odds in trying to enforce compliance with traffic laws. At mid-decade the section had a strength of 410, which was 123 under its authorized complement. Equipped with sedans and motorcycles, the Traffic Section used electronic devices in combating speeders, but the section needed more equipment and more modern equipment. The greatest need, however, was for more personnel.

Criminal Law and the Penal Code

In the precolonial period antisocial and criminal behavior were defined by the group or community, and cases against wrongdoers were heard by chiefs or elders who more often than not sentenced guilty persons to compensate victims. During the colonial period the British superimposed their legal system on the existing customary law, and all but the most minor cases were taken out of the hands of the tribal authorities. The colonial authorities redefined antisocial and criminal behavior and determined punishments from a European rather than an African perspective. Imprisonment became a favored form of punishment for many specified criminal acts, and compensation of victims rarely occurred except in cases where civil suits were processed in addition to criminal complaints.

After independence there were some minor organizational changes, but the distinction between criminal and civil substantive and procedural law remained well established, and the basic structure of Zambian law continued to resemble that of its British model (see The Judicial System, ch. 3). During the 1960s court decisions were guided by British precedent; but during the 1970s more Zambians graduated from the University of Zambia Law School, more Zambians were appointed as judges in the country's court system, and a body of Zambian case law was being amassed gradually and was available to be tapped as precedent in criminal and civil trials.

As a consequence of the newly independent government's desire for universal application of a uniform substantive code of criminal law, the application of customary law concerning crime diminished in importance and practically disappeared. The original constitution provided that no person could be tried and convicted of a criminal offense unless that offense was defined and a penalty prescribed in written law. Violations of customary law could no longer lead to criminal charges unless those elements of customary law had been codified. Moreover customary law offenses could not stand in court if they were considered contrary to justice, equity, or good conscience or if they were considered incompatible with statutes or local laws. The Constitution of 1973 restated these provisions.

The basic source of Zambian criminal law is the Penal Code, which is an integral part of the *Laws of Zambia.* It is a modification of the colonial penal code introduced by the British authorities in 1930. Modified and amended many times during the thirty-four years before independence, the code—with some additions and deletions—was incorporated into Zambian law in 1964. It is divided into two parts: Part I—General Provisions—deals with interpretation and application of the code, rules of criminal responsibility, and punishments; Part II—Crimes—is a listing and definition of all crimes covered by the code. It is interesting to note that the code states that the "principles of English law" apply in Zambia's courts. For example, the burden of proof in a criminal trial rests on the government, proof beyond any reasonable doubt is required, and an accused person may not be placed in double jeopardy. Children under the age of eight cannot be charged with a crime. Juveniles between eight and eighteen may be charged, but punishment upon conviction is less severe than for adults. The number of juvenile offenders between the ages of eight and eleven brought to trial during 1974 was very small, and most were accused of some kind of theft.

Punishments are covered in detail in the code, and the range of penalties is carefully defined although the courts generally have some latitude in sentencing. Penalties include death by hanging, imprisonment with or without hard labor, corporal punishment (caning), fine, forfeiture of property, payment of compensation, and deportation. A conviction of murder carries with it a mandatory death sentence. Persons under the age of eighteen at the time of commission of a crime cannot be sentenced to death; pregnant women are also exempted from that penalty.

The code specifies the conditions under which corporal punishment may be imposed and prohibits its use in all other cases. Corporal punishment consists of whipping with a rod or cane in a manner approved by the minister of home affairs. The number of strokes must be specified as part of the sentence and cannot exceed twelve for a person under nineteen years of age or twenty-four for older persons. The code prohibits the caning of females, males over the age of forty-five, and males sentenced to death. When practicable, caning is inflicted in the presence of a professional medical officer who must certify in writing that the prisoner is medically fit to undergo corporal punishment. The code prohibits inflicting more than twelve strokes unless a medical officer is present. Medical officers also may halt a caning in progress, and authorities are not allowed to resume caning after it has been halted.

Subsidiary legislation prohibiting the importation of specific newspapers, magazines, books, and other printed materials appears at the end of the Penal Code. Most of the publications listed apparently are viewed by the government as contrary to the public interest. The majority of the materials consists of publications of the Watch Tower Bible and Tract Society (Jehovah's Witnesses), an organization that had a history of religious and political agitation in the area even before Zambia became independent (see Religion, ch. 2). Many of those publications were prohibited by colonial authorities and were retained on the list after independence. Several other items on the list are publications of various international communist organizations, and a few are comic books published in the United States. During the 1970s Rhodesian newspapers have also been proscribed.

Incidence of Crime

In early 1979 the latest available statistics on crime were those covering calendar year 1974, published by the Zambian government in 1976. In presenting the annual report for 1974, the inspector general of police at that time, Fabiano Chela, stated that crimes against the Penal Code had been higher than during the previous year but that crimes against other laws had been somewhat lower. He also reported that juveniles had been involved in more crimes during 1974 than before. Offenses covered by the Penal Code were listed under eight general headings: Offenses Against Public Order; Offenses Against Lawful Authority; Offenses Injurious to the Public in General; Offenses Against the Person; Offenses Relating to Property; Malicious Injury to Property; Forgery, Coining, and Impersonation; and Offenses Relating to Corrupt Practices. In addition to more than 62,000 arrests made for Penal Code violations in 1974, there were almost 12,500 arrests for Offenses Under Other Laws—which included inter alia crimes involving dangerous drugs, explosives, or firearms; accusing others of witchcraft; and poaching. Although no official statistics existed for the years after 1974, news reports and magazine articles indicated that as the economy has deteriorated, crime has increased, and the situation in 1978 was described as serious.

Included under the heading of Offenses Against Public Order

were the crimes of affray (fighting and brawling), proposing or threatening violence, rioting, sedition, and unlawful assembly. By far the greatest number of arrests under this general heading and the greatest number of cases handled by the courts resulted from fights and brawls that were reported to the police. Most defendants brought to trial on charges of affray were found guilty in 1974 (about 98 percent) and, of those, 74 percent were fined rather than imprisoned. Proposing or threatening violence was the next most serious crime but accounted for fewer than 250 arrests as opposed to almost 8,500 for affray. Arrests and convictions for other listed crimes were: rioting—seventy-seven arrests and fifty convicitions; sedition—fifteen arrests and six convictions; and unlawful assembly—fifty-two arrests and twenty-one convictions. Several cases in each classification were carried over at the end of the year; only a few had resulted in acquittal. The incidence of affray seemed to be so common that it often went unreported, but it was reasonable to assume in early 1979 that not much change had occurred since 1974. Incidence of the other crimes, using news reports as indicators, was probably lower, particularly rioting and sedition.

The category of Offenses Against Lawful Authority included escape from lawful custody, perjury, and official corruption. The largest number of arrests resulted from escapes; those for perjury were negligible; and those made on charges of official corruption appeared to be low, and the number was certainly not cause for grave concern. The low number of arrests on corruption charges was believed to reflect accurately the low level of such crimes rather than a lack of interest in such affairs on the part of police or prosecutors. The periodical *Africa* in its January 1977 issue referred to Zambia as "a country in which corrupt practices are the exception rather than the rule," and Zambia has been noted for this attribute particularly when compared with other nations at the same stage of development. Despite the low incidence of such crime, the government and UNIP constantly monitor official dealings in an ongoing effort to stamp out corruption and abuse of power. The Office of the Investigator General is responsible for guarding the interests of the people against corrupt officials and illegal use of office.

The next major heading, Offenses Injurious to the Public in General, included gross indecency, indecent assault on a female, rape, attempted rape, and drunk and disorderly conduct. Almost one-third of all arrests in 1974, whether for Penal Code offenses or for offenses under other laws, resulted from overindulgence in alcohol, and news accounts of police activities in 1978 indicated that if anything the problem had grown worse. Drunkenness has been a national problem in Zambia for several years, and political leaders, including President Kaunda, periodically decry the abuse of alcohol. Out of a total of almost 25,000 arrests made under this general category, more than 96 percent dealt with drunkenness. The vast majority of cases handled by the courts resulted in fines, but 444 men, 173 women, and eight juveniles were sent to prison on such charges in 1974. Concerning the other crimes in this category, 437 reported cases of indecent assault on a female resulted in 270 arrests and 156 trials (fifty-two others awaited trial at the end of the year); 135 adults and four juveniles were sentenced to prison, one adult and thirteen juveniles were caned, five were fined, and one was remanded. Three had received dual sentences. Of 376 reported cases of rape, only eighty-one eventually reached trial; but of those, seventy-five defendants were sent to prison. Aside from crimes involving alcohol, it was impossible to tell whether other crimes in this general category had increased or decreased by the late 1970s.

Listed under the heading of Offenses Against the Person were the crimes of common assault, assault causing bodily harm, assault causing grievous bodily harm, manslaughter, murder, attempted murder, and unlawful wounding. Assault causing bodily harm accounted for the greatest number of arrests, which resulted in prison terms for 2,498 men, eighty-two women, and seventy-seven juveniles. Eighty-five men and 180 juveniles were caned under these charges, and more than 2,700 other persons paid fines. The incidence of murder during 1974 did not seem disproportionate to the size of the population, the unsettled conditions existing in the country, or the incidence of crime in general. Out of 329 arrests for murder, twenty-three cases were dropped by the prosecutor, eighty-eight defendants were acquitted, 195 awaited trial at the end of the year, and twenty-three others were tried, convicted, and executed. Once again it was impossible to estimate accurately the rate of criminal activity listed as Offenses Against the Person in 1978 and early 1979 but, because of increased unrest in the country and because of a reported increase in crime generally, it is safe to assume that crimes of violence were also on the increase. Murders of expatriate miners in the copperbelt early in the year and a rash of attacks on whites after the Rhodesian raids of October and November 1978 were particularly disturbing to the government because of racial overtones. Some ritual murders in North-Western and Copperbelt provinces also shocked the country during that year.

The fifth general heading under Penal Code violations— Offenses Relating to Property—covered a long list of property crimes (fifteen in all) including burglary, robbery, illegal possession of diamonds, receiving stolen goods, and a wide variety of theft, such as motor vehicle, bicycle, stock, postal material, and theft in general. Almost 5,500 of the 15,437 arrests made under this heading were for common theft; ranking second in number of arrests was the subcategory listed as "stealing by clerks, servants, or agents." News accounts in the late 1970s gave the impression that the ranking of property crimes would be about the same but that the incidence had increased. In 1974 most adults convicted of property crimes were sent to prison; of 1,534 juveniles convicted of property offenses, only about one-third were sent to prison, and the remaining two-thirds were caned.

Examples that showed the extent of the theft problem throughout the country and also showed the extent of official and public concern over the problem appeared regularly in the press. In November 1977 an exposé in the *Zambia Daily Mail* charged that "pilfering among Zambia Airways employees and those working for clearing agents at Lusaka International Airport had reached alarming proportions." In early 1978 a member of parliament asked the public to "declare war on thefts in parastatal bodies." Later in the year Chinese construction workers building a bridge across the Luapula River requested police protection for the site because of the constant disappearance of construction materials. In addition to the nonviolent property crimes that worried officials in the late 1970s, news reports and editorials also referred frequently to the increase in armed robbery that had become evident in various urban centers. Official concern over the incidence of armed robbery had grown to such an extent that by 1976 the death penalty was authorized as a permissible punishment. No doubt some of the illegal activities could be attributed to the unsettled conditions that stemmed from the operations of guerrilla armies operating from Zambian bases and the attacks on those bases by Rhodesian forces. Such conditions fostered an atmosphere of lawlessness that, added to the deterioration of the economy, led some ordinary citizens into criminal activities.

The crimes of arson, malicious damage, and threats to burn or destroy were under the general heading of Malicious Injury to Property. The incidence of arson was not considered serious, but cases were not dealt with lightly: ninety-one convictions resulted in seventy-two imprisonments. Malicious damage to property (vandalism) was common, and of about 500 convictions a few more defendants received prison sentences than fines. Forty juveniles were caned after being found guilty of malicious damage. There were no arrests for threats to burn or destroy during 1974. Accurate estimates concerning the extent of such crimes in 1978 were not available.

The seventh general heading under Penal Code crimes dealt with forgery, counterfeiting, and impersonation. The first two crimes accounted for most of the cases in this category, but of the few persons convicted of impersonation the majority were sent to prison, a general outcome of most rulings for adults in Zambian courts. Conviction of forgery resulted in prison terms for 184 men, two women, and seven juveniles in 1974, and twelve other juveniles were caned for the same offense. Conviction on charges of distributing counterfeit money sent 130 men, three women, and six juveniles to prison; twelve juveniles were caned for the same crime. The eighth and final general heading—Offenses Relating to Corrupt Practices—was not broken down into subcategories and accounted for only twenty-eight arrests during 1974.

In the category of Offenses Under Other Laws 12,474 arrests were made, and 11,889 convictions in court were secured. As opposed to violators of Penal Code crimes, however, persons convicted of breaking this wide variety of laws were much more frequently fined than imprisoned. Convictions for violations of the Dangerous Drug Act, for example, resulted in fines for 215 defendants, whereas only 100 received prison sentences on similar charges. For violations of the Animal Conservation Act, 372 persons were fined and 117 imprisoned. Of forty-six convictions under the Witchcraft Act, however, twenty-seven prison sentences resulted. This act followed the pattern established under colonial rule that defined not witchcraft but the accusing of others of witchcraft as an offense. Out of the total of 11,889 convictions for Offenses Under Other Laws, 888 men, 204 women, and thirty juveniles were imprisoned; the remainder were either caned (only twelve) or fined (the vast majority).

One of the particularly serious crimes covered under this category was poaching and, from newspaper accounts during the period since the last publication of official statistics, it has been obvious that government and party officials were deeply concerned about the apparent wanton destruction of wildlife. Despite the stringent law, poachers were conducting wholesale slaughter of game in the country's national parks and game reserves. A judge of the High Court in Lusaka said in late 1978 that "the law against poaching was one of the toughest laws we had in this country." Responding to critics who faulted the law as too lenient, the judge attributed the alarming increase in the rate of poaching to the greater sophistication of the poachers, who were well armed and well equipped for their illegal activities. From other statements by officials and reports in the press in 1978 it was obvious that game wardens and park rangers were at a disadvantage because of their small numbers and their lack of transport. According to government spokesmen some progress had been made in enlisting the aid of villagers in the antipoaching campaign, but more needed to be done to educate people to the seriousness of the situation because of the plummeting number of animals of all species.

Also drawing considerable attention in the Zambian press in 1978 was the widespread smuggling of all kinds of goods along the country's frontiers and the illegal mining of emeralds, arrests for which were increasing in frequency. According to an article in the *Zambia Sunday Times* of October 29, 1978, illegal dealings in emeralds were conducted almost openly in Kitwe hotels and restaurants not far from the areas where the illegal mining was taking place. The article stressed that the big operators in the illegal emerald handling were either expatriates or visiting foreigners but that those illegally digging the stones were Zambians.

During 1978 the crime situation in general was referred to by officials as an "increased wave of crime," in a newspaper editorial as "the alarming high incidence of crime," and in a magazine as "the rampant crime." No matter what the words used to describe it, there was no doubt that the incidence of crime had become of prime concern to authorities. Some UNIP officials blamed some of this on dissident elements who desired to embarrass Kaunda as the December elections approached. Some police officials blamed the increased criminal activity on the fact that the police were understaffed and poorly equipped. Most Zambians agreed, however, that much of the crime problem resulted from the number of aliens resident in the country, and during the year there were mass roundups and deportations of illegal aliens. In March parliament authorized the Ministry of Home Affairs "to hunt down all illegal residents and flush them out of Zambia immediately." Minister of Home Affairs Phiri said that most crime was committed by aliens and promised that his ministry would be diligent in repatriating undesirables. An editorial in the *Times of Zambia* shortly thereafter blamed Zambia's crime on its open society that allowed undesirable foreigners to flow into the country at will. The editorial called for a campaign against the "alien menace" but also warned against mass xenophobia.

By summer a campaign against aliens was in full swing, backed by the press, the party, and the police. Near the end of July Operation Clean-up began when a joint force of police and immigration officers in Kitwe rounded up 300 aliens for inspection of papers and possible deportation. The *Zambia Sunday Times* of August 6, 1978, noted that many aliens were illegally obtaining identification cards; officials then called on the public to aid authorities in making sure that identity documents were not acquired by unauthorized aliens. A few days later another joint operation in which members of the ZNDF joined the police and immigration officers rounded up a total of 819 aliens in Lusaka, Ndola, and Kabwe. The minister of home affairs said that the security forces conducted block-to-block searches, entering every house looking for illegal aliens and in the process searching for illegal firearms and contraband. The operation was carried out under the direction of Inspector General of Police Crispin Katukula. Minister of Home Affairs Phiri, whose ministry oversees police activities, announced that such operations would continue until all criminal aliens had been deported. A *Zambia Daily Mail* editorial congratulated the police and called on Zambians to cooperate in ridding the country of undesirable elements.

The number of aliens actually deported during the security sweeps of late summer 1978 was not publicized. Many of those arrested were later released after properly identifying themselves and proving that they were in the country legally. There were reports of several hundred unemployed Tanzanians voluntarily returning to their own country, and earlier in the year several hundred Somalis reportedly left Zambia complaining that they could no longer put up with police harassment. How many aliens departed voluntarily, how many were deported, and how the crime rate was affected were questions that had not been answered at the end of the year.

Penal System

The penal system, a carryover from colonial times, is essentially British in structure and in principles of operation. It was originally staffed at top levels by British officials, but the process of zambianization increased rapidly during the late 1960s, and by 1970 most senior positions were held by Zambians. Responsibility for the Prison Service was vested in the Ministry of Home Affairs. The minister was advised and assisted by the constitutionally appointed Police and Prison Service Commission (see Zambia Police Force, this ch.).

Prison staffs were a career element of the civil service, but no figures were available on either the authorized or the actual strength of the Prison Service at the beginning of 1979. The efficiency of the Prison Service did not appear to have suffered from a lack of qualified personnel in the years after independence, and it was unlikely that any serious personnel shortages could occur because the law provided that police officers could be brought in to run the prisons if necessary. The law governing the operation of the Prison Service was a single chapter of the *Laws of Zambia* titled simply "Prisons." The service maintains the Prison Staff Training School at Kabwe for the primary purpose of training Prison Service recruits, but the school also offers advanced courses for personnel needing refresher training or preparing for promotions.

At the beginning of 1975 there were fifty-two penal institutions under the control of the Prison Service. Because there has been no publicity concerning the closing of old installations or the opening of new ones, the number was assumed to be about the same in the late 1970s. The law governing the operation of the system decrees that male and female prisoners are kept separate and that prisoners are classified as juveniles, adults, first offenders, and those of unsound mind. The service attempted to provide appropriate installations for the segregation of different classes of prisoners of both sexes; twelve prisons distributed among provincial capitals or major cities were designed to house male convicts. Kabwe Maximum Security Prison provided facilities for the most difficult cases. All female offenders whose sentences exceeded three months were sent to Kasama Prison in Northern Province. Juvenile offenders were sent to a reformatory at Katambora near Livingstone.

Conditions in Zambian prisons in 1978 were said to be crowded and unsanitary, and health care was reported as inadequate. There was no evidence of systematized maltreatment or torture, but some Rhodesian detainees had complained of beatings in the mid-1970s. The president has wide powers of detention and, although detainees have some rights, habeas corpus is not available to persons held under presidential order. Kaunda has sometimes used the presidential detention powers against political opponents. Amnesty International investigated reports of political detentions in 1976 and 1977, but the Zambian government did not respond to its queries. It was believed, however, that most if not all political prisoners had been released.

Internal Threats to National Security

At the beginning of 1979 no organized dissident group was operating against the legal government of Zambia from within the country, although there was some political opposition to it (see Political Developments, 1975–79; Political Dynamics, ch. 3). Internal threats to security came from the presence of large numbers of ZAPU guerrillas and from ethnic tensions, although the latter were latent rather than salient. Political opposition parties were banned in favor of the one-party state, making opposition disorganized and diffuse; nevertheless it existed. Kaunda's one-sided victory in the presidential election of December 1978 served notice to his opponents that they had little overt support among the people. Kaunda has often said that the presence of ZAPU guerrillas in the country presented no threat, and in fact there seemed to have been few threatening incidents. Nevertheless the mere presence of a foreign army of such size and over such an extended period of time in itself tended to be a potential threat. Kaunda often spoke out against ethnic divisiveness, which he considered dangerous, but Zambia has not been torn by what Zambians speak of pejoratively as tribalism (see The Politics of Independence, ch. 1; see "Tribes" and "Tribalism," ch. 2). Kaunda has always deplored ethnic extremism and has pleaded for a nationwide commitment to zambianism, but the national consciousness that he has worked so hard to foster still seemed to be of the future in early 1979.

Threats to security are not always easily divisible into categories such as internal and external, and that was the case in Zambia in the late 1970s. The danger of raids into Zambia by Rhodesian armed forces seemed to be properly classified as an external threat, but such raids often led to dangerous situations within the country, which then became internal threats. Even though the Rhodesian attacks have most often been directed against guerrilla camps, they have been perceived by Zambians as infringements on the country's sovereignty, and some citizens have therefore demanded that force be answered by force. A continuation of the Rhodesian raids could increase such feelings and possibly create a dissident movement that could become a threat to the government. Although little has been heard from military spokesmen, the raids could create attitudes among armed forces personnel that would be counter to Kaunda's announced policy of nonretaliation. John Darnton, writing from Lusaka for the *New York Times,* stated that Kaunda's announcement in late November

1978 that he was diverting funds from other projects to buy weapons was "a move to assuage public fears and also to the feelings of army officers, angry at not being allowed to strike back at the attackers." The replacement of General Zuze as commander of the ZNDF at the beginning of 1979 was also rumored to be a reaction to his alleged discontent with the policy of nonretaliation against the Rhodesians.

In December 1978 the *Zambia Daily Mail* reported that heavily armed gangs of young people had created a "wave of terror" east of Lusaka along the highway that connects the capital with Lilongwe, the capital of Malawi. The newspaper said that motorists had been attacked and women raped, but the terrorists were not identified. David Ottaway, *Washington Post* Africa correspondent, reported from Lusaka in January 1979 that motorists on the same highway were formed into convoys and escorted by Zambia Army troops because of the depredations of the bands of armed youth. The Zambian government claimed, as it had often in the past, that the armed gangs were Selous Scouts, a commando group of the Rhodesian army. Ottaway said that some Western diplomats as well as some Zambian officials expressed the opinion that the armed gangs were deserters from the ZAPU guerrilla army who had fled their camps during the Rhodesian raids of October and November 1978 and had roamed the area as bandit gangs ever since. ZAPU spokesmen strongly denied the allegation, saying that it was a deliberate ploy to sow dissension, but the attacks on motorists reportedly began in October and increased steadily during the next two months. In January twelve deserters from Nkomo's guerrilla army were arrested in the area, ending that particular crime wave.

Nkomo reported in early 1979 that he had completed a reorganization and dispersal of his forces that would make them less vulnerable to Rhodesian raids. This move would also serve to lessen tensions among Zambians living in areas where large ZAPU camps had previously been located. According to ZAPU reports, several thousand recruits had been moved from camps around Lusaka to remote areas in northern Zambia where they would be trained in small camps rather than in large concentrations that had made easy targets for enemy bombers.

*   *   *

Zambia: Security and Conflict by Jan Pettman and *Politics in Zambia* edited by William Tordoff are helpful in setting the national security scene in Zambia in the early 1970s. For the security affairs of the mid- and late 1970s newspapers, periodicals, and the *Africa Research Bulletin* have been relied on heavily. The *Africa Contemporary Record* is always a handy reference in pinning down what happened and when. There are no books dealing specifically with the security forces in Zambia. (For further information see Bibliography.)

Appendix

Table

Table 1. Conversion Coefficients and Factors

When you know	Multiply by	To find
Millimeters....................	0.04	inches
Centimeters...................	0.39	inches
Meters........................	3.3	feet
Kilometers....................	0.62	miles
Hectares (10,000 m²)............	2.47	acres
Square kilometers..............	0.39	square miles
Cubic meters..................	35.3	cubic feet
Liters........................	0.26	gallons
Kilograms.....................	2.2	pounds
Metric tons...................	0.98	long tons
....	1.1	short tons
....	2,204.	pounds
Degrees Celsius	9	degrees Fahrenheit
(Centigrade)	divide by 5 and add 32	

Table 2. Population and Growth Rates of Provinces, 1963, 1969, and 1974

Province	Population			Average Annual Growth Rate (in percent)	
	1963	1969	1974	1963–69	1969–74
Central[1]	505,164	712,630	920,000	5.9	5.2
Copperbelt.......	543,465	816,309	1,046,000	7.0	5.1
Eastern	479,866	509,515	568,000	1.0	2.2
Luapula..........	357,018	335,584	321,000	−1.0	−0.9
Northern.........	563,995	545,096	580,000	−0.6	1.3
North-Western ...	211,189	231,733	256,000	1.6	2.0
Southern.........	466,327	496,041	540,000	1.0	1.7
Western	362,480	410,087	463,000	2.1	2.5
TOTAL......	3,489,504	4,056,995[2]	4,695,000[3]	2.5[4]	3.0[4]

[1]In January 1976 Lusaka and its immediate environs, formerly a part of Central Province, became Zambia's ninth province. In 1974 Lusaka had an estimated population of 401,000.
[2]This is the original total, unadjusted for an estimated 2.1-percent underenumeration.
[3]The total as given in the source exceeds the actual sum of provincial populations by 1,000.
[4]The provincial variations in average annual growth, 1963–69 and 1969–74, reflect the substantial migration in these periods, chiefly toward the urban centers of Copperbelt and Central provinces.

Source: Based on information from Zambia, Central Statistical Office, *Sample Census of Population 1974: Preliminary Report*, Lusaka, 1975, p. 6.

Table 3. Population and Growth Rates of Urban Areas, 1963, 1969, and 1974

Urban Area[1]	Population[2]			Average Annual Growth Rate[3] (in percent)	
	1963	1969	1974	1963–69	1969–74
Lusaka...........	123,146	262,425	401,000	13.4	8.9
Kitwe............	123,027	199,798	251,000	8.4	4.7
Ndola...........	92,691	159,786	229,000	9.5	7.5
Mufulira	80,609	107,802	136,000	5.0	4.8
Chingola........	59,517	103,292	134,000	9.6	5.3
Luanshya	75,332	96,282	121,000	4.2	4.7
Kabwe..........	39,522	65,974	98,000	8.9	8.2
Livingstone	33,026	45,243	58,000	5.4	5.1
Chililabombwe ...	34,165	44,862	56,000	4.7	4.5
Kalulushi.........	21,303	32,272	41,000	7.2	4.9
Total Urban....	682,338	1,117,736	1,525,000	8.6	6.4
Other towns[4].....	32,682	74,380	131,000	14.7	12.0
TOTAL......	715,020	1,192,116	1,656,000	8.9	6.8

[1]Except for Lusaka, Kabwe, and Livingstone, all large urban areas are in the copperbelt.
[2]Figures from 1963 and 1969 censuses are unadjusted for undercounting. Figures for 1974 are estimates based on sample census.
[3]Growth rates are not wholly comparable because boundaries of some towns have been changed between censuses.
[4]In 1974 these towns ranged from roughly 5,000 to just under 20,000.

Source: Based on information from Zambia, Central Statistical Office, *Sample Census of Population 1974: Preliminary Report,* Lusaka, 1975, p. 6.

Table 4. Student Enrollment, 1964 and 1971–76
(in thousands)

	1964	1971	1972	1973	1974	1975	1976
Primary School							
Male	215.4	402.3	428.7	445.0	470.2	476.0	n.a.
Female	163.3	327.5	349.2	365.2	388.0	396.4	n.a.
Total Primary School	378.6[1]	729.8	777.9	810.2	858.2	872.4	n.a.
Secondary School							
Male	9.8	37.5	39.9	40.3	43.6	48.0	51.9
Female	4.1	18.5	20.1	21.0	22.2	25.1	26.9
Total Secondary School	13.9	56.0	60.1[1]	61.4[1]	65.8	73.0[1]	78.8
Teacher Training							
Male	1.0	1.4	1.4	1.6	1.7	1.8	n.a.
Female	0.5	1.0	1.0	1.1	1.2	1.2	n.a.
Total Teacher Training	1.5	2.5[1]	2.4	2.7	2.9	3.1[1]	n.a.
University of Zambia[2]	—	1.6	1.7	2.2	2.6	2.4	2.6

Adult Education							
Primary							
Male	—	19.3	21.4	21.1	22.8	24.1	15.0
Female	—	8.1	9.4	10.0	10.8	13.4	7.9
Total Primary	2.7	27.4	30.8	31.0[1]	33.6	37.5	22.9
Secondary							
Male	—	11.5	12.6	16.6	18.6	18.7	12.9
Female	—	3.6	4.3	6.4	7.8	9.6	6.5
Total Secondary	1.8	15.1	16.9	22.9[1]	26.4	28.2[1]	19.4
Total Adult Education	4.5	42.5	47.7	54.0[1]	60.0	65.7	42.3[3]
Technical and trades training institutes	0.8	3.2	1.9[4]	4.8	5.7	5.4[3]	5.6
TOTAL	399.3	835.6	891.6[1]	935.3	995.1[1]	1,022.0	n.a.

n.a.—not available.
—means not applicable.
[1] Figures do not add to total because of rounding.
[2] At the establishment of the University of Zambia in 1966, enrollment was 312. Information accounting for the decline in enrollment from 1974 to 1975 is not available.
[3] Decrease cannot be accounted for because of lack of information.
[4] Evelyn Hone College (oriented to business education) was not included in 1972.

Source: Based on information from Zambia, Central Statistical Office, *Monthly Digest of Statistics*, Lusaka, XIV, 3-6, March-June 1978.

Table 5. *Employees by Industry, 1972–76*[1]

Industry	Zambian	Non-Zambian	Total
1972			
Agriculture, forestry, and fisheries.....	29,640	1,500	31,140
Mining and quarrying...............	49,470	11,180	60,650
Manufacturing......................	40,020	3,280	43,300
Electricity and water................	4,000	530	4,530
Construction and allied repairs........	68,230	4,090	72,320
Distribution, restaurants, and hotels ...	29,670	4,020	33,690
Transport and communications........	23,240	1,800	25,040
Finance, insurance, real estate, and business services..............	12,420	1,890	14,310
Community, social, and personal services[2]	77,100	5,850	82,950
TOTAL 1972.....................	333,790	34,140	367,930
1973			
Agriculture, forestry, and fisheries.....	30,330	1,400	31,730
Mining and quarrying...............	50,420	11,320	61,740
Manufacturing......................	40,460	3,140	43,600
Electricity and water................	4,150	530	4,680
Construction and allied repairs........	66,630	3,860	70,490
Distribution, restaurants, and hotels ...	31,160	3,700	34,860
Transport and communications........	22,470	1,740	24,210
Finance, insurance, real estate, and business services..............	13,110	1,900	15,010
Community, social, and personal services[2]	81,320	5,800	87,120
TOTAL 1973.....................	340,050	33,390	373,440
1974			
Agriculture, forestry, and fisheries.....	32,160	1,450	33,610
Mining and quarrying...............	54,270	10,840	65,110
Manufacturing......................	40,970	3,100	44,070
Electricity and water................	4,240	510	4,750
Construction and allied repairs........	66,270	4,310	70,580
Distribution, restaurants, and hotels ...	32,180	3,400	35,580
Transport and communications........	20,530	1,620	22,150
Finance, insurance, real estate, and business services..............	14,540	1,910	16,450
Community, social, and personal services[2]	86,430	6,160	92,590
TOTAL 1974.....................	351,590	33,300	384,890

Table 5—Continued

Industry	Zambian	Non-Zambian	Total
1975			
Agriculture, forestry, and fisheries.....	34,790	1,310	36,100
Mining and quarrying...............	54,440	10,310	64,750
Manufacturing......................	41,230	3,100	44,330
Electricity and water................	4,720	410	5,130
Construction and allied repairs........	67,790	3,960	71,750
Distribution, restaurants, and hotels ...	30,230	2,730	32,960
Transport and communications........	20,490	1,560	22,050
Finance, insurance, real estate, and business services..............	16,820	1,880	18,700
Community, social, and personal services[2]	90,660	7,060	97,720
TOTAL 1975.....................	361,170	32,320	393,490
1976			
Agriculture, forestry, and fisheries.....	31,230	1,270	32,500
Mining and quarrying...............	55,580	9,000	64,580
Manufacturing......................	38,960	2,700	41,660
Electricity and water................	5,090	320	5,410
Construction and allied repairs........	47,150	3,120	50,270
Distribution, restaurants, and hotels ...	33,880	2,220	36,100
Transport and communications........	19,840	1,240	21,080
Finance, insurance, real estate, and business services..............	17,300	1,600	18,900
Community, social, and personal services[2]	91,490	6,480	97,970
TOTAL 1976.....................	340,520	27,950	368,470

[1]Based on quarter ending December.
[2]Excludes domestic service.
[3]Preliminary.

Source: Based on information from Zambia, Central Statistical Office,
Monthly Digest of Statistics, Lusaka, XIV, 3–6, March-June 1978,
p. 5, Supplement, p. 1.

Table 6. Balance of
(in millions

Item	1974 Credit	1974 Debit	1975 Credit	1975 Debit
Goods and Services	963.6	833.9	567.6	926.6
Merchandise (FOB)	898.2	508.6	512.9	593.4
Exports and imports	900.4	506.6	518.0	597.6
Reexports	4.7	—	3.1	—
Adjustments	−6.9	2.0	−8.2	−4.2
Freight and insurance on merchandise	22.9	127.6	26.0	154.3
Other transportation	9.8	31.2	9.7	33.0
Travel	4.8	14.1	6.0	10.0
Investment income	19.2	81.4	5.0	68.6
Other government	5.0	3.2	6.0	5.7
Other private	3.7	67.8	2.0	61.6
Unrequited Transfers	7.9	89.1	6.0	85.3
Private	2.0	88.5	2.0	85.3
Government	5.9	0.6	4.0	—
Current Account Balance	+48.5		−438.3	
Capital (excluding reserves and related items)	9.7	...	195.8[3]	...
Nonmonetary Sectors	10.9	...	188.3[3]	...
Private capital	...	25.9	103.5[3]	...
Central government	36.8	...	84.8	...
Monetary Sectors	...	...	7.5	...
Monetary institutions (other than central)	...	1.2	7.5	...
Liabilities	5.0	...	0.4	...
Assets	...	6.2	7.1	...
Reserves and related items	...	8.2	242.5	...
Liabilities	...	0.2	108.3	...
Use of fund credit	...	—	—	...
Other	...	0.2	108.3	...
Assets	...	8.0	35.8	...
Monetary gold	...	...	...	...
SDRs[4]	...	9.0	...	2.9
Foreign exchange (Bank of Zambia)	2.7	...	38.0	...
Foreign exchange (government)	...	1.7	0.7	...
Payment arrears	...	...	102.1	...
Currency realignment changes	...	...	...	3.7
Net Errors and Omissions	...	50.0	...	...

—means none.
[1] For value of the kwacha—see Glossary.
[2] Preliminary.
[3] Includes errors and omissions.
[4] Special drawing rights.

Source: Based on information from Zambia, Central Statistical Office, *Monthly Digest of Statistics,* Lusaka, XIV, 3–6, March-June 1978, p. 54.

Payments, 1974–77
of kwacha)[1]

1976[2]		1977[2]		Item
Credit	Debit	Credit	Debit	
798.1	863.5	784.5	976.9	Goods and Services
733.7	496.0	715.5	554.4	Merchandise (FOB)
748.6	468.6	706.4	536.7	Exports and imports
3.3	—	2.1	—	Reexports
−18.2	27.4	7.0	17.7	Adjustments
30.0	148.8	33.0	165.7	Freight and insurance on merchandise
13.4	39.4	15.0	42.0	Other transportation
9.0	14.0	9.0	22.8	Travel
3.0	98.6	3.0	106.7	Investment income
7.0	6.7	7.0	7.0	Other government
2.0	60.0	2.0	78.3	Other private
7.2	90.2	14.0	79.2	Unrequited Transfers
2.0	89.4	2.0	79.2	Private
5.2	0.8	12.0	—	Government
−143.4		−257.6		Current Account Balance
				Capital (excluding reserves
12.3[3]	...	57.8[3]	...	and related items)
12.2[3]	...	42.9[3]	...	Nonmonetary Sectors
...	42.7[3]	...	...	Private capital
30.5	...	...	...	Central government
0.1	...	14.9	...	Monetary Sectors
				Monetary institutions (other than
0.1	...	14.9	...	central)
5.1	...	13.1	...	Liabilities
...	5.0	1.8	...	Assets
136.1	...	199.8	...	Reserves and related items
23.0	...	19.6	...	Liabilities
—	...	...	...	Use of fund credit
23.0	...	...	...	Other
16.7	...	23.3	...	Assets
...	0.9	...	...	Monetary gold
...	5.7	...	...	SDRs[4]
22.1	...	...	...	Foreign exchange (Bank of Zambia)
1.2	...	...	...	Foreign exchange (government)
103.6	...	156.9	...	Payment arrears
...	7.2	...	...	Currency realignment changes
...	...	...	...	Net Errors and Omissions

Table 7. Mineral Production, 1965–77
(in thousands of tons)

Year	Copper			Zinc	Lead	Coal	Cobalt
	Blister	Electrolytic	Total				
1965.....	164	521	685	48	21	—	1.5
1966.....	88	498	586	42	19	118	1.5
1967.....	82	534	616	45	20	399	1.5
1968.....	93	572	665	53	22	573	1.2
1969.....	105	643	748	50	23	397	1.5
1970.....	103	580	683	54	27	623	2.1
1971.....	99	535	633*	57	28	812	2.1
1972.....	84	614	698	56	26	937	2.1
1973.....	43	638	681	54	25	940	1.9
1974.....	34	669	703	58	25	810	2.0
1975.....	21	619	640	47	19	814	1.8
1976.....	18	695	713	37	14	762	1.7
1977.....	11	649	660	40	13	708	1.7

—means none.
*Figures do not add to total because of rounding.

Table 8. Principal Exports, Selected Years, 1965–77[1]
(in millions of kwacha)[2]

Year	Copper	Zinc	Lead	Cobalt	Tobacco	Maize	Other	Total
1965....	343.2	9.6	3.4	3.6	4.9	1.9	8.4	375.0
1967....	434.0	8.1	2.7	5.6	3.7	8.7	4.2	467.0
1969....	724.5	12.4	6.1	4.5	3.2	0.4	3.4	754.5
1971....	450.2	11.5	4.6	4.1	3.5	0.2	5.9	480.0
1973....	698.3	16.7	5.4	4.9	4.8	2.6	5.4	738.1
1974....	838.5	25.2	7.2	7.9	5.8	7.6	8.2	900.4
1975....	472.0	20.3	5.7	7.1	5.0	1.4	6.5	518.0
1976....	688.6	26.4	4.4	15.9	5.1	0.5	7.7	748.6
1977....	645.9	17.9	5.7	15.3	5.8	3.5	12.3	706.4

[1]Excludes reexports.
[2]For value of the kwacha—see Glossary.

Table 9. Imports by SITC Division, 1966–77[1]
(in millions of kwacha)[2]

Division	1966	1967	1968
Food	19.79	21.37	24.13
Beverages and tobacco	3.02	2.13	2.17
Crude materials	4.59	4.42	4.41
Electricity and mineral fuels	19.60	31.23	33.21
Oils and fats	2.63	2.35	1.94
Chemicals	19.24	20.90	22.65
Manufactured goods classified by materials	55.12	65.51	74.12
Machinery and transport equipment	97.94	126.33	134.44
Miscellaneous manufactured articles	23.82	28.39	23.96
Miscellaneous transactions	0.37	3.82	4.17
TOTAL	246.12	306.45	325.20

Division	1969	1970	1971
Food	30.41	30.45	48.19
Beverages and tobacco	2.20	1.18	1.42
Crude materials	4.49	5.28	7.63
Electricity and mineral fuels	35.58	35.18	32.24
Oils and fats	2.88	4.46	4.52
Chemicals	22.56	26.02	31.69
Manufactured goods classified by materials	62.79	74.80	84.79
Machinery and transport equipment	123.04	131.72	160.12
Miscellaneous manufactured articles	25.61	30.54	27.76
Miscellaneous transactions	2.23	1.09	1.45
TOTAL	311.79	340.72	399.31[3]

Division	1972	1973	1974
Food	37.14	24.34	43.80
Beverages and tobacco	1.25	0.97	1.13
Crude materials	7.94	5.42	10.36
Electricity and mineral fuels	26.52	33.29	61.10
Oils and fats	3.91	4.32	6.77
Chemicals	33.04	35.14	48.45
Manufactured goods classified by materials	87.92	77.34	130.00
Machinery and transport equipment	168.01	138.91	167.80
Miscellaneous manufactured articles	35.38	25.38	36.43
Miscellaneous transactions	1.37	1.75	2.81
TOTAL	402.48	346.86	506.64[3]

Table 9—(continued)

Division	1975	1976	1977
Food	35.75	24.47	29.66
Beverages and tobacco	1.02	0.88	0.97
Crude materials	9.89	7.21	8.81
Electricity and mineral fuels	81.12	72.62	87.72
Oils and fats	9.09	10.68	10.12
Chemicals	77.29	68.18	58.81
Manufactured goods classified by materials	140.21	96.81	116.47
Machinery and transport equipment	211.30	166.92	205.15
Miscellaneous manufactured articles	28.70	19.00	19.42
Miscellaneous transactions	3.25	0.78	0.54
TOTAL	597.62	467.54[3]	536.67[3]

[1]SITC—Standard International Trade Classification.
[2]For value of the kwacha—see Glossary.
[3]Figures do not add to total because of rounding.

Table 10. Destination of Exports, Selected Years, 1970–77
(in millions of kwacha)[1]

Country	1970	1972	1974	1976	1977
United Kingdom	160.1	107.7	195.8	103.7	113.5
European Economic Community[2]	227.3	170.9	324.0	253.3	276.0
West Germany[3]	(84.2)	(45.5)	(114.7)	(106.0)	(101.9)
European Free Trade Association	38.6	28.7	33.2	35.3	32.2
South Africa	8.7	10.8	3.4	1.8	1.8
United States	1.4	2.3	5.3	116.4	72.9
Japan	166.5	110.6	176.3	125.9	I24.1
China[4]	34.1	12.6	21.9	19.0	22.9
Soviet bloc	4.6	2.6	0.03	1.2	3.0
Other	73.7	95.4	145.2	95.3	62.1
TOTAL	715.0	541.6	905.1	751.9	708.5

[1]For value of the kwacha—see Glossary.
[2]EEC, also called the Common Market; United Kingdom excluded.
[3]Federal Republic of Germany.
[4]People's Republic of China.

Source: Based on information from Zambia, Central Statistical Office, *Monthly Digest of Statistics,* Lusaka, XIV, 3–6, March–June 1978, pp. 23–24.

Table 11. Sources of Imports, Selected Years, 1970–77
(in millions of kwacha)[1]

Country	1970	1972	1974	1976	1977
United Kingdom	80.6	94.9	99.4	112.3	122.8
European Economic Community[2]	43.9	61.6	96.1	86.2	113.5
West Germany[3]	(16.5)	(21.5)	(41.0)	(33.7)	(62.6)
European Free Trade Association	14.5	15.6	27.7	25.0	31.4
South Africa	59.1	59.3	38.7	36.0	38.5
United States	32.9	35.0	39.7	50.7	57.5
Japan	21.8	38.8	48.6	22.1	25.3
China[4]	2.2	9.8	24.3	9.0	6.6
Soviet bloc	4.2	6.1	2.4	1.7	1.7
Other	81.5	81.4	129.7	124.5	139.4
TOTAL	340.7	402.5	506.6	467.5	536.7

[1]For value of the kwacha—see Glossary.
[2]EEC, also called the Common Market; United Kingdom excluded.
[3]Federal Republic of Germany.
[4]People's Republic of China.

Source: Based on information from Zambia, Central Statistical Office, *Monthly Digest of Statistics,* Lusaka, XIV, 3–6, March–June 1978, pp. 23–24.

Table 12. *Central Government Recurrent Budget, Fiscal Years 1965/66 and 1970–77*
(in millions of kwacha)[1]

	1965/6	1970	1971	1972	1973	1974	1975	1976	1977
Recurrent Revenue									
Mineral revenue	141.6	251.1	114.1	55.7	107.6	332.8	59.4	11.6	15.0
Income taxes	21.3	70.0	80.1	91.2	116.0	116.8	142.6	159.1	173.0
Customs duties	16.6	32.5	36.7	49.8	46.0	60.9	48.4	29.0	30.0
Excise and sales taxes	8.6	35.6	38.1	48.7	63.1	86.1	139.9	183.1	215.0
Other	29.4	43.2	40.0	65.7	52.5	52.9	57.9	60.2	70.8
Total Recurrent Revenue	217.4[2]	432.4	309.0	311.1	385.2	649.5	448.2	443.1[2]	503.8
Recurrent Expenditure									
General Services	50.2	95.3	128.3	137.5	135.1	164.0	238.2	207.0	210.8
Social Services									
Education	19.6	43.8	53.6	60.9	65.5	69.7	75.4	81.7	92.8
Health	8.9	20.2	24.1	25.8	28.2	31.8	34.8	37.8	47.3
Other	1.4	1.8	1.6	1.5	1.4	2.8	2.7	3.2	3.2
Total Social Services	29.9	65.8	79.3	88.2	95.1	104.3	112.9	122.7	143.3

Economic Services

Agriculture and rural development	5.6	26.3	48.2	37.8	46.9	45.4	78.1	66.2	75.3
Land, mines, and natural resources	6.2	4.4	6.1	5.8	5.8	10.3	8.0	9.9	9.4
Trade and industry	0.5	4.7	1.1	2.4	1.0	1.2	14.6	1.7	1.5
Transport, communications, and power	11.9	40.9	44.0	35.8	33.4	37.3	43.2	37.7	41.4
Other	10.4	3.5	3.0	0.1	26.0	7.0	15.0	5.0	0.5
Total Economic Services	34.5[2]	79.8	102.4	81.9	113.1	101.2	158.9	120.5	128.1
Other Expenditure	7.7	14.4	17.3	20.9	26.7	36.2	36.9	43.4	82.2
Total Recurrent Expenditure	122.2[2]	256.1[2]	327.3	328.5	370.1[2]	405.8[2]	546.9	493.6[3]	564.4[3]

[1]For value of the kwacha—see Glossary.
[2]Figures do not add to total because of rounding.
[3]Budget. Preliminary results for 1976 show expenditure at K562.6 million, and the provisional total for 1977 is reported at K593.6 million.

Table 13. *Average Annual Earnings of Employees by Industry, 1972–76*[1]
(in kwacha)[2]

Industry	Zambian	Non-Zambian	All Employees
1972			
Agriculture, forestry, and fisheries......	434	3,148	529
Mining and quarrying................	1,601	5,014	2,230
Manufacturing.......................	1,025	5,248	1,159
Electricity and water.................	825	5,483	1,370
Construction and allied repairs........	703	4,377	911
Distribution, restaurants, and hotels	1,081	4,680	1,510
Transport and communications........	1,204	4,143	1,415
Finance, insurance, real estate, and business services...............	1,298	6,339	1,964
Community, social, and personal services[3]	1,129	3,303	1,282
Average, all industries............	1,014	4,548	1,342
1973			
Agriculture, forestry, and fisheries......	419	2,596	515
Mining and quarrying................	1,685	5,406	2,367
Manufacturing.......................	1,064	6,119	1,428
Electricity and water.................	922	6,194	1,519
Construction and allied repairs........	724	4,324	921
Distribution, restaurants, and hotels	1,147	4,866	1,542
Transport and communications........	1,292	4,377	1,514
Finance, insurance, real estate, and business services...............	1,328	6,623	1,998
Community, social, and personal services[3]	1,318	3,956	1,494
Average, all industries............	1,135	4,949	1,476
1974			
Agriculture, forestry, and fisheries......	445	2,602	538
Mining and quarrying................	1,701	6,629	2,522
Manufacturing.......................	1,071	5,866	1,408
Electricity and water.................	803	6,062	1,368
Construction and allied repairs........	716	4,371	939
Distribution, restaurants, and hotels	1,019	5,066	1,406
Transport and communications........	1,397	4,653	1,635
Finance, insurance, real estate, and business services...............	1,356	6,947	2,005
Community, social, and personal services[3]	1,299	4,168	1,490
Average, all industries............	1,122	5,389	1,491

Table 13—Continued

Industry	Zambian	Non-Zambian	All Employees
1975			
Agriculture, forestry, and fisheries......	453	2,524	528
Mining and quarrying.................	1,478	6,784	2,322
Manufacturing.......................	1,179	5,657	1,445
Electricity and water.................	1,042	7,835	1,569
Construction and allied repairs.........	764	6,868	983
Distribution, restaurants, and hotels	1,018	5,316	1,373
Transport and communications.........	1,834	7,377	2,226
Finance, insurance, real estate, and business services...............	1,641	7,528	2,233
Community, social, and personal services[3]	1,259	3,859	1,446
Average, all industries............	1,140	5,572	1,504
1976			
Agriculture, forestry, and fisheries......	604	3,490	717
Mining and quarrying.................	2,507	10,300	3,593
Manufacturing.......................	1,382	6,652	1,724
Electricity and water.................	1,471	7,475	1,826
Construction and allied repairs.........	906	4,109	1,105
Distribution, restaurants, and hotels	1,274	7,762	1,673
Transport and communications.........	1,818	5,282	2,022
Finance, insurance, real estate, and business services...............	1,927	6,696	2,331
Community, social, and personal services[3]	1,370	4,149	1,554
Average, all industries............	1,469	6,858	1,878

[1]Based on quarter ending December.
[2]For value of the kwacha—see Glossary.
[3]Excludes domestic service.

Source: Based on information from Zambia, Central Statistical Office, *Monthly Digest of Statistics,* Lusaka, XIV, 3–6, March–June 1978, p. 6, Supplement, p. 3.

Table 14. Zambia Air Force Aircraft Inventory, 1978

Designation	Manufacturer or Designer	Country of Origin	Kind	Quantity
Galeb (Seagull)	SOKO	Yugoslavia	Two-seat jet armed trainer	6
Jastreb (Hawk)	—do—	—do—	Single-seat jet light attack	6
MB-326G	Aermacchi	Italy	Dual-role jet trainer and ground attack	18
SF-260MZ	SIAI Marchetti	—do—	Single-engine conventional trainer	8
Yak-40	Yakovlev	Soviet Union	Three-engine jet short-haul transport	2
DC-6	Douglas	United States	Four-engine conventional transport	2
C-47 (Dakota) . .	—do—	—do—	Twin-engine conventional transport	10
DHC-2 (Beaver)	de Haviland	Canada	Single-engine utility	7

DHC-4 (Caribou)	—do—	—do—	Twin-engine conventional STOL[1] transport	5
DHC-5 (Buffalo)	—do—	—do—	Twin-turboprop STOL[1] transport	7
HS-748.........	Hawker Siddeley	United Kingdom	Twin-turboprop transport	1
Do-28..........	Dornier	West Germany[2]	Twin-engine STOL[1] transport	10
—(Supporter)...	Saab	Sweden	n.a.	20
AB-205.........	Agusta-Bell	Italy	Helicopter	3
AB-206.........	—do—	—do—	—do—	5
AB-212.........	—do—	—do—	—do—	3
Bell 47G........	Bell	United States	—do—	21
Mi-8...........	Mikoyan	Soviet Union	—do—	7

n.a.—not available.
[1]Short takeoff and landing.
[2]Federal Republic of Germany.

Table 15. Police Force Grade Structure and Strength, January 1975

Police	Strength		Police Reserve*
	Authorized	Actual	
Superior Officers			
Inspector general	1	1	—
Commissioner	1	0	—
Deputy commissioner	1	1	—
Senior assistant commissioner	2	2	—
Assistant commissioner	9	9	—
Senior superintendent.	31	30	—
Superintendent.	54	42	Superintendent
Quartermaster.	1	1	—
Assistant superintendent.	101	68	Assistant super- intendent
Subordinate Officers			
Chief inspector	127	112	Chief inspector
Inspector, assistant inspector	528	501	Inspector
. . . .			Assistant in- spector
Other Ranks			
Subinspector	623	631	Subinspector
Sergeant	992	958	Sergeant
Constable	7,244	7,321	Constable
Bugler.	50	50	—

—means not applicable.
*Strength figures for the police reserve were not known.

Source: Based on information from Zambia, Zambia Police Force, *Zambia Police Annual Report*, 1974, Lusaka, 1976.

Bibliography
Chapter 1

Baldwin, Robert E. *Economic Development and Export Growth: A Study of Modern Rhodesia, 1920–1960.* Berkeley and Los Angeles: University of California Press, 1966.

Bates, Robert H. *Unions, Parties and Political Development: A Study of Mineworkers in Zambia.* New Haven: Yale University Press, 1971.

Berger, Elena L. *Labour, Race and Colonial Rule: The Copperbelt from 1924 to Independence.* London: Oxford University Press, 1974.

Bond, George C. *The Politics of Change in a Zambian Community.* Chicago: University of Chicago Press, 1976.

Bontinck, F. "Le voyage des pombeiros: essai de réinterprétation," *Cultures au Zaire et en Afrique* [Kinshasa], 5, 1974, 39–70.

Caplan, Gerald L. *The Elites of Barotseland, 1878–1969.* Berkeley and Los Angeles: University of California Press, 1970.

Clark, J.D. *The Prehistory of Africa.* New York: Praeger, 1970.

Fagan, Brian, et al. *Iron Age Cultures in Zambia.* 2 vols. London: Chatto and Windus, 1967, 1969.

Fagan, Brian M. "Zambia and Rhodesia." Pages 215–244 in P.L. Shinnie, *The African Iron Age.* London: Oxford University Press, 1971.

Fagan, Brian M. (ed.) *A Short History of Zambia from the Earliest Times until A.D. 1900.* London: Oxford University Press, 1966 (reprinted with revision, 1968).

Gann, Lewis H. *The Birth of a Plural Society: The Development of Northern Rhodesia under the British South Africa Company, 1894–1914.* Manchester: Manchester University Press, 1958.

————. *A History of Northern Rhodesia: Early Days to 1953.* London: Chatto and Windus, 1964.

Hall, Richard S. *The High Price of Principles: Kenneth Kaunda and the White South.* (Rev. ed.) Baltimore: Penguin Books, 1973.

————. *Zambia.* New York: Praeger, 1965.

Kaplan, Irving, et al. *Area Handbook for Zambia.* (2d ed., DA Pam 550–75.) Washington: GPO for Foreign Area Studies, The American University, 1974.

Kaunda, Kenneth. *Humanism in Zambia and a Guide to its Implementation,* I. Lusaka: Zambia Information Service, 1967.

————. *A Humanist in Africa: Letters to Colin Morris.* London: Longman, 1966.

————. *Zambia Shall be Free, An Autobiography.* New York: Praeger, 1963.

Kaunda, Kenneth D. *Zambia: Independence and Beyond.* London: Nelson and Sons, 1966.

Kay, George. *A Social Geography of Zambia.* London: University of London Press, 1967.

Keatley, Patrick. *The Politics of Partnership.* Baltimore: Penguin Books, 1963.

MacPherson, Fergus. *Kenneth Kaunda of Zambia: The Times and the Man.* London and Lusaka: Oxford University Press, 1974.

Mainga [Bull], Mutumba. *Bulozi under the Luyana Kings: Political Evolution and State Formation in Pre-Colonial Zambia.* London: Longman, 1973.

Meebelo, Henry S. *Reaction to Colonialism: A Prelude to the Politics of Independence in Northern Zambia, 1893–1939.* Manchester: Manchester University Press, 1971.

Meebelo, Henry S. (ed.) *Main Currents of Zambian Humanist Thought.* London and Lusaka: Oxford University Press, 1973.

Miller, Joseph C. *Equatorial Africa.* (AHA Pamphlet 518.) Washington: American Historical Association, 1976.

Mulford, David C. *Zambia: The Politics of Independence, 1957–1964.* London: Oxford University Press, 1967.

Oliver, Roland, and Brian M. Fagan. *Africa in the Iron Age, c. 500 B.C. to 1400.* Cambridge: Cambridge University Press, 1975.

Pettman, Jan. *Zambia: Security and Conflict.* New York: St. Martin's Press, 1974.

Phillipson, David W. *The Later Prehistory of Eastern and Southern Africa.* New York: Africana Publishing, 1978.

———. *The Prehistory of Eastern Zambia.* Nairobi: British Institute in Eastern Africa, 1976.

Roberts, Andrew D. *A History of the Bemba.* Madison: University of Wisconsin Press, 1974.

———. *A History of Zambia.* New York: Africana Publishing, 1976.

Rotberg, Robert I. *Christian Missionaries and the Creation of Northern Rhodesia, 1880–1924.* Princeton: Princeton University Press, 1965.

———. *The Rise of Nationalism in Central Africa: The Making of Malawi and Zambia, 1873–1964.* Cambridge: Harvard University Press, 1965.

Sklar, Richard L. *Corporate Power in an African State: The Political Impact of Multinational Mining Companies in Zambia.* Berkeley and Los Angeles: University of California Press, 1975.

Stokes, Eric, and Richard B. Brown (eds.). *The Zambesian Past: Studies in Central African History.* Manchester: Manchester University Press, 1966.

Tindall, P.E.N. *A History of Central Africa.* New York: Praeger, 1968.

Tordoff, William (ed.). *Politics in Zambia.* (Perspectives on Southern Africa Series.) Berkeley and Los Angeles: University of California Press, 1975.

U.S. Department of State. Agency for International Development.

Gross National Product: Growth Rates and Trend Data by Region and Country. Washington: May 1, 1974.
————. *U.S. Overseas Loans and Grants and Assistance from International Organizations, July 1, 1945-June 30, 1975.* Washington: Office of Financial Management, Statistics and Reports Division, 1976.

U.S. Department of State. Arms Control and Disarmament Agency. *World Military Expenditures and Arms Transfers, 1965–1974.* (ACDA Publication 84.) Washington: 1976.

U.S. Department of State. Bureau of Intelligence and Research. *Communist States and Developing Countries: Aid and Trade in 1974.* (Report No. 298.) Washington: January 27, 1976.

Chapter 2

"Adequacy of Age and Sex Data in the 1969 Population Census of Zambia for Estimates of Fertility." Chapter VI in *Techniques of Evolution of Basic Demographic Data.* (African Population Studies Series, No. 2.) Addis Ababa: United Nations Economic Commission for Africa, 1975.

Annuario Pontifico. Vatican City: Liberia Editrice Vaticana, 1978.

Anthony, Kenneth R.M., and Victor C. Uchendu. "Agricultural Change in Mazabuka District, Zambia," *Food Research Institute Studies in Agricultural Economics, Trade, and Development,* 9, No. 3, 1970, 215–267.

Apthorpe, Raymond. "Clanship, Chieftainship and Nsenga Political Adaptation." Pages 69–98 in Raymond Apthorpe (ed.), *From Tribal Rule to Modern Government.* Lusaka: Rhodes-Livingstone Institute, 1958.

Atlas for Zambia. Glasgow: William Collins Sons, 1973.

Bates, Robert H. *Rural Responses to Industrialization: A Study of Village Zambia.* New Haven: Yale University Press, 1976.

Bethlehem, Douglas W., and Phillip R. Kingsley. "Zambian Student Attitudes Toward Others, Based on Tribe, Class and Rural-Urban Dwelling," *Journal of Social Psychology,* No. 100, 1976, 189–198.

Bhagavan, M.R. *Zambia: Impact of Industrial Strategy on Regional Imbalance and Social Inequality.* (Research Report, Vol. 44.) Uppsala: Nordiska afrikainstitutet, 1978.

Bloom, L. "Some Values and Attitudes of Young Zambians, Studies Through Spontaneous Autobiographies," *African Social Research* [Lusaka], No. 14, December 1972, 288–300.

Bond, George. "Minor Prophets and Yombe Cultural Dynamics." Pages 145–162 in Maxwell Owusu, *Colonialism and Change: Essays Presented to Lucy Mair.* (Studies in Anthropology, 4.) Atlantic Highlands, N.J.: Humanities Press, 1975.

Bond, George C. *The Politics of Change in a Zambian Community.* Chicago: University of Chicago Press, 1976.

271

Brelsford, William Vernon. *The Tribes of Zambia.* (2d ed.) Lusaka: Government Printer, 1965.

Burawoy, Michael. *The Colour of Class on the Copper Mines: From African Advancement to Zambianization.* (Zambian Papers, Vol. 7.) Manchester: University of Manchester Press, 1972.

Carpenter, Frances. "The Introduction of Commercial Farming into Zambia and Its Effects, to 1970." Pages 1–13 in *Zambian Land and Labour Studies,* 1. (National Archives Occasional Paper, 2.) Lusaka: 1973 (mimeo.).

Chawama Self-Help Housing Project. Philadelphia: American Friends Service Committee, 1975.

Chibesakunda, Lombe. "The Rights of Divorcées under Statutory Law." Pages 53–58 in *Women in Zambia.* (Report of Consultation on Women's Rights in Zambia.) Kitwe: Mindolo Ecumenical Centre, 1970 (mimeo.).

―――. "The Rights of Married Women under Statutory Law." Pages 45–52 in *Women in Zambia.* (Report of Consultation on Women's Rights in Zambia.) Kitwe: Mindolo Ecumenical Centre, 1970 (mimeo.).

―――. "The Rights of Widows under Statutory Law." Pages 59–64 in *Women in Zambia.* (Report of Consultation on Women's Rights in Zambia.) Kitwe: Mindolo Ecumenical Centre, 1970 (mimeo.).

Cliffe, Lionel R. "Labour Migration and Peasant Differentiation: Zambian Experiences," *Journal of Peasant Studies* [London], 5, No. 3, April 1978, 326–346.

Colson, Elizabeth. "The Alien Diviner and Local Politics among the Tonga of Zambia." Pages 221–228 in Marc Swartz, Victor W. Turner, and Arthur Tuden (eds.), *Political Anthropology.* Chicago: Aldine Publishing, 1966.

―――. "A Continuing Dialogue: Prophets and Local Shrines among the Tonga of Zambia." Pages 119–139 in R.P. Werbner (ed.), *Regional Cults.* (Association of Social Anthropologists Monograph, 16.) London: Academic Press, 1977.

―――. "From Chief's Court to Local Court: The Evolution of Local Courts in Southern Zambia." Pages 14–29 in Myron J. Aronoff (ed.), *Freedom and Constraint: A Memorial Tribute to Max Gluckman.* Assen, Netherlands: Van Gorcum, 1976.

―――. "The Plateau Tonga of Northern Rhodesia." Pages 94–162 in Elizabeth Colson and Max Gluckman (eds.), *Seven Tribes of Central Africa.* London: Oxford University Press, 1951.

―――. *Social Organization of the Gwembe Tonga.* Manchester: Manchester University Press, 1960.

Colson, Elizabeth, and T. Scudder. "New Economic Relationships between the Gwembe Valley and the Line of Rail." Pages 190–212 in David Parkin (ed.), *Town and Country in Central and Eastern Africa.* London: Oxford University Press for International African Institute, 1975.

Conaty, Joseph Clement. "Alienation among Factory Workers: Comparisons between the United States and Zambia." Unpublished Ph.D. dissertation. Madison: Department of Sociology, University of Wisconsin, 1977.

Crockford's Clerical Dictionary. London: Oxford University Press, 1976.

Cunnison, Ian. "History and Genealogies in a Conquest State," *American Anthropologist,* 49, No. 1, February 1957, 20–31.

———. *History on the Luapula.* (Rhodes-Livingstone Papers, Vol. 21.) Manchester: Manchester University Press, 1951.

———. *The Luapula Peoples of Northern Rhodesia: Custom and History in Tribal Politics.* Manchester: Manchester University Press for the Rhodes-Livingstone Institute, 1959.

———. "Perpetual Kinship: A Political Institution of the Luapula Peoples," *Rhodes-Livingstone Journal* [Lusaka], No. 20, 1956, 28–48.

Datta, Ansuk. "Languages Used by Zambian Asians." Pages 244–267 in Sirarpi Ohannessian and Mubanga E. Kashoki (eds.), *Language in Zambia.* London: International African Institute, 1978.

Davies, D. Hywel (ed.). *Zambia in Maps: Graphic Perspectives of a Developing Country.* New York: Africana Publishing, 1971.

Derricourt, Robin M. "Archaeology in Zambia: An Historical Outline," *Africa Social Research* [Lusaka], No. 21, June 1976, 31–50.

Dotson, Floyd, and Lillian O. Dotson. *The Indian Minority of Zambia, Rhodesia, and Malawi.* New Haven: Yale University Press, 1968.

Dresang, Dennis L. "Ethnic Politics, Representative Bureaucracy and Development Administration: The Zambian Case," *American Political Science Review,* 68, No. 4, December 1974, 1605–1617.

Dresang, Eliza T. *The Land and People of Zambia.* Philadelphia: Lippincott, 1975.

"Drive Against Illegal Immigrants," *New African* [London], No. 134, October 1978, 35–36.

Eriksen, Karen. "Zambia: Class Formation and Détente," *Review of African Political Economy* [London], No. 9, 1978, 4–26.

Fortman, Clasina de Gaay. "Oral Competence in Nyanja Among Lusaka Schoolchildren." Pages 182–206 in Sirarpi Ohannessian and Mubanga E. Kashoki (eds.), *Language in Zambia.* London: International African Institute, 1978.

Garrison, Howard H. "Patterns of Ethnic and Socioeconomic Association in Urban Zambia: The Structural Basis of Friendship Choice." Unpublished Ph.D. dissertation. Madison: Department of Sociology, University of Wisconsin, 1976.

Gertzel, Cherry. "Labour and the State: The Case of Zambia's Mineworkers' Union," *Journal of Commonwealth and Comparative Politics* [London], 13, No. 3, November 1975, 290–304.

Gluckman, Max. *The Economy of the Central Barotse Plain.* (Rhodes-Livingstone Papers, Vol. 7.) Livingstone: Rhodes-Livingstone Institute, 1941.

————. "The Lozi of Barotseland in North-Western Rhodesia." Pages 1–93 in Elizabeth Colson and Max Gluckman (eds.), *Seven Tribes of British Central Africa.* London: Oxford University Press, 1951.

————. "Tribalism, Ruralism and Urbanism in South and Central Africa." Pages 127–166 in Victor W. Turner, *Colonialism in Africa, 1870–1960,* Vol. 3. Cambridge: Cambridge University Press, 1971.

Grimsdell, J.J.R., and R.H.V. Bell. "The Bangweulu Basin of Zambia," *Botswana Notes and Records* [Gaberones], 2 (special edition), 1977, 257–262.

Handbook of Member Churches. Geneva: World Alliance of Reformed Churches, 1972.

Heisler, H. "The Pattern of Migration in Zambia," *Cahiers d'é-tudes africains* [Paris], 13, No. 2, 1973, 193–212.

Heisler, Helmuth. *Urbanization and the Government of Migration: The Inter-relation of Urban and Rural Life in Zambia.* New York: St. Martin's Press, 1974.

Hellen, John A. *Rural Economic Development in Zambia* (Afrika-Studien Series, Vol. 32.) Munich: Weltforum Verlag, 1968.

Hooker, J.R. *Population Problems in Zambia.* (American Universities Field Staff. Fieldstaff Reports. Central and Southern Africa Series, XV, No. 7.) Hanover, N.H.: AUFS, July 1971.

Hoover, J. Jeffrey. "The Seduction of Ruwej: Reconstructing Ruund History (The Nuclear Lunda: Zaïre, Angola, Zambia)." Unpublished Ph.D. dissertation. New Haven: Department of History, Yale University, 1978.

Jackman, Mary E. *Recent Population Movements in Zambia.* Manchester: Manchester University Press, 1973.

Johnson, Walton R. *Worship and Freedom: A Black American Church in Zambia.* London: International African Institute, 1977.

Jones, A.D. "Social Networks of Farmers among the Plateau Tonga of Zambia." Pages 272–285 in Peter Cutt Lloyd (ed.), *The New Elites of Tropical Africa.* London: Oxford University Press, 1964.

Kapferer, Bruce. "Conflict and Process in a Zambian Mine Community: An Appreciation of Some of Max Gluckman's Theories of Conflict." Pages 50–82 in Myron J. Aronoff (ed.), *Freedom and Constraint: A Memorial Tribute to Max Gluckman.* Assen, Netherlands: Van Gorcum, 1976.

————. *Co-operation, Leadership and Village Structure.* (Zambian Papers, No. 1). Lusaka: Institute for Social Research, University of Zambia, 1967.

————. "Social Network and Conjugal Role in Urban Zambia: Towards a Reformulation of the Bott Hypothesis." Pages 83–110 in

Jeremy Boissevain and Clyde J. Mitchell (eds.), *Network Analysis Studies in Human Interaction.* The Hague: Mouton, 1973.

———. *Strategy and Transaction in an African Factory: African Workers and Indian Management in a Zambian Town.* Manchester: Manchester University Press, 1972.

Kashoki, Mubanga E. "Between-Language Communication in Zambia." Pages 123–143 in Sirarpi Ohannessian and Mubanga E. Kashoki (eds.), *Language in Zambia.* London: International African Institute, 1978.

———. "In What Language is Zambia's Copper Produced?: A Linguist Looks at Language Adaptation in the Mining Industry," *Enterprise* [Lusaka], October 1973, 32–35.

———. "The Language Situation in Zambia." Pages 9–46 in Sirarpi Ohannessian and Mubanga E. Kashoki (eds.), *Language in Zambia.* London: International African Institute, 1978.

———. "Migration and Language Change: The Interaction of Town and Country [Bemba]," *Africa Social Research* [Lusaka], No. 19, June 1975, 707–729.

———. "Migration and Language Change: The Interaction of Town and Country [Bemba]." Pages 228–249 in David Parkin (ed.), *Town and Country in Central and Eastern Africa.* London: Oxford University Press for International African Institute, 1975.

———. "The Zambia Adult Literacy Programme." Pages 398–423 in Sirarpi Ohannessian and Mubanga E. Kashoki (eds.), *Language in Zambia.* London: International African Institute, 1978.

Kashoki, Mubanga E., and Michael Mann. "A General Sketch of the Bantu Languages of Zambia." Pages 47–100 in Sirarpi Ohannessian and Mubanga E. Kashoki (eds.), *Language in Zambia.* London: International African Institute, 1978.

Lancaster, Chet S. "Brideservice, Residence, and Authority among the Goba (N. Shona) of the Zambezi Valley," *Africa* [London], 44, No. 1, 1974, 46–64.

———. "The Economies of Social Organization in an Ethnic Border Zone: The Goba (Northern Shona) of the Zambezi Valley," *Ethnology,* 10, No. 4, October 1971, 445–465.

———. "Ethnic Identity, History and 'Tribe' in the Middle Zambezi Valley," *American Ethnologist,* 1, No. 3, 1974, 707–730.

———. "Women, Horticulture, and Society in Sub-Saharan Africa," *American Anthropologist,* 78, No. 3, 1976, 539–564.

———. "The Zambezi Goba Ancestral Cult," *Africa* [London], 47, No. 3, 1977, 229–241.

Lehmann, D.A. "Languages of the Kafue Basin: Introductory Notes." Pages 101–120 in Sirarpi Ohannessian and Mubanga E. Kashoki (eds.), *Language in Zambia.* London: International African Institute, 1978.

Lifanu, Likotola Nawa. "Self-Reliance and Social Development in Zambia's Western Province." Unpublished Ph.D. dissertation.

Waltham, Mass.: The Florence Heller Graduate School for Advanced Studies in Social Welfare, Brandeis University, 1978.

Mabaso, Sylvia A.N. "The Urbanisation of William Mubita and Isaac Banda." Pages 14–31 in *Zambian Land and Labour Studies*, 1. (National Archives Occasional Paper 2.) Lusaka: 1973 (mimeo.).

McAdam, Bryson. "The New Zambia Primary Course." Pages 329–354 in Sirarpi Ohannessian and Mubanga E. Kashoki (eds.), *Language in Zambia.* London: International African Institute, 1978.

McClain, W.T. "The Legal Position of Women and Children under Zambia's Customary Laws." Pages 65–84 in *Women in Zambia.* (Report of Consultation on Women's Rights in Zambia.) Kitwe: Mindolo Ecumenical Centre, 1970 (mimeo.).

————. "The Rights of Widows under Customary Law." Pages 85–93 in *Women in Zambia.* (Report of Consultation on Women's Rights in Zambia.) Kitwe: Mindolo Ecumenical Centre, 1970 (mimeo.).

Mainga [Bull], Mutumba. *Bulozi under the Luyana Kings: Political Evolution and State Formation in Pre-Colonial Zambia.* London: Longman, 1973.

————. "A History of Lozi Religion to the End of the Nineteenth Century." Pages 95–107 in Terrence O. Ranger and Isaria N. Kimambo (eds.), *The Historical Study of African Religion.* Berkeley and Los Angeles: University of California Press, 1972.

Marks, Stuart A. *Large Mammals and a Brave People: Subsistence Hunters in Zambia.* Seattle: University of Washington Press, 1976.

————. "Profile and Process: Subsistence Hunters in a Zambian Community." (Paper prepared for African Studies Association Annual Meeting, Baltimore, November 1–4, 1978.) Waltham, Mass: ASA, 1978 (mimeo.).

Mitchell, J.C. "Prestige in a Plural Society." Pages 256–271 in Peter Cutt Lloyd (ed.), *The New Elites of Tropical Africa.* London: Oxford University Press, 1964.

Mitchell, J. Clyde. *The Kalela Dance: Aspects of Social Relationships among Urban Africans in Northern Rhodesia.* (Rhodes-Livingstone Papers, Vol. 27.) Manchester: Manchester University Press, 1959.

Molteno, Robert V. *Studies in Zambian Government and Administration.* Lusaka: NECZAM (National Educational Company of Zambia), 1973.

Mulenga, M.S.C. "Population Policies in Zambia," *African Population Newsletter* [Addis Ababa], No. 24, March 1977, 6–14.

Muntemba, Maud. "Thwarted Development: A Case Study of Economic Change in the Kabwe Rural District of Zambia, 1902–1970." Pages 345–364 in Robin Palmer and Neil Parsons (eds.), *The Roots of Rural Poverty in Central and Southern Africa.* Berkeley and Los Angeles: University of California Press, 1977.

Muntemba, Maud Shimwaayi. "Rural Underdevelopment in Zambia: Kabwe Rural District, 1850–1970." Unpublished Ph.D. dissertation. Los Angeles: Department of History, University of California, 1977.

Musonda, Moses. "A Study of Language Use among Local Students at the University of Zambia." Pages 228–243 in Sirarpi Ohannessian and Mubanga E. Kashoki (eds.), *Language in Zambia.* London: International African Institute, 1978.

Mutsau, J. "The Shona and Ndebele Settlements in Kabwe Rural Area, 1953–1963." Pages 41–47 in *Zambian Land and Labour Studies,* 1. (National Archives Occasional Paper 2.) Lusaka: 1973 (mimeo.).

Mutukwa, Kasuka S. *Politics of the Tanzania-Zambia Rail Project: A Study of Tanzania-China-Zambia Relations.* Washington: University Press of America, 1977.

Muyangana, G.M. "A Survey of Land Tenure among the Ila of Chief Mungaila in the Namwala District." Pages 48–55 in *Zambian Land and Labour Studies,* 1. (National Archives Occasional Paper 2.) Lusaka: 1973 (mimeo.).

Mytton, Graham. "Language and the Media in Zambia." Pages 207–227 in Sirarpi Ohannessian and Mubanga E. Kashoki (eds.), *Language in Zambia.* London: International African Institute, 1978.

Naidoo, M.R., and M. Mumbwe. *A Secondary Geography of Zambia.* Lusaka: Longman, 1969.

Ng'andwe, Chiselebwe O.M. "African Traditional Land Tenure and Agricultural Development: Case Study of the Kunda People in Jumbe," *African Social Research* [Lusaka], 21, June 1976, 51–67.

Ngwisha, Kaluba John. "Urbanization and Family Structure: A Study of the Family on the Copperbelt of Zambia." Unpublished Ph.D. dissertation. Waltham, Mass.: The Florence Heller Graduate School for Advanced Studies in Social Welfare, Brandeis University, 1978.

1978 Yearbook of Jehovah's Witnesses. Brooklyn: Watch Tower Bible and Tract Society of Pennsylvania, 1977.

Ohadike, P.O. "Migrants in the Copper Mines of Zambia, 1940–66." Pages 252–261 in S. H. Omande and C. N. Ejiogu (eds.), *Population and Economic Development in Africa.* London: Heineman, 1972.

Ohadike, Patrick O. "The Evolving Phenomena of Migration and Urbanization in Central Africa: A Zambian Case." Pages 125–244 in David Parkin (ed.), *Town and Country in Central and Eastern Africa.* London: Oxford University Press for International African Institute, 1975.

——. *The Population of Zambia.* The Hague: Institute of Social Studies, 1977.

Ohadike, Patrick O., and Habtemarian Tesfaghiorghis. *The Population of Zambia.* Paris: CICRED, 1975.

Ohannessian, Sirarpi. "English and Zambian Languages in Secondary Schools." Pages 355–375 in Sirarpi Ohannessian and Mubanga E. Kashoki (eds.), *Language in Zambia.* London: International African Institute, 1978.

———. "Historical Background [to Language in Education]." Pages 271–291 in Sirarpi Ohannessian and Mubanga E. Kashoki (eds.), *Language in Zambia.* London: International African Institute, 1978.

———. "The Teaching of Zambian Languages and the Preparation of Teachers for Language Teaching in Primary Schools." Pages 292–328 in Sirarpi Ohannessian and Mubanga E. Kashoki (eds.), *Language in Zambia.* London: International African Institute, 1978.

———. "Zambian Languages in Secondary Schools: Attitudes of Teachers in Training." Pages 376–397 in Sirarpi Ohannessian and Mubanga E. Kashoki (eds.), *Language in Zambia.* London: International African Institute, 1978.

Ohannessian, Sirarpi, and Mubanga E. Kashoki. *Language in Zambia.* London: International African Institute, 1978.

Ollawa, Patrick. *Rural Development Policies and Performance in Zambia: A Critical Inventory.* (Occasional Papers, No. 59.) The Hague: Institute of Social Studies, January 1977.

Palmer, Robin. "Land in Zambia." Pages 56–66 in *Zambian Land and Labour Studies,* 1. (National Archives Occasional Paper 2.) Lusaka: 1973 (mimeo.).

———. "Robert H. Bates, *Rural Responses to Industrialization: A Study of Village Zambia*" (review), *African Economic History,* No. 3, Spring 1977, 85–87.

Papart, Jane. "Class Formation and Class Consciousness among African Miners on the Copperbelt during the Colonial Period." Draft chapters of unpublished Ph.D. dissertation. Boston: Department of History, Boston University, 1979.

Papstein, Robert Joseph. "The Upper Zambezi: A History of the Luvale People, 1000–1900." Unpublished Ph.D. dissertation. Los Angeles: Department of History, University of California, 1978.

Peters, Harold Eugene. "The Contributions of Education to the Development of Elites among the Plateau Tonga of Zambia: A Comparative Study of School-Leavers from Two Mission Schools, 1930 to 1965." Unpublished Ph.D. dissertation. Urbana-Champaign: Department of Education, University of Illinois, 1976.

Poewe, Karla O. "Matriliny in the Throes of Change: Kinship, Descent, and Marriage in Luapula, Zambia," *Africa* [London], 48, No. 3, 1978, 205–218; No. 4, 1978, 353–367.

———. "Religion, Matriliny, and Change: Jehovah's Witnesses and Seventh-Day Adventists in Luapula, Zambia," *American Ethnology,* 5, No. 2, 1978, 303–321.

Prins, Gwyn I.T. "Bulozi under the Luyana Kings," *Africa Social Research* [Lusaka], No. 21, June 1976, 89–92.

———. "Disease at the Crossroads: Towards a History of Therapeutics in Bulozi since 1976." (Paper prepared for African Studies Association Annual Meeting, Baltimore, November 1–4, 1978.) Waltham, Mass.: ASA, 1978 (mimeo.).

Prives, Moshe Z. "A Project in Zambia: Integrated Area Settlement in the Copperbelt," *Journal of Rural Cooperation* [Jerusalem], 4, No. 1, 1976, 17–41.

Quick, Stephen Adee. "Bureaucracy and Rural Socialism: The Zambian Experience." Unpublished Ph.D. dissertation. Palo Alto, Cal.: Department of Political Science, Stanford University, 1975.

Read, Margaret. *The Ngoni of Nyasaland.* London: Oxford University Press, 1956.

Rees, W.A. "Kafue Flats," *Black Lechwe* [Kitwe], 11, No. 3, (n.d.), 27–35.

Richards, Audrey I. "The Bemba of North-Eastern Rhodesia." Pages 163–193 in Elizabeth Colson and Max Gluckman (eds.), *Seven Tribes of Central Africa.* London: Oxford University Press, 1951.

———. "The Political System of the Bemba Tribe, Northeastern Rhodesia." Pages 83–120 in Meyer Fortes and E.E. Evans-Pritchard (eds.), *African Political Systems.* London: International Institute of African Languages and Cultures, 1940.

Roberts, Andrew. "Robert H. Bates, *Rural Responses to Industrialization: A Study of Village Zambia*" (review), *African Affairs* [London], 76, No. 303, April 1977, 271–272.

Sanyal, Bikas C., et al. *Higher Education and the Labour Market in Zambia: Expectations and Performance.* Lusaka: University of Zambia, 1976.

Schuster, Isla M. Glazer. *New Women of Lusaka.* (Explorations in World Ethnology Series.) Palo Alto, Cal.: Mayfield Publishing, 1979.

Scott, Ian. "Middle-Class Politics in Zambia," *African Affairs* [London], 77, No. 308, July 1978, 321–334.

Scudder, T. "Social Anthropology and the Reconstruction of Prehistoric Land Use Systems in Tropical Africa: A Cautionary Case Study from Zambia." Pages 357–381 in J. R. Harlan, Jan M. J. de Wet, and B. L. Stemler (eds.), *Origins of African Plant Domestication.* The Hague: Mouton, 1976.

Serpell, Robert. "Comprehension of Nyanja by Lusaka School Children." Pages 144–181 in Sirarpi Ohannessian and Mubanga E. Kashoki (eds.), *Language in Zambia.* London: International African Institute, 1978.

———. "Some Developments in Zambia." Pages 424–447 in Sirarpi Ohannessian and Mubanga E. Kashoki (eds.), *Language in Zambia.* London: International African Institute, 1978.

Seventh-Day Adventist Encyclopedia, Vol. 10. Washington: Review and Herald Publishing Association, 1976.

Shaw, Timothy M. *Dependence and Underdevelopment: The Development and Foreign Policy of Zambia.* (Africa Series, No. 28.) Athens: Center for International Studies, Ohio University, 1976.

Shewmaker, Stan. *Tonga Christianity.* South Pasadena, Cal.: Carey Library, 1970.

Simons, H. J. "A Statistical Comment on the Position of Women in Zambia." Pages 27–36 in *Women in Zambia.* (Report of Consultation on Women's Rights in Zambia.) Kitwe: Mindolo Ecumenical Centre, 1970 (mimeo.).

———. "Women in a Changing Society." Pages 9–13 in *Women's Rights in Zambia.* (Report of Consultation on Women's Rights in Zambia.) Kitwe: Mindolo Ecumenical Centre, 1970 (mimeo.).

Small, N. J. "Getting Ideas Across: Limitations to Social Engineering in a New State," *African Affairs* [London], 77, No. 309, October 1978, 531–553.

Spring, Anita. "Faith and Participation in Traditional Versus Cosmopolitan Medical Systems in Northwest Zambia." (Paper prepared for African Studies Association Annual Meeting, Baltimore, November 1–4, 1978). Waltham, Mass.: ASA, 1978 (mimeo.).

Tench, Andrew W.B. *Socio-Economic Factors Influencing Agricultural Output, with Special Reference to Zambia.* (Sozialökonomische Schriften zur Agrarentwicklung, 12.) Saarbrücken: Verlag der SSIP-Schriften, 1975.

Tiberondwa, Ado K., and Lyson P. Tembo. "The Role of Youth in Zambia's Agrarian Revolution," *Rural Affairs,* No. 30, Spring 1976, 99–108.

Turner, Victor W. *The Drum of Affliction.* London: Oxford University Press, 1968.

———. *The Forest of Symbols: Aspects of Ndembu Ritual.* Ithaca: Cornell University Press, 1967.

———. *Revelation and Divination in Ndembu Ritual.* Ithaca: Cornell University Press, 1975.

———. "Ritual Aspects of Conflict Control in African Micropolitics." Pages 239–246 in Marc Swartz, Victor W. Turner, and Arthur Tuden (eds.), *Political Anthropology.* Chicago: Aldine Publishing, 1966.

———. *Schism and Continuity in an African Society: A Study of Ndembu Village Life.* Manchester: Manchester University Press for the Rhodes-Livingstone Institute, 1957.

van Binsbergen, Wim M. J. "Occam, Francis Bacon and the Transformation of Zambian Society," *Cultures et Developpement* [Louvain, Belgium], 9, No. 3, 1977, 520.

———. "Regional and Non-Regional Cults of Affliction in Western Zambia." Pages 141–175 in R.P. Werbner (ed.), *Regional Cults.*

(Association of Social Anthropologists Monograph 16.) London: Academic Press, 1977.

Van Horn, Laurel. "The Agricultural History of Barotseland, 1840–1964." Pages 144–170 in Robin Palmer and Neil Parsons (eds.), *The Roots of Rural Poverty in Central and Southern Africa.* Berkeley and Los Angeles: University of California Press, 1977.

Van Velsen, Jaap. "Urban Squatters: Problem or Solution." Pages 294–307 in David Parkin (ed.), *Town and Country in Central and Eastern Africa.* London: Oxford University Press for International African Institute, 1975.

Verboon, W.C. "The Barotse Loose Sands of Western Province, Zambia," *Zambia Geographical Association Magazine* [Lusaka], 27, July 1974, 1–12.

Verstraelen, F.J. *An African Church in Transition from Missionary Dependence to Mutuality in Mission: A Case Study on the Roman Catholic Church in Zambia.* Tilburg, Netherlands: Developmental Research Institute, 1975.

Vickery, Kenneth Powers. "The Making of a Peasantry: Imperialism and the Tonga Plateau Economy." Unpublished Ph.D. dissertation. New Haven: Department of History, Yale University, 1978.

Vrydogh, P. André. "La fabrication des costumes et des masques *makisi* des Mbunda de Zambie," *Bulletin de la Société Royale Belge d'Anthropologie et Préhistoire* [Brussels], No. 82, 1971, 193–212; No. 83, 1972, 157–166.

Watson, William. "British Colonial Policy and Tribal Organization." Pages 169–181 in W. Arens (ed.), *A Century of Change in East Africa.* The Hague: Mouton, 1977.

————. *Tribal Cohesion in a Money Economy: A Study of the Mambwe People of Northern Rhodesia.* Manchester: Manchester University Press, 1958.

Williams, G.J., and G.W. Howard. *Development and Ecology in the Lower Kafue Basin in the 1970s.* (2d ed.) Lusaka: Kafue Basin Research Committee, University of Zambia, 1977.

Williams, Jerry Lee. "A Retail Landscape in Rural Zambia." Unpublished Ph.D. dissertation. Eugene: Department of Social Geography, University of Oregon, 1977.

Wilson, Godfrey. *The Constitution of Ngonde.* (Rhodes-Livingstone Papers, Vol. 2.) Livingstone: Rhodes-Livingstone Institute, 1939.

Women's Rights in Zambia. (Report of Consultation on Women's Rights in Zambia.) Kitwe: Mindolo Ecumenical Centre, 1970 (mimeo.).

World Health Organization. *World Health Statistics Annual, 1977.* 3 vols. Geneva: 1977.

Zambia. Central Statistical Office. *Census of Population and Housing, 1969.* Lusaka: 1970.

————. *Monthly Digest of Statistics* [Lusaka], XIV, 3–6, March-June 1978.

————. *Sample Census of Population 1974: Preliminary Report.* Lusaka: February 1975.

Zulu, Gertrude, and Janet Mfula. "Changing Patterns of Marriage in Zambia." Pages 37–44 in *Women in Zambia* (Report of Consultation on Women's Rights in Zambia.) Kitwe: Mindolo Ecumenical Centre, 1970 (mimeo.).

(Various issues of the following periodicals were also used in the preparation of this chapter: *Africa Research Bulletin* (Political, Social and Cultural Series) [Exeter], January 1976–January 1979; *Times of Zambia* [Ndola/Lusaka], October 1978–February 1979; U.S. Department of Commerce, Office of Technical Services, Joint Publications Research Service—JPRS [Washington], *Translations on Sub-Saharan Africa,* Nos. 1798–2049, September 9, 1977–January 9, 1979; and *Zambia Daily Mail* [Lusaka], October 1978–February 1979.)

Chapter 3

Africa Yearbook Who's Who 1977. London: Africa Journal, 1977.

Anglin, Douglas G. "Confrontation in Southern Africa: Zambia and Portugal," *International Journal* [Toronto], 25, No. 3, Summer 1970, 497–513.

————. "Zambia and the Recognition of Biafra," *African Review* [Nairobi], 1, No. 2, September 1971, 102–136.

Anglin, Douglas G., and Timothy M. Shaw. *Studies in Diplomacy and Dependence.* Boulder: Westview Press, 1979.

————. *Zambia's Foreign Policy.* Boulder: Westview Press, 1979.

Azevedo, Mario J. "Zambia, Zaïre and the Angolan Crisis Reconsidered: From Alvor to Shaba," *Journal of Southern African Affairs* [London], 2, No. 3, July 1977, 275–293.

Breytenbach, W.J. "The Government and Single Party System in Zambia," *Bulletin of the Africa Institute of South Africa* [Pretoria], No. 6, 1975, 210–214.

Burawoy, Michael. "Consciousness and Contradiction: A Study of Student Protest in Zambia," *British Journal of Sociology* [London], No. 27, March 1976, 78–98.

Campagne, François. "Les Institutions politiques zambiennes et leur évolution," *Revue Française d'Etudes Politiques Africaines* [Paris], 11, No. 130, October 1976, 72–83.

de Rham, Gérard. *La Politique étrangère de la Republique de Zambia.* Bern: Peter Lang, 1977.

Dresang, Dennis L. "Ethnic Politics, Representative Bureaucracy and Development Administration: The Zambian Case," *American Political Science Review,* 68, No. 4, December 1974, 1605–1617.

Eriksen, Karen. "Zambia: Class Formation and Détente," *Review of African Political Economy* [London], No. 9, 1978, 4–26.

Grundy, Trevor. "Political Impasse—and Zambia Sinks Deeper," *African Development* [London], 9, No. 11, 1975, 9–11.

Gudel, Christoph. "Zambia: Signs of Crisis," *Swiss Review of World Affairs* [Zurich], XXVIII, No. 3, June 1978, 23–25.

Hatch, John Charles. *Two African Statesmen.* Chicago: Henry Regnery, 1976.

Hawkesworth, Nigel R. *Local Government in Zambia.* Lusaka: Lusaka City Council, 1974.

Kaunda, K.D. *Humanism in Zambia and a Guide to its Implementation,* I. Lusaka: Zambia Information Service, 1967.

Kaunda, Kenneth D. *Humanism in Zambia and a Guide to its Implementation,* II. Lusaka: Government Printer, 1974.

———. *A Path for the Future.* Lusaka: Zambia Information Service, 1971.

———. *You Hold the Key to the Success of Participatory Democracy.* Lusaka: Zambia Information Service, 1972.

———. *Zambia's Guidelines for the Next Decade.* Lusaka: Government Printer, 1968.

Lewis, Roy. "Kenneth Kaunda in 1976," *Round Table* [London], No. 263, July 1976, 283–288.

MacPherson, Fergus. *Kenneth Kaunda of Zambia: The Times and the Man.* London and Lusaka: Oxford University Press, 1974.

Martin, Robert. "The Ombudsman in Zambia," *Journal of Modern African Studies* [Cambridge], 15, No. 2, June 1977, 239–259.

Meebelo, Henry S. (ed.) *Main Currents of Zambian Humanist Thought.* London and Lusaka: Oxford University Press, 1973.

Molteno, Robert. "Cleavage and Conflict in Zambian Politics: a Study in Sectionalism." Pages 62–106 in William Tordoff (ed.), *Politics in Zambia.* Berkeley and Los Angeles: University of California Press, 1974.

———. *The Zambian Community and Its Government.* Lusaka: NECZAM (National Educational Company of Zambia), 1974.

Molteno, Robert, and William Tordoff. "Independent Zambia: Achievements and Prospects." Pages 363–401 in William Tordoff (ed.), *Politics in Zambia.* Berkeley and Los Angeles: University of California Press, 1974.

Moolman, J.H. "One Zambia—One Nation," *Bulletin of the Africa Institute of South Africa* [Pretoria], 13, No. 6, August-September 1975, 199–239.

Mutukwa, Kasuka S. *Politics of the Tanzania-Zambia Rail Project: A Study of Tanzania-China-Zambia Relations.* Washington: University Press of America, 1977.

Nabulyato, R.M. "The Speakership in Zambia," *Parliamentarian* [London], 69, No. 1, January 1978, 14–19.

Nyalugwe, Naphy. "Zambia under UNIP," *Africa* [London], No. 86, October 1978, 37–42.

Ollawa, Patrick. *Rural Development Policies and Performance in Zambia: A Critical Inventory.* (Occasional Papers, No. 59.) The Hague: Institute of Social Studies, January 1977.

Ollawa, Patrick E. "Politics, Institutions, and Participatory Development in Rural Zambia," *Labour Society* [Geneva], 2, No. 3, July 1977, 225–251.

Pettman, Jan. "Zambia Second Republic—The Establishment of a One Party State," *Journal of Modern African Studies* [London], 12, No. 2, 1974, 231–244.

———. *Zambia: Security and Conflict.* New York: St. Martin's Press, 1974.

Quick, Stephen A. "Bureaucracy and Rural Socialism in Zambia," *Journal of Modern African Studies* [London], 15, No. 3, September 1977, 379–400.

Saidi, W. "Zambia: Parliament and Party," *Parliamentarian* [London], 57, No. 1, 1976, 26–29.

Scarritt, James R. "Political Legitimacy in Zambia: An Explanation of Change based on Incomplete Data." (Paper No. 25946, prepared for African Studies Association Annual Meeting, Boston, November 1976.)

Scott, Ian. "Middle-Class Politics in Zambia," *African Affairs* [London], 77, No. 308, July 1978, 321–334.

———. "Party Functions and Capabilities: The Local-Level UNIP Organisation during the first Zambian Republic," *African Social Research* [Lusaka], No. 22, December 1976, 107–129.

Seidlitz, Peter. "Tears for Zambia," *Review of World Affairs* [Switzerland], XXVII, No. 2, February 1978, 21–22.

Shaw, Timothy. "The Foreign Policy of Zambia: An Events Analysis of a New State," *Comparative Political Studies,* 11, No. 2, July 1978, 181–210.

Shaw, Timothy M. *Dependence and Underdevelopment: The Development and Foreign Policy of Zambia.* (Africa Series, No. 28.) Athens: Center for International Studies, Ohio University, 1976.

———. "The Foreign Policy of Zambia: Interests and Ideology," *Journal of Modern African Studies* [London], 14, No. 1, April 1976, 79–105.

———. "Zambia's Foreign Policy." Pages 220–234 in Olajide Aluko (ed.), *The Foreign Policies of African States.* Atlantic Highlands, N.J.: Humanities Press, 1977.

Sircar, Parbati K. "The Great Uhuru (Freedom) Railway: China's Link to Africa," *China Report,* 14, March-April 1978, 15–24.

Sklar, Richard L. *Corporate Power in an African State: The Political Impact of Multinational Mining Companies in Zambia.* Berkeley and Los Angeles: University of California Press, 1975.

Small, N.J. "Zambia—Trouble on Campus," *Index on Censorship* [London], 6, No. 6, November-December 1977, 8–14.

Tordoff, William. "Provincial and Local Government in Zambia," *Journal of Administration Overseas* [London], IX, No. 1, January 1978, 23–35.

———. "Residual Legislatures: The Cases of Tanzania and

Zambia," *Journal of Commonwealth and Comparative Politics* [London], 15, No. 3, November 1977, 235–249.

————. "Zambia: The Politics of Disengagement," *African Affairs* [London], 76, No. 302, January 1977, 60–69.

Tordoff, William (ed.). *Politics in Zambia*. (Perspectives on Southern Africa Series.) Berkeley and Los Angeles: University of California Press, 1975.

(Various issues of the following periodicals were also used in the preparation of this chapter: *Africa* [London], January 1975–December 1978; *Christian Science Monitor*, January 1975–December 1978; *Facts and Reports* [Amsterdam], January 1975–November 1978; *New York Times*, July 1975–January 1979; U.S. Department of Commerce, Office of Technical Services, Joint Publications Research Service—JPRS [Washington], *Translations on Sub-Saharan Africa*, Nos. 1673–2036, September 13, 1976–December 12, 1978; and *Washington Post*, August 1975–January 1979.)

Chapter 4

Africa South of the Sahara, 1978–79. London: Europa Publications, 1978.

Allan, William. *The African Husbandman*. Edinburgh: Oliver and Boyd, 1965.

Arnold, Guy, and Ruth Weiss. *Strategic Highways of Africa*. London: Julian Friedmann, 1977.

Atlas for Zambia. Glasgow: William Collins Sons, 1973.

Bank of Zambia. *Report and Statement of Accounts for the Year Ended 31st December 1976*. N. pl.: UNACC, n.d.

Bates, Robert H. *Rural Responses to Industrialization: A Study of Village Zambia*. New Haven: Yale University Press, 1976.

Beveridge, Andrew A. "Economic Independence, Indigenization, and the African Businessman: Some of Zambia's Economic Reforms," *African Studies Review*, XVII, No. 3, December 1974, 477–490.

Campagne, François. "L'Economie de la Zambie," *Revue Française d'Etudes Politiques Africaines* [Paris], 13, March 1978, 44–55.

Cliffe, Lionel R. "Labour Migration and Peasant Differentiation: Zambian Experiences." *Journal of Peasant Studies* [London], 5, No. 3, April 1978, 326–346.

Damachi, Ukandi G., Guy Routh, and Abdel-Rahman E. Ali Taha (eds.). *Development Paths in Africa and China*. Boulder: Westview Press, 1976.

Davies, D. Hywel (ed.). *Zambia in Maps: Graphic Perspectives of a Developing Country*. New York: Africana Publishing, 1971.

Dodge, Doris Jansen. *Agricultural Policy and Performance in Zambia: History, Prospects, and Proposals for Change*. (Research Series, No. 32.) Berkeley: Institute of International Studies, University of California, 1977.

Federal Republic of Germany. *Statistisches Bundesamt. Länderkurzberichte: Sambia, 1976.* (Allgemeine Statistik des Auslandes.) Stuttgart: W. Kohlhammer, October 1976.

Gertzel, Cherry. "Labour and the State: The Case of Zambia's Mineworkers' Union," *Journal of Commonwealth and Comparative Politics* [London], 13, No. 3, November 1975, 290–304.

Harvey, Charles. "Rural Credit in Zambia: Access and Exit," *Development and Change* [The Hague], VI, No. 2, April 1975, 89–105.

————. "The Structure of Zambian Development." Pages 136–151 in Ukandi G. Damachi, Guy Routh, and Abdel-Rahman E. Ali Taha (eds.), *Development Paths in Africa and China.* Boulder: Westview Press, 1976.

Heisler, Helmuth. *Urbanization and the Government of Migration: The Inter-relation of Urban and Rural Life in Zambia.* New York: St. Martin's Press, 1974.

Katzenellenbogen, S.E. *Railways and the Copper Mines of Katanga.* Oxford: Clarendon Press, 1973.

"Kaunda's Dilemma," *Africa: An International Business, Economic and Political Monthly* [London], No. 87, November 1978, 40, 45.

Kessel, N. "Financial Aspects of the Mining Industry in Zambia." Pages 311–323 in W. T. Newlyn et al., *The Financing of Economic Development.* Oxford: Clarendon Press, 1977.

Legum, Colin (ed.). *Africa Contemporary Record: Annual Survey and Documents, 1973–74.* New York: Africana Publishing, 1974.

Lombard, C.S., and A.H.C. Tweedie. *Agriculture in Zambia Since Independence.* Lusaka. NECZAM (National Educational Company of Zambia), 1974.

Markakis, John, and Robert L. Curry, Jr. "The Global Economy's Impact on Recent Budgetary Politics in Zambia," *Journal of African Studies,* 3, No. 4, Winter 1976, 403–427.

Martin, Anthony. *Minding Their Own Business: Zambia's Struggle Against Western Control.* London: Hutchinson, 1972.

Mihalyi, Louis J. "Electricity and Electrification for Zambia," *Geographical Review,* LXVII, No. 1, January 1977, 63–70.

Murupa, Rukudzo. "Nationalization of the Zambian Mining Industry,," *Review of Black Political Economy,* 7, No. 1, Fall 1976, 40–52.

Nadeau, E.G. "Prospects for Agricultural Cooperatives in Zambia," *Land Tenure Center Newsletter,* No. 51, January–March 1976, 25–30.

Ndulo, Muna. "The Requirement of Domestic Participation in New Mining Ventures in Zambia," *African Social Research* [Lusaka], No. 25, June 1978, 399–427.

Newlyn, W.T., et al. *The Financing of Economic Development.* Oxford: Clarendon Press, 1977.

Ng'andwe, Chiselebwe O.M. "African Traditional Land Tenure and Agricultural Development: Case Study of the Kunda People in Jumbe," *African Social Research* [Lusaka], 21, June 1976, 51–67.

Nkowani, Windsor K. "Planning Techniques in Zambia," *Economic Bulletin for Africa*, XII, No. 1, 1976, 67–92.

Ollawa, Patrick. *Rural Development Policies and Performance in Zambia: A Critical Inventory.* (Occasional Papers, No. 59.) The Hague: Institute of Social Studies, January 1977.

Ollawa, Patrick E. "Politics, Institutions, and Participatory Development in Rural Zambia," *Labour and Society* [Geneva], 2, No. 3, July 1977, 225–251.

Ollawa, Patrick Eze. "Rural Development Strategy and Performance in Zambia: An Evaluation of Past Efforts," *African Studies Review*, XXI, No. 2, September 1978, 101–124.

Priestley, J.R. "The Transfer of Agricultural Land in the Eastern Province of Zambia," *Journal of Tropical Geography* [Singapore], 46, June 1978, 47–60.

Quarterly Economic Review of Zambia: Annual Supplement 1977. London: Economist Intelligence Unit, 1977.

Quick, Stephen A. "Bureaucracy and Rural Socialism in Zambia," *Journal of Modern African Studies* [London], 15, No. 3, September 1977, 379–400.

Scarritt, James R. "European Adjustment to Economic Reforms and Political Consolidation in Zambia," *Issue*, 3, No. 2, Summer 1973, 18–22.

Schultz, Jürgen. *Land Use in Zambia.* Munich: Weltforum Verlag, 1976.

Sedjo, Roger A. *Zambia.* Washington: U.S. Agency for International Development, February 1977.

Seidman, Ann. "The Distorted Growth of Import-Substitution Industry: The Zambian Case," *Journal of Modern African Studies* [London], 12, December 1974, 601–631.

Shaw, Timothy M. *Dependence and Underdevelopment: The Development and Foreign Policies of Zambia.* (Africa Series, No. 28.) Athens: Center for International Studies, Ohio University, 1976.

Sircar, Parbati K. "The Great Uhuru (Freedom) Railway: China's Link to Africa," *China Report*, 14, March–April 1978, 15–24.

Sklar, Richard L. *Corporate Power in an African State: The Political Impact of Multinational Mining Companies in Zambia.* Berkeley and Los Angeles: University of California Press, 1975.

United Nations. Economic and Social Council. *Assistance to Zambia.* (Document No. E/1978/114/Rev. 1 and Annex.) New York: October 3, 1978.

U.S. Department of Agriculture. Economics, Statistics, and Cooperatives Service. *Africa and West Asia: Agricultural Situation, Review of 1977 and Outlook for 1978.* Washington: July 1978.

U.S. Department of Commerce. Industry and Trade Administration. *Marketing in Zambia.* (Overseas Business Reports, OBR 78–24.) Washington: GPO, June 1978.

U.S. Department of State. Embassy in Lusaka. *Foreign Economic Trends and Their Implications for the United States: Zambia.* (International Marketing Information, 77-094.) Washington: GPO, August 1977.

Williams, Mike. "State Participation and the Zambian Economy," *World Development,* 1, No. 10, October 1973, 43–54.

World Bank. *World Development Report, 1978.* Washington: World Bank, August 1978.

World Bank. External Debt Division. *World Debt Tables—Supplements: External Public Debt of Developing Countries.* Washington: World Bank, November 7, 1978.

Young, Alistair. *Industrial Diversification in Zambia.* New York: Praeger, 1973.

Zambia. *The Current Economic Crisis, Government Response and Approach to the Third Plan.* N. pl.: Government of the Republic of Zambia, May 8, 1978.

——. *Estimates of Revenue and Expenditure for the Year 1st January, 1978, to 31st December, 1978.* Lusaka: Government Printer, 1978.

Zambia. Central Statistical Office. *Census of Agriculture, 1970–71 (First Report).* Lusaka: Central Statistical Office, May 1974.

——. *Chemicals, Rubber and Plastic Industries.* (Industry Monograph No. 5.) Lusaka: Central Statistical Office, March 1976.

——. *Manufacture of Non-Metallic Mineral Products.* (Industry Monograph No. 6.) Lusaka: Central Statistical Office, March 1977.

——. *Monthly Digest of Statistics* [Lusaka], XIV, 3–6, March-June 1978.

——. *Paper, Paper Products, Printing and Publishing Industries.* (Industry Monograph No. 4.) Lusaka: Central Statistical Office, February 1976.

——. *Textile, Wearing Apparel and Leather Industries.* (Industry Monograph No. 2.) Lusaka: Central Statistical Office, September 1975.

——. *Wood, Wood Products and Furniture Industries.* (Industry Monograph No. 3.) Lusaka: Central Statistical Office, January 1976.

Zambia. Ministry of Development Planning and National Guidance. *Second National Development Plan, January, 1972–December, 1976.* Lusaka: Government Printer, December 1971.

Zambia. Ministry of Lands and Natural Resources. *Annual Report of the Department of Lands for the Year 1964.* Lusaka: Government Printer, 1965.

——. *Annual Report of the Lands Department for the Year 1970.* Lusaka: Government Printer, 1972.

Zambia. Ministry of Lands, Natural Resources and Tourism. *Annual Report of the Forest Department for the Year 1973.* Lusaka: Government Printer, 1976.

Zambia. Ministry of Lands, Natural Resources and Tourism. Department of Fisheries. *Annual Report 1974.* Lusaka: Government Printer, n.d.

————. *Annual Report 1975.* Lusaka: Government Printer, 1977.

Zambia. Ministry of Power, Transport and Works. *Annual Report of the Roads Branch for the Period 1st January, 1973, to 31st December, 1973.* Lusaka: Government Printer, 1976.

————. *Annual Report of the Roads Department for the Period 1st January, 1974 to 31st December, 1974.* Lusaka: Government Printer, 1977.

"Zambian Economic Survey," *African Development* [London], 10, No. 10, October 1976, 995–1023.

"La Zambie de l'incertitude," *Marchés Tropicaux et Méditerranéens* [Paris], No. 1692, April 14, 1978, 1003–1005.

(Various issues of the following periodicals were also used in the preparation of this chapter: *Africa Research Bulletin* (Economic, Financial and Technical Series) [Exeter], March 15–April 14, 1967 and December 15, 1978–January 14, 1979; *Quarterly Economic Review of Zambia*, [London], first quarter 1977–third quarter 1978; *Sunday Times* [Ndola/Lusaka], October 22, 1978–February 25, 1979; *Times of Zambia* [Ndola/Lusaka], October 27, 1978–February 28, 1979; and U.S. Department of Commerce, Office of Technical Services, Joint Publications Research Service—JPRS [Washington], *Translations on Sub-Saharan Africa*, Nos. 1798–2042, September 9, 1977–December 22, 1978; and *Zambia Daily Mail* [Lusaka], October 21, 1978–February 28, 1979.)

Chapter 5

Amnesty International Report 1977. London: Amnesty International Publications, 1977.

Brelsford, W.V. (ed.) *The Story of the Northern Rhodesia Regiment.* Lusaka: Government Printer, 1954.

Darnton, John. "Rhodesian Bombers Humiliate Zambia," *New York Times,* December 15, 1978, A3.

Legum, Colin (ed.). *Africa Contemporary Record: Annual Survey and Documents, 1968–69.* Exeter: Africa Research Limited, 1969.

————. *Africa Contemporary Record: Annual Survey and Documents, 1969–1970.* Exeter: Africa Research Limited, 1970.

————. *Africa Contemporary Record: Annual Survey and Documents, 1970–1971.* London: Rex Collings, 1971.

————. *Africa Contemporary Record: Annual Survey and Documents, 1971–1972.* London: Rex Collings, 1972.

————. *Africa Contemporary Record: Annual Survey and Documents, 1972–1973.* New York: Africana Publishing, 1973.

————. *Africa Contemporary Record: Annual Survey and Documents, 1973–1974.* New York: Africana Publishing, 1974.

————. *Africa Contemporary Record: Annual Survey and Documents, 1974–1975.* New York: Africana Publishing, 1975.

————. *Africa Contemporary Record: Annual Survey and Documents, 1975–1976.* New York: Africana Publishing, 1976.

————. *Africa Contemporary Record: Annual Survey and Documents, 1976–1977.* New York: Africana Publishing, 1977.

Leh, Robert G. *Weapons Transfers in Africa, With Emphasis on Bloc and Front-Line Example States.* (Paper prepared for Midwest Political Science Association Annual Meeting, Chicago, April 20–22, 1978; U.S. Department of State, Office of External Research, Foreign Affairs Research Paper, No. FAR 23883.)

Moolman, J.H. "One Zambia—One Nation," *Bulletin of the Africa Institute of South Africa* [Pretoria], 13, No. 6, August–September 1975, 199–239.

Morris, Michael. *Armed Conflict in Southern Africa.* Cape Town, South Africa: Jeremy Spense, 1974.

Ottaway, David B. "Zambia Provides Armed Escorts," *Washington Post,* January 11, 1979, A17.

Pettman, Jan. *Zambia: Security and Conflict.* New York: St. Martin's Press, 1974.D.

Roberts, Andrew *A History of Zambia.* New York: Africana Publishing, 1976.

Schutz, Barry M. "The Military Conflict in Southern Africa—1978: Zones, Actors and Roles." (Paper prepared for African Studies Association Annual Meeting, Baltimore, November 1–4, 1978.) Waltham, Mass.: ASA, 1978 (mimeo.).

Shaw, Timothy M. *Dependence and Underdevelopment: The Development and Foreign Policies of Zambia.* (Africa Series, No. 28.) Athens: Center for International Studies, Ohio University, 1976.

Small, N.J. "Getting Ideas Across: Limitations to Social Engineering in a New State," *African Affairs* [London], 77, No. 309, October 1978, 531–553.

————. "Zambia—Trouble on Campus," *Index on Censorship* [London], 6, No. 6, November–December 1977, 8–14.

Stockholm International Peace Research Institute. *World Armaments and Disarmament: SIPRI Yearbook 1977.* Cambridge: MIT Press, 1977.

Tordoff, William (ed.). *Politics in Zambia.* (Perspectives on Southern Africa Series.) Berkeley and Los Angeles: University of California Press, 1975.

U.S. Department of State. "Zambia." Pages 131–135 in *Country Reports On Human Rights Practices.* (Report submitted to the Committee on International Relations, U.S. House of Representatives, and the Committee on Foreign Relations, U.S. Senate, February 3, 1978.) Washington: GPO, 1978.

Zambia. "The Home Guard Act, 1971." (Dated December 20,

1971.) In *Government Gazette,* Supplement. Lusaka: Government of Zambia, December 24, 1971.

Zambia. Ministry of Home Affairs. *Prisons Department Annual Report. 1974.* Lusaka: 1976.

Zambia. Zambia Police Force. *Zambia Police Annual Report, 1974.* Lusaka: 1976.

(Various issues of the following periodicals were also used in the preparation of this chapter: *Africa Research Bulletin* (Political, Social and Cultural Series) [Exeter], 1963–1978; *Times of Zambia* [Ndola/Lusaka]. October and November 1978; U.S. Department of Commerce, Office of Technical Services, Joint Publications Research Service—JPRS [Washington], *Translations on Sub-Saharan Africa,* Nos. 1632–2050, January 1976–January 1979; and *Zambia Daily Mail* [Lusaka], October and November 1978.)

Glossary

African—Standard term applied to black Zambians.

Asian—A Zambian resident of Indian or Pakistani origin or descent. The term replaced *Indian* after the partition and independence of British India in 1947.

citemene (also seen as *chitemene*)—A system of slash-and-burn cultivation, common to the watershed area of the Zaïre and Zambezi rivers, in which the vegetation is cut over and burned primarily for the purpose of increasing soil fertility. The term *citemene* is derived from the Bemba language and has the general meaning of "to cut."

clan—A descent group whose members are putatively descended in either the male or the female line from a common ancestor without all links being known; often comprises a number of lineages *(q.v.)*.

copperbelt—Region in north central Zambia, southwest of Zaïre Pedicle *(q.v.)*; locus of most of the country's mining and much of its industry and urban population.

emergent farmer—Cultivator in the subsistence subsector who uses improved methods and regularly grows, although on a small to medium scale, a substantial part of his crops for sale in the cash market.

European—Standard term applied to whites regardless of country of origin.

fiscal year (FY)—Until June 30, 1966, the fiscal year ran from July 1 to June 30 of the following year. Fiscal year 1966/67, however, covered the period from July 1, 1966, through December 31, 1967, as prelude to making the fiscal year conform to the calendar year.

GDP—Gross domestic product. The total value of goods and services produced within a country's borders during a fixed period, usually one year. Obtained by adding the value contributed by each sector of the economy in the form of compensation of employees, profits, and depreciation (consumption of capital). Subsistence production is included and consists of the imputed value of production by the farm family for its own use and the imputed rental value of owner-occupied dwellings. In countries lacking sophisticated data-gathering techniques the total value of GDP is often estimated.

GNP—Gross national product. GDP *(q.v.)* plus the income received from abroad by residents less payments to nonresidents remitted abroad.

Humanism—The name given by President Kenneth Kaunda to his philosophy (which has become the official philosophy of the ruling party and government). Broadly it urges community, harmony, and egalitarianism and emphasizes common humanity as opposed to "tribalism."

kwacha (K)—Zambian currency unit introduced on January 16, 1968, to replace the Zambian pound. The kwacha is a decimal currency and consists of 100 ngwee (n). The Zambian pound was equivalent to US$2.40. From January 1968 through 1971 the kwacha was equivalent to US$1.40. It maintained this ratio until devaluation of the dollar in March 1973 when the equivalency of K1 rose to US$1.55, a value that it held until mid-1976. In July 1976 the kwacha was devalued by 20 percent and was linked to the Special Drawing Rights (SDRs) of the International Monetary Fund (IMF). Thereafter K1 equaled US$1.25 to US$1.26 based on the SDR-dollar relationship until late 1977; from then through 1978 the kwacha-dollar rate varied, roughly within a range of 5 percent in either direction.

lineage—A descent group whose members can, in principle, trace their descent through males from a common male ancestor (a patrilineage) or through females from a common female ancester (a matrilineage).

line of rail—The area roughly within forty kilometers of the north-south railroad (and on either side of it) running from the copperbelt *(q.v.)* in the north to Livingstone on the Zambezi River.

supertribe—A regional political bloc or constituency, often identified as a "tribe" in national context according to the largest ethnic group in the region; each supertribe consists of disparate peoples and is evoked in discussion of contemporary national political issues rather than of traditional cultures and identities.

World Bank—Name commonly used for the International Bank for Reconstruction and Development (IBRD), which is part of the World Bank Group *(q.v.)*.

World Bank Group—Consists of the World Bank *(q.v.)* and its two financial affiliates, the International Finance Corporation (IFC) and the International Development Association (IDA). IFC works with the private sector in developing countries. IDA operates in the same sectors and with the same policies as the World Bank but provides credits only to the poorer developing countries and on easier terms than conventional World Bank loans.

Zaïre Pedicle—Southeastward extension of Zaïre intruding between northeastern Zambia and its copperbelt *(q.v.);* formerly Congo Pedicle.

Index

Published Country Studies
(Area Handbook Series)

550–65	Afghanistan		550–82	Guyana
550–98	Albania			
550–44	Algeria		550–164	Haiti
550–59	Angola		550–151	Honduras
550–73	Argentina		550–165	Hungary
550–169	Australia			
550–176	Austria		550–21	India
			550–154	Indian Ocean Territories
550–175	Bangladesh		550–39	Indonesia
550–170	Belgium		550–68	Iran
550–66	Bolivia		550–31	Iraq
550–20	Brazil		550–25	Israel
550–168	Bulgaria		550–182	Italy
550–61	Burma		550–69	Ivory Coast
550–83	Burundi			
			550–177	Jamaica
550–166	Cameroon		550–30	Japan
550–96	Ceylon		550–34	Jordan
550–159	Chad			
550–77	Chile		550–56	Kenya
550–60	China, People's Republic of		550–50	Khmer Republic (Cambodia)
550–63	China, Republic of		550–81	Korea, North
550–26	Colombia		550–41	Korea, South
550–91	Congo, People's Republic of		550–58	Laos
550–90	Costa Rica		550–24	Lebanon
550–152	Cuba		550–38	Liberia
550–22	Cyprus		550–85	Libya
550–158	Czechoslovakia			
			550–163	Malagasy Republic
550–54	Dominican Republic		550–172	Malawi
			550–45	Malaysia
550–52	Ecuador		550–161	Mauritania
550–43	Egypt		550–79	Mexico
550–150	El Salvador		550–76	Mongolia
550–28	Ethiopia		550–49	Morocco
			550–64	Mozambique
550–167	Finland			
			550–35	Nepal, Bhutan, and Sikkim
550–155	Germany, East		550–88	Nicaragua
550–173	Germany, Federal Republic of		550–157	Nigeria
550–153	Ghana		550–94	Oceania
550–87	Greece			
550–78	Guatemala		550–48	Pakistan
550–174	Guinea		550–46	Panama

550–156	Paraguay		550–47	Syria
550–185	Persian Gulf States			
550–42	Peru		550–62	Tanzania
550–72	Philippines		550–53	Thailand
550–162	Poland		550–178	Trinidad and Tobago
550–181	Portugal		550–89	Tunisia
			550–80	Turkey
550–160	Romania			
550–84	Rwanda		550–74	Uganda
			550–97	Uruguay
550–51	Saudi Arabia			
550–70	Senegal		550–71	Venezuela
550–180	Sierra Leone		550–57	Vietnam, North
550–184	Singapore		550–55	Vietnam, South
550–86	Somalia			
550–93	South Africa, Republic of		550–183	Yemens, The
550–171	Southern Rhodesia		550–99	Yugoslavia
550–95	Soviet Union			
550–179	Spain		550–67	Zaïre
550–27	Sudan		550–75	Zambia

☆ U.S. GOVERNMENT PRINTING OFFICE : 1979 O—311-009 (108)